INDIE REFRAMED

Traditions in American Cinema

Series Editors Linda Badley and R. Barton Palmer

Titles in the series include:

The 'War on Terror' and American Film: 9/11 Frames Per Second
by Terence McSweeney

American Postfeminist Cinema: Women, Romance and Contemporary Culture
by Michele Schreiber

Film Noir
by Homer B. Pettey and R. Barton Palmer (eds)

In Secrecy's Shadow: The OSS and CIA in Hollywood Cinema 1941–1979
by Simon Willmetts

Indie Reframed: Women's Filmmaking and Contemporary American Independent Cinema
by Linda Badley, Claire Perkins and Michele Schreiber (eds)

www.edinburghuniversitypress.com/series/tiac

INDIE REFRAMED

Women's Filmmaking and Contemporary American Independent Cinema

Edited by Linda Badley, Claire Perkins and Michele Schreiber

EDINBURGH
University Press

For Lydia – LB
For Alistair and Huck – CP
For Brian and Ella – MS

Edinburgh University Press is one of the leading university presses in the UK. We publish academic books and journals in our selected subject areas across the humanities and social sciences, combining cutting-edge scholarship with high editorial and production values to produce academic works of lasting importance. For more information visit our website: edinburghuniversitypress.com

Edinburgh University Press Ltd
The Tun – Holyrood Road
12 (2f) Jackson's Entry
Edinburgh EH8 8PJ

Typeset in 10/12.5pt Sabon by
Servis Filmsetting Ltd, Stockport, Cheshire,
Printed and bound in the United States of America

A CIP record for this book is available from the British Library

ISBN 978 1 4744 0392 4 (hardback)
ISBN 978 1 4744 0394 8 (paperback)
ISBN 978 1 4744 0393 1 (webready PDF)
ISBN 978 1 4744 0395 5 (epub)

CONTENTS

PART IV COLLABORATIONS

LIST OF ILLUSTRATIONS

ACKNOWLEDGEMENTS

We would like to thank our commissioning editor Gillian Leslie and series editor Barton Palmer for their enthusiastic support and assistance on this project from its inception. Thank you also to Yannis Tzioumakis and Chris Holmlund for their generous work as (respectively) respondent and chair on the 2014 SCMS panel at which this material was first previewed and discussed. We would like to acknowledge the production support that we have received from the School of Media, Film & Journalism at Monash University and the Department of Film and Media Studies at Emory University, as well as the sharp work of the production team at Edinburgh University Press. Most of all, we wish to thank our contributors, who have each worked with such keen interest and innovation to illuminate the personas and practice of this incredible group of female filmmakers.

NOTES ON THE CONTRIBUTORS

John Alberti is Professor and Director of Cinema Studies in the Department of English at Northern Kentucky University. His research interests include constructions of gender in cinema, composition in the digital age and the pedagogy of multicultural American literature. He is the author of *Screen Ages: A Survey of American Cinema* (2105), *Masculinity in the Contemporary Romantic Comedy: Gender as Genre* (2013) and editor of *Leaving Springfield: The Simpsons and the Possibility of Oppositional Culture* (2004).

Linda Badley is Professor of English and Film Studies at Middle Tennessee State University. She has published widely in film studies, popular culture, and gender studies, and is the author of *Film, Horror, and the Body Fantastic* (1995), *Writing Horror and the Body* (1996), and *Lars von Trier* (2011), and the co-editor of *Traditions in World Cinema* (2006). With R. Barton Palmer, she co-edits Traditions in World Cinema and Traditions in American Cinema, companion series at Edinburgh University Press.

Cynthia Baron is Professor of Film at Bowling Green State University. She is the co-author, with Yannis Tzioumakis, of *Acting Indie: Aesthetics, Industry, and Performance in American Independent Cinema* (2017). She is the author of *Modern Acting: The Lost Chapter in American Film and Theatre* (2016) and *Denzel Washington* (2015). She is also the co-author of *Reframing Screen Performance* (2008) and *Appetites and Anxieties: Food, Film, and the Politics of Representation* (2014). She is the co-editor of *More Than a Method*

(2004) and founding editor of *The Projector: A Journal on Film, Media, and Culture*.

Shelley Cobb is associate professor in Film and English at the University of Southampton, UK. She has published widely in the areas of adaptation, women filmmakers, postfeminist cinema and celebrity studies. She is the author of *Adaptation, Authorship and Contemporary Women Filmmakers* (2014); co-editor, with Neil Ewen, of *First Comes Love: Power Couples, Celebrity Kinship and Cultural Politics* (2015); and Principal Investigator of the Arts and Humanities Research Council funded four-year project 'Calling the Shots: Women and Contemporary Film Culture in the UK, 2000–2015'.

Corinn Columpar is Director of the Cinema Studies Institute and Associate Professor of Cinema Studies at University of Toronto, where she regularly teaches courses on film theory, the politics of representation, corporeality and film, and various counter-cinematic traditions. She is author of *Unsettling Sights: The Fourth World on Film* (2010) and co-editor, with Sophie Mayer, of *There She Goes: Feminist Filmmaking and Beyond* (2009). Additionally, she has published articles in numerous anthologies and in journals such as *Camera Obscura*, *Quarterly Review of Film and Video*, *Women Studies Quarterly*, and *Refractory*.

Chris Holmlund is Arts and Sciences' Excellence Professor of Film, Women's Studies and French at the University of Tennessee-Knoxville. She is the author of *Impossible Bodies* (2005) and editor of *American Cinema in the 1990s* (2008), *Contemporary American Independent Film: From the Margins to the Mainstream* (2005) and *Between the Sheets, In the Streets: Queer, Lesbian, Gay Documentary* (1997). Her current projects include books on *Female Trouble*, *Being John Malkovich* and Sylvester Stallone.

Geoff King is Professor of Film Studies at Brunel University, London, and author of books including *American Independent Cinema* (2005), *Indiewood, USA: Where Hollywood Meets Independent Cinema* (2009) and *Indie 2.0: Change and Continuity in Contemporary American Indie Film* (2013). He has also written monographs on the indie features *Donnie Darko* and *Lost in Translation*, is co-editor of *American Independent Cinema: Indie, Indiewood and Beyond* (2013) and editor of the Blackwell *Companion to Indie Film* (forthcoming 2016).

Christina Lane is Associate Professor in the Department of Cinema and Interactive Media at the University of Miami. She is the author of the books *Feminist Hollywood: From Born in Flames to Point Break* (2000) and

Magnolia (2011), which is the first full-length study of the Paul Thomas Anderson film. She has published articles in *Cinema Journal*, *Mississippi Quarterly*, *The Journal of Popular Film and TV*, and *Film and History*. She also has numerous essays in edited collections, most recently *Feminism at the Movies: Understanding Gender in Contemporary Popular Culture* (2011) and *Hitchcock and Adaptation* (forthcoming).

James Lyons is Senior Lecturer in Film Studies at the University of Exeter. He is the author of *Selling Seattle* (2004) and *Miami Vice* (2010) and co-editor of *Quality Popular Television* (2003), *Multimedia Histories: From the Magic Lantern to the Internet* (2007), and *The Rise of the American Comics Artist: Creators and Contexts* (2010). He is working on a new book on performance in independent documentary.

Kathleen A. McHugh, Professor of English and Cinema and Media Studies at UCLA, is the author of *Jane Campion* (2007), *American Domesticity: From How-To Manual to Hollywood Melodrama* (1999), the co-editor of *South Korean Golden Age Melodrama: Gender, Genre and National Cinema* (2005, 2008) and the co-editor of a special issue of SIGNS on Film Feminisms. She has published articles on feminist filmmakers, experimental autobiography, domesticity, transnational media feminisms, global melodrama, and the avant-garde in *Camera Obscura*, *Cultural Studies*, *Jump Cut*, *Screen*, *South Atlantic Quarterly*, and *Velvet Light Trap*.

Kent A. Ono is Professor in and Chair of the Department of Communication at the University of Utah. He conducts critical and theoretical research of print, film and television media, specifically focusing on representations of race, gender, sexuality, class and nation. He is the author of *Contemporary Media Culture and the Remnants of a Colonial Past* (2009) and co-author of *Asian Americans and the Media* (2009) and *Shifting Borders: Rhetoric, Immigration, and California's Proposition 187* (2002) and has contributed articles to numerous journals including *Critical Studies in Mass Communication*, *Communication Inquiry* and *Journal of Asian American Studies*.

Lydia Papadimitriou is Senior Lecturer and Programme Leader of Film Studies at Liverpool John Moores University. Her monograph *The Greek Film Musical: A Critical and Cultural History* (2006) has been translated into Greek (2009). She is the Principal Editor of the new *Journal of Greek Media and Culture* (Intellect). She has co-edited (with Yannis Tzioumakis) the collection of essays *Greek Cinema: Texts, Forms and Identities* (2011). She has published articles and reviews in *New Review of Film and Television Studies*, *Screen*, *NECSUS*, *Sight & Sound* and *Senses of Cinema* and contributed chapters in a number of edited collections. She is co-editor of the special issue of *Interactions* (3.2) on Contemporary Greek culture (2012).

Claudia Costa Pederson is Assistant Professor of Art History at Wichita State University and the Finger Lakes Environmental Film Festival Assistant Curator for New Media. Her writings on play, videogames, digital photography, and techno-ecological art are published in *Review: Literature and Art of the Americas*, *Journal of Peer Production*, *Afterimage*, *Intelligent Agent*, *Eludamos*, as well as the ISEA, DAC, and CHI conference proceedings. Recent curatorial projects include, Gün, with Turkish women working in the intersections of media and feminism, and Home/s, a collaboration with Turkish and Greek women at the Benaki Museum, Athens, Greece.

Claire Perkins is Senior Lecturer in Film and Screen Studies at Monash University, Melbourne. She is the author of *American Smart Cinema* (2012) and co-editor of *U.S. Independent Film After 1989: Possible Films* (2015), *B is for Bad Cinema: Aesthetics, Politics and Cultural Value* (2014) and *Film Trilogies: New Critical Approaches* (2012). Her writing on aspects of American independent cinema has also appeared in the journals *Camera Obscura, Celebrity Studies, Critical Studies in Television, Continuum* and *The Velvet Light Trap.*

Sarah Projansky is Associate Dean of Faculty & Academic Affairs in the College of Fine Arts and holds a joint appointment as professor in the Film and Media Arts Department and the Gender Studies Program at the University of Utah. She is the author of *Spectacular Girls: Media Fascination and Celebrity Culture* (2014) and *Watching Rape: Film and Television in Postfeminist Culture* (2001) and has published articles on gender, race and sexuality in film, television and US popular culture and convergence media in the *Journal of Children and Media, Women's Studies in Communication, Cinema Journal, Velvet Light Trap, Signs* and various anthologies.

Maria San Filippo is Assistant Professor of Communication and Media Studies at Goucher College. She is author of *The B Word: Bisexuality in Contemporary Film and Television* (2013), winner of a Lambda Literary Award. Her article on queer film criticism and AfterEllen.com, published in *Film Criticism in the Digital Age* (2015), received the Best Essay in an Edited Collection Award from the Society for Cinema and Media Studies. Her new book project examines sexual provocation in twenty-first-century screen media.

Michele Schreiber is Associate Professor of Film and Media Studies at Emory University. She is the author of *American Postfeminist Cinema: Women, Romance and Contemporary Culture* (2014) and multiple articles on postfeminist media and contemporary independent and Hollywood filmmakers. Her work has appeared in *Journal of Film and Video* and various anthologies including *American Independent Cinema: Indie, Indiewood and Beyond, Feminism at the Movies* and *Reclaiming the Archive: Feminism and Film History*.

Sarah E. S. Sinwell is an Assistant Professor in the Department of Film and Media Arts at the University of Utah. She has published essays on *Being John Malkovich*, *Green Porno* and cell phone culture in *Film and Sexual Politics*, *Women's Studies Quarterly* and *In Media Res*. Her research examines shifting modes of independent film distribution and exhibition on YouTube, Hulu, Netflix and the Sundance Channel website as a means of redefining independent cinema in an era of media convergence.

Yannis Tzioumakis is Senior Lecturer in Communication and Media at the University of Liverpool. He is the author and co-editor of six books, including *American Independent Cinema: An Introduction* (2006) and *Hollywood's Indies: Classics Divisions, Specialty Labels and the American Film Market* (2012). He is currently co-authoring *Acting Indie* and co-editing the *Routledge Companion to Film and Politics*. He also co-edits the American Indies book series (2009–).

Patricia White is Eugene Lang Research Professor of Film and Media Studies at Swarthmore College. She is a longtime member of the editorial collective of *Camera Obscura* and the board of Women Make Movies, and the author of *Uninvited: Classical Hollywood Cinema and Lesbian Representability* (1999) and *Women's Cinema/World Cinema: Projecting 21st Century Feminisms* (2015). She is also co-author of *The Film Experience* (4th edn, 2014) and co-editor of *Critical Visions in Film Theory: Classic and Contemporary Readings* (2011).

Patricia R. Zimmermann is Professor of Screen Studies at Ithaca College and co-director of the Finger Lakes Environmental Film Festival. She is the author of *Reel Families: A Social History of Amateur Film* (1995); *States of Emergency: Documentaries, Wars, Democracies* (2000); and *Thinking Through Digital Media: Transnational Environments and Locative Places* (2015) with Dale Hudson. With Karen Ishizuka, she co-edited *Mining the Home Movie: Excavations in Histories and Memories* (2007). She was the Ida Beam Professor in Cinema at the University of Iowa and the Shaw Foundation Professor of New Media in the School of Communication and Information at Nanyang Technological University in Singapore. She has published over 200 essays on documentary, amateur history, screen theory, and new media.

INTRODUCTION

Linda Badley, Claire Perkins and Michele Schreiber

Reframing Indie

In April 2015 the tumblr account 'Shit People Say to Women Directors' debuted online and promptly went viral. Cataloguing anonymous stories of sexism and inequity encountered by female practitioners working on film sets around the world, the space was 'designed for catharsis and to raise awareness about the barriers women face in the film industry' and instantly identified some common themes in discrimination – named elsewhere by Mynette Louie, president of the female-focused Gamechanger Films, to include 'the babysitting barrier', 'the mini-me problem', 'knee-jerk disrespect' and 'spotty solidarity' (Louie 2015). The account reportedly received a year's worth of public content overnight and gained an immediate media profile through being featured in outlets such as *Vanity Fair*, *The New York Times*, *Fortune Magazine*, *The Huffington Post*, *The Guardian*, *Mashable*, *Glamour Magazine* and *Cosmopolitan*. While this reach and profile distinguishes it, the tumblr account is but one example of a wide range of initiatives, stories and projects that have sprung up in the industry and on social media and popular news sites over the past few years to highlight the plight of women practitioners working in moving images. From quizzes like BuzzFeed's 'How Many Of These Movies by Female Directors Have You Seen?' (Willmore 2014) and stories like *Indiewire*'s '10 Female Directors Who Deserve More Attention From Hollywood' (King 2014) to schemes like Meryl Streep's Writer's Lab – designed to nurture female screenwriters over the age of 40 – and Amy Schumer's popular 'Last Fuckable

Day' sketch from *Inside Amy Schumer* (2013–), all expose the entrenched gender inequality of the filmmaking industry and aim to begin conversations on this problem and how to address it. They demonstrate how the labour and status of women in this environment is a vital issue for liberal feminism in the second decade of the twenty-first century.

At a specific level, these initiatives are authorised and inspired by the journalistic and academic activity of women like Manohla Dargis, Melissa Silverstein, Martha Lauzen and Stacy L. Smith. As chief film critic for *The New York Times*, Dargis routinely advocates for female filmmakers and representation in articles and reviews that identify phenomena such as 'the new, post-female American cinema' (Dargis 2008) and the 'Director Gap' (Dargis 2014a; Dargis 2014b; Dargis 2015), while Silverstein 'educates, advocates and agitates for gender parity across the entertainment industry' from her widely read 'Women and Hollywood' site. This work in turn draws on the statistical analyses of Lauzen and Smith, who both run media labs that annually produce comprehensive, quantitative data on the numbers of women working on and off screen in Hollywood – showing, for instance, how in 2014 women comprised just 17% of all practitioners working on the top 250 (US domestic) grossing films (Lauzen 2015a) and how, in 2012, only 28.4% of speaking characters in the top 100 films were women (Smith et al 2013). At a more general level, the initiatives find context in the popular feminism that online culture has produced in the millennial era through developments such as the Everyday Sexism Project (everydaysexism.com), the HeForShe movement (heforshe.org) and the Everyday Feminism media site (everydayfeminism.com). The principles of equality that the Hollywood-specific stories and activity are based upon is articulated in these more general feminist developments as a backlash against postfeminist culture – perceived as an environment where, in the words of the Everyday Sexism Project, 'it seems to be increasingly difficult to talk about sexism, equality and women's rights in a modern society that perceives itself to have achieved gender equality'.

Indie Reframed: Women's Filmmaking and Contemporary American Independent Cinema contributes to and intervenes in the gender politics of this critical milieu by attending to the specific work and practice of female practitioners in the independent or 'indie' sphere of contemporary US filmmaking. This is a topic that has its own clear narrative within accounts of women in Hollywood, where it is frequently stated or implied that women fare 'better' in the worlds of the studio speciality divisions and genuinely independent companies than in the top-tier tentpole environment that is responsible for the highest grossing, and most visible, products. Further studies by Lauzen provide the numbers for this narrative, demonstrating, for instance, that women made up 26% of the practitioners working on independent films in 2013–14 – a figure that was the same as 2011–12 and up two points from 2008–9 (Lauzen

2015b). While initially encouraging, a breakdown of these numbers shows that it is only in the categories of producer and executive producer that the figures are increasing; the numbers of female writers, editors, cinematographers and directors is actually decreasing. This trend rationalises the downside of the popular female indie narrative where, as Silverstein has written, 'women struggle to get tapped for the big films', and thereby demonstrate how the indie world is not the same 'pipeline to Hollywood gigs' that it is for men (Silverstein 2014).

The essays in this collection extrapolate and interrogate both the positive and negative sides of this popular understanding of women in the indie sphere. On the negative side, they examine how better representation for women both on and off screen does not necessarily equate to prominent female stories and biographies in the indie world, which remains popularly and critically branded by the powerful narratives of the white, male 'maverick' auteur and male identity politics. The work of women filmmakers operating at the intersection of mainstream, art and independent film does not often align with the particular qualities of irony, 'quirk' and mannerism that have emerged from these imperatives to define the narrative image of the indie sector. But indie women's films also typically defy association with the formulaic myths of the mainstream 'chick flick' *and* the ideological and experimental radicalism of feminist counter-cinema – meaning they are rarely ironic, popular or political enough to be readily absorbed into any pre-existing categories, and thereby struggle to gain visibility in the increasingly crowded marketplace of American cinemas.

On the positive side, these essays work to reclaim this 'in-betweenness' as a mark of distinction and intervention. With the goal of mobilising these women's work to expand the parameters of how 'indie' is currently understood, contributors illustrate how the perspectives, sensibilities, ideologies and industrial practices of a range of female practitioners disrupt and reframe the dominant narratives and traditions of this sector. The goal here is not to locate the 'difference' of this work in an essentialised conception of femininity, but to examine how strategies of women's labour such as hybridisation and collaboration give rise to an alternative set of narratives, both real and fictional. This attention represents a first dedicated and sustained examination of female practitioners in indie scholarship, which has for the most part sidelined specific questions of both gender politics and female practice in favour of interrogating broader issues of industries and aesthetics and constructing a male-dominated canon of frequently discussed films and directors.

This collection, then, approaches the work of female practitioners in the indie sphere as a form of women's cinema. In this, it draws its context not just from the environment of popular feminism described above but, more instructively, from the revitalisation of feminist film discourse on women filmmakers that has occurred in the post–2000 era. In this contemporary landscape, the agency and activity of female practitioners has been embraced as a pathway for analysis in film theory in a way that differs substantially from historical film feminisms. As Catherine Grant has shown, this contemporary work operates as a 'reverse discourse' on women's authorship, 'enabling agency, after decades of embarrassed deconstruction, finally to be subjected to analysis in the form of its textual, biographical traces' (Grant 2001: 123). Here, female practitioners are considered not as a site of 'enunciation' bound by the theoretical terms of psychoanalysis and structuralism but as *agents*: 'female subjects who have direct and reflexive, if obviously not completely "intentional" or determining, relationships to the cultural products they help to produce, as well as to their reception' (Grant 2001: 124). In this schema, authorship is reimagined as a discourse with the potential to repay feminist investigation, rather than as the Romantic cult of (male) personality that film feminisms have traditionally avoided.

Indie Reframed takes up a conception of women's cinema that emerges from this reimagining to acknowledge the importance of discussing women's cultural production. As Alison Butler describes, it has often been argued that understanding women's work as distinct from men's is counter-productive for both the egalitarian goals of feminism and the potentially androgynous creativity of the individual artist. On the other hand, she continues, it is 'only the most conservative of feminisms [that] approaches the goal of equality via the denial of social differences' (Butler 2002: 22). In Butler's own work, the issue of difference is theorised through the concept of marginalisation, where she proposes that women's cinema is a 'minor' cinema insofar as it is the work of a marginalised group who write in the major language of the cinematic apparatus – mobilising a relationship that is neither alienated nor oppositional, but 'mediated and contestatory' (Butler 2002: 21).

As Patricia White identifies, though, this deterritorialising potential of women's cinema to '[resist] totalizing narratives of the world system' has to be matched by an awareness of how women's filmmaking is also *reterritorialised* through contemporary film culture. The ways in which women rupture and reframe the categories familiar within discourses of women's cinema – authorship, aesthetics, address – 'must be supplemented by consideration and theorization of institutional questions – of production, distribution, exhibition and reception' (White 2015: 13). As White and other feminist screen theorists have shown, the change in conceptions of film feminism in the late twentieth and early twenty-first centuries has been contextualised and impacted by industrial, social and technological changes in the formations of cinema itself. These include the emergence of new and flexible pathways for production and distribution via digital technologies, the institutionalisation of film festival cultures, and the rise of the Internet as a site for promotion, commentary and criticism. These systemic developments have produced a new transnational environment and a new set of discourses for understanding the work and image of the female practitioner, where once stable terms of 'art', 'popular', 'world' and 'national' cinema are now mutable. As a discursive formation that is typically dated to around 1990 (Perkins and Verevis 2015), the rise of 'indie' as a critical and cultural category is a central development in this contemporary environment, and a consideration of the 'cinefeminisms' that operate within it is thus overdue.

Pioneers and Precursors

We define 'independence' in this volume as the realm of financing, production and artistic intent that exists in between avant-garde and experimental films and studio-financed Hollywood production. Indeed, as previously noted, this book embraces the many ways in which women filmmakers fall 'in between' or represent 'in-betweenness' in its many forms. This space in between mainstream Hollywood production and experimental cinema is a fairly new one for women filmmakers to occupy. As the wide variety of pieces in this study evince, the filmmakers discussed here have very diverse backgrounds, approaches to filmmaking, and perhaps most importantly, different interpretations of and positions towards the term 'independent'; and of course there still are too few of them. However, they do collectively occupy an unprecedented space in the filmmaking landscape. When looking at the history of women's cinema, at no other time has it been possible to talk about a substantial group of American women filmmakers who work in the same mode of production in the same general historical period. Prior to the recent past, it has been necessary to speak about them only in isolated case studies or in scholarly anthologies that are specific either to mode of production or historical period.

Director Dorothy Arzner, for instance, has been the subject of several influential articles and one major book that focus on her pioneering status as a woman director of women's films in Hollywood in the 1920s through to the 1940s. Arzner is a unique figure not just because she was the sole women director working during this period but because she resisted normative conceptions of female behaviour and femininity both in her public persona and in her films' depiction of female characters. As Judith Mayne discusses in her influential book on Arzner, 'Arzner's films are consistently provocative . . . they reflect both Arzner's unique achievement and the extent to which she remained, throughout her lifetime, the exception in Hollywood' (Mayne 1994: 1). Indeed Arzner's status as the 'exception' has allowed her and her films to be the subject of extensive analyses by feminist film historians and theoreticians like Mayne. In an early piece of feminist film theory, Claire Johnston uses Arzner's films to argue for the potential for a woman's 'counter-cinema' within otherwise conventional classical films, where female characters challenge patriarchal narrative models and structures of looking and 'render strange' the 'universe of the male' (Johnston 1988, [1973]/1999). In 'Approaching the Work of Dorothy Arzner', Pam Cook talks about the ways in which Arzner's films consist of narrative disruptions, such as 'gags' and 'pregnant moments' that call attention to the contradictions inherent in 'female desire under patriarchy' (Cook 1988: 48, 51–2). Mayne also discusses Arzner's films but is more invested in her complicated public persona where her 'masculine' appearance and lesbian identity are both visible and invisible (Mayne 1994). Arzner's career, and the critical work that takes her as its subject, is instructive because it demonstrates how much value and energy is associated with her 'exceptional' position as a woman filmmaker in a time and mode of production when there was little to no diversity in American cinema. Despite the historical differences, the scholarly evaluation of Arzner has a great deal of relevance for the work detailed in this volume: it introduces various methodologies for reading feminist or counter-narratives in her films, collaborative relationships with her female co-stars (Billie Burke and Rosalind Russell, specifically), and the degree to which her public identity as a 'masculine' woman who 'flaunted a style that signified "lesbian"' influenced the way in which she was received by the press at the time. It also establishes a lens through which we can view her films now (Mayne 1994: 2).

On the other side of the spectrum is Maya Deren, who made films during the same general historical period as Arzner but was a pioneer in avant-garde and experimental cinema. Both filmmakers have been 'rewritten' into film history through the work of film scholars over the last thirty years. However, they are rarely, if ever, paired together in critical conversations because they work in different modes of production. Like Arzner, Deren was interested in finding new ways of representing the female figure and she sought to make abstract connections between cinematic language, dance and movement. In this way, Deren's work (much like that of subsequent women experimental filmmakers) resided in between film and another art form – in this case, dance. Deren also left a more practical legacy for later independent filmmaking: in 1955 she founded of the Creative Film Foundation, which provided support for avant-garde and experimental filmmakers. As Geoff King notes, the organisation serves as a model for later foundations that would support independent filmmakers such as the Independent Feature Project and Women Make Movies (King 2005: 16, 20). There have been few scholarly books on Deren; these include an anthology, *Maya Deren and the American Avant-garde* (ed. Bill Nichols, 2001) and a monograph, Sarah Keller's *Maya Deren: Incomplete Control* (2014). Much of the work on her has been in scholarly anthologies on women's avant-garde and experimental filmmaking more generally. These rich volumes focus on avant-garde and experimental work across a broad historical spectrum, and Deren is discussed alongside more contemporary filmmakers or filmmakers working in other national cinemas. For instance, in Maureen Turim's article 'The Violence of Desire in Avant-Garde Films' in *Women and Experimental Filmmaking*, Deren is discussed together with classic French filmmaker Germaine Dulac, contemporary American filmmaker Yvonne Rainer and contemporary Serbian performance artist, Marina Abramovic. Comparisons involving such a broad range of women artists as this point to the fact that filmmakers working in the experimental mode of production are often discussed together regardless of national origins or historical periodisation because their approach to film form (however diverse it might be) is often outside the boundaries of traditional Hollywood channels of production, distribution and exhibition. The Petrolle/Wexman anthology also reveals the frequent overlap between films that are referred to as avant-garde/experimental and those referred to as 'independent'. All experimental and avant-garde films are technically independent films because they are not financed by any commercial infrastructure; however they are not referred to as such because they are made in an artisanal mode of production.

Cheryl Dunye is a filmmaker whose work complicates this distinction, as she is classified as both 'independent' and 'avant-garde/experimental'. Dunye's best-known film *The Watermelon Woman* (1996) adopts some experimental techniques but did receive limited theatrical distribution and was a modest financial success. She is seen as an influential player in the 'New Queer Cinema' that falls firmly into the category of independent cinema but is also discussed in articles, both written by Kathleen McHugh, in the aforementioned Petrolle/Wexman experimental cinema anthology as well as in Robin Blaetz's anthology, *Women's Experimental Filmmaking: Critical Frameworks*. Dunye's case points to how the 'in-between' status that is discussed throughout this volume can be as applicable to the relationship between independent cinema and avant-garde and experimental modes of production, as it is to that between independent cinema and Hollywood, or 'Indiewood'.

The most significant predecessor of the women discussed in this volume is Ida Lupino, who worked in the limited realm of independent filmmaking during the studio system and whose entire career was predicated on 'in-betweenness'. She is sometimes mentioned in the same conversation as Arzner because these two are the only two female directors to work in the Classical Hollywood cinema. However, because of the different historical periods in which they worked and their different sensibilities and career trajectories, they are rarely discussed side by side. Lupino has always been a thornier figure than Arzner for film scholars and for feminist scholars in particular, because she doesn't fit very neatly into pre-ordained categories. Not only did she take on many different roles throughout her career – actress, writer, producer and director – but she also actively resisted labels that would characterise her as a pioneering female figure. In fact, in press interviews, she would often go out of her way to paint herself as willingly subservient to men, and her films, as Molly Haskell puts it, are 'conventional, even sexist' (Haskell 1973: 201).

In 1948, while in the middle of a successful acting career, she and her then husband, Collier Young, along with Anson Bond, founded Emerald Productions, which later became the Filmakers Company, an independent production company whose films were distributed by RKO studios until 1954. Between 1949 and 1954, Emerald/Filmakers made twelve feature films; Lupino directed or co-directed six of these, wrote or co-wrote at least five, produced or co-produced at least one, and acted in three (Kuhn 1995: 2). Lupino is best known for her work in the melodrama genre but her films were quite diverse, ranging from the love triangle melodrama *The Bigamist* (1953) to the exclusively male-starring *The Hitchhiker* (1954). After Filmakers failed, she capitalised on her adaptability by directing episodes of a vast array of television programmes in the 1960s, including *Gilligan's Island* (1964–7), *Have Gun – Will Travel* (1958–61), *Hong Kong* (1960–1), and *Thriller* (1960–2), among many others. Lupino may have been a reluctant pioneer but her career points to the kind of blurred boundaries between independent cinema, Hollywood cinema, and television that characterise the careers of many of the filmmakers discussed in *Indie Reframed.*

There are isolated cases of American women directors and producers making Hollywood and independent films in the 1960s and 1970s, including exploitation filmmaker Doris Wishman (*Bad Girls Go to Hell* (1965), *Satan Was a Lady* (1975), and *Let Me Die a Woman* (1978)), Barbara Loden (*Wanda* (1970)), Elaine May (*A New Leaf* (1970) and *The Heartbreak Kid* (1972)) and Joan Micklin Silver (*Between the Lines* (1977)), but few women filmmakers were able to establish substantial bodies of work again until the 1980s. Most of these filmmakers emerged as a result of the burgeoning infrastructure of American independent cinema, although many, such as those who came from film movements such as the L. A. Rebellion, like Julie Dash, emerged outside of this realm. As has been well documented by the scholarship on the topic, the 1980s saw a new phase of independent cinema emerge that was bolstered by the formation of the Sundance Film Festival, Independent Feature Project, and 'mini-major' companies such as Orion, Miramax and New Line films. These organisations helped create more opportunities for filmmakers who wanted to challenge and/or deviate from classical Hollywood conventions but still strived to appeal to a broader audience, and eventually led to what Yannis Tzioumakis has called the 'institutionalisation' of independent cinema (Tzioumakis 2006: 246). As Geoff King puts it, 'from the mid-1980s . . . the more arty, quirky, sometimes politically inflected, brand of independent cinema began to gain a higher profile and more sustained institutionalised base in the broadly off–Hollywood arena' (King 2005:8).

The 1980s saw a generation of women filmmakers make their mark on independent cinema, and their paths forward through the industry can be seen as predicative of the subsequent generation of filmmakers discussed in *Indie Reframed*. For instance, filmmaker Donna Deitch was celebrated for her LGBT-themed film *Desert Hearts*, which won the Special Jury Prize at the Sundance Film Festival in 1986. After this success, she directed only one additional narrative feature, 1994's *Criminal Passion*, but has worked steadily for the last twenty years directing television series and mini-series. Another example is director Susan Seidelman (the subject of Christina Lane's study in Chapter 4), whose 1982 film *Smithereens* was the first American independent film invited into competition for the Palme d'Or at the Cannes Film Festival. This led to Seidelman helming a number of high-profile Hollywood films during the 1980s including *Desperately Seeking Susan* (1985) and *Making Mr. Right* (1987) only to see opportunities dry up towards the end of the decade. Seidelman, like Deitch, went on to work in television directing but, as Lane's chapter discusses, she remains determined to make films even if she needs to do this without the traditional models of exhibition and distribution. Director Kathryn Bigelow is probably the most visible success story of women independent filmmakers during the 1980s. Her first three features – 1981's *The Loveless*, 1987's *Near Dark* and 1989's *Blue Steel* – were independently financed, with *Blue Steel* receiving distribution by MGM. Bigelow then went on to make a number of big budget Hollywood features, including *Point Break* (1991), *Strange Days* (1995) and *The Hurt Locker* (2008), which won the Academy Award for Best Picture, as well as a Best Director Oscar for Bigelow, the first ever to be awarded to a woman. The very different career trajectories of Deitch, Seidelman, and Bigelow tell the story of how independent cinema doesn't necessarily serve as a launchpad for a successful career in Hollywood for women as often as it does for their male counterparts.

Most of the women discussed in this volume emerged in the independent cinema scene of the 1990s. They have benefited from studying the films and career paths of their predecessors and learned their own lessons about the difficulties of making films in an independent film landscape in which the career trajectories of their Caucasian male counterparts have dominated both journalistic and scholarly narratives. However, despite the evidence of both roadblocks and discrimination against them, American women filmmakers are, for the first time, making their mark on cinematic storytelling as a very diverse and loosely unified group. They navigate the crossover between independent and Hollywood filmmaking very carefully; some successfully move into Hollywood while others are able to make only one film, and then they see opportunities dry up. Many resist the crossover and choose to stay in the independent realm of production, waiting and thus using the lengthy amount of time it takes to secure financing for a film to remain close to their artistic vision. And, others continue to make films independently but move over into the commercial realm by directing for television.

Reading Women's Filmmaking through Four Lenses

The work of women filmmakers rarely fits into the dominant model that exemplifies the indie 'brand', and often goes unrecognised. This is because they work through multiple vectors, forms and roles, whether this is to effect social and political change or merely to survive. In the interest of illuminating the range and variety of women's cinema and thereby challenging that model, the chapters in this volume are organised into four parts: 'Production and Distribution Contexts', 'Genres and Modalities', 'Identities' and 'Collaborations'.

The chapters in Part I address the labour and leadership of women in individual movements and companies between the 1970s and the present, examining how these channels enable the financing and distribution of work by female practitioners. Authors observe how individual figures and companies work with and against traditions of feminism and counter-cinema, and within new contexts of industrial convergence and digital technology. Sarah Sinwell opens with an analysis of the pioneering and continuing importance of legendary non-profit Women Make Movies, founded in 1972 as the first production and distribution company devoted to films by and about women, before turning to two recently founded companies. Chicken & Egg Pictures, created in 2005 to support the work of female nonfiction filmmakers, continues a tradition of activism in which feminist documentary figures centrally by mentoring and awarding grants to filmmakers who address social, political, and global human rights issues. In contrast, Gamechanger Films, the first for-profit fund exclusively for narrative films scripted and directed by women, is aimed at intervening in the gender imbalance in the feature film industry. Set up in 2013 to create a community of investors to support new and coming generations of female filmmakers, it has already supported the 2014 Independent Spirit John Cassavetes Award-winning *Land Ho!* (2014), by Martha Stephens and Aaron Katz, and recent projects by Karyn Kusama, Jamie Babbit, and So Yong Kim.

In the next two chapters, Patricia White and James Lyons argue for a perspective that recognises pivotal and multifaceted roles of key female producers. Celebrated in accounts of the American indie heyday of the 1990s and through the 2000s, Killer Films is headed by the equally feted partnership of producers Christine Vachon and Pam Koffler. Drawing on interviews and other primary source material, White seeks to integrate the story of Killer as a butch-lesbian woman's company into the history of feminist filmmaking. This history includes not only the New Queer Cinema but trailblazing lesbian and transgender features such as *Go Fish* (1994), *High Art* (1998) and *Boys Don't Cry* (1999) and 'women's films' made by women (Mary Harron) and queer men (Todd Haynes). Next, James Lyons turns to the career and production strategies of heiress Megan Ellison, whose powerhouse Annapurna Pictures was established with the goal of creating a sophisticated, risk-taking art cinema of auteurs. Although, like Vachon, Ellison has become an unconventional figurehead for the company, she strategically moderates her image, as Lyons demonstrates, through various social media as well as through Annapurna's impressive stream of award-winning films such as *Zero Dark Thirty* (Kathryn Bigelow, 2012), *The Master* (Paul Thomas Anderson, 2012), and *Her* (Spike Jonze, 2013).

In the final two chapters in this part, Christina Lane and Michele Schreiber examine the recent alternative routes taken by veteran filmmakers who were celebrated for their first features but, in a depressing cycle examined in Lane's pivotal 2005 article 'Just Another Girl outside the Neo Indie', found themselves struggling afterwards. Filmmakers like Julie Dash, Allison Anders and, as noted above, Susan Seidelman among others, inspired by second-wave feminism and once poised to lead a vibrant women's film culture, came to be regarded as one-hit wonders as their follow-up projects failed through poor distribution or because they never reached production. In her chapter, Lane focuses on Seidelman's long-term response to this dilemma through self-reinvention. Capitalising on new technologies including digital, social and emergent media and micro-budget strategies such as crowdsourcing and self-distribution, her most recent films are often low-budget 'high concept' endeavours that, in the case of *Boynton Beach Club* (2005) and *The Hot Flashes* (2013) appeal to niche audiences – seniors, Latinos and disabled rights groups – whom she engages in the creative process. Yet like her earlier mainstream indie hit *Desperately Seeking Susan*, her recent projects are attuned to the marketplace and blend elements of commercial and independent film. In a similar way, Michele Schreiber updates the careers of Allison Anders and Mary Harron, whose careers took off in the early-to-mid 1990s but who have subsequently turned to television. Schreiber details how both found a workspace in the much-maligned Lifetime Movie Network's made-for-television film aimed at women and, specifically, the celebrity biopic subgenre. Like Seidelman, Anders and Harron have targeted an older female demographic in order to make films about women whose stories have been marginalised (June Carter in Anders' *Ring of Fire*, 2013) or discredited (Anna Nicole Smith in Harron's *Anna Nicole*, 2013), reaching appreciative audiences. Harron moreover exploits the subversive potential of the 'notorious' celebrity biopic to expose the media's role in constructing the self-destructing Anna Nicole. In such ways, the chapters in this part reveal how indie women's filmmaking can play an interventionist role and even change the traditions, paradigms and institutions in which it is embedded.

The chapters in Part II, 'Genres and Modalities', consider diverse ways in which women in the contemporary independent realm resist and negotiate industrial boundaries and obstacles that obscure their visibility. Authors attend to how individual filmmakers interrogate and hybridise and thus defy the generic frames that have constructed and sustained Hollywood and indie discourse as a male-dominated narrative. While analysing two features by Megan Griffiths, Geoff King challenges essentialist assumptions that are often imposed on films directed by women. Griffiths' first feature *The Off Hours* (2011) might seem to support the expectation that the female 'sensibility' results in films with a realistic, low-key aesthetic focused on characterisation and relationships and fostered by a collaborative style of filmmaking. Nevertheless, as King observes, a large swathe of the (male) indie sector might be accounted for through these same characteristics and production methods. Griffiths' *Eden* (2012), on the other hand, adapts the male thriller genre to a film based on one woman's experience as a victim of the international sex trade. Hence Griffiths' practice overall suggests that, rather than sharing some essential predisposition, female filmmakers transform and hybridise 'indie' modalities and existing genres to their own feminist ends. With similarly anti-essentialist assumptions, Linda Badley examines a resurgence of the venerable American independent tradition of documentary-style social realism that inspired and enabled female pioneers in the 1980s. Focusing on critically and popularly successful films by Debra Granik (*Winter's Bone*, 2010), Courtney Hunt (*Frozen River*, 2008), and Kelly Reichardt (*Meek's Cutoff*, 2011), among others, she explores how their adaptation of an international 'neo–neorealist' aesthetic and ethos has exposed the detrimental effects of neoliberal austerity on working-class women's lives. Such realism is by no means 'pure', however, as these films incorporate melodrama and reappropriate mainstream 'male' genre tropes in the interest of highlighting feminist characterisations and 'moments' within their films, while appealing to a wider audience than otherwise, to offer visible interventions within the Indiewood sector. Next, Claire Perkins investigates women's infiltration of mumblecore, a predominantly 'male' subgenre associated with auteurs such as Andrew Bujalski, Mark and Jay Duplass and Joe Swanberg, for feminist ends. Like the new neo-neorealism, the subgenre's cheap, lo-fi digital aesthetic and anti-mainstream values of 'authenticity' in representing relationships among twenty-something millennials is congenial to indie female practitioners including Lynn Shelton, So Yong Kim and Desiree Akhavan. Rather than simple appropriations of a 'male' genre, their work represents a 'reframing' not only of mumblecore but indie cinema generally, which mumblecore has recently epitomised. In films with a feminist focus on female aspirations and insecurities but that also accommodate queer and racial perspectives, these practitioners transpose the mumblecore 'ethos' to accommodate otherwise marginalised subjectivities and experiences. Concluding this part, Shelley Cobb turns to Sanaa Hamri's Indiewood productions *Something New* (2006) and *Just Wright* (2010) as innovations within the mainstream genre of the postfeminist romantic comedy, which has omitted or sidelined black women's stories. Compatible with a trend for 'feel-good' films about middle-class blacks, Hamri's films are neither formally innovative nor politically progressive and are therefore ignored in studies of contemporary black film and women's cinema alike. Yet simply by existing, as films about black women made by black female filmmakers who are thereby made visible, Hamri's films intervene in a pervasively white postfeminist media culture. They also transfigure the black romantic comedy by challenging the dominant stereotype of the middle-class black woman's negotiation of love and career in which she must give up one to have the other.

Expanding on themes from the previous part, Part III attends to how contemporary female independent practitioners represent and negotiate diverse issues of identity in their films and working practices. Across a range of case studies, chapters address ways in which nationality, race, gender, and sexuality is constructed and interrogated, and how the question of 'difference' is engaged, while considering the pragmatic and self-conscious ways in which individual filmmakers manage and mediate their professional and artistic identities. The transnational figure and rich, thirty-seven-year career of Mira Nair might well be prototypical: Nair is an Indian filmmaker whose production company Mirabai Films is based in New York City and whose works cross multiple borders, whether nation, race, class, sexuality or genre, to promote social activism. Emphasising Nair's documentary film production and methods and her career-long investment in non-profit organisations, Sarah Projansky and Kent Ono claim that her popular fictional features such as *Salaam Bombay!* (1988), *Monsoon Wedding* (2001), or *Vanity Fair* (2004) and *The Reluctant Fundamentalist* (2012) share with her documentaries and outreach programmes a fundamentally political sensibility and socially confrontational aims. Like Christina Lane and Michele Schreiber in Part I, Projansky and Ono conclude that women filmmakers must work in between nationalities and genres through a variety of forms, vectors and roles whether to effect social change or simply to survive.

Identities in several senses are at stake in the issues surrounding *My Big Fat Greek Wedding* (2002). Remembered as the highest-grossing romantic comedy of all time rather than as an indie – in fact, one of the indie sector's biggest box office successes – the film has been critically overlooked. Challenging this marginalisation, which results in part from the indie sector's emphasis on the director as auteur, Yannis Tzioumakis and Lydia Papadimitriou reclaim the film as an expression of the intersectional perspective of its writer and lead actor, Greek-American Nia Vardalos, rather than its male director, and unpack the film's overlooked ethnic, social and gender concerns. While examining the much more obvious and widespread marginalisation of African-American women's cinema, Cynthia Baron explores the feature films of Dee Rees, Ava DuVernay and Kasi Lemmons. Intersecting women's, independent, and black independent cinema, their films reveal how the independent sector remains socially relevant, providing a space for the critique of race, class, gender and sexuality. If their early films, as in Rees' *Pariah* (2011), Lemmons' *Eve's Bayou* (1997) and DuVernay's *Middle of Nowhere* (2012), place black women's subjectivities at the centre of intimate narratives, their recent work assumes a 'womanist' perspective that encompasses the lives and experiences of a people regardless of gender. In Rees' HBO film *Bessie* (2015), Lemmons' *Talk to Me* (2007) and DuVernay's *Selma* (2014), the latter a fusion of biopic and historical epic, they craft intimate portraits amidst historical contexts, conveying the scale and impact of events on a range of black subjectivities.

Turning to the problematically queer cinema of Lisa Cholodenko, Maria San Filippo argues that her earliest and most recent films *High Art* (1998) and *The Kids Are All Right* (2010) as well as her underdiscussed *Laurel Canyon* and recent television work, exemplify the sort of 'in-betweenness' that resists and challenges established categories. Identified with the lesbian branch of the new Queer Cinema of the early 1990s while evoking equal praise and divisive reactions, Cholodenko's *High Art*, about the intense and fraught professional and sexual relationship between a young straight female art critic and journalist and a brilliant lesbian artist/heroin addict, was controversial at a time when lesbian indies were mostly lo-fi romances like *Go Fish* (Rose Troche, 1994). Likewise, the more mainstream lesbian family drama *The Kids Are All Right* has been accused of compromising with heteronormative patriarchal values. Rather than 'betraying' lesbian cinema, San Filippo maintains, her characters and films resist sexual, ideological and industrial categories, whether for pragmatic, political and/or personal reasons. Traversing the boundaries, Cholodenko offers a model of 'in-betweenness' for female indie practitioners.

Approaching the concept of 'in-betweenness' from the opposite direction, Kathleen McHugh singles out the brilliant, idiosyncratic multimedial work of Miranda July as nothing less than exemplary of American independent cinema as it currently stands. Defining the latter in terms of the emerging indie culture of the twenty-first century's second decade, she argues that July's oeuvre reframes the masculinist rhetoric that has dominated the discussion until now. Manifesting itself communally, through informal networks rather than through self-stylisation, July's creative work is collaborative, improvisational, and distributed across a broad range of platforms including, besides film and video, writing, acting, performance and conceptual art, all of which are represented in her two feature films *Me and You and Everyone We Know* (2005) and *The Future* (2011). Throughout, McHugh concludes, July exemplifies the past and the future of indie cinema as 'a mode of communal expression and interaction; as a method of financing; and, perhaps most importantly, as a way of feeling free'.

Focusing on the cooperative practices through which women in the contemporary indie sector work, the filmmakers discussed in the final part, 'Collaborations', move fluidly between roles, whether of director, producer, writer, or actor, and between film, television, Internet and new media production to engage multiple communities in the creative process. Their workplace practices are examined as interventions into the historical systems that continue to reproduce an ideology of the male 'maverick' director as the lynchpin of indie discourse. In 'Mutual Muses', having noted the conventional definition of a muse as a woman who inspires a male artist, Christine Holmlund explores mutual inspiration and collaboration between female directors and actresses, singling out two pairs, Nicole Holofcener and Catherine Keener (*Walking and Talking* (1996), *Lovely & Amazing* (2001), *Friends with Money* (2006), *Please Give* (2010), *Enough Said* (2013)) and Kelly Reichardt and Michelle Williams (*Wendy and Lucy* (2008), *Meek's Cutoff* (2010)). Applying the feminist ethics of Luce Irigaray's later work (in *I Love to You*, 1995, and *To Be Two*, 1998), which advocates that relationships acknowledge difference by leaving an interval between partners, by partners, eliminating the objectification of the other, Holmlund proposes that the films of Holofcener/Keener and Reichardt/Williams are produced in this spirit and are in some sense about it. Rather than assuming positions of dominance and submission, their partnerships and films explore human relationships while valuing an Irigarayan 'difference *for*' others, if in different ways, with Holofcener/Keener performing the subtle minutia of everyday encounters and Reichardt/Williams exploring relationships across class, race, species and the biosphere. In contrast to this model, Lena Dunham, the film and television celebrity, showrunner, director and star who is often described as postfeminist and narcissistic, seems to epitomise the singular auteur. Corinn Columpar begs to differ, however, through a rigorous examination of the feminist collaborative practices integral to Dunham's productions as illustrated in her breakthrough film *Tiny Furniture* (2010). Including family members and friends as well as their art and ideas (her mother Laurie Simmons' photography, for example), the film has characteristics of the autobiographical documentary and engages self-reflexively with the multiple communities that make up intersubjective and intertextual experience, including intergenerational feminisms.

Too often dismissed as expressions of a 'female sensibility', as John Alberti notes, women's collaborative methods should be understood as political interventions into the production and marketing practices that privilege the white male 'auteur'. Working from his interviews with Lynn Shelton, he focuses on the workplace practices of a director who functions more as a facilitator and curator for films that are often improvised collectively. Alberti's chapter also features an analysis of *Humpday* (2008), a deconstruction of the indie bromance and a film about men making a (porn) film – one that exploits mumblecore dramedy to place the auteurist director in an ironic perspective. In the volume's final chapter, Claudia Costa Pederson and Patricia Zimmermann draw on their work as programmers for the Finger Lakes Environmental Film

Festival, a multi-disciplinary, multi-arts, cross-platform festival, to examine women's new feminist media 'ecologies' – environments, ventures and practices that reject the goal of producing a fixed object such as an analog feature film. Instead, practitioners work within relational and participatory models, with the role of director yielding to that of designer or convener within place-based encounters and workshops. Highlighting intersectional connections between feminism and a host of other issues, projects also range across media platforms as in *The Lunch Love Community Project* (an online mosaic promoting healthy food in schools) and *Children of Srikandi* (a collaborative multimedia LBGT project in Indonesia).

Taken together, these chapters redirect the argument about the lack of options for women directors. In Chapter 1, having delineated the historical importance of Women Make Movies, and while noting that investment in women's independent production is growing, Sarah Sinwell nevertheless predicts, in a supposition validated by several other contributors, that alternative distribution and exhibition venues such as Netflix, Hulu, Video on Demand and cross-media platforms will become increasingly necessary options. In this light, the Finger Lakes Environmental Film Festival's shift to new media fittingly concludes a volume whose chapters demonstrate how social, industrial and technological changes in cinema have altered feminist practice and, with it, conceptions of film feminism. Yet throughout, these chapters reveal women working within the marginal spaces and intersections, whether of the industry, genres, or identities, rather than assimilating to existing models or opposing them in the sense in which feminist 'counter-cinema' once did. The 'difference' of American women's independent cinema is usefully approached by way of the Deleuzo-Guattarian term 'minor', which, as Alison Butler has identified, frees the practice from both an essentialist understanding of the category 'women' *and* the binarisms – 'popular/elitist, avant-garde/mainstream, positive/negative' – that frame it as a parallel or oppositional cinema (Butler 2002: 21–2). A women's minor cinema operates instead as an 'inflected mode' that reworks and contests the conventions of a major language from within, and is thereby distinguished not on the basis of an essentialised subjectivity but on the cultural positions of the women it projects: 'neither included within nor excluded from cultural traditions, lacking a cohesive collective identity, but yet not absolutely differentiated from one another' (Butler 2002: 22).

Far from taking an 'oppositional' stance, veterans like Susan Seidelman, Allison Anders and Mary Harron now occupy such cultural positions, operating between Hollywood and art film, between Indiewood and television, much as precursors like Ida Lupino did in the 1950s, yet to the extent that the current concept of 'independence' – and even 'filmmaking' – begs to be redefined. Like them, younger practitioners including Megan Griffiths, Debra Granik, Courtney Hunt, Karen Moncrieff, Lynn Shelton, So Yong Kim, Desiree

Akhavan and Sanaa Hamri rework Hollywood and indie genres and modalities, male, white, and black, contesting, redirecting and intersecting them to feminist ends while utilising their power to attract and affect audiences. Mira Nair, Nia Vardalos, Lisa Cholodenko and Miranda July mobilise the concept of 'in-betweenness' as a site of potential and transformation in mediating their multitudes of professional and artistic identities. And Kelly Reichardt, Nicole Holofcener, Lena Dunham and Lynn Shelton and their 'muses' demonstrate a range of collaborative creative methods – not to demolish or even to circumvent, but to *reframe* the now hoary model of the maverick male auteur.

This volume celebrates the differences of its subjects but also demonstrates the historical importance of being able to talk about these women together. They represent one of the first groups of American women filmmakers who share something in common. They are attempting to navigate the murky waters of self-expression versus commercialism and feminist ideals versus mainstream acceptance, to push the boundaries of genre versus remaining within conventional expectations, and to challenge preconceived notions of gender, race, ethnicity, class, and sexual orientation without antagonising an audience. The fact that they necessarily share these concerns represents a new phase in the trajectory of American women filmmakers that, until now, has gone unexplored.

References

Blaetz, Robin (ed.) (2007), *Women's Experimental Cinema: Critical Frameworks*, Durham, NC: Duke University Press.

Butler, Alison (2002), *Women's Cinema: The Contested Screen*, London: Wallflower.

Cook, Pam (1988), 'Approaching the Work of Dorothy Arzner', in Constance Penley (ed.), *Feminism and Film Theory*, New York: Routledge, 1988, pp. 46–56.

Dargis, Manohla (2008), 'Is There a Real Woman in this Multiplex?', *The New York Times*, 4 May, <http://www.nytimes.com/2008/05/04/movies/moviesspecial/04dargi.html?_r=0> (last accessed 27 July 2015).

Dargis, Manohla (2014a), 'Making History: With "Selma", Ava DuVernay Seeks a Different Equality', *The New York Times*, 3 December, <http://www.nytimes.com/2014/12/07/movies/ava-duvernay-makes-a-mark-with-selma.html> (last accessed 27 July 2015).

Dargis, Manohla (2014b), 'In Hollywood, it's a Men's, Men's, Men's World', *The New York Times*, 24 December, <http://www.nytimes.com/2014/12/28/movies/in-hollywood-its-a-mens-mens-mens-world.html> (last accessed 27 July 2015).

Dargis, Manohla (2015), 'Lights, Camera, Taking Action: On Many Fronts, Women are Fighting for Better Opportunity in Hollywood', *The New York Times*, 21 January, <http://www.nytimes.com/2015/01/25/movies/on-many-fronts-women-are-fighting-for-better-opportunity-in-hollywood.html?ref=arts> (last accessed 27 July, 2015).

Davis, Therese, Belinda Smaill and Patricia White (eds) (2014), 'The Place of the Contemporary Female Director', *Camera Obscura* special issue, 85.

Grant, Catherine (2001), 'Secret Agents: Feminist Theories of Women's Film Authorship', *Feminist Theory*, 2: 1, pp. 113–30.

Haskell, Molly (1973), *From Reverence to Rape: The Treatment of Women in the Movies*, Harmondsworth: Penguin Books.

Johnston, Claire (1988), 'Dorothy Arzner: Critical Strategies', in Constance Penley (ed.), *Feminism and Film Theory*, New York: Routledge, pp. 36–45.

Johnston, Claire ([1973]/1999), 'Women's Cinema as Counter-Cinema', in Sue Thornham (ed.), *Feminist Film Theory: A Reader*, Edinburgh: Edinburgh University Press, pp. 31–40.

Keller, Sarah (2014), *Maya Deren: Incomplete Control*, New York: Columbia University Press.

Kiang, Jessica (2014), '10 Female Directors Who Deserve More Attention From Hollywood', *Indiewire*, 24 September <http://blogs.indiewire.com/theplaylist/10-female-directors-who-deserve-more-attention-from-hollywood-20140924> (last accessed 27 July, 2015).

King, Geoff (2005), *American Independent Cinema*, Bloomington: Indiana University Press.

Kuhn, Annette (1995), 'Introduction: Intestinal Fortitude', in Annette Kuhn (ed.), *Queen of the 'B's: Ida Lupino Behind the Camera*, Westport, CT: Praeger, pp. 1–12.

Lauzen, Martha M. (2015a), 'The Celluloid Ceiling: Behind-the-Scenes Employment of Women on the Top 250 Films of 2014', *Center for the Study of Women in Television & Film*, <http://womenintvfilm.sdsu.edu/files/2014_Celluloid_Ceiling_Report.pdf> (last accessed 27 July 2015).

Lauzen, Martha M. (2015b), 'Independent Women: Behind-the-Scenes Employment on Independent Films in 2014–15', *Center for the Study of Women in Television & Film*, <http://womenintvfilm.sdsu.edu/files/2015_Independent_Women_Report.pdf> (last accessed 27 July 2015).

Louie, Mynette (2015), 'A Female Producer Explains 4 Ways Women Get a Raw Deal in Hollywood', *Vulture*, 7 July, <http://www.vulture.com/2015/07/how-hollywood-discriminates-female-filmmakers.html> (last accessed 27 July 2015).

Mayne, Judith (1994), *Directed by Dorothy Arzner*, Bloomington: Indiana University Press.

McHugh, Kathleen (2005), 'History and Falsehood in Experimental Documentaries', in Jean Petrolle and Virginia Wright Wexman (eds), *Women and Experimental Filmmaking*, Urbana: University of Illinois Press, pp. 107–27.

McHugh, Kathleen (2007), 'The Experimental "Dunyementary": A Cinematic Signature Event', in *Women's Experimental Cinema: Critical Frameworks*, Durham, NC: Duke University Press, pp. 339–59.

Nichols, Bill (ed.) (2001), *Maya Deren and the American Avant-Garde*, Berkeley: University of California Press.

Perkins, Claire and Constantine Verevis (eds) (2014), 'Introduction: Possible Films', in C. Perkins and C. Verevis (eds), *US Independent Film After 1989: Possible Films*, Edinburgh: Edinburgh University Press.

Petrolle, Jean and Virginia Wright Wexman (ed.) (2005), *Women and Experimental Filmmaking*. Urbana: University of Illinois Press.

Silverstein, Melissa (2014), 'Women Filmmakers Fare Much Better in the Indie World – But It's Still Not Good Enough', *Forbes*, 7 May, <http://www.forbes.com/sites/melissasilverstein/2014/05/06/women-filmmakers-fare-much-better-in-the-indie-world-but-its-still-not-good-enough/> (last accessed 27 July, 2015).

Smith, Stacy L, Marc Choueiti, Elizabeth Scofield and Katherine Pieper (2013), 'Gender Inequality in 500 Popular Films: Examining On-Screen Portrayals and Behind-the-Scenes Employment Patterns in Motion Pictures Released between 2007–2012', *Annenberg School for Communication and Journalism*, <http://annenberg.

usc.edu/sites/default/files/2015/04/28/Gender%20Inequality%20in%20500%20 Popular%20Films.pdf> (last accessed 27 July 2015).

Turim, Maureen (2005), 'The Violence of Desire in Avant-Garde Films', in Jean Petrolle and Virginia Wright Wexman (eds), *Women and Experimental Filmmaking*, Urbana: University of Illinois Press, pp. 71–90.

Tzioumakis, Yannis (2006), *American Independent Cinema: An Introduction*, New Brunswick, NJ: Rutgers University Press.

White, Patricia (2015), *Women's Cinema, World Cinema: Projecting Contemporary Feminisms*, Durham, NC: Duke University Press.

Willmore, Alison (2014), 'How Many of These Movies by Female Directors Have You Seen?', *BuzzFeed*, 18 April, <http://www.buzzfeed.com/alisonwillmore/how-many-of-these-movies-by-female-directors-have-you-seen#.tvqNg9QxG> (last accessed 27 July 2015).

PART I

PRODUCTION AND DISTRIBUTION CONTEXTS

1. WOMEN MAKE MOVIES: CHICKEN & EGG PICTURES, GAMECHANGER FILMS AND THE FUTURE OF FEMALE INDEPENDENT FILMMAKING

Sarah E. S. Sinwell

As numerous critics and studies have noted, though women now represent 50% of film school graduates, there is still a limited number of films directed by women within the cultural marketplace. For instance, only 5% of the directors of the Top 100 grossing films of 1994–2013 and only 7% of directors of the 250 top grossing films of 2009–12 were women. In addition, women comprise only 13.5% of the Director's Guild of America. The independent film industry only marginally increases these numbers, with women comprising 18% of the directors of narrative features at film festivals between 2011 and 2012 and 10% of directors of indie features between 2009 and 2013 (Gamechanger Films 2015).

In 2001, the feminist group of artists and activists the Guerrilla Girls drew attention to this gender disparity within the industry by targeting the sexist hiring and promotional practices for film directors noting that no Best Director Oscar had ever been awarded to a woman. Although in 2010, Kathryn Bigelow became the first woman to win the Best Director Oscar for *The Hurt Locker*, only three other female filmmakers have ever been nominated for Best Director (Lina Wertmuller, Jane Campion, and Sofia Coppola). However, it is also important to note that when given the same budget, feature films by women do as well at the box office as those by men (Kelly and Robson 2014: 18). Citing a recent study by USC's Media, Diversity, and Social Change Initiative, Stacy L. Smith argues that 'The No. 1 barrier is financial . . . The people who fund films and greenlight content are mostly male. Women are perceived to lack confidence and to be less trustworthy with resources' (Keegan 2014). Thus, female film directors are not only less likely to get their projects funded, but they also lack the financial and industrial resources necessary to get their films produced, distributed and exhibited. This chapter examines three for-profit and not-for-profit organisations that are attempting to shift this gender disparity within the film industry: Women Make Movies, Chicken & Egg Pictures and Gamechanger Films.

Taking an industrial and historical approach to the work of female practitioners within the independent film industry, this essay traces a history of female independent filmmaking from the creation of Women Make Movies in 1972 to the introduction of for-profit and not-for-profit organisations Chicken & Egg Pictures and Gamechanger Films in the past decade. To this end, this study draws attention to the ways in which the financial, economic, and industrial constraints and support networks for women's filmmaking have impacted the presence of women in the independent film industry. Whereas many critics have addressed the lack of women in the industry (especially in directorial positions), few critics have analysed the role that these not-for-profit and for-profit organisations have played in the history, present and future of female independent filmmaking.

Perhaps most famously, Women Make Movies was started in 1972 to address the under representation and misrepresentation of women in the media industry (Women Make Movies 2015). Although this organisation focuses primarily on the distribution of women's films, it also includes a production assistance programme that provides fiscal sponsorship, media workshops, and information services for independent filmmakers. Female filmmakers such as Jane Campion, Julie Dash, Sally Potter, Trinh T. Minh-ha, Lourdes Portillo, Tracey Moffatt, Valie Export, Kim Longinotto, Pratibha Parmar, Ngozi Onwurah and Ulrike Ottinger are included within the Women Make Movies Collection. To date, this organisation continues to be one of the primary distribution outlets for movies made by female filmmakers.

Chicken & Egg Pictures was created in 2005 to support the work of female nonfiction filmmakers. Chicken & Egg Pictures has awarded over $3.7 million in grants to nearly 160 film projects and has provided over 4,500 hours of mentorship directly to filmmakers (Chicken & Egg Pictures 2015a). Backing the presence of women filmmakers in the documentary film market, one of the central tenets of Chicken & Egg Pictures is to provide funding for films directed by women that focus on social issues such as environmental change and global human rights. For instance, films such as *Orgasm, Inc.* (Elizabeth Canner, 2009), *Children in No Man's Land* (Anayansi Prado, 2009), *Semper Fi: Always Faithful* (Rachel Liber and Tony Hardmon, 2011), and *Brooklyn Castle* (Katie Dellamaggiore, 2012) have all received funding from Chicken & Egg Pictures.

In 2013, the first for-profit film fund exclusively targeting narrative feature-length films directed by women, Gamechanger Films, was created. Focusing on scripted films, this organisation will fund up to ten narrative features directed by women in the coming years. The goal of this organisation is to create a new community of investors who will provide a support structure for a new generation of women filmmakers. In 2013, Gamechanger funded the Independent Spirit and John Cassavetes Award-winning film *Land Ho!* (Martha Stephens and Aaron Katz, 2014). As of this writing, Gamechanger has also financed *The Invitation* (Karyn Kusama, 2014), *Fresno* (Jamie Babbit, 2014), and *Lovesong* (So Yong Kim, 2014), all of which are currently in post-production.

This essay studies the industrial and financial contexts and constraints facing these organisations and the ways in which these organisations are impacting the future of female independent filmmaking. Taking a three-pronged approach to this study, I will first examine the ways in which Women Make Movies pioneered funding for the production and distribution of female independent films. Next, I will focus on Chicken & Egg Pictures and the interrelationships between documentary filmmaking and feminist practice. Then I will examine the ways in which Gamechanger Films has promoted a for-profit model of female independent filmmaking. I will conclude by discussing strategies for the future of female independent filmmaking.

Women Make Movies: Pioneers and Precursors

As Anthony Slide has noted in *Early Women Directors*, women were not always so under-represented within the film industry. He argues, 'During the silent era, women can be said to have dominated the industry. There were over thirty women directors prior to 1920, more than at any other period of film history' (1977: 9). In fact, at that time, Film Director was considered a viable career choice for women (Lauzen 2012: 310). Female filmmakers such as Lois Weber, Ida May Park, Lillian Gish, and Dorothy Arzner all made films within the constraints of the Hollywood studio system (Kelly 2014: 106). Since the 1920s, however, the number of female filmmakers has continued to dwindle. Though the creation of international women's film festivals, conferences, and film journals since the 1970s has contributed to the success of female independent filmmaking, many of these female independent filmmakers have had to seek out additional funding and resources in order to get their films produced and distributed (Kaplan 2002).

Established in 1972 by Ariel Dougherty and Sheila Page to address the under representation and misrepresentation of women in the media industry, Women Make Movies started with 'the specific mission of training women to become film and video makers' (Women Make Movies 2015c). From its inception, Women Make Movies was engaged with the intersections between feminist theory and filmmaking practice. As noted on its website, the organisation supports films by and about women. To this end, the website explains,

> We believe that women's media, in both traditional and non-traditional forms, presents social, political, and aesthetic visions of women that are not generally available in mainstream media. Reflecting an understanding of women's experience, women's independent films reveal the complexity and diversity of women's lives and artistic visions. We remain steadfast in our belief that media can inform and engage, inspire action and challenge reigning perspectives. (Women Make Movies 2015a)

As Debra Zimmerman, Executive Director of Women Make Movies since 1983, has noted, not only do women making films about women get less money, but 'Men making films about women get less money than women making films about men' (Zimmerman and White 2013: 154). Thus, to be distributed by Women Make Movies, a film must not only be directed or co-directed by a woman, but it must also include a subject or issue of specific relevance to women's lives. Thus, many of these films address social and political issues such as international human rights, environmentalism, activism, body image, domestic violence, criminal justice, global feminism, labour studies, medical ethics, and reproductive rights.

Supporting feminist conferences, film festivals, and touring theatrical programmes at museums, galleries, libraries, colleges, universities and media arts organisations across the United States and abroad, Women Make Movies encourages collaboration among artists, activists, theorists, teachers, and filmmakers. According to its website, 'Women Make Movies is a multicultural, multiracial, non-profit media arts organisation which facilitates the production, promotion, distribution and exhibition of independent films and videotapes by and about women. The organisation provides services to both users and makers of film and video programs, with a special emphasis on supporting work by women of colour' (Women Make Movies 2015c). Though the Distribution Service is its primary programme, Women Make Movies also provides Production Assistance for female filmmakers as well.

The Women Make Movies Production Assistance Program provides low-cost media workshops and information services to female independent filmmakers. Acting as a non-profit tax-exempt umbrella organisation, Women Make Movies provides individualised fundraising and ongoing project consultations, fundraising sources, grant resource materials and production information, and networking opportunities with other women media makers (Women Make Movies 2015b). Despite its growing lack of governmental support from organisations like the National Endowment for the Arts, the New York State Council on the Arts, and the Educational Foundation of America, Women Make Movies continues to work as an advocacy organisation to support female independent filmmaking and is the foremost distributor of films made by and about women in both the US and abroad (Aufderheide 2004: 1455).

Since the 1970s, Women Make Movies has funded, produced and distributed films such as Lizzie Borden's *Born in Flames* (1983), Trinh Minh-ha's *Surname Viet Given Name Nam* (1989), and Lourdes Portillo's Sundance Film Festival award-winning *Señorita Extraviada* (2011). In the 1980s, the Women Make Movies catalogue included about forty films. Now, it includes 550 films and distributes about eighteen to twenty-five films a year (Zimmerman 2013: 1511). In addition, Women Make Movies now distributes the work of over 400 female filmmakers from over thirty countries (Women Make Movies 2015c). Recently, the films that Women Make Movies has assisted in producing include *Which Way Home* (Rebecca Cammisa, 2009), *Pariah* (Dee Rees, 2011), *Citizenfour* (Lara Poltras, 2014), and *The Diary of a Teenage Girl* (Marielle Heller, 2015). Some of its most popular recent releases include films such as *Regarding Susan Sontag* (Patricia Clarkson, 2015), *India's Daughter* (Leslee Udwin, 2015), and *Golden Gate Girls* (S. Louisa Wei, 2014). More than half of the Women Make Movies collection was produced by women of diverse cultures, representing not only national and ethnic diversity, but also the work of women of different ages, sexualities, abilities, and so on. Perhaps most significantly, according to its website, Women Make Movies has returned more than $1.5 million to women producers in royalty payments over the last three years (Women Make Movies 2015c). Thus, Women Make Movies has consistently been a driving force in the production and distribution of independent films made by women. However, it is also important to note that many of these films fail to reach the wider audiences of other independent films within the marketplace because the distribution and exhibition of the films from Women Make Movies is often limited to small art cinemas and college campuses. More recently, Chicken & Egg Pictures and Gamechanger Films have joined Women Make Movies in the attempt to give more financial and industrial support to female independent filmmakers.

Chicken & Egg Pictures: Documentary Film and Feminist Practice

The connections between female documentary filmmaking and activism are often overlooked. In her essay, 'Women's Film Production: Going Mainstream', Michelle Citron points out that many female filmmakers have turned to documentary in an attempt to represent 'real' women onscreen, 'something that Hollywood not only failed to do, but actively worked against' (1988: 50). As Kelly Hankin notes in her essay, 'And Introducing . . . The Female Director: Documentaries About Women Filmmakers as Feminist Activism', 'Statistical and anecdotal evidence suggest that, in both Hollywood and commercial independent film industries, female directors are not given the same support and opportunities as their male counterparts' (2007: 59). Thus, the films that are funded by Chicken & Egg contribute to a long-standing tradition of documentary, activism and feminist filmmaking. Addressing such topics as criminal justice, disability rights, poverty, education, food security and access, Internet freedom, health care, immigration, labour rights, and reproductive justice, Chicken & Egg Pictures works to catalyse social change on a global scale.

Founded in 2005 by Julie Parker Benello, Wendy Ettinger, and Judith Helfand in order to support women non-fiction filmmakers who tell stories that encourage social change, Chicken & Egg Pictures is the only non-profit film fund devoted solely to supporting women documentary directors (Bernstein 2014). In 2005, Chicken & Egg funded its first film, *The Forest for the Trees* (*Der Wald vor lauter Bäumen*, Maren Ade, 2003). As noted on its website, 'Since 2005, Chicken & Egg Pictures has awarded $3.7 million and 5,220 hours of mentorship to over 180 films' (Chicken & Egg Pictures 2015b). Chicken & Egg funds about ten to fifteen new projects a year with an average grant of $10,000 matched with ten hours of mentorship (Chicken & Egg Pictures 2015b). Not only does Chicken & Egg provide start-up money for female filmmakers, but it also provides additional grants so that directors who have almost completed their films may complete the final stages of editing and post-production. Like Women Make Movies, Chicken & Egg provides mentoring for its grant winners with the goal of creating sustainable filmmaking practices for female filmmakers. And, unlike many other film funds, Chicken & Egg also provides additional grants for outreach and community engagement efforts (Chicken & Egg Pictures 2015b).

Tackling issues such as human rights, environmentalism, and social justice, Chicken & Egg also promotes the intersections between activism, philanthropy, and film. To this end, Chicken & Egg also backs two specific issue-driven film funds, the Mother With Human Rights Film Fund (which supports diverse filmmakers from around the world who are making films on human rights) and the Which Came First Environmental Film Fund (which supports projects that take on environmental justice issues). In 2014, Chicken & Egg partnered with the India Documentary Foundation to create a new fund to support women documentarians from India.

Partnered with such organisations as the Athena Film Festival, DOC NYC, the Indian Documentary Film Foundation, and the True/False Film Fest, films funded by Chicken & Egg have played at the Sundance Film Festival, South by Southwest Festival, Hot Docs International Documentary Festival, and Tribeca Film Festival. Some of Chicken & Egg's most popular films to date include *Orgasm, Inc.* (Elizabeth Canner, 2009), *Children in No Man's Land* (Anayansi Prado, 2009), *Semper Fi: Always Faithful* (Rachel Liber and Tony Hardmon, 2011), and *Brooklyn Castle* (Katie Dellamaggiore, 2012). In addition, Chicken & Egg backed the Oscar-winning short films, *Freeheld* (Cynthia Wade, 2007) about a lesbian couple's battle for pension benefits, and *Saving*

Figure 1.1 *Hot Girls Wanted* (2015) © Courtesy of Hot Girls Wanted.

Face (Sharmeen Obaid Chinoy and Daniel Junge, 2012) about acid attacks on women in Pakistan.

Chicken & Egg Pictures has also worked to distribute many of its films on both Netflix and Video on Demand (VOD), acknowledging the growing role of video streaming in the independent and documentary filmmaking marketplace. Since a small percentage of these documentary films screen theatrically, Chicken & Egg is also making deals with Netflix and other digital and video on demand services so that these films may be screened online. For instance, *Hot Girls Wanted* (Jill Bauer and Ronna Gradus, 2015) and *Sexy Baby* (Jill Bauer and Ronna Gradus, 2012) have both been picked up by Netflix. When announcing the acquisition of *Hot Girls Wanted*, Netflix Vice President of Global Independent Content Erik Barmack said, 'Jill and Ronna have exposed a shocking world of hope and heartbreak. The filmmakers gained unprecedented access into a world never documented until now, and we are proud to bring their unflinching work to a global audience' (Chicken & Egg Pictures 2015c). In January 2015, *American Revolutionary: The Evolution of Grace Lee Boggs* (Grace Lee, 2013) and *Vessel* (Diana Whitten, 2013) were also released for download on digital platforms such as iTunes, Amazon Instant Video, VUDU, and Google Play. Chicken & Egg's awareness and utilisation of multiple platforms of distribution and exhibition also reflects their awareness of the independent film marketplace and creates a new space for viewing female independent documentaries online.

Gamechanger Films: Gender and Financial Equity

Founded in 2013 by the co-founders of Chicken & Egg Pictures, Julie Parker Benello and Wendy Ettinger (together with fellow veteran documentary producers Dan Cogan and Geralyn Dreyfous), Gamechanger Films is the first equity fund that exclusively finances narrative features directed by women (Gamechanger Films 2015a). However, unlike Women Make Movies and Chicken & Egg Pictures, Gamechanger only finances fictional narrative films. With the goal of shifting the gender disparity within the film industry, Gamechanger provides production financing for female independent filmmakers 'no matter what kinds of stories they choose to tell' (Gamechanger Films 2015a). Gamechanger is committed to financing all genres of films with no restrictions on their content, so films do not have to be female-themed or have female protagonists in order to be financed. This mission is quite different from the missions of Women Make Movies and Chicken & Egg Pictures in that both fund only stories by and *about* women. According to Gamechanger President Mynette Louie, Gamechanger aims to create a new community of sophisticated and empowered film financiers by making investor education an integral part of their Gamechanger experience.

> We want to create a new source of 'smart money' that can support a new generation of women directors while making a return on their investment. We believe, and studies show, that more women at the helm will influence the sort of films that are made, the way those stories are told, and the POV of the characters that inhabit those stories. More women at the helm will also spark a trickle-down effect of greater female representation among the entire crew – cinematographers, editors, sound mixers, production designers, and more. By investing in women-directed features, Gamechanger is investing in the leadership and employment of women behind the camera, as well as in a greater diversity of perspectives on screen. (Fernandez, 2014)

Gamechanger is committed to funding female directors not only because there is a paucity of women in the industry, but also because 'When a woman is in the director's chair, there is likely to be a higher proportion of women in all other departments, and female characters on screen are likely to be more multidimensional' (Gamechanger Films 2015a). As stated in the *Los Angeles Times*, 'Gamechanger aims to fully or partly finance up to 10 narrative feature films in the coming years, in budgets generally ranging from $1 million to $5 million, across all genres' (Zeitchik 2013). Although Gamechanger President Mynette Louie cited '*Frozen River* [Courtney Hunt, 2008] and *Winter's Bone* [Debra Granik, 2010] – both movies by and from women – as models for

Gamechanger films, stories about or starring women are not a prerequisite. The selection committee – which includes Louie, Skalski, Cogan, Dreyfous and Chicken & Egg's Julie Parker Benello and Wendy Ettinger – will give equal weight to scripts focusing on either gender and on any subject' (Zeitchik 2013). Thus, Gamechanger's Independent Spirit Award-winning first feature *Land Ho!* was funded despite the fact that it is a buddy comedy focusing on the story of two ex-brothers-in-law who go on a road trip through Iceland.

Gamechanger acts as an executive producer and this is why it is only involved in production and post-production and not film development, packaging, or distribution. However, the Gamechanger website notes that *Land Ho!*, the only Gamechanger film released theatrically to date, was distributed by Sony Pictures Classics. The Gamechanger website also notes the Blu-Ray and VOD Release dates for *Land Ho!* This certainly points to the significance of VOD releases for the future of the independent film market (Gamechanger Films 2015b). As award-winning filmmaker of *Gideon's Army* (2013) and *Spies of Mississippi* (2014) Dawn Porter notes, 'So who controls the message matters not just in some fuzzy world of feel good sunshine, but because the social and political questions of our time are impacted by the commercial market' (Porter 2014). And, it is these demands of the commercial market that Gamechanger is concerned with.

Also, unlike Women Make Movies and Chicken & Egg Pictures, Gamechanger does not accept unsolicited submissions. Rather, it scouts for projects via film festivals, agents, managers, filmmaker programmes and other established film professionals and project markets. To date, the funding for many of these Gamechanger films, Martha Stephens' *Land Ho!*, as well as Karyn Kusama's *The Invitation* (2014), Jamie Babbit's *Fresno* (2014) and So Yong Kim's *Lovesong* (2014), went to female filmmakers who had already proven their successes in the independent film industry, as well as on television and via the Hollywood studios. For instance, Kusama won the Director's Prize and shared the Grand Jury Prize at the 2000 Sundance Film Festival for *Girlfight* (1999). She also directed *Aeon Flux* (2004) for Paramount Pictures and *Jennifer's Body* (2009) for Twentieth Century-Fox. And Babbit, director of *But I'm a Cheerleader* (1999) and *The Itty Bitty Titty Committee* (2007), also directs for popular TV series such as *Girls* (HBO, 2012–present), *Looking* (HBO, 2014–present), *The United States of Tara* (Showtime, 2009–11), and *Brooklyn 99* (Fox, 2013–present). Korean-American filmmaker So Yong Kim received the Special Jury Prize at the Sundance Film Festival for her debut feature *In Between Days* in 2006 and was nominated for the John Cassavetes Award and Best Cinematography at the Independent Spirit Awards for her 2008 film, *Treeless Mountain*. Thus, to date, Gamechanger has not taken on any risks in its financing of female independent filmmakers. However, because it has only financed four films as of 2015, the future of Gamechanger remains to be seen.

Strategies for Independence: The Future of Female Independent Filmmaking

As Gabrielle Kelly has noted in *Celluloid Ceiling*, the key issue facing independent filmmakers today is distribution (Kelly 2014: 116). Members of the International Documentary Association recognise that Video on Demand (VOD) is the future of independent and documentary distribution (Valenti 2012). At a SXSW panel in 2012, founder of the Film Collaborative, Orly Ravid, President of Magnolia Pictures Eamonn Bowles and a variety of other independent filmmakers and professionals gave a presentation entitled, 'How I Learned to Stop Worrying and Love VOD' (The Film Colllaborative 2012). Using their release of *American: The Bill Hicks Story* (Matt Harlock and Paul Thomas, 2009) as a model, they argue that the future of independent and documentary film distribution is VOD. Advocating ad-supported VOD strategies for independent and documentary films such as Netflix and Hulu, these industry professionals noted that VOD distribution strategies often provide significant revenue generators and may lead to additional viewing on cable and satellite services.

Filmmaker, media strategist and author of *Think Outside the Box Office: The Ultimate Guide to Film Distribution and Marketing for the Digital Era,* Jon Reiss warns that these models are constantly changing and encourages filmmakers to read the fine print and exhaust multiple options, including not only ad-supported streaming but direct distribution models, and encourages filmmakers to consider digital rights in relation to foreign sales (2010). But, for many unknown independent (and female) filmmakers, Netflix, Hulu, and Video on Demand may be the best options among these, especially if the film has not received much critical acclaim or if its content is not immediately marketable to wider audiences.

In fact, as more and more independent filmmakers turn to Video on Demand options, independent cinema's meaning is continuing to change as it becomes more immediately available and more accessible via streaming and digital distribution on sites such as Amazon, Netflix and Hulu. In this context, these forms of media convergence 'represent a paradigm shift' towards the interdependence of different media delivery channels and more complex relationships between corporate and independent media (Jenkins 2002). Without the well defined and guaranteed audiences of larger media franchises, independent films made by women must often engage with the advent of these digital technologies in their own unique ways.

Thus, female independent filmmakers may choose to release their films on Amazon, Netflix or Hulu in the hopes of not only getting their films seen by a larger audience, but also with the possibility of earning enough money to recoup the costs of making these films and financing their DVD releases. These alternative distribution and exhibition venues and cross-media platforms are especially significant given the high costs of both theatrical exhibition and DVD distribution. The success of films such as *Hot Girls Wanted* and *Sexy Baby* on Netflix, as well as Jill Soloway's television series *Transparent* (2014) on Amazon, point to the possibilities that alternative distribution and exhibition practices may hold for female independent filmmakers. And, in an era in which video streaming is now outperforming DVD sales, the use of online distribution and exhibition spaces have become even more necessary as female independent filmmakers attempt to navigate a variety of film distribution and exhibition sites online.

Interestingly, many filmmakers have noted that it is easier for women to succeed at documentary filmmaking than narrative feature filmmaking. As Dawn Porter discussed in her keynote address at the 'Getting Real' Documentary Film Conference in Los Angeles, 'The difference with documentary is you don't have to ask permission to star . . . There is still a lot of work involved, but you don't have to get that first "yes" to pursue the project and there's not as much of an initial financial commitment. So to eliminate those hurdles makes a big difference' (Porter 2014).

Lynn Shelton, director of *Humpday* (2009), *Your Sister's Sister* (2011) and *Touchy Feely* (2013) 'believes in starting small and developing a distinctive body of work supported by a web of ongoing relationships. "I've really built my career on my own terms and stayed true to my vision, and that has been the best calling card ever", she says. "I'd recommend this approach to any person who wants to have a filmmaking career" (Dawes 2014). Director of *Salaam Bombay!* (1988), *Monsoon Wedding* (2001), and *The Reluctant Fundamentalist* (2013), Mira Nair states, 'But if your movie has muscularity and some sort of emotional power, and people go see it, then other people take you seriously, and they come to you with studio financing and whatever' (Dawes 2014).

The future of female independent filmmaking also lies in the possibilities for film production, exhibition and distribution globally. In their introduction to *Celluloid Ceiling*, female film producers Gabrielle Kelly and Cheryl Robson note that 'The percentage of women film directors in Iran is higher than the percentage of women directors making films in the USA [and] the percentage of women directors is higher in countries (like India) where the upper classes are involved in film production' (2014: 18). Thus, the financial support of organisations like Women Make Movies, Chicken & Egg Pictures and Gamechanger Films is particularly important as it provides opportunities for female independent filmmakers across the globe.

Of course, the future of female independent filmmaking is unknown. However, it is clear that in the contemporary market, online streaming and on-demand video services are continuing to grow. As Gamechanger President Mynette Louie stated in an interview in *Rolling Stone*, 'It's such a difficult landscape right now . . . With audience behaviour shifting, with TV getting better, with Netflix and Hulu getting into the distribution game, it's hard to get yourself known as a filmmaker' (Susman 2013). However, access to female independent filmmaking instantly and on demand is creating wider audiences for female independent films online (Chicken & Egg Pictures Grants 2015). Thus, women's place in the independent filmmaking marketplace is still up for negotiation. At least for the moment, investment in indie female filmmaking continues to grow.

References

Aufderheide, Pat and Debra Zimmerman (2004), 'From A to Z: A Conversation on Women's Filmmaking', *Signs*, 30: 1, pp. 1,455–72.

Bernstein, Paula (2014), 'Chicken & Egg Pictures: The Force Behind Women Directed Documentaries at Sundance and Beyond', *Indiewire*, <http://www.indiewire.com/article/meet-the-funders-chicken-egg-is-the-force-behind-women-directed-documentaries> (last accessed 1 April 2015).

Chicken & Egg Pictures (2015a), <http://Chickeneggpics.org> (last accessed 1 April 2015).

Chicken & Egg Pictures (2015b), 'Grants', <http://Chickeneggpics.org/grants> (last accessed 1 April 2015).

Chicken & Egg Pictures (2015c), 'Netflix Acquires Hot Girls Wanted', blog entry, <http://chickeneggpics.org/netflix-acquires-hot-girls-wanted/> (last accessed 1 April 2015).

Citron, Michelle (1988), 'Women's Film Production: Going Mainstream', in E. Deidre Pribram (ed.), *Female Spectators: Looking at Film and Television*, London and New York: Verso, pp. 45–63.

Dargis, Manohla (2014), 'In Hollywood, It's a Men's, Men's, Men's World', *The New York Times*, 24 December, <http://www.nytimes.com/2014/12/28/movies/in-hollywood-its-a-mens-mens-mens-world.html?ref=arts&_r=1> (last accessed 1 April 2015).

Dawes, Amy (2014), 'Women's Movement?' Director's Guild of America, <http://www.dga.org/Craft/DGAQ/All-Articles/1403-Summer-2014/Womens-Movement.aspx> (last accessed 1 April 2015).

Fernandez, Rebecca (2014), Interview, 'Mynette Louie: President, Gamechanger Films.' <http://thewomentakeover.com/mynette-louie-president-gamechanger-films> (last accessed 1 April 2015).

Gamechanger Films (2015b), <http://gamechanger-films.com> (last accessed 7 April 2015).

Gamechanger Films (2015b), *'Land Ho!'*, <http://gamechanger-films.com/land-ho> (last accessed 7 April 2015).

Hankin, Kelly (2007), 'And Introducing . . . The Female Director: Documentaries about Women Filmmakers as Feminist Activism', *National Women's Studies Association Journal*, Spring, 19:1, pp. 59–88.

The Film Collaborative (2012), 'How I Learned to Stop Worrying and Love VOD', *SXSW*, <http://www.thefilmcollaborative.org/sxsw/American_VOD_SXSW2012.pdf> (last accessed 1 April 2015).

Jenkins, Henry (2006), *Convergence Culture: Where Old and New Media Collide*, New York and London: New York University Press.

Kaplan, E. Ann (1983), *Women and Film: Both Sides of the Camera*, London and New York: Routledge.

Kaplan, E. Ann (2002), 'Women, Film, Resistance: Changing Paradigms', in Jacqueline Levitin, Judith Plessis and Valerie Raoul (eds), *Women Filmmakers*, Vancouver: University of British Columbia Press, pp. 15–28.

Keegan, Rebecca (2014), 'Women are Underrepresented in Key Movie Positions, USC Study Finds, *Los Angeles Times*, <http://www.latimes.com/entertainment/movies/la-et-mn-women-hollywood-usc-study-20140724-story.html> (last accessed 1 April 2015).

Kelly, Gabrielle. 'From Hollywood to Indiewood to Chinawood', in Gabrielle Kelly and Cheryl Robson (eds), *Celluloid Ceiling: Women Directors Breaking Through*, Twickenham: Supernova Books, pp. 106–25.

Kelly, Gabrielle and Cheryl Robson (2014), 'Introduction', in Gabrielle Kelly and Cheryl Robson (eds), *Celluloid Ceiling: Women Directors Breaking Through*, Twickenham: Supernova Books, pp. 9–18.

Lauzen, Martha (2012), 'Where are the Film Directors (Who Happen to be Women*)*?', *Quarterly Review of Film and Video*, 29: 4, pp. 310–19.

Porter, Dawn (2014), 'Here's Why We Need More Women and Minority Filmmakers', *Indiewire*, 4 October, <http://www.indiewire.com/article/heres-why-we-need-more-women-and-minority-filmmakers-20141002> (last accessed 1 April 2015).

Reiss, Jon (2010), *Think Outside the Box Office: Ultimate Guide to Film Distribution and Marketing for the Digital Era*, New York: Hybrid Cinema Publishing.

Rich, B. Ruby (1998), *Chick Flicks: Theories and Memories of the Feminist Film Movement*, Durham, NC and London: Duke University Press.

Rich, B. Ruby (2013), 'The Confidence Game', *Camera Obscura: Feminism, Culture, and Media Studies* 28(1 82): 157–65.

Sheppard, Kate (2013), 'How to Crack the Film World's Glass Ceiling: Chicken & Egg Pictures incubates women filmmakers – and has Oscars to show for it', *Mother Jones*, September/October, <http://www.motherjones.com/media/2013/09/chicken-egg-pictures-women-filmmakers-documentary-after-tiller> (last accessed 1 April 2015).

Slide, Anthony (1977), *Early Women Directors*, New York: Thomas Yoseloff Ltd.

Susman, Gary (2014), 'Where are all the Female Filmmakers', *Rolling Stone*, 29 November, <http://www.rollingstone.com/movies/news/where-are-all-the-female-filmmakers-20131129#ixzz3XFCiutOA> (last accessed 1 April 2015).

Valentina Valenti (2012), 'In VOD We Trust. Navigating the Minefield of the Ever-Changing Distribution Platform', *Documentary Magazine*, <http://www.documentary.org/magazine/vod-we-trust-navigating-minefield-ever-changing-distribution-platform> (last accessed 1 April 2015).

Zimmerman, Debra and Patricia White (2013), 'Looking Back and Forward: A Conversation about Women Make Movies', *Camera Obscura: Feminism, Culture, and Media Studies*, 28, 1:82, pp. 147–55.

Women Make Movies (2015a), 'Filmmakers', <http://www.wmm.com/filmmakers/distribution.shtml> (last accessed 1 April 2015).

Women Make Movies (2015b), 'Fiscal Sponsorship', <http://www.wmm.com/filmmakers/fiscal_sponsorship.shtml> (last accessed 1 April 2015).

Women Make Movies (2015c), 'General Info', <http://www.wmm.com/about/general_info.shtml> (last accessed 1 April 2015).

Zeitchik, Steven (2013), 'New Movie Fund Gamechanger Films is Formed to Back Women Directors', *Los Angeles Times*, 27 September, <http://www.latimes.com/entertainment/envelope/cotown/la-et-ct-film-fund-gamechanger-female-directors-20130926-story.html#page=1> (last accessed 1 April 2015).

2. KILLER FEMINISM

Patricia White

In coverage of independent film in both trade and independent outlets in the US, words like 'powerhouse' and 'stalwart' regularly appear in conjunction with the twenty-year-old production house Killer Films (Jones 2008). The aggressive attitude signalled in the company name is reinforced by co-founder Christine Vachon's persona. A lifelong New Yorker, she can be intimidating – habitually clad in black jeans, T-shirt, and combat boots, Blackberry at the ready. She is also a beguiling raconteur with a keen sense of irony about her standing – she jokes that there are people working in her office who weren't even born when Killer started up. Missing from the standard Killer profile is the explicit invocation of feminism, even of the 'lean in' sort that the mainstream press tolerates in reportage of female executives and entrepreneurs. While Vachon and her partner Pamela Koffler are often included in tributes to prominent women in film, such as *Variety*'s annual New York Women's Impact Report (*Variety* staff 2015), the company narrative is identified most closely with the emergence of independent queer cinema and especially with Vachon's close collaboration with auteur Todd Haynes, whom she met at Brown University in the early 1980s. Advocacy of women filmmakers for its own sake is not a major strain of Vachon's self-narration in her two autobiographical books on indie producing, *Shooting to Kill* (1998) and *A Killer Life* (2007), which deal pragmatically and even-handedly with the problems plaguing low-budget productions helmed by men and women. (If the villains tend to be men – sales agents, talent managers, Harvey Weinstein – it is an apt characterisation of an independent film scene defined by male posturing and agon.)

Figure 2.1 Pam Koffler, Todd Haynes and Christine Vachon.

Is Vachon's toughness defensive, a disavowal of female (market?) weakness and/or feminist debt? I'll take it rather as butch swagger and explore the feminist forcefield surrounding Killer Films and its principals, connecting the production house to histories of feminist critique, aesthetic production, political affiliation and cultural work, while remarking on its position within independent film.

Four dimensions of Killer's relation to feminism are considered here: 1) New York City independent film culture, where women have played key roles historically; 2) the emergence of lesbian feature filmmaking in the 1990s; 3) collaboration within the company, with directors, and with other independent film entities, and 4) the shaping of contemporary women's cinema through the work of Todd Haynes. While postfeminist discourses of individual female merit inform Killer's success in the market economy of independent film, its woman-led, project-driven, hands-on, team-oriented culture warrants feminist consideration. At a moment when gender equity in filmmaking has become much more widely scrutinised (Smith 2014; Smith 2015; Lauzen 2014; Lauzen 2015), Killer exemplifies 'not Hollywood' practices on the level of labour, content, form, and conceptualisation of the audience (Ortner 2013). This case study offers a feminist reading of Killer's place within this culture while foregrounding political contradictions within its profile and the current independent film world.

New York Stories

Vachon and Koffler started Killer in 1995, building on Vachon's early successes in the 90s. That work captured the activist energy of ACT-UP and participated in a surge of New York independent feature production alongside and sometimes in collaboration with maverick companies like Good Machine. Vachon and Haynes' first feature, *Poison* (1991), had won the Grand Jury Prize at Sundance in 1991, marking a swerve in the festival's burgeoning brand. *Poison* is a queer narrative in form and subject matter, indebted to Genet, addressed to HIV hysteria, and stylishly mounted on location in New York – including at an abandoned military facility on Governors Island – for a budget of around $250,000. Vachon and Haynes had been working with Brown classmate Barry Ellsworth as producers of low-budget short films by emerging artists through their company Apparatus Productions. While financing independent films in the US has never been easy, in the 80s artists could get grants from places like the New York State Council on the Arts (NYSCA), and the National Endowment for the Arts (NEA). *Poison* became a flashpoint in the culture wars when the religious right latched onto its 'filthy' homosexual content (Vachon 2007: 4).

Vachon was back at Sundance a year later with her second feature as producer, Tom Kalin's *Swoon* (1992), a stylised interpretation of the notorious Leopold-Loeb murder case. Critic and former NYSCA programme officer B. Ruby Rich christened these boldly experimental, anti-assimilationist, and successful independent features the New Queer Cinema (Rich 1992). The first film in the wave that was by and about lesbians rather than gay men – Rose Troche and Guinevere Turner's *Go Fish,* produced by Vachon and Kalin – made market history in 1994 as the first film to sell *during* the Sundance festival. Not long after, Vachon and Koffler, who worked as line producer with Kalin and Vachon on *I Shot Andy Warhol* (Mary Harron, 1996) and several other projects, decided it was time to keep the production company's shingle out fulltime and start developing projects. The name came from photographer Cindy Sherman's debut feature film *Office Killer* – Vachon's fondness for true-crime can be seen across the Killer oeuvre.

Killer did more than define and fill a queer niche, however. The sheer number of films on which Killer has received a production credit – seventy-five and counting – proves it a central player in the Sundance-Miramax era of independent film. The story Peter Biskind tells in *Down and Dirty Pictures* is of how in this period independent film – emblematised by the Sundance Film Festival, ski-trip distance away from Hollywood – emerged from a crucible of risk-taking to become an auxiliary to the studio system (Biskind 2004). Killer certainly was part of this mainstreaming – casting stars in independent productions, signing with a talent agency, and selling films to mini-majors, including the New York-based Miramax. But its position in the ecosystem was more like that of the Poverty Row studios during the classical Hollywood era – producing low-budget, tawdry tales marked with the visual panache of new talent. The scandal of Todd Solondz's sensibility defined the early Killer as much as did that of Todd Haynes. After acquiring independent distributor October Films, Universal notoriously dropped Solondz's tale of suburban paedophilia, *Happiness* (1998), leaving Killer scrambling to release the film.

After twenty years Killer maintains its vanguard position, working with the post-Miramax The Weinstein Company, which financed and planned the savvy release strategy of Killer's biggest Cannes success to date, Haynes' *Carol* (2015). But while Harvey Weinstein earned notoriety and the nickname Harvey Scissorhands for wresting creative control away from filmmakers in his awards-driven vision of independent film commerce, Vachon represented his antithesis: fidelity to directors' visions – often those of first-timers with correspondingly low budget projects – was the central plank of Killer's platform. This principled stance has been possible because Killer remains far from Hollywood in ethos and location. Being based in New York facilitates its edgy aesthetic; filmmakers come from art and activist circles, fashion and film schools, and Killer draws on a talented pool of crew, actors, and post-production professionals who are often less imprinted by the hierarchies of the Los Angeles industry. It has also meant, however, that its business model hovers on the brink of sustainability.

New York is the setting of a romantic story of independent film whose leading men are Jim Jarmusch and Spike Lee. But as Emanuel Levy acknowledges in *Cinema of Outsiders*, a significant number of women, including feminists like Susan Seidelman (*Desperately Seeking Susan,* 1985), were active at the New York film schools and especially in the downtown art scene that stirred up the wave of independent film in the 1980s (Levy 1999). Avant-garde film, video art, and activist documentary were thriving even as the push towards a viable theatrically exhibited independent feature film culture intensified, again with major contributions from women like director Martha Coolidge and producer Sandra Schulberg. The Association of Independent Film and Videomakers and the Independent Feature Project were founded a decade before Angelika Film Center opened its doors in 1989 and ushered in the era of the 'indieplex' (Newman 2011: 77). The threads of alternative film histories in New York crisscross Killer's more industry-oriented practices, connecting with feminist networks that fall away in more standard chronicles. As B. Ruby Rich remarks: 'Women were such a key part of that movement that it's infuriating to see it reduced in the telling to Jim Jarmusch and Spike Lee' (Rich 2015).

Vachon's entrée to New York independent film was through the avant-garde venues her older sister – artist Gail Vachon – took her to in high school (Vachon

2007: 22). Later, in Brown's Art and Semiotics programme, Mary Ann Doane and Leslie Thornton exposed her to feminist film theory and practice. A figure like dancer/choreographer Yvonne Rainer, who stood at the intersection of this feminist-art-theory world and feature-length filmmaking, arguably paved the way for Apparatus and Killer as they sought a wider public. While the introduction of narrative elements into experimental practice had been almost heretical in modernist circles, Vachon understood it as given. She got started in the indie film scene after graduation by synching dailies for feminist filmmaker Jill Godmilow, who hooked her up with Bill Sherwood on the production of *Parting Glances* (1985). The film was the first independent feature by a queer filmmaker to confront the AIDS epidemic, and producer's representative John Pierson, who was instrumental in gaining attention for Lee, found Sherwood's film a distribution deal. Amid this elevation of the visibility of independent features, Vachon realised she wanted to produce.

Today the hegemony of narrative in independent media is undisputed; Vachon readily uses the term 'storyteller' instead of filmmaker to acknowledge rapidly changing platforms. But the deconstruction of visual pleasure and narrative convention undertaken in academic feminist film theory and experimental film practice continues to haunt Killer as a New York-based producer of films on the cutting edge of film form and politics. Not incidentally, this context strongly informs the visual art of Vachon's partner Marlene McCarty, a frequent collaborator on Killer films' title sequences and designer of the firm's graphic identity. McCarty, Kalin, and Haynes were members of the influential AIDS activist art collective, Gran Fury, and ACT-UP New York and its diverse constituency were a decisive aesthetic and political catalyst for their work with Killer.

Feminist art practice was an important context for what Douglas Crimp calls ACT-UP's 'demo graphics' (Crimp 1990). While feminist critiques of representation, heteronormativity, and spectatorship are more likely to be articulated by Haynes than by the pragmatic Vachon and her relatively silent partner Koffler, both producers are attuned to these discourses. The provocative nature of Killer's feminism finds its emblems in Bettie Page and Valerie Solanas, subjects of two biopics by Mary Harron, a key director on Killer's early roster. These 'sex positive' historical figures can be placed in a New York feminist genealogy with filmmakers Bette Gordon and Sheila McLaughlin, who confronted the politics of the gaze in their experimental features *Variety* (1983) and *She Must Be Seeing Things* (1987), on which Vachon worked as a PA. To sum up, Downtown New York in the 1980s was a key place and time for the emergence of the independent feature ecosystem that Killer would help anchor, and a strong history and networked culture of feminist image-making informed its aesthetic and mission. Both traditions contributed to what I would call the conditions of lesbian representability in independent film of the early 1990s (White 1999).

Lesbian Representation in New Queer Cinema

If it weren't for the fact that B. Ruby Rich, who coined the term New Queer Cinema, was a lesbian writing from a feminist perspective, the male-skewing momentum of the movement might have gone unremarked. Instead, Rich raised the question of gender equity from the beginning; in a sidebar to Rich's original essay in *Sight & Sound*, Cherry Smythe amplified the concern that 'in the New Queer Wave, lesbians are drowning' (Rich 2013: 202; Smythe 1992). The imbalance could be understood partly in economic and technological terms, measured by material access to the theatrically exhibited feature film form and to the authoritative position of director.

In the late 1980s and early 1990s, when I worked at the New York-based non-theatrical distributor Women Make Movies, lesbian films were in demand. Experimental filmmaker Su Friedrich's *Damned if You Don't* (1987), Michelle Parkerson's documentary video *Stormé: The Lady of the Jewel Box* (1987), and AIDS activist video artist Jean Carlomusto's hybrid *L Is for the Way You Look* (1991), all had deep roots in New York's downtown queer culture. Soon, the corpus and diversity of lesbian work available to the North American festival and educational audiences served through Women Make Movies' collection expanded. WMM distributed Pratibha Parmar's films about South Asian queer diaspora and women of colour feminism – including *Khush* (1991) and *A Place of Rage* (1991) – films made possible by government support of queer and Black and South Asian programming in Britain. Several lesbian feature films, including Cheryl Dunye's *The Watermelon Woman* (1995) and Alex Sichel's *All Over Me* (1997) were moving through Women Make Movies' production assistance programme. Theatrically, however, the wave had yet to crest. There had been a few breakthroughs. Samuel Goldwyn released Donna Deitch's 1950s lesbian romance *Desert Hearts* in 1985; more representative of the New York ethos were the anti-racist, coalitional politics and documentary-style indie aesthetics of Lizzie Borden's *Born in Flames* (Rich 1998; Rich 2013: 7). That film was released by First Run Features in 1983 when the infrastructure for exhibiting queer independent film and video was yet to emerge and feminist festival networks were proving unsustainable.

As Rich and others have documented, the expansion of queer grassroots media production and of the international network of community-based LGBT film festivals were spurred on by new video formats and AIDS activism at least as much as by growing niche markets and mainstream political credibility for gay men and lesbians. When New York's gay film festival was revived as the New Festival in 1989 by Women Make Movies board member Susan Horowitz, I helped programme it, with an eye for inclusivity and gender equity. Energised by the efflorescence and diversity of short work by lesbians,

I was nevertheless keenly aware of the lack of feature-length, theatrical quality films by and about lesbians.

In 1992, Chicago film school graduate Rose Troche and her romantic and producing partner, writer Guinevere Turner, reached out for help finishing their hybrid documentary/fiction film *Ely and Max,* about sex and community among a group of young Chicago dykes. Vachon and Kalin knew audiences were waiting for it and jumped on the project. They formed Killer's antecedent, KVPI Productions, to complete what would become the first theatrically released feature by and about lesbians trumpeted in the New Queer Cinema, *Go Fish* (1994).

Lisa Henderson writes astutely about how this film met dyke audiences where they were; its 'narrative and stylistic gestures . . . animate utopic thoughts of community and a life within it', she observes (Henderson 1999: 37). The New Festival's opening night screening of the film was joyous, especially since many of the women involved in the film's production had relocated from Chicago to New York and their energy was infectious. *Go Fish* was scrappy and low budget, stylish and sex positive, and literate in women of colour feminism, and it made money – grossing $2.4 million on an initial $53,000 investment (Pierson 1996: 297). In fact, the story of the film's sale to Samuel Goldwyn at Sundance 1994 – recounted by John Pierson in his book *Spike, Mike, Slackers & Dykes* as a harbinger of deal-making to come – arguably overshadowed its breakthrough status in feminist film history.

By the time Pierson revised his book in 2004 as *Spike Mike Reloaded,* dropping the dykes from his title, *Go Fish* might have seemed less relevant to the course the history of independent film had taken, one marked by male mavericks and mini-majors. Selling a film at Sundance for $400,000 was no longer news. Troche has directed only two subsequent features to date, certainly an indicator of the difficulty women directors face sustaining careers in film. 'The situation is dire for women', she notes, 'I don't even know if it is harder for women of color . . . Film school costs at least $100,000 . . . it's a class thing more than a race thing' (Troche 2015). But in a parallel development Troche and Turner joined executive producer Ilene Chaiken at the launch of the Showtime series *The L Word* (2004–9), with Troche serving as co-executive producer and the series' most frequent director. The move signalled the migration of lesbian talent to premium cable and of the aesthetics and staging of lesbian media visibility from New York to Los Angeles. Showtime's niche, carved out as a major sponsor of the US LGBT film festival circuit, helped the show capitalise on the truth of *Go Fish*'s slogan in demographic terms: 'the girl is out there.'

Go Fish's impact signals the contribution Vachon and her co-producers made at the precise historical intersection of New Queer Cinema and an energetic, if not necessarily lucrative, feminist film culture energised by a new generation of producers, many of them film-school educated. While the AIDS crisis is correctly invoked as context and catalyst for New Queer Cinema's rise in the 1990s, the less remarked upon but crucial co-currents of lesbian activism and the DIY aesthetic and feminist savvy of riot grrrl also inform the lesbian feature films Vachon produced. *Go Fish*, *I Shot Andy Warhol*, and *Boys Don't Cry* (Kimberly Peirce, 1999) – all directed by women – challenged the visual politics and critical understanding of lesbian representation within LGBT communities, engaged with academic queer theory and fractious queer politics, and smashed through to larger publics via art-plex release and the advent of DVD distribution.

Harron, an experienced documentary producer when she teamed up with Vachon and Kalin, made her debut feature with *I Shot Andy Warhol*. Like *Go Fish*, the film made artistic use of black and white cinematography and ignored political correctness: the 'I' of the film's title is Valerie Solanas, radical lesbian feminist author of the SCUM Manifesto (Society for Cutting Up Men). With its dyke anti-hero, Warhol factory setting, and creative team – straight feminist director Harron; queer co-writer Dan Minahan; cast of indie icons including Lili Taylor, Jared Harris and Martha Plimpton; Ellen Kuras as cinematographer; plus Koffler, Vachon and Kalin – *I Shot Andy Warhol* epitomises Killer Films' and New Queer Cinema's polymorphous appeal.

Soon after, recent Columbia film-school graduate Kimberly Peirce's *Boys Don't Cry*, about the life and tragic death of trans man Brandon Teena in Nebraska in 1993, earned Killer its first Academy Award and secured the company's place in the history of lesbian feature filmmaking, even though the film wasn't about lesbians. Rather, *Boys Don't Cry* engaged and ignited debates about lesbian and transgender identities that had emerged within feminist, queer, radical, and anti-racist theory and politics in the 2000s. Jack Halberstam positioned the film in terms of female masculinity and metronormativity, and many other scholars wrote about the film's race, class, and gender politics (Halberstam 2007; Stacey and Street 2007). The film also galvanised audiences beyond the queer community, 'crossing over' spectacularly with Hilary Swank's Oscar for Best Performance by an Actress in a Leading Role.

As Vachon details, *Boys Don't Cry* was also one of Killer's most problem-plagued productions (Vachon 2007: 93–107). First time director Peirce, who was adapting her short thesis film, *Take It Like a Man*, had a single-minded passion for the project that was both an asset and a liability. Script revisions and casting caused delays. Peirce's intensity presented challenges to the star, the crew, and the budget. The MPAA threatened the film with an NC-17 rating, in part because of an orgasmic facial close-up of Chloë Sevigny, as Brandon's girlfriend Lana. But the results of this difficult production were incandescent. Executive produced by Killer lawyer and sales agent John Sloss, a key player in the sustainability of independent film through his company Cinetic, *Boys*

Don't Cry was released by Fox Searchlight to critical acclaim and a worldwide gross of over $20 million (on a $1.7 million budget).

Without Vachon and the female-dominated producing team at Killer, there would not have been a New Queer Cinema, and certainly not one in which lesbians had much say. This is not to minimise the contributions made by directors like Derek Jarman and Jennie Livingston whose formally and politically audacious work helped Rich name a corpus that would quickly become a market trend. But it took Killer's commitments to art and market, to lesbian features and women filmmakers, to blatant gay male niche films (*Kiss Me Guido*, Tony Vitale 1997) and tasteful ones (*A Home at the End of the World*, Michael Mayer 2004), to films that were queer in the fullest sense – *Stonewall* (Nigel Finch, 1995), *Hedwig and the Angry Inch* (John Cameron Mitchell, 2001), *Camp* (Todd Graff, 2003), and *A Dirty Shame* (John Waters, 2004), and to auteur-directors like Kalin and Haynes – to sustain this sea change in queer self-representation.

By 2000 Rich was writing in 'Queer and Present Danger' about the death of New Queer Cinema; the changing face and fortunes of indie cinema since then have shaped this evolution along with assimilationist LGBT politics and small-screen breakthroughs in queer representation (Rich 2013: 130–7). The economic downturn of 2008 had a deep impact on independent film financing, and digital technologies and corporate consolidation have destabilised the distribution terrain. Though it is hard to pinpoint how gender hierarchies in independent film influenced what got made and who got to make it during this period, it is interesting to observe that Killer didn't produce another lesbian feature until *Carol* in 2014. The project was a long time in the making. Producer Dorothy Berwin optioned Patricia Highsmith's book *The Price of Salt* (1952) around 2000 and asked London-based lesbian playwright Phyllis Nagy to write the script under the title of the book's British reissue, *Carol*. She approached Troche, with whom she had twice worked as producer, to direct. Nagy had known Highsmith in New York and had discussed the book with her – she later successfully adapted the author's *The Talented Mr. Ripley* for the London stage. After acquiring the project in 2008, the film's British producer, Elizabeth Karlsen, fought hard to get the film made until Vachon and Haynes joined the production. The delays – extraordinary even for an indie film – were caused by rights issues and the availability of a package of script, stars and director that would appeal to financiers. Even with Cate Blanchett attached, biased industry assumptions against the earning power of films headlined by women played their part – lesbian films have *two* female leads. The Killer brand gave the project credibility within the genealogy of New Queer Cinema, but it is telling that the project only got made with Killer's most prestigious collaborator, a male director, attached.

The question of authorship is a key dimension of lesbian representability, not because of an essentialist definition of creativity, but because of historical lack of opportunity. Troche, Turner, and their collaborators drew on their own experiences to create the lesbian verisimilitude that Henderson prizes in *Go Fish;* Chaiken's lesbian identity was the basis of her pitch for *The L Word;* and Peirce speaks of her almost mystical connection with Brandon Teena. Auteur theory favours the director, but *Carol*'s authorship, as with any media text, and especially with adaptations, is multi-dimensional. As I shall discuss below, the film fits like a glove into Haynes' oeuvre. Yet obviously Highsmith has formidable authority as a rival signatory, and screenwriter Nagy has a strong proprietary claim on *Carol*, especially given the project's long gestation. Even the status of *The Price of Salt* as a pseudonymously published, 'neglected' Highsmith makes its generations of lesbian readers feel like *they* own it. With Karlsen's passionate involvement in the project, Berwin's executive production, the support of executive Tessa Ross at Film 4, and Vachon as producer, *Carol* was significantly shaped by women in aesthetic and material terms.

The example of Killer and *Carol* underscores the importance of female producers in independent film culture. *Carol* debuted during a moment of increasingly vocal protests against gender disparities in directing in Hollywood, with the ACLU (American Civil Liberties Union) calling for an investigation into the industry for discrimination. Sundance Senior Programmer Caroline Libresco believes that nurturing women producers is key to building a film culture in which women directors can have sustainable careers: 'The presence of strong creative producers (who understand story and the cinematic art form as well as the business) elevate the work of a director from merely good to great. Killer's body of work is a massive contribution to the culture' (Libresco 2015). Killer's statistics – thirteen features by women in the can and counting, or roughly 26% of their output – are much better than Hollywood's and consistent with the percentage of dramatic features by women shown at Sundance over the twelve years reported by the Institute's groundbreaking Female Filmmakers Initiative (Smith 2014). A later phase of the report confirmed that productions with women in key creative positions tend to employ more women, which is true of Killer's crews (Smith 2015).

But the women directors they've worked with have had a harder time in feature filming in comparison to their male cohort, with both Harron and Troche finding work in television. In a revealing profile in *The New York Times Magazine* timed with the release of her *Carrie* remake in 2012, Kimberly Peirce spoke frankly of her struggles as a woman in Hollywood. Despite several exciting prospects and numerous almost-deals, *Carrie* is only her third feature: the second, *Stop-Loss*, didn't make it to the screen till 2008, nine years after *Boys Don't Cry*. Neither was a lesbian project (though *Carrie* has its moments): Peirce's queer script *Butch Academy* languishes in development at Universal.

Discussing Peirce's direct experience of the disrespect shown to women in Hollywood, author Mary Kaye Schilling asked whether being butch is an advantage in the profession. 'There's a picture of me with David O. Russell, Spike Jonze and Alexander Payne,' Peirce answered. 'We're all hanging out, and I'm in the middle, and I respect these guys, and it *is* a boy's club' (Schilling 2015). She explained that if she projected any kind of femininity, the balance changed, acknowledging that authorship is performance as well as filmography.

The exchange on butchness bears on the question of lesbian authorship's visibility and indeed authority, a matter I see as germane to valuing Vachon's persona and her work with Killer. Peirce's assertion about modern day Hollywood feels both anachronistic and like common sense. In the 1930s and 1940s 'mannish' directors like Dorothy Arzner and the recently rediscovered Chinese-American Esther Eng claimed masculine entitlement for themselves on film sets through their dress and manner (Mayne 1994; Wei 2013). Although these codes have relaxed, I posit a modern day parallel in Vachon's manner of negotiating gender norms and protocols in the male dominated worlds of both industry and independent filmmaking. (A minor controversy bubbled up at Cannes 2015 around the requirement that women wear heels to red carpet galas. Vachon wore her customary combat boots.) I am not arguing that a butch persona is a necessity, discounting the role of Killer partner Pam Koffler, or even staking a feminist argument on this characterisation. I'm simply accruing evidence that, though her work with Killer, Christine Vachon has indisputably produced the oeuvre of a lesbian auteur.

Independent Collaborators

This part sets out to correct any previous over-emphasis on Vachon's singular agency by foregrounding the practice of collaboration at Killer on material as well as symbolic levels. Both 'female' and 'producer' trouble the conventional vision of the auteur-hero of indie film as male director. At Killer these categories do not take a back seat; the female-led company's twenty-year history shows the central role of hands-on creative producing to the history and practice of US independent filmmaking.

A primary theme of Vachon's books is the multifarious nature of the producer's job. 'What *don't* they do?' she asks (Vachon 1998: 2). *Shooting to Kill* starts with a record of 'a day in the life', tracking meetings with talent, disputes with distributors, crises with the bond company. Vachon's writing, teaching, and lecturing aim to demystify the filmmaking process and make it seem accessible to anyone willing to work hard. She and Koffler are regularly called upon as mentors at programmes like Sundance's annual Creative Producing Summit and Feature Film Program Lab. Vachon doesn't comment on the fact that collaboration, multi-tasking, and caretaking are also qualities of female socialisation. She does note that she doesn't care when money people condescend to her – as a woman she's used to it. But the perception that women are good at hands-on producing also affects the prestige of the profession. Status and credit hierarchies range from the line producer who has responsibility for every penny of the budget to the executive producer who may have 'earned' his credit by investing in the film. Vachon recognises that: 'The bottom line is, you cannot be a producer unless you understand that it's all your fault' (Vachon 1998: 9).

At the core of Killer is the partnership and seemingly intuitive working relationship between Vachon and Koffler. Vachon knew she wanted a partner in the venture and found their temperaments and outlooks worked well together. In interviews, both use the term 'organic' to describe how they collaborate on everything from selecting projects to deciding who will be on-set producer. Yet Koffler's personality and role contrast with Vachon's; she avoids confrontation and seems content to stay out of the limelight. She describes two aspects of her role:

> I try to step back now and then and assess the big picture. How are we doing: how are we going to get the bills paid, are our employees happy? I . . . see where Christine's energies are going and follow that – she is a very instinctual, visceral person . . . [A]t the other end of the spectrum, I tend to dive into a project and be a bit more soup to nuts on a particular movie than she is.

While they will both work on a large production like *Mildred Pierce* (2011), they also divide responsibilities with an eye towards work-life balance.

Through several moves following the fortunes of independent film and Manhattan real estate, the Killer office floor plan has always been open. Vachon and Koffler look out across their desks at each other, consulting 'back and forth all day long' as Vachon comments, and involving other staff in whatever capacity they are needed. This work style has facilitated the advancement of other women at Killer, where the assumption of responsibility is a key dimension of the labour culture. It has also demanded a thick skin. Over Killer's twenty-year history, employees who started as entry-level assistants or interns have gone on to receive full producer credits on Killer Films (not only line producer, co-producer or executive producer, though sometimes those as well). Eva Kolodner rose to producer on *Boys Don't Cry*. Katie Roumel got her first producer credit on *Hedwig and the Angry Inch* and became a third partner before leaving in 2007. Koffler herself started as a line producer. Balancing those who have moved up the ranks are the many others who found the work pace and style too demanding.

Killer's mode of production foregrounds the fundamentally collaborative nature of independent – indeed all – filmmaking. New York-based female crew such as DPs Maryse Alberti and Ellen Kuras, production designers Thérèse DePrez and Judy Becker have risen to prominence on Killer productions, and casting director Laura Rosenthal is a regular collaborator. And as we will discuss in more detail below, actors see in Killer projects a chance to do challenging work. Low-budget filmmaking requires everyone to pitch in, highly trained and highly trainable personnel alike.

It would be a stretch to call Killer's culture feminist, however. Killer has worked with women-led companies like the New York distributor Zeitgeist, which released *Poison,* and, recently, with Adrienne Becker's Glass Elevator Media to produce for new platforms. But in an effort to stay afloat it has cycled through a series of industry alliances and partnerships that push identity politics and experimental tastes aside. Vachon's attraction to edgy material translates into projects like *Kids* (Larry Clark, 1995) whose gender politics are questionable. Overall Killer fosters what might be called queer collaborations – driven by economic necessity and animated by creativity – that do not necessarily conform to expectations of gendered work.

Vachon sees her role as producer as facilitating the director's artistic vision. While her temperament bucks traditional notions of feminine supportiveness, she is a deeply loyal advocate, especially in her storied collaboration with Haynes. Trust is paramount between producer and director, she explains. 'With Todd it is a lot about protecting his vision, but also, because the trust goes both ways, I can just . . . tell him the truth . . . he's got a lot of people around him who would say yes'. Inevitably the discourse of expressive auteur pushes her into the background, something to which Haynes objects. But it is clear that certain components of Haynes' amiable and intellectual authorial persona are enabled by the steely and pragmatic qualities of Vachon's. And it is Killer's efficiency and expertise that have enabled Haynes to maintain his independence. On set with *Far From Heaven* (2002) in Bayonne, New Jersey just after 9/11, Vachon writes, 'Everybody is jumpy: our days are punctuated by the wail of police sirens, anthrax alerts, and Code Orange. At least Todd is our one saving grace. He's completely calm and focused' (Vachon 2007: 170). Their professional collaboration is fortified by a deep personal friendship and a moving allegiance: together they have weathered the deaths of their mothers, of Haynes' partner and editor Jim Lyons, health scares, and major surgeries, all set against the vicissitudes of development, production, and promotion – and extravagantly positive reception.

Vachon recounts: 'People think that if you're not in a state of crisis on a movie, you're not really working. I learned from Todd that it didn't have to be that way. When we started making movies together, he said. "Don't yell at me and I won't yell at you. Let's not be like that . . . ". That said, I yell at people all the time' (Vachon 1998: 9). For Haynes, Vachon's legendary fierceness is chivalric. He describes the shift in scale on the production of *Mildred Pierce*:

> It was a great experience working with HBO in the end . . . it felt finally for the first time maybe ever that we were [o]n intensely solid ground, I don't think I've ever felt that before – I don't think Christine has ever felt that before. Even just for her, I was thinking, you have so earned this, man! . . . [W]here there are other people worrying about every cent and you can be there for the creative experiences, like she was on *Poison* . . . But she was often dueling with the dragons and slaying the beasts on most of the films we've made together since. (Leyda 2014: 226)

The Haynes/Vachon collaboration – and Killer's approach to collaboration more generally –challenges gendered discourses as much as it conforms to them. In fact it renews debates on the nature of women's cinema that characterised feminist film theory and practice from their emergence in the 70s.

Killer Films and Women's Cinema

As a female-owned company Killer makes 'women's cinema' of a kind, though signature titles like *Kids*, *Happiness*, and *One Hour Photo* (2002) would be hard to assimilate to a generic characterisation. As a director collaborating closely with female artists on women-centred stories that appeal to spectators keyed to experiences of socialised femininity, Haynes makes a very specific kind of 'women's cinema' at Killer. Both of these definitions can leave explicit feminism to the side – Killer doesn't privilege female makers, stories, genres, or spectators per se; Haynes' films are often period dramas with relatively disempowered heroines. Nevertheless feminism informs the work at many levels, including, as we've seen, that of collaboration itself.

Haynes is arguably the most significant director of women's pictures in world cinema today. In *Superstar* (1987), *Safe* (1995), *Far From Heaven, Mildred Pierce*, and *Carol*, Haynes has explored the self-reflexive dimensions of the classic genre – the expressivity of décor, music and costume and performance codes – and the revolutionary implications of films in which 'women think', as Fassbinder memorably characterised Sirk's oeuvre (Fassbinder 1992: 81). The period settings of Haynes' women's films function as historical pastiche and as thought experiments – how do these white, middle-class American women cope without access to feminist discourse? Mildred and the lovers in *Carol* are fighters; Karen Carpenter, Carol White and Cathy Whitaker suffer. These are roles that recall the 'superfemales' and 'superwomen' Bette Davis and Katharine Hepburn infused with critical passion in the 1930s and 1940s (Haskell 1974; Dyer 1986: 61–64). And one dimension of Haynes' genius is a

Cukor-like queer rapport with actresses, transposed to a vastly different political universe.

Certainly any definition of Killer feminism has to include the contributions of stars Julianne Moore, Kate Winslet, and Cate Blanchett in Haynes' films: these women are his public face, even as the women producers have his back. Of course their prominence is on one level an index of the importance of star casting to the sustainability of independent film, a demand that can compromise a film's integrity. But Haynes has adapted his mode of working to this reality in a way that would do honour to his fellow queer auteurs Warhol and Fassbinder, with their ironic takes on studio glamour and ensemble work. This female scaffolding, this multi-pronged collaboration, makes Haynes' authorial persona significantly more feminist than that of other male mavericks of indie cinema from Steven Soderbergh to Quentin Tarantino.

As a lesbian film, *Carol* teases out some of the ramifications of Killer's contribution to women's cinema. As I noted, the project didn't start out with the company – although Patricia Highsmith is a quintessential Killer author, one of Vachon's favourites. *The Price of Salt*, the 1952 lesbian romance written under the pseudonym Claire Morgan, is Highsmith's only novel lacking an actual killer. Written after a chance encounter with an elegant female customer in the store where Highsmith was earning extra cash, the novel is a fever dream of first love tinged with anxiety. Although *Carol* was finished in fall 2014, the Weinstein Company, always canny about Oscar potential, held the film for a holiday 2015 release, building on festival dates and critical acclaim. Although it came up short at the Academy Awards, Rooney Mara shared the award for best actress at Cannes and Cate Blanchett, in the title role of the beloved, garnered rapturous press. The triangulation of the two female stars and director Haynes made for some good red carpet photo opportunities. Outside the press bubble, these relationships, gendered and queered, intertextual and material, became a fascinating roundelay – producer protecting director, director tendering a rare intellectual respect for stars – ripe for feminist interpretation.

Even as Vachon was back and forth from Cincinnati for the *Carol* shoot, where Karlsen stayed fulltime, Koffler was on the set of *Still Alice*, Richard Glatzer and Wash Westmoreland's adaptation of Lisa Genova's 2007 bestseller about a fifty-year-old linguistics professor struggling with early onset Alzheimer's. Koffler, a French literature major at Yale who loves psychologically compelling material along the lines of *Madame Bovary* and *Portrait of a Lady*, puts her mark on Killer cinema as women's cinema with this film. Koffler took on an especially difficult role with *Still Alice*: to get the film made during the crisis of Glatzer's rapid decline with ALS. Glatzer had been diagnosed in 2011 while making the couple's first Killer film, *The Last of Robin Hood* (2013), with Koffler producing. Koffler says of the strains on the couple directing, 'Making the movie was enough – like *dayenu* – "it would have been enough!"' The creative and personal collaboration was tragically affected by the illness – with one of the directors literally losing his voice by the end – and trust was paramount. Koffler said: 'I dealt with our VFX and our Toronto deadlines and then I would be finding someone from the ALS community who knew how to get this particular breathing machine so Richard could get on a plane'. The race to finish *Still Alice* mirrored that of the protagonist of the film to communicate her sense of self before losing the power to do so.

Julianne Moore finally won her Oscar for her role in *Still Alice*. Glatzer and Westmoreland are close friends of Haynes, so Moore's casting in *Still Alice* has an almost dizzying intertextuality, her performance of suffering a symbolic tie between the films and filmmakers materially grounded in Koffler's work as producer. Star of *Safe* and *Far From Heaven* and featured as Joan Baez in *I'm Not There*, Moore is often considered a muse to Haynes. Based in New York, Moore has worked on other Killer films, notably starring in Kalin's *Savage Grace* (2007) as an incestuous mother finally murdered by her son. Moore's star persona is as rich as any classic women's picture star, and goes beyond to comprise archetypes of damaged femininity achieved collaboratively with gay male filmmakers (Çakırlar 2015). The fact that *Still Alice* was finished and released and Glatzer saw Moore thank him in her Oscar acceptance speech was at once unspeakably sad and a fairy-tale ending. Kind of like a women's picture.

These nuanced feminist dramas are onscreen projections of queer worlds built from intimate friendships, hard and unpredictable work, and a rough and tumble production culture. But melodrama is ultimately not Killer's primary genre – on the uncertain terrain of independent film in the age of media convergence, their approach is necessarily realistic. I interviewed Christine in 2015 just before Cannes; I came back to interview Pam two weeks later – in between *Carol* had been tipped for the Palme d'Or, and although things didn't go that way, the Killer team was pleased with the film's profile and ready for what would come next. Down to a staff of four in difficult times for independent film, and occupying part of Moxie's Pictures' Union Square space, Killer's resourcefulness was on full display. A white board listed eight feature films in the works, several by women. Once again Killer is collaborating, developing work for new platforms through Killer Content. Koffler says there are parallel motivations. The material is cool and challenging, and 'you can't just make small independent features and run a business.' For their first project, they have compiled a list of directors that excite them – all of whom are women.

Is it a paradox that the most fearless women producers in independent film are turning to the stereotypically feminised format of non-theatrical serial drama for a livelihood (a terrain that has already lured some of their most talented female directors)? It is a feminist truism that in TV women play bigger roles both in front of and behind the camera – television drama inherits the cultural space of the women's picture. And, as Troche told me, the paycheck is bigger. But Killer's brand of feminism goes beyond concerns with gender equity and identity politics: its institutional, political, and formal affiliations and proclivities; its intertextual (bordering on incestuous) bonds; its queerness – all put the company on dangerous ground in the current climate of independent media production. Just where it feels most safe.

References

American Civil Liberties Union, 'ACLU asks state and federal civil rights agencies to investigate gender discrimination in Hollywood', <https://www.aclusocal.org/pr-film-equality/> (last accessed 20 April 2015).

Biskind, Peter (2004), *Down and Dirty Pictures: Miramax, Sundance, and the Rise of Independent Film*, New York: Simon and Schuster.

Çakırlar, Cüneyt (2016), 'Mothers on the Line: The Allure of Julianne Moore', [*In*] *Transition: Journal of Videographic Film and Moving Image Studies* 3.1, <http://mediacommons.futureofthebook.org/intransition/2016/03/14/mothers-line-allure-julianne-moore> (last accessed 3 June 2016).

Crimp, Douglas with Adam Ralston (1990), *AIDS Demo Graphics*, Seattle: Bay Press.

Cvetkovich, Ann (2003), *An Archive of Feelings: Trauma, Sexuality, and Lesbian Public Cultures*, Durham, NC: Duke University Press.

Dyer, Richard (1979), *Stars*, London: BFI.

Ellis-Petersen, Hannah (2015), 'Passion Project: Meet the Indie Super-producer behind Cannes Hot Ticket *Carol*', *The Guardian*, 14 May, <http://www.theguardian.com/film/2015/may/14/carol-film-cannes-karlsen-cate-blanchett> (last accessed 20 May 2015).

Fassbinder, R. W. (1992), *The Anarchy of the Imagination: Interviews, Essays, Notes*, Michael Tötenberg and Leo Lensing (eds), Baltimore: Johns Hopkins University Press.

Halberstam, J. (2007), *In a Queer Time and Place: Transgender Bodies, Subcultural Lives*, Durham, NC: Duke University Press.

Haskell, Molly (1974), *From Reverence to Rape: The Treatment of Women in the Movies*, Chicago: University of Chicago Press.

Henderson, Lisa (1999), 'Simple Pleasures: Lesbian Community and *Go Fish*', *Signs*, 25: 1, pp. 37–64.

Jones, Michael (2014), 'Vachon, Koffler Sell 50% of Company', *Variety*, 16 November.

Lauzen, Martha M. (2014), 'The Celluloid Ceiling: Behind-the-Scenes Employment of Women on the Top 25 Films of 2014', <http://womenintvfilm.sdsu.edu/files/2014_Celluloid_Ceiling_Report.pdf> (last accessed 20 April 2015).

Lauzen, Martha M. (2015), 'Independent Women: Behind-the-Scenes Employment on Festival Films in 2014–15', <http://womenintvfilm.sdsu.edu/files/2015_Independent_Women_Report.pdf> (last accessed 20 April 2015).

Levy, Emmanuel (1999), *Cinema of Outsiders: The Rise of American Independent Film*, New York: New York University Press.

Leyda, Julia (2012), 'Something That Is Dangerous and Arousing and Transgressive': An Interview with Todd Haynes, in Julia Leyda (ed.), *Todd Haynes: Interviews*, Wayne State University Press, 201–26.

Libresco, Caroline (2015), email communication, 17 July.

Mayne, Judith (1994), *Directed by Dorothy Arzner*, Bloomington, IN: Indiana University Press.

Newman, Michael Z. (2011), *Indie: An American Film Culture*, New York: Columbia University Press.

Ortner, Sherry B. (2013), *Not Hollywood: Independent Film at the Twilight of the America Dream,* Durham, NC: Duke University Press.

Pierson, John (1996), *Spike, Mike, Slackers & Dykes*, New York: Hyperion/Miramax Books.

Rich B. Ruby (1998), *Chick Flicks: Theories and Memories of the Feminist Film Movement*, Durham, NC: Duke University Press.

Rich B. Ruby (2015), email communication, 12 July.

Rich, B. Ruby (2013), *New Queer Cinema: The Director's Cut*, Durham, NC: Duke University Press.

Schilling, Mary Kaye (2013), '*Carrie* Is Back. So Is Kimberly Peirce', *The New York Times Magazine,* 26 September, <http://www.nytimes.com/2013/09/29/magazine/carrie-is-back-so-is-kimberly-peirce.html> (last accessed 25 April 2015).

Smith, Stacy I. et al. (2014), 'Exploring the Barriers and Opportunities for Independent Women Filmmakers Phase I and II', <http://www.sundance.org/pdf/artist-programs/wfi/phase-i-ii-research---exploring-the-barriers.pdf> (last accessed 25 April 2015).

Smith, Stacy I. et al. (2015), 'Exploring the Careers of Female Directors: Phase III', <http://www.sundance.org/pdf/artist-programs/wfi/phase-iii-research---female-filmmakers-initiative.pdf> (last accessed 20 April 2015).

Smythe, Cherry (1992), 'Trash Femme Cocktail', *Sight & Sound*, 2: 5, September, p. 30.

Stacey, Jackie and Sarah Street (eds) (2007), 'Dossier on *Boys Don't Cry*', *Queer Screen: A* Screen *Reader*, London: Routledge.

Thompson, Anne (2015), '"Carol" Producer Christine Vachon Talks Being Queen of the Croisette', Thompson on Hollywood, *Indiewire*, 26 May 2015.

Troche, Rose (2015), telephone interview, 7 July.

Vachon, Christine (2015), interview with author, 11 May.

Vachon, Christine and David Edelstein (1998), *Shooting to Kill*, New York: Harpers.

Vachon, Christine with Austin Bunn (2007), *A Killer Life: How an Independent Film Producer Survives Deals and Disasters in Hollywood and Beyond*, New York: Hal Leonard Corporation.

Variety staff (2015), 'Christine Vachon and Pamel Koffler, Toppers, Killer Films', 'New York Women's Impact Report', *Variety* online, <http://variety.com/gallery/new-york-womens-impact-report/#!43/christine-vachon-pamela-koffler-toppers-killer-films/> (last accessed 20 May 2015).

Wei, S. Louisa (2013). 'Esther Eng', in Jane Gaines, Radha Vatsal and Monica Dall'Asta (eds), *Women Film Pioneers Project*, Center for Digital Research and Scholarship. New York: Columbia University Libraries, <https://wfpp.cdrs.columbia.edu/pioneer/esther-eng-2/> (last accessed 20 April 2015).

White, Patricia (1999), *Uninvited: Classical Hollywood Cinema and Lesbian Representability*, Bloomington, IN: Indiana University Press.

White, Patricia (2015), *Women's Cinema, World Cinema*, Durham, NC: Duke University Press.

3. 'A WOMAN WITH AN ENDGAME': MEGAN ELLISON, ANNAPURNA PICTURES AND AMERICAN INDEPENDENT FILM PRODUCTION

James Lyons

In 2014 Megan Ellison made headlines by becoming the first woman to receive two best picture Academy Award nominations in the same year, in recognition of her role as producer of *Her* (Spike Jonze, 2013) and *American Hustle* (David O. Russell, 2013). She had also been nominated in 2012 for producing Kathryn Bigelow's *Zero Dark Thirty* (2012). Ellison was the only film producer included in *Time* magazine's 2014 list of 'The 100 Most Influential People in the World', placed in the 'Pioneers' category alongside NSA whistleblower Edward Snowden and José Mujica, Uruguay's marijuana-legalising president (*Time* 2014). She was profiled in *Fortune* magazine's '40 under 40' list of 'the most influential young people in business' (*Fortune* 2014), while also making *Out* magazine's list of 'The Top 50 most powerful gay people' (*Out* 2014), sharing the plaudits with Apple CEO Tim Cook. This flurry of recognition reflected the fact that Ellison, daughter of software billionaire Larry Ellison, was beginning to assert an unquestionable impact on the ecology of the American independent/specialty film business, via her production company Annapurna Pictures. Titles such as *Her*, *American Hustle*, and *Zero Dark Thirty*, placed alongside others such as *The Master* (Paul Thomas Anderson, 2012), *Spring Breakers* (Harmony Korine, 2013), *The Grandmaster* (Wong Kar Wai, 2013) and *Foxcatcher* (Bennett Miller, 2014), conveyed emphatically the company's objective, stated on its website, of 'creating sophisticated, high-quality films that might otherwise be deemed risky by contemporary Hollywood studios' (*Annapurna* 2015).

That broader context of risk, referred to in the company's mission statement,

Figure 3.1 Megan Ellison, founder and producer, Annapurna Pictures.

is one that provides the narrative backdrop for Annapurna's and Ellison's rapid rise to prominence. The wake of the 2008 global financial crisis saw what Yannis Tzioumakis describes as an 'extensive shakeout' (2013: 28) of the American specialty film market, as evident in the folding of a number of the major studios' specialty divisions, such as Warner Independent Pictures and Paramount Vantage. Allied to coterminous developments such as the parlous decline of DVD sales, Alisa Perren diagnosed the 'near collapse of the specialty sector' (2012: 231) at this time. With hindsight, it appears that rumours of its (near) death may have been greatly exaggerated: indeed, Geoff King argues that episodic narratives of crisis are one of the sector's enduring characteristics (2013). But what is clear is that the aftermath of 2008 has seen some discernible shifts in film financing and production.

In the following pages I set out a consideration of Megan Ellison that situates her, distinctively, within this emergent set of contexts. In the first part, I examine the configurations of industry and activity that helped shape Ellison's rapid rise to prominence, before turning to the question of how her identity as a producer has been negotiated within the gendered discourses of the independent film sector. In the final part, I seek to bring these questions of industry and identity together with a close examination of Ellison's use of social media, most specifically her extensive activity on Twitter where she is, by some distance, the most followed female independent/specialty film producer.[1] I draw on the work of Alice Marwick and danah boyd in theorising the strategic functions of Twitter for high-profile individuals, and the efficacy of what Jan-Hinrik Schmidt terms Twitter's constitution of the 'personal public' (2013). Twitter's conflation of the promotional and the private, the shrewd and the sincere makes it a fascinating medium for the mobilisation of the producer persona, and Ellison's usage, particularly shaped around articulations of taste, authenticity, sexual preference and gender identity, require us to rethink how business is conducted in the upper echelons of the contemporary American independent/specialty film sector.

Financing 'Smart Art' – the Rise of Annapurna

Over the last decade the major studios, steered by ever more risk-averse corporate parents, have concentrated on producing 'big-budget tentpoles that can perform as franchises at the box office and in retail sales' (Kroll and Graser 2012: 9). As one unnamed studio boss told *Variety*, 'I can't make certain movies anymore, no matter how profitable they might become. I make movies that turn into toys' (Graser 2012: 8). While this sentiment suggests that we are unlikely to see the next Paramount Vantage anytime soon, Marc Graser notes the ongoing requirement for an arguably more diversified but certainly greater quantity of movies to supply the majors' 'distribution pipelines' (2012: 8). As Graser states, 'that's where Hollywood's new bankrollers come in' (2012: 8), citing Thomas Tull (Legendary Entertainment), Tim Headington (FilmDistrict), Amit Khanna (Reliance Group), and Philip Anschulz (Walden) as part of a 'new crop of investors boasting their own rich bank accounts' (8) and filling the gap left by the majors' own shrinking production slate. In some respects, these autonomous financiers offer a more clear-cut basis for arguing the case for 'independent' film production than entities such as the risibly-named, now-extinct Warner Independent. But, as Tzioumakis cautions, 'rhetoric aside, much of American independent cinema has always operated at close range with the Hollywood majors' (2013: 30), and the frequency of co-financing pacts with majors eager to share profits but offset risk, together with distribution deals, is clear evidence of this ongoing reality.

Speculative investment in film production from individuals and entities outside the industry is of course nothing new; writing a cheque in exchange for a sprinkling of Hollywood glitter is a phenomenon long referred to derogatively by insiders as 'dumb money'. But as TWC chief operating officer David Glasser states, 'there's a lot of smart money in the indie market right now – people like Megan Ellison' (*Variety* 2011: 22). While Glasser's remark could be dismissed as self-seeking (TWC is partly capitalised by supermarket magnate Ronald Burkle), the adjective 'smart' gains greater credence when corroborated by the specifics of investment activity, and in particular the role of the industry's leading talent agencies in brokering agreements. The rapid evolution of Ellison's own film-financing arrangements offers a case in point. Her first investment in film production came in 2007 with *Waking Madison* (Katherine Brooks, 2010), a psychological drama about a young woman suffering from dissociative identity disorder. Ellison underwrote the production (a reported $2 million) after developing the project with Brooks, whom she had contacted via MySpace (Cieply and Barnes 2011). Three subsequent film productions, *Passion Play* (Mitch Glazer, 2010) *Main Street* (John Doyle, 2010), and *Catch .44* (Aaron Harvey, 2011) were also modestly budgeted adult dramas (all under $10 million) that had lukewarm reviews and failed to find audiences. But another production, the Coen brothers' remake of *True Grit* (2010), signalled an important shift. Helmed by auteur filmmakers of major standing, *True Grit* was a much more lavishly resourced production (a reported $38 million budget). Ellison invested in the film together with her brother David, who had recently agreed a four-year co-financing, production and distribution agreement with Paramount Pictures, underwritten by a reported $350 million fund used to support his new company Skydance productions (Eller 2010). Larry Ellison reportedly provided an undisclosed portion of the equity used to secure a $200–million credit facility for Skydance (Eller 2010). David Ellison described the company's founding objective as being 'to deliver the highest level of commercial, event entertainment' (Eller 2010), an ambition apparent in subsequent releases with Paramount such as *Mission Impossible: Ghost Protocol* (Brad Bird, 2011) *Jack Reacher* (Christopher McQuarrie, 2012) or *World War Z* (Marc Forster, 2013).

Although securely generic and star-led, *True Grit* appears positively aberrant in such company; certainly nothing else on the Skydance production slate to date could be described as a film by a recognised auteur filmmaker and appealing to the specialty/independent end of the exhibition market. By contrast, Megan Ellison's Annupurna Pictures, founded in 2012, and named after the Hindu Goddess of food and nourishment, has concentrated on financing films Anthony Kaufman terms 'smart art': mid-range budgeted ($20–$40 million) 'auteur-pics', which have the potential to 'yield foreign presales' (Kaufman 2013: 18). Occupying what Kaufman terms 'the high-end indie space', Annapurna has sought to operate in the echelon once heavily populated by the majors' largely defunct specialty divisions, beginning with *Lawless* (2012), John Hillcoat's prohibition-era crime drama scripted by Nick Cave. A powerful historical drama full of strong star performances, *Lawless* would appear a logical next step after *True Grit*, but the fact that Hillcoat is represented by Creative Artists Agency (CAA), one of the industry's leading talent agencies, may be the more pertinent detail. As reported by *The New York Times*, Ellison's acquisition of a substantial film investment fund, an undisclosed sum assumed to be from her father, and reported to be anywhere between $200 million and $2 billion according to the source (Grigoriadis 2013), coincided with meetings at CAA, where the advice was to use her money to take 'creative chances' but only with 'filmmakers in the top rank' (Cieply and Barnes 2011). Moreover, the producer was to operate 'not as a client, but as a well-heeled adjunct to the agency's film finance group' (Cieply and Barnes, 2011). The fact that virtually all Annapurna's films to date have been directed by CAA clients (Andrew Dominik, Katherine Bigelow, Paul Thomas Anderson, David O. Russell, Wong Kar Wai, Harmony Korine and Bennett Miller) could be seen as corroborating the notion that the agency has been instrumental in brokering Ellison's investments, although CAA's predominance in the 'top' talent market rather presupposes its presence for anyone wishing to secure the services of such individuals. As Tom Kemper's work on the rise of Hollywood's talent agents reveals, leading agencies have long been an integral but critically neglected component of industry practice (2010). Indeed, there is an overdue assessment of the function of such power brokers in the recent history of the specialty film sector, offering additional nuance to the conceptualising of 'independent' production.

While David Ellison's Skydance has, through its slate production agreement, contracted to develop its projects with one major studio (comparable with Warner Bros.' agreement with Tull's Legendary Entertainment), Annapurna has pursued a different strategy. Its first three releases (*Lawless*, *The Master*, and *Killing them Softly* (Andrew Dominik, 2012) were independently produced (the last a co-production with Brad Pitt's Plan B. Entertainment), and distributed in the US by The Weinstein Company. A number of subsequent projects were either produced independently (*Zero Dark Thirty*, *Her*, *Spring Breakers*, and *The Grand Master*) or packaged in advance of individual co-financing or distribution agreements with a studio (*American Hustle*, *Foxcatcher*). The well-documented dwindling of studio development money, and what *Variety* termed the incentive of 'faster greenlights' have both been identified as contributing more generally to a recent upswing in 'pre-packaged projects' (Kroll and Graser 2012: 9) being brought to studios. But it is important also to recognise the extent to which this strategy is articulated as one affording creative autonomy and control, which, as Michael Z. Newman notes, are attributes that have remained central to 'indie' cinema's rhetoric of 'artistic authenticity' (2011: 5). If anything, the coalescence of studio and independent operations has only served to enhance their value.

Vision and Values – Producing Independence

The image of Kathryn Bigelow, John Hillcoat, or Spike Jonze holed up, editing their films in one of Ellison's three multi-million dollar homes in the Hollywood Hills – all sold in 2013 for a reported $47 million which was then used to purchase the 'super-villainish' $20 million mega-mansion featured in *I Love You, Man* (John Hamburg, 2009), (Kudler 2013) – is vividly at variance with the corporate topography and dynamics of the studio lot. Jonze commented that 'normally, the idea of the financier coming by the editing room all the time isn't very comforting . . . but with Megan, if she'd be walking up to work from her house, I'd get my feelings hurt if she didn't stop in and say hi' (Grigoriadis 2013). Producer Ted Hope, whose varied career in many respects expresses the vicissitudes of the contemporary independent film business from its early 1990s boom, stated in 2013 that Ellison is 'the only one out there putting reasonable budgets behind adventurous movies for adults that are 100% their directors' visions' (Leigh 2013). As Sherry Ortner points out, the language of 'protecting directors', and helping to 'realize his or her "vision"' (2013: 147) is one spoken widely by producers in the sector, even if the reality is inevitably more fraught and complex. Implicit in such statements is the notion that the director's 'vision' is worth realising in the first place, which, speaking bifocally, is dependent upon the producer's 'vision' (one of the attributes, incidentally, used to judge nominations for the Independent Spirit's Producer's Award). Ortner translates the nebulousness of 'vision-speak' into something more sociologically concrete, namely taste and judgement, after Pierre Bourdieu's theorising of cultural distinction. As Ortner notes, in the independent sector 'one cannot overestimate the importance for a producer of being viewed by one's peers of [sic]having good taste', defined as 'the ability to find the highest-quality material and/or to back the highest-quality filmmakers' (2013: 154–5). As Jane Feuer has argued, within this echelon of cultural production the concept of '"quality"' is . . . ideological . . . seen as more literate, more stylistically complex, and more psychologically "deep"' (1984: 56), and these are all terms that apply readily to the films in the Annapurna stable (so much so that Seth Rogen's upcoming R-rated animated *Sausage Party* (2016) feels like a calculated exception). And one doesn't have to search too far to find quotes from individuals happy to go on record proclaiming, as Amy Pascal, Mark Boal or Sharon Waxman do, that one of Ellison's major attributes is 'really good taste' (McGurk 2013).

Ortner also makes the point that the notion of 'protecting directors' is part of the 'intimate language of producing – of marrying and mothering . . . with (female) gendered overtones, even when the producer is male' (2013: 167). The symbolism of Annapurna, Hindu goddess of food and nourishment, rather speaks to this idea (as does the nominative determinism of Disruption Entertainment Inc.'s Mary Parent). Ortner's observation is made in the context of a discussion of the fact that while 'women form a relatively small percent of directors and filmmakers . . . [they] constitute almost half the ranks of producers', arguing that the rise from 'nearly zero in the 1970s' is 'clearly one of the payoffs' of the second-wave women's movement (2013: 150). Yet it is not entirely apparent from Ortner's argument why this 'payoff' should be so strikingly bifurcated between directing and producing, which, if anything, evidences the failure to overturn gendered assumptions about the skillsets necessary to undertake these jobs. Recent research by Martha Lauzen indicates that for feature-length independent fiction films screening at high-profile film festivals in the United States in 2013–14, 18% were directed by women, as opposed to 30% being produced by them, which suggests greater parity *between* roles, albeit less gender parity for women producers overall (Lauzen 2014).

What is clear is that in the rarefied air of high-end independent film financing, Ellison's gender has contributed significantly to her media attention. Amy Pascal, one of only two female heads of a major studio until her resignation in February 2015 as Motion Pictures Group Chairman for Sony Pictures Entertainment, stated that 'if she was a guy, nobody would be talking her age at all' (Hertz 2014), an opinion rather borne out by the lack of such focus on her similarly youthful and well-resourced brother. For the trade press this is couched positively; the 2014 edition of *Variety*'s annual 'Power of Women' issue included the section 'Indie Flame Burns Bright', with Ellison profiled alongside OddLot Entertainment's Gigi Pritzker, and Black Label Media's Molly Smith; all three women described as 'creative, hands-on producers with dirt under their fingernails, many notches in their belts, and a keen understanding of the art and commerce of making movies' (Foundas 2014: 46). Given that all are also, in *Variety*'s words, 'the scions of three of America's wealthiest families' (Pritzker is daughter of Jay Pritzker, founder of Hyatt hotels, while Smith's father is FedEx founder Fred Smith), the reference to dirty fingernails and belt notches appears more aimed at correcting assumptions of lofty patronage than feminine decorum. For *Variety*, the more meaningful link between the women is their shared role in 'revitalizing . . . a space – the midbudget, adult-skewing drama – that the studios have largely abandoned' (Foundas 2014: 46). Notably, the trade publication makes no reference to whether or not they are invested in empowering *other* women through their projects, either as directors, screenwriters, or in leading roles – comparable to the explicit mission of Reese Witherspoon and Bruna Papandrea's Pacific Standard, formed in 2012 (Riley 2014).

By contrast, for the mainstream news media, the underlying discourse on the figure of the producer skews towards self-promotion, or, in Matthew Bernstein's terms, the producer 'as a brand name . . . marketed to the moviegoing public' (2008: 188). Here, Ellison plays as the anti-Harvey Weinstein/Jerry Bruckheimer/Scott Rudin; youthful, enigmatic, taciturn, but also distinct from other notable high-profile women producers and studio executives such as Gale Anne Hurd, Mary Parent, Donna Langley and Amy Pascal in her avoidance of customary public relations and profile management activities. In this context, it is interesting that screenwriter Mark Boal refers to Ellison's 'Silicon Valley style' (Grigoriadis 2013), suggesting the producer's adoption of the tech world's casual, informal, and understated approach to business culture. As

Mark Zuckerberg's widely-reported uniform of grey T-shirt and hoodie makes evident, this finds embodiment in sartorial semiotics: according to *Vanity Fair* Ellison 'usually wears a uniform of army boots, denim jeans, and a hoodie pulled over the T-shirt of an old-school rock band' (Grigoriadis 2013), while the *Hollywood Reporter* notes that in Hollywood 'only the talent can wear whatever they want' (Swart 2014). More substantively, 'Silicon Valley style' is used to pinpoint an ethos of investment in innovation – the 'freewheeling world of technology start-ups' (Cieply and Barnes 2011) – that appears to offer a direct contrast to Hollywood's cautious strategy of risk avoidance. A *GQ* profile on Ellison sought significance in the fact that she 'grew up around the pioneers of Silicon Valley rather than the moguls of the Hollywood Hills,' schooled in 'dotcom entrepreneurship . . . backing talent and innovation in the hope something previously unknown can become huge' (McGurk 2013). While this makes for good copy, it is somewhat facile, and fails to acknowledge the extent to which Annapurna's investment in 'smart art', allegedly brokered by CAA, appears more considered and disciplined than the term 'freewheeling' would glibly imply.

@meganellison – Producing a 'Personal Public'

A stronger evidential basis for Ellison's 'Silicon Valley style' lies in her use of social media, brought spectacularly to public attention in the wake of the cyber attack on Sony Pictures Entertainment in November 2014. The work of a group calling themselves 'the Guardians of Peace' targeted the company's release of *The Interview* (Seth Rogen and Evan Goldberg, 2014), and the resulting security breach saw a reported 100 terabytes of data stolen from the corporation (Bernstein 2014). Among the flood of sensitive documents and communications leaked onto the web was an email conversation between film producer Scott Rudin and Sony's Amy Pascal, about the plans for *Jobs*, Aaron Sorkin's adaptation of the biography of the late Apple CEO. In the middle of an exchange about possible co-financing arrangements for the picture, Rudin referred to Ellison, who had partnered with the studio for *American Hustle* and *Foxcatcher*. The notoriously bellicose Rudin goaded Pascal over a potential approach to Annapurna, describing Ellison as a 'bipolar 28 year old lunatic', adding that 'maybe if she likes you and if she took her meds, there's some vague chance you can start this movie in ten weeks?' (Biddle 2014). On the same day that this exchange appeared on media gossip blog *Gawker* and was disseminated rapidly by news outlets worldwide, Ellison offered by way of riposte a dispatch from @meganellison, tweeting 'Bipolar 28 year old lunatic . . . ? I always thought of myself more as eccentric' (2014).

Putting to one side the apparent insensitivity of Rudin to mental health issues and the ethics of publishing documents obtained through criminal activity, the decision by Ellison to take to Twitter to offer an arch, no-more-than 140-character response (seventy-five characters, to be exact), was one that came as no surprise to those observers who had been following her rapid rise to the top rank of independent film producers. For instance, there was her widely reported use of the micro-blogging site to comment on Kathryn Bigelow's failure to get an Oscar nomination for Annapurna's *Zero Dark Thirty* in 2013: she tweeted 'Kathryn Bigelow was robbed. So fucked up. #recount' (Zakarin 2013). Indeed, beginning with her initial communication with *Waking Madison*'s director Katherine Brooks through MySpace, Ellison's persistent use of social media requires us to qualify claims for her well-publicised diffidence (she doesn't grant personal interviews, requiring numerous profile pieces to circumnavigate her absence). This stance is typically represented as one motivated not by media hostility but a desire for inconspicuousness; *The Wrap*'s founder Sharon Waxman, recounting a meeting with Ellison at Cannes, writes that she stated she 'just didn't want to be in the limelight' (Waxman 2012). Yet Ellison's decision to have an individual, public Twitter account arguably complicates that sentiment. Annapurna Pictures, a company comprised of Ellison and no more than a handful of associates, has its own Twitter account, and would seem to be the ideal de-personalised channel of communication for a producer eager to shun the limelight but still promote her movies.

In their work on the use of Twitter by prominent individuals, Alice Marwick and danah boyd characterise it as a form of 'strategically managed self-disclosure' through the 'appearance and performance of "backstage"' access, while noting that 'highly followed accounts vary in performed intimacy' (2011: 147). In those terms, and given Ellison's apparently calculated absence from other, more traditional forms of public self-disclosure such as press interviews and personal appearances (Annapurna's film premieres aside), her use of the micro-blogging site needs to be understood as a privileged, tactically-useful site of 'performative practice'. Tellingly, neither Pascal nor Rudin has a Twitter feed. Both are corporate Hollywood veterans, and high-profile casualties of a blisteringly-paced, post-Snowden digital world. By contrast, Twitter enables Ellison to show she is young, hip, tech-savvy, self-knowing and in control – amply demonstrated by the artful, instantly retweetable message that skewered the graceless efforts (embarrassing emails *and* subsequent apologetic communiqués) of Pascal and Rudin.

An analysis of Ellison's use of Twitter offers a useful illustration of its value in the terms described by Marwick and boyd. Over the period between 19 April 2011 (the date of Ellison's first public use of Twitter) and 3 March 2015, Ellison tweeted/retweeted 1,433 times, at an average rate of about six tweets per week. Of those, 506 (35%) were directly related to Annapurna films, either in production, at the point of release, or involved in competition for awards (e.g., 'Watch out for the premiere of the AMERICAN HUSTLE trailer today at 4pm pst on @YahooMovies'; 'I recommend anyone interested in seeing the first trailer for Spike Jonze's HER check out <http://apple.com/trailers at 9am pst. Breath taking'). These tweets saw Ellison straightforwardly adopt the public persona of film producer. Many such messages were in fact retweets of postings on Annapurna's own twitter feed, indicating an intention to extend the promotional reach of such information to Ellison's own followers. Yet as a category, they offer little reason to 'follow' Ellison rather than Annapurna. But it is how such instances of professional communication combine in 'the same space with personal musings, phatic communication and social grooming', that serves to organise Twitter as a site for what Jan-Hinrik Schmidt calls the 'personal public', where 'information is selected by criteria of personal relevance for a known, networked audience in a conversational mode' (2013: 7).

For example, a further 450 tweets/retweets (31%) were references to pop culture, the overwhelming majority about movies. These ranged from those that offered a generalised declaration of personal taste ('Hulu has the Criterion Collection. For Free. For real. <http://bit.ly/X8Mn01'), to more specific preferences (e.g., 'Goonies never say die'; 'Frodo lives'; 'I saw Cabaret last night. Incredible. Emma Stone is a triple threat, endlessly charismatic and @ Alancumming is a god.'). A preponderance of such tweets were dialogue quotations, often unattributed ('For the night is dark and full of terror' [*Game of Thrones*]), to 1980s movies (*Goonies*, *Back to the Future*, *Never Ending Story*, *Terminator*) or more recent fantasy and adventure stories (*Lord of the Rings*; *Game of Thrones*). In contrast to the preceding cluster of tweets, these messages positioned Ellison as a fan, someone deeply and personally invested in movie culture. And not primarily arthouse fare, but in large part what Peter Kramer calls 'family-adventure movies', aimed 'at kids – the kid in everybody' (2004: 358) which serve to foreground a sense of unalloyed enchantment with cinema. Nevertheless, it is hard not to characterise such tweets as what Marwick and boyd call 'strategic revealing' (2011: 147) that necessarily complicates a sense of the clear division between 'frontstage' and 'backstage' access. For example, Ellison tweeted 'I grew up in the era of VHS, making 80s cinema at my core. Goonies, Back to the Future, Overboard. All staples of my youth. What are yours?' This reads like fan-to-fan communication, inviting a connection to be built on the shared personal significance of childhood movie watching to a sense of self. But it is also the case that at the time of posting, Annapurna was producing Richard Linklater's *That's What I'm Talking About*, set in the 1980s, and an alleged 'spiritual sequel' (Sneider 2014) to *Dazed and Confused* (Richard Linklater, 1993). Indeed, Ellison had tweeted previously 'Day 2 of shooting on THAT'S WHAT I'M TALKING ABOUT. Looking good, feeling good. Welcome to the 80s.' One way to interpret this would be to see Ellison as cannily 'cuing up' up potential audience for

the film. But it also serves to corroborate Ellison as a 'producer-fan', someone for whom movie-making is a sincere extension of personal tastes and passions.

A similar blurring of 'frontstage' and 'backstage' might be detected in the third category of tweets made by Ellison. These are best described as quotations from famous people, and comprise 24% (346 tweets) of her postings during the period in question. The quotations are notably eclectic in provenance, ranging from Walt Whitman ('Resist much, obey little'), to Friedrich Nietzsche ('Blessed are the forgetful: for they get the better even of their blunders'), to Dr Seuss ('I like nonsense; it wakes up the brain cells'). Douglas Adams and Oscar Wilde are the most frequently quoted. Ellison is also not above poking fun at her tendency to tweet such quotations, posting '"A witty saying proves nothing." – Voltaire.' On one level these quotations fit normatively into the 'thoughts on life' (Marwick and boyd 2011: 142) category deployed by many twitter users, famous or otherwise. But particularly noteworthy is Ellison's tendency to tweet quotations about artistic production, for instance, '"Without art, the crudeness of reality would make the world unbearable." – George Bernard Shaw'; '"If art is to nourish the roots of our culture, society must set the artist free to follow his vision wherever it takes him." – JFK.' Perhaps most pertinent of all is '"The arts are not a way to make a living. They are a very human way of making life more bearable." – Kurt Vonnegut.' For someone heavily involved in financing 'smart art', not always with spectacular investment-to-profit ratios – Sharon Waxman publicly criticised Ellison for spending 'too much' (2012) to make *Zero Dark Thirty* and *The Master* – this quotation articulates a personalised *raison d'être*, and one which also positions her within the indie film sector's own espoused set of values. As Newman notes, indie cinema's rhetoric of uncompromised personal expression valorises 'the film-maker as a creative artist working unhampered by corporate influence' (2009: 24). Extended to the figure of the producer, this involves, as Mirasol Enriquez contends, 'collaboration on a single vision' (2015) – that of the auteur-filmmaker. Annapurna's roster of auteur 'filmmakers in the top rank' (Cieply and Barnes 2011) thus establishes the conditions for letting the artists get on with making art for art's sake. Notable also is the way in which indie's aforementioned privileging of artistic authenticity aligns with what Nancy K. Baym describes as Twitter's 'site-wide norm of "authenticity" created through both official rhetoric and user practices' (2013: 222). As Baym's analysis of the use of Twitter by indie musicians makes clear, many such individuals have readily applied the maxim that 'connecting with your fans in an authentic way is one key to your success' (222).

The remaining 131 tweets/retweets (9%) made by Ellison could be described as comprising personal information, although over a third of that number are little more than references to locations (e.g., 'meanwhile . . . the current view from my hotel room'; 'selfie in the Sahara'; 'Enjoying a beautiful day in Rome';

'Dolphins!!'), and many are places Ellison is visiting for film shoots or awards ceremonies, emphasising again the blurring of 'frontstage' and 'backstage' access. Only a very small percentage – perhaps ten tweets out of 1,433 (0.7%) constitute personally intimate information, such as 'I went to visit my Mom on her ranch and saw my old horse' or 'Looking forward to my 10 year high school reunion . . . tonight.' Among these is a notable tweet that fulfills one of the functions of 'performative intimacy' identified by Marwick and boyd, namely 'addressing rumors' (2011: 148). On 8 June 2014, Ellison tweeted 'In the spirit of pride let me clear something up. I'm not bisexual. I'm a full blown gay . . . lesbian . . . what have you. And I love it.' Prompted by media speculation over Ellison's sexuality (for instance, *Out* magazine's April 2014 'power list' had assuredly declared her bisexual), the tweet was sandwiched between two others that referenced *Hedwig and the Angry Inch* ('Fuck yes "@TheTonyAwards: #TonyAwards Win: Leading Actor in a Musical – @ ActuallyNPH in (@HedwigOnBway)"'; and lyrics 'Breathe Feel Love Give Free Know in your soul Like your blood knows the way From your heart to your brain Know that you're whole'). The Broadway production has been a major contributor to LGBT charities, while star Neil Patrick Harris announced publically in 2006 that he was gay in order to dispel rumours and assert a sense of pride (*People* 2006). Again, this appears strategic, in that it allows Ellison to contextualise 'backstage' with a 'frontstage' that redirects the story away from her private life to the public issue of LGBT acceptance and equality, but also does so with reference to the love of pop culture and celebration of exceptional artistry.

One final noteworthy tweet demonstrates the micro-blogging site's distinct communicative mode, and the way that it can be harnessed to shape a distinct 'meta-narrative and meta-image of self' (Marwick and boyd 2010: 119). On 1 April 2014 (a date that might in fact lead one to treat its veracity with caution), Ellison tweeted, cryptically, 'INFP'. No contiguous tweets served to elucidate its meaning. Easily mistaken for the name of some hipster Brooklyn eatery, the acronym has in fact one widely known referent, which is a specific type on the Myers-Briggs personality assessment instrument, derived from the work of Carl Jung, and used worldwide in careers counselling and personal development. INFP stands for Introverted, iNtuitive, Feeling, Perceiving, and the Internet abounds with sites devoted to coalescing these attributes into an unambiguous personality, characteristically typified as 'true idealists . . . calm, reserved or even shy . . . [with] an inner flame and passion', for whom 'the risk of feeling misunderstood is unfortunately high' (*16personalities* 'INFP Personality ("The Mediator")'. Reservations over such reductiveness aside, the key point is Ellison's desire to seemingly self-identify as 'INFP', and to communicate this to her personal public (tellingly, Ellison's second ever post on Twitter had been a link to an article from *Psychology Today*, entitled

'Revenge of the Introvert', which is a striking gesture for someone embarking upon a new social media platform). While the corpus of indie cinema is undoubtedly heterogeneous, it would not be untrue to suggest that one of its dominant strains could be described as cinema *for* and *about* INFPs, from *Eternal Sunshine of the Spotless Mind* (Michel Gondry, 2004), *Sun Don't Shine* (Amy Seimetz, 2012) to Annapurna's *Her*, whose Theodore Twombly (Joaquin Phoenix) appears the embodiment of 'INFP'. Indeed, the film that helped spearhead the contemporary independent film sector's growth back in the 1990s, *sex, lies, and videotape* (Steven Soderbergh, 1989), could itself be seen to champion the INFP personality type. Notably, its producer, Harvey Weinstein, is a pugnacious huckster, and thus strikingly at odds with the film's own set of values, though, as Alisa Perren has shown, savvy in his skewing of its content for promotional purposes (2001). Twenty-five years on, Twitter demonstrates Ellison's capacity to build a 'personal public', and thus a potential audience constituency for Annapurna's movies, around a set of attributes and values that are in many ways more congruent with the sector's idealised self-image.

Conclusion

While Ellison, as an uncloseted lesbian multi-millionaire financier is a figure without precedent in the history of independent cinema, the issue faced by Annupurna Pictures, namely how to mitigate the uncertainty inherent in film production, is one widely shared. Baym writes that 'Twitter seems ideal for those careers that are increasingly dependent on audience relationships' (2013: 222), and Ellison's use of the site suggests a keen understanding of how best to navigate a rapidly transforming landscape 'in which digital technology and social media allow for new ways to program for and reach audiences in theaters and online' (Astle 2012: 76). *Variety*'s description of her as 'elusive' thus appears wide of the mark, and fails to acknowledge the degree to which Ellison's social media profile gives her a quotidian presence far more extensive than even the most boosterish producer of an earlier era.

More broadly, Ellison's use of Twitter to respond to the leaked Pascal-Rudin exchange should be understood as consonant with social media's emergence as a conspicuous platform for publically questioning behavioural norms in the film industry, as evinced by the tumblr site 'Shit People Say to Women Directors', or actress and independent director Rose McGowan's use of Twitter to publicise being fired by her agent for divulging sexist casting notes (Kang 2015). The latter, which allegedly prompted the agent's own dismissal, led Ellison to tweet '@rosemcgowan you're a fucking badass', and makes her own investment in that evolving discourse emphatically clear. How Ellison continues to shape and deploy her profile remains to be seen, but, typically, she took to Twitter in May 2014 to reply to Manohla Dargis' and A. O. Scott's request to 'take a few more risks' (Dargis and Scott 2014), rejoining 'Just give me a minute, I'm getting to that.' Indeed, the shape and form that Ellison's response takes will do much to substantiate Mark Boal's memorable description of her as a 'woman with an endgame' (Cieply and Barnes 2011).

Note

1. At the time of writing Ellison has 84,000 followers on Twitter. Her closest comparator is Christine Vachon, with 15,900 followers, while Alicia Van Couvering and Adele Romanski have 2,101 and 1,047 followers respectively.

References

'About' (2015), *Annapurna Pictures*, <http://annapurnapics.com/main/#about> (last accessed 6 July 2015).

Astle, Randy (2012), 'Alternate Routes', *Filmmaker*, Summer, p. 76.

Baym, Nancy K. (2014), 'The Perils and Pleasures of Tweeting with Fans', in Katrin Weller, Axel Bruns, Jean Burgess, Merja Mahrt, and Cornelius Puschmann (eds), *Twitter and Society*, New York: Peter Lang, pp. 221–35.

Bernstein, Matthew (2008), 'The Producer as Auteur', in Barry Keith Grant (ed.), *Auteurs and Authorship: A Film Reader*, London: Blackwell.

Bernstein, Paula (2014), 'Is the Day-and-Date Release of "The Interview' a Success?"', *Indiewire*, 29 December, <http://www.indiewire.com/article/is-the-day-and-date-release-of-the-interview-a-success-that-depends-20141229> (last accessed 6 July 2015).

Biddle, Sam (2014), 'Leaked: The Nightmare Email Drama Behind Sony's Steve Jobs Disaster', *Defamer*, 9 December, <http://defamer.gawker.com/leaked-the-nightmare-email-drama-behind-sonys-steve-jo-1668882936> (last accessed 4 August 2015).

Cieply, Michael and Brooks Barnes (2011), 'Silicon Valley Scion Tackles Hollywood', *The New York Times*, 29 August, <http://www.nytimes.com/2011/08/29/business/media/megan-ellison-and-annapurna-pictures-tackle-hollywood.html> (last accessed 6 July 2015).

Dargis, Manohla and A. O. Scott (2014), 'Memos to Hollywood', *The New York Times*, 2 May, <http://mobile.nytimes.com/2014/05/04/movies/critics-weigh-in-on-patriarchy-and-the-vanished-film-print.html?referrer=&_r=0> (last accessed 4 August 2015).

Eller, Claudia (2010), 'David Ellison raises $350 million to co-fund movies with Paramount', *Los Angeles Times*, 16 August, <http://latimesblogs.latimes.com/entertainmentnewsbuzz/2010/08/david-ellison-raises-350-million-to-cofund-movies-with-paramount.html> (last accessed 6 July 2015)

Enriquez, Mirasol (2015), 'Elizabeth Avellán: Independent Troublemaking to Hollywood and Back Again,' SCMS Conference, Montreal, CA, 26 March.

'EXCLUSIVE: Neil Patrick Harris Tells PEOPLE He Is Gay' (2006), *People*, 11 March, <http://www.people.com/people/article/0,26334,1554852,00.html> (last accessed 6 July 2015).

Feuer, Jane, Paul Kerr and Tise Vahimagi (1984), *MTM 'Quality Television'*, London: BFI.

Finney, Angus (2010), *The International Film Business*, London: Routledge.

'40 Under 40' (2014), *Fortune*, <http://fortune.com/40-under-40/megan-ellison-20/> (last accessed 4 August 2015).

Foundas, Scott (2014), 'Indie Flame Burns Bright', *Variety*, 14 October, p. 46.

'Full Sale Ahead' (2011), *Variety*, 5 September, p. 22.

Graser, Marc (2012), 'Heavy hitters', *Variety*, 27 February–4 March, p. 8.

Grigoriadis, Vanessa (2013), 'Caution: Heiress at Work', *Vanity Fair*, March, <http://www.vanityfair.com/hollywood/2013/03/megan-ellison-27-producer-zero-dark-thirty?mbid=social_twitter> (last accessed 6 July 2015).

Hertz, Barry (2014), 'Oscars 2014: How best picture maker Megan Ellison became the most powerful woman in movies', *National Post*, 28 February, <http://news.nationalpost.com/2014/02/28/oscars-2014-how-best-picture-maker-megan-ellison-became-the-most-powerful-woman-in-movies/> (last accessed 6 July 2015).

'INFP Personality ("The Mediator")' (ND), *16Personalities*, <http://www.16personalities.com/infp-personality> (last accessed 4 August 2015).

Kaufman, Anthony (2013), 'Smart Art Thrives at the Right Price', *Variety*, 14 May, pp. 117–18.

Kang, Inkoo (2015), 'Rose McGowan Clarifies Claim She Was Dropped by Agents for Speaking Out Against Sexism (UPDATED)', *Indiewire*, 25 June, <http://blogs.indiewire.com/womenandhollywood/rose-mcgowan-dropped-by-agents-for-speaking-out-against-sexism-in-hollywood-20150625> (last accessed 25 June 2015).

Kemper, Tom (2010), *Hidden Talent: The Emergence of Hollywood Agents*, Los Angeles: University of California Press.

King, Geoff (2013), 'Thriving or in permanent crisis? Discourses on the state of indie cinema,' in Geoff King, Claire Malloy and Yannis Tzioumakis (eds), *American Independent Cinema: indie, Indiewood, and beyond*, London: Routledge, pp. 41–52.

Kramer, Peter (2004), '"It's Aimed at Kids – the Kid in Everybody": George Lucas, Star Wars and Children's Entertainment', in Yvonne Tasker (ed.), *Action and Adventure Cinema*, London: Routledge, pp. 358–70.

Kroll, Justin and Marc Graser (2012), 'Pre-packaged projects give producers more pic control', *Variety*, 27 February–4 March, p. 9.

Kudler, Adrian (2013), 'Heiress Megan Ellison Buys Infamous Party Palace for $30M,' *Curbed*, 31 December, <http://la.curbed.com/archives/2013/12/megan_ellison_buys_mt_olympus_supervillain_lair_for_30_million.php> (last accessed 4 August 2015).

Lauzen, Martha (2014), 'Independent women: behind-the-scenes employment on festival films in 2013–14', <http://womenintvfilm.sdsu.edu/files/2014_Independent_Women_Report.pdf> (last accessed 6 July 2015).

Leigh, Danny (2013), 'Megan Ellison, the most powerful new force in Hollywood', *The Guardian*, 18 February, <http://www.theguardian.com/theguardian/2013/feb/18/megan-ellison-producer-the-master> (last accessed 6 July 2015).

McGurk, Stuart (2013), 'The socialite saving cinema', *GQ*, 8 March, <http://www.gq-magazine.co.uk/entertainment/articles/2013-03/08/megan-ellison-annapurna-billionaire-movie-mogul/viewall> (last accessed 6 July 2015).

Marwick, Alice, and danah boyd (2010), 'To See and Be Seen: Celebrity Practice on Twitter', *Convergence*, 17: 2, pp. 139–58.

Marwick, Alice, and danah boyd (2011), 'I Tweet Honestly, I Tweet Passionately: Twitter Users, Context Collapse, and the Imagined Audience', *New Media and Society*, 13: 1, pp. 114–33.

Newman, Michael Z. (2009), 'Indie Culture: In Pursuit of the Authentic Autonomous Alternative', *Cinema Journal*, 48: 3, pp. 16–34.

Newman, Michael Z. (2011), *Indie: An American Film Culture*, New York: Columbia University Press.

Ortner, Sherry B. (2013), *Not Hollywood: Independent Film at the Twilight of the American Dream*, Durham, NC and London: Duke University Press.

Perren, Alisa (2001), 'sex, lies and marketing: Miramax and the Development of the Quality Indie Blockbuster', *Film Quarterly*, 55: 2, pp. 30–9.

Perren, Alisa (2012), *Indie, Inc., Miramax and the Transformation of Hollywood in the 1990s*, Austin: University of Texas Press.

'Power List 2014: MEGAN ELLISON' (2014), *Out*, <http://www.out.com/out-exclusives/power-50/2014/04/07/power-list-2014-megan-ellison> (last accessed 4 August 2015).

Riley, Jenelle (2014), 'Reese Witherspoon, Bruna Papandrea Push for Female-Driven Material With Pacific Standard', *Variety*, 7 October, <http://variety.com/2014/film/features/reese-witherspoon-production-company-female-driven-material-1201323117/> (last accessed 4 August 2015).

Schmidt, Jan-Hinrik (2014), 'Twitter and the Rise of Personal Publics', in Katrin Weller, Axel Bruns, Jean Burgess, Merja Mahrt and Cornelius Puschmann (eds), *Twitter and Society*, New York: Peter Lang, pp. 3–14.

Sneider, Jeff (2014), 'Megan Ellison, Paramount Board Richard Linklater's Spiritual Sequel to "Dazed and Confused"', *The Wrap*, 29 September, <http://www.thewrap.com/megan-ellison-paramount-board-richard-linklaters-spiritual-sequel-to-dazed-and-confused/> (last accessed 6 July 2015).

Swart, Sharon (2014), 'Silicon Valley vs. Hollywood: Clash of the Corporate Cultures', *The Hollywood Reporter*, 29 May, <http://www.hollywoodreporter.com/news/silicon-valley-hollywood-clash-corporate-707147> (last accessed 6 July 2015).

'The 100 Most Influential People' (2014), *Time*, 23 April, <http://time.com/70887/megan-ellison-2014-time-100/> (last accessed 6 July 2015).

Travers, Ben (2014), '"American Hustle" Producer Megan Ellison Developing TV Series on Greta Garbo & Marlene Dietrich', *Indiewire*, 17 April, <http://www.indiewire.com/article/television/american-hustle-producer-megan-ellison-developing-tv-series-on-greta-garbo-marlene-dietrich>

Tzioumakis, Yannis (2013), '"Independent", "Indie" and "Indiewood": Towards a periodisation of (post-1980) American independent cinema', in Geoff King, Claire Malloy and Yannis Tzioumakis (eds), *American Independent Cinema: indie, Indiewood, and beyond*, London: Routledge, pp. 28–40.

Waxman, Sharon (2012), 'Why Well-Meaning Billionaires Like Megan Ellison May Ruin the Movie Business', *The Wrap*, 17 October, <http://www.thewrap.com/movies/column-post/megan-ellison-and-hollywood-or-when-billionaire-run-movie-business-61041/> (last accessed 4 August 2015).

Zakarin, Jordan (2013), 'Megan Ellison Calls Kathryn Bigelow Oscar Snub "F***ed Up," Jessica Chastain Praises Her Direction', *The Hollywood Reporter*, 10 January, <http://www.hollywoodreporter.com/race/megan-ellison-kathryn-bigelow-oscar-411107> (last accessed 6 July 2015).

4. SUSAN SEIDELMAN'S CONTEMPORARY FILMS: THE FEMINIST ART OF SELF-REINVENTION IN A CHANGING TECHNOLOGICAL LANDSCAPE

Christina Lane

The renaissance of American, quasi-indie cinema in the 1990s – an era that ushered in young mavericks like Kevin Smith, Quentin Tarantino, Robert Rodriguez, and David O. Russell – often overshadows the 1980s wave that preceded it: a vibrant, flourishing spell of activity for independent women filmmakers.[1] From approximately 1982 to 1992, numerous institutional, political, economic, and cultural forces aligned, creating a climate in which self-identified feminists such as Lizzie Borden, Joyce Chopra, Martha Coolidge, Julie Dash, Donna Deitch, Lisa Gottleib, Nancy Savoca, and Susan Seidelman enjoyed remarkable critical and festival circuit success.

These filmmakers were the progeny of second-wave feminism, having embraced progressive (Marxist, radical, progressive, liberal, humanist) politics. This was not a perfect environment, informed as it was by white, middle-class feminism. It excluded many women of colour; lesbians, bisexuals, and transgender individuals; and those lacking in financial or educational resources. It was not free of corporate, economic, or political considerations. But it was a powerful moment in American film history, nonetheless.

Many contextual factors bred the conditions for such a successful wave of 1980s feminist independent cinema: robust funding by government sources (e.g., NEH, NEA) as well as public and private foundations; film collectives; a still-thriving public television network; emerging festivals and marketplaces; investment tax structures; grassroots connections; independent reviewers; an entire apparatus for non-commercial exhibition (through libraries, galleries, museums, schools, and underground spaces), not to mention a growing appetite for feminist films within mass culture.

Seidelman's debut feature (*Smithereens*, 1982) was the first American independent film to be invited to enter the competition at Cannes. Borden's second feature (*Working Girls*, 1985) premiered at Cannes in the Directors' Fortnight and won the Special Jury Prize at Sundance. Deitch's narrative turn, *Desert Hearts*, took top prizes at Sundance, Toronto, and the Independent Spirit Awards, and was picked up for distribution by the Samuel Goldwyn Company. Savoca's initial feature (*True Love*, 1989) won the Grand Jury Prize at Sundance. Dash's *Daughters of the Dust* (1991) was funded by American Playhouse and aired nationally on PBS. There was promise in the air.

What most likely felt like 'just the beginning' for these filmmakers, however, was essentially over within a few short years (though many of their careers survived in other forms). By the early 1990s, 'maverick' cinema arrived with full force, privileging young, white, male directors, and witnessing a massive corporatisation and privatisation of the independent and crossover Indiewood spheres. A renewed 'cult of the auteur' took hold (Perren 2012: 13–14, 106–7).

Some women directors (Allison Anders, Rebecca Miller, Darnelle Martin) turned to television. Other 1990s newcomers, such as Leslie Harris and Rose Troche, made impressive two- or three-picture studio deals only to languish in the development phase. Women's independent cinema had been labelled 'niche' in quick time, and deemed 'outdated' just as rapidly.

But a broader 'othering' of feminism was occurring, as mass culture took a postfeminist turn, in many ways relegating to the past and demonising second-wave feminist politics (and in many cases translating female power into a hyper-consumerist, me-directed discourse) (Tasker and Negra 2007: 1–26). By the first decade of the twenty-first century, many of these indie women, now in their forties, fifties, or sixties, were not only 'too old' in the eyes of ageist gatekeepers within Indiewood and Hollywood, but 'yesterday's news.' In the midst of these many challenges, the seismic technological, millennial shift – towards digitalism, interactivity, connectivity, and the Web – posed perhaps the most important question of all. Would emergent technologies (and co-optive practices by transnational corporations) serve a final blow to women whose careers originated in the 1980s – those stalwarts who believed fervently that it was imperative to make media by and for women – or would they open a new door?

This chapter considers the case of Susan Seidelman, a constructive example of filmmakers from her generation who have seized on the challenge of reinventing their professional lives by capitalising on digital, social, and emergent media.[2] I examine the production, distribution, marketing, and exhibition of three of Seidelman's features: *Boynton Beach Club* (2006), *Musical Chairs* (2011), and *The Hot Flashes* (2013). Each represents a series of challenges and opportunities for feminist filmmaking in a digital age. The creative ways in which she approached these projects offer powerful models for working within as well as around existing institutional structures while at the same time pushing beyond the limits of what seems possible. They often occur at the local, niche, or ground level. The kinds of micro-strategies deployed by Seidelman – many of which are little known because they are underpublicised or trivialised in more commercial streams – might be adopted or adapted by other women invested in indie practices.

Seidelman has shown a willingness to experiment in an extremely unsettled marketplace. Her recent work illuminates the kinds of savvy and entrepreneurial techniques that commercially minded feminist media-makers might harness in order to survive and succeed within the ever-expanding spaces beyond the major studios. My aim is not to suggest that Seidelman is naïve or that she subscribes to utopian discourses heralding 'hyper-textual society' and a new democratisation of the camera.[3] Rather, Seidelman's emphasis on professional transformation captures a sense of purpose and perseverance in the face of deep ambivalence towards rapid technological (and concurrent economic, industry, and cultural) change. While this case study sets out to specifically address the climate faced by women over forty who are not "digital natives," it can be extrapolated – or reframed – to speak more generally to contemporary feminist indie practices in the commercial, digital realm.

Apprehension towards emergent media is warranted, given the degree to which the enormous role played by women in the development of digital and Web media forms in the experimental, 'frontier' days (when such forms were seen as risky ventures by business and government) has been overlooked. As Lynn Hershman Leeson puts it, 'Computer language was invented by Ada Lovelace. Cell phone technology was invented by Hedy Lamarr. Artificial intelligence was invented by Mary Shelley (or, at least, the first concept of it). Women invent technology. Then when it gets to a point of marketing it, men step in and . . . get the jobs' (Callahan 2012: 424).[4] As a result, the historical involvement of women has traditionally been erased from the public narrative of developing technologies.

In an attempt to chart a course for scholars, critics, and media-makers interested in feminist, digital, commercial work, I aim to counteract such omission by recounting Seidelman's activities, obstacles, experiences, and (rare) triumphs. As Anne Balsamo contends, 'Feminists need reliable maps and innovative tools to navigate the technocultural terrain . . . I am absolutely convinced that this territory is exactly where feminists need to venture' (Balsamo 2011: 31). She continues, 'Most people simply don't see the women who have been there and still are there, creating significant inventions and innovations' (ibid. p. 32).

For the sake of both recognition and record, I examine the way that *Boynton*

Beach Club, *Musical Chairs*, and *The Hot Flashes* were conceived and pushed out into the world, especially through crowdsourcing, alternative financing, self-distribution, and travelling exhibitions. I incorporate trade reports, news articles, and interviews with the filmmaker in an effort to bring together a map of Seidelman's movements through relatively uncharted territory. Seidelman is a logical choice for study, given her long history of crisscrossing the often-underlineated lines between commercial and independent. She has demonstrated a sustained investment in conventional storytelling and an attunement to the marketplace. She often captures zeitgeist-moments (*Desperately Seeking Susan* in 1985, *Sex and the City* in 1998) or low-budget 'high concepts' (*Boynton Beach Club*, *The Hot Flashes*). Her filmic perspective is heavily informed by progressive politics and integrates feminist theory and aesthetics. Yet she strives to make accessible movies (working in the $1–6 million dollar budget range) that are character- and star-driven, and has helped 'make' stars out of relatively unknown actresses.

In the process, Seidelman has been insistent that an audience exists for her work. When told by executives that *Boynton Beach Club*'s 'fifty years and over' target demographic would not yield enough profit, she proved them wrong by initially self-distributing. When most directors passed on *Musical Chairs*, a fictional movie structured around a wheelchair ballroom dance competition, she signed on with the belief that multiple niche audiences could be cultivated. When studios rejected *The Hot Flashes* (in which a group of middle-aged women set out to recapture their high school basketball prowess) citing its lack of box office appeal, she championed the aging female demographic for whom it was conceived. In each example, Seidelman's intended audiences – whether certain female subsets or other specific niches, such as seniors, Latinos, or disabled rights groups – guide the creative process. She projects or imagines her target viewers, forms deep identificatory ties with them, and embarks on a personal mission to prove their value. Her willingness to cultivate and subsequently reward her intended audiences is a distinctive trait of her feminist authorship.

It is an uphill battle to combat the industry notion that adult women are not worth reaching. This is a strange position when trade research shows that most film and television products need a strong female demographic to survive, the majority of viewing decisions are made by women, many of the biggest industry success stories are female-driven films and television series, and 73% of women aged thirty-five to forty-nine have household purchasing power (Brody 2015; Dargis 2015; Consoli 2013).

Media executives with the ability to green-light projects may know all of this on some level, as evidenced by much of their product (especially in cable/premium television), yet they often invoke the fourteen-to-thirty-five-year-old male demographic in knee-jerk fashion. As a result, a self-reinforcing cycle occurs: 'niche' audiences are not well cultivated, evidence of their importance is ignored, and the widely sought-after young, white, male demographic continues to dominate the marketplace . . . and the industrial imagination (Harris 2014; Lauzen 2008; Lauzen 2015). This dynamic is replicated in very low- and micro-budget sectors where the reigning genres are horror, sci-fi, techie, and teen male rite-of-passage tales. Though exceptions exist, the micro-budget features that are held up as exemplars of the do-it-yourself (DIY) ethos are generally made by young, white, male directors for mirroring demographics.[5]

Feminists are more armed than ever before with research that challenges the mythical hold of such self-reinforcing attitudes. Owing to endeavours by San Diego State University's Center for the Study of Women in Television and Film, University of Southern California's Media, Diversity, and Social Change Initiative, the Geena Davis Institute on Gender in Media, and others, extensive metadata has started to amass, indicating the specific nature of professional obstacles for women and how they might be counteracted. However, dismissive attitudes about women remain deeply entrenched. It is in this space – between the prevailing attitudes of the present and the radical possibilities offered by technology – that Seidelman continues to toil.

Engineering a Comeback: Boynton Beach Club

Seidelman was arguably the most successful feminist, crossover, indie-commercial filmmaker of the 1980s. Graduating from New York University in 1977, she took part in a 1970s wave of film school feminists. Her first feature, *Smithereens* (1982), became the first independent feature by an American director ever to be invited into the Cannes Palm D'Or competition. A $60,000 film financed through a funding pool from family, friends, and crew, it was intended as a portfolio sample.[6] The crew was comprised of well-trained students and recent graduates. From Cannes, the film went on to be picked up by New Line Cinema, a relative newcomer to (and harbinger within) American commercial distribution. After fielding numerous studio deals for her next project, Seidelman signed to direct *Desperately Seeking Susan* (1986) with fledgling mini-major Orion Pictures. There, she was mentored by executive producer Barbara Boyle, whose stated mission was to increase women's Hollywood presence (Cole and Dale 1994: 194). For Seidelman, the critical success of *Desperately Seeking Susan* was followed by the box office failures (and professional struggles) associated with the studio features *Making Mr. Right* (1989) and *She-Devil* (1991), setbacks which have been well documented (Redding 1997: 145–57; Foster 1995: 334–5; Cole and Dale, 1936).

Seidelman took a hiatus from feature filmmaking in 1992 in part to start a family and in part to regroup from *She-Devil*'s tepid reception, though she continued to direct shorts and television, including several notable successes.[7]

By the time she embarked on the 2005 commercial feature *Boynton Beach Club*, she confronted an entirely different industry climate, defined by emergent technologies and uncertain organisational structures (author interview).[8] And she was fifty years old. Originally titled *The Boynton Beach Bereavement Club*, the film follows the romantic exploits of a group of recently widowed or divorced senior citizens in a Florida retirement community. The comedy was inspired by her mother Florence's anecdotal experience living in an active, adult community in Boynton Beach, Florida.[9] Seidelman co-wrote the script with her mother as well as local widower (and former TV actor) David Cramer and Miami writer Shelly Gitlow. Seidelman's producers raised the estimated $1.5 million budget through equity financing, provided by South Florida-based private investors with personal interest (a limited liability company named The Snowbirds) (author interview). Having garnered tremendous community support, the filmmakers cut costs by shooting on location, borrowing residential spaces for prep, hair, and make-up, and rounding up scores of senior citizens to serve as extras and assistants (Sick 2006).

Shooting on 35 mm film and casting established stars like Dyan Cannon, Brenda Vaccaro, Sally Kellerman and Joseph Bologna, Seidelman may have hoped for a traditional theatrical release, but she quickly found that reps and distributors did not view the senior citizen market as viable. Major and boutique distributors insisted there was no audience for *Boynton Beach Club*. Seidelman believed she had concrete evidence to the contrary, namely the outpouring of support by seniors helping to bring to the screen the kind of film they wanted to see. She told the *South Florida Sun-Sentinel*, 'I think Hollywood is operating under an old model – the idea that thirteen- to twenty-five year-olds are the ones who are going to movies. The fact is, Hollywood is underestimating the over-thirty-five audience. A sixteen-year-old doesn't go to the movies as often as I do, and I don't go as much as my mother does' (Sick).

The distribution and exhibition stages proved to be most crucial, precisely because Seidelman took it upon herself to prove her audience existed. After countless rejections, where executives would say, 'It's a nice movie but we don't believe there is enough commercial potential there,' she employed an entrepreneurial self-distribution strategy, with the goal of demonstrating the senior citizen market (author interview). Having paid for a digital transfer through the initial production budget, she produced several DVD copies on her home computer. In the spring of 2006, she and her producer team arranged limited digital-projection screenings at local Florida theatres, eventually building to twenty-five screens in the region, sustained over several weeks (author interview). Through localised advertising and aggressive word of mouth (including Florence's 'one-woman' grassroots promotional activities), audience response was considerable, with lines around the block (Shatzman 2006).

Taking cues from the classic 1970s roadshow model, this strategy capitalised on the hyper-mobility and lower cost (and risk) of digital technology. Based on the box office numbers, and per screen averages, Roadside Attractions-Samuel Goldwyn signed on to distribute in the US (author interview). The $1.5 million film made just over $3 million in its theatrical run, according to boxofficemojo.com.

Roadside Attractions-Samuel Goldwyn had ironically been one of the distributors that passed on Seidelman's original pitch, but they were soon hailing it as a new paradigm for digital age cinema. Samuel Goldwyn, Jr enthused in *Variety* that the company had 'found the audience that has been stranded' (Archerd 2006). *Boynton Beach Club* modelled unconventional business practices, its success suggesting an effective approach for bypassing standard gatekeepers such as producer reps, agents, distributors, and festival markets, through low-cost self-distribution, on-the-ground promotion, and crowd-sourcing. These ingredients have subsequently become staples for low-budget filmmaking in the context of emergent media. Seidelman observes that one of 'the biggest changes between 2005 and 2015 is the crucial role of crowdsourcing, reaching out to total strangers for support without having to go through the usual channels (such as LLCs or studios). When I made *Boynton Beach*, I did my own kind of crowdsourcing with retirees in South Florida. Cut to ten years later, it's the same method, but on the Internet, instead of on the ground' (author interview).

Even as *Boynton Beach Club* serves as a success story, pointing to empowered and creative opportunities for exploiting a transitional marketplace, it signals an additional burden placed on filmmakers. The DIY route typically requires directors to know more about each stage, and to manage every phase as a conductor leads an orchestra. Seidelman remarks, 'I now involve myself more in the business side than ever before. When I came out of film school in the 1980s, all I knew was that I wanted to "be an artist." The business part was the producer's job. But today, and *Boynton Beach* exemplifies this, before I even begin, I need to ask, "Who will be watching this?" "How and where will they be watching it?" and "Who wants to see this movie get made?"' (author interview).

Musical Chairs: Playing to Multiple Niches

Seidelman's next film, *Musical Chairs*, represents something of an aberration in that the completed script came to her fully funded by a private financier. It tells the story of Mia (Leah Pipes), an aspiring dancer who, after a car accident, becomes a paraplegic and takes up wheelchair ballroom dancing. Following a *Romeo and Juliet*-style plot, the film pairs her with Armando (E. J. Bonilla), a Puerto Rican young man working as a custodian in the dance studio. He shares her love of dancing and inspires her to confront the challenges brought on by her injury. While winning her heart, he galvanises an entire physical rehab unit of disabled patients into dance-action. A subplot features a black, disabled, transgender woman named Chantelle (Laverne Cox) overcoming her fear of coming out to her newfound love, Armando's uncle.

Developed by the relatively unknown writer Marty Madden, *Musical Chairs* became a passion project for investor Janet Carrus, a competitive amateur dancer deeply engaged with disability charities (author interview). With an approximate budget of $2.5 million, the film's costs were kept down by shooting digitally and using lesser-known actors. Though Seidelman had little to do with development, one of her chief assets was her savvy navigation of New York's local and state tax incentives and support structures. *Musical Chairs* benefited from official support from the New York Governor's Office and made use of lenient New York City permitting for location shooting. In exchange, Seidelman's film publicity promoted the area, declaring for example, 'Everywhere you point the camera, there's great production design. New York offers a very inexpensive backdrop' (Brooks 2012).

Musical Chairs was not a financial winner. Producers signed on to a service deal – where they pay for their own release – with the distributor Palladin. It initially opened theatrically in South Florida in March 2012, before seeing limited rollout the following week in New York, Chicago, and various California cities.[10] There was little publicity, suggesting a minimal promotional budget, and its four-week run earned $31,478, according to boxofficemojo.com. In December 2012, producers made a countermove with a 'mini-media blitz,' streaming *Musical Chairs* for free through an Internet homepage for two weeks. The LGBT publication *The Advocate* named the event one of the 'Top Ten Highlights of the Year' ('Hot Sheet' 2012).[11] In November 2013, HBO Latino, HBO On-Demand, and the streaming channel HBO-GO distributed it. Amazon acquired DVD retail rights.

Seidelman's association with *Musical Chairs* is most instructive in terms of her continued struggles to make films for underserved audiences. She saw it as an opportunity to target multiple niches, including Latinos, dance and music enthusiasts, LGBT communities, and disability rights groups. Indeed, many individual screenings (at dance festivals, disability charities, LGBT film festivals) sought to capture one market slice. There were several festival showings, including the Miami International Film Festival and the Havana Film Festival. The movie was nominated for a Fred and Adele Astaire Award and won a GLAAD award for Outstanding Film in Limited Release. This may have been an instance, however, of too many niches spread too thin, which overly fragmented an already underfunded marketing process. The next case, *The Hot Flashes*, offers an auspicious contrast: a clearly defined premise with a precise demographic that feeds a concentrated, coherent distribution and marketing plan.

Figure 4.1 *The Hot Flashes* (2013) was released through vigorous advance marketing and social media campaigns.

The Hot Flashes

Released in 2013, *The Hot Flashes* stars Brooke Shields, Daryl Hannah, Wanda Sykes, Camryn Manheim and Virginia Madsen in an ensemble comedy-drama about former all-state basketball champions – all underappreciated, middle-aged women living in the fictional small town of Burning Bush, Texas – who team up to raise money for breast cancer prevention. The eclectic crew challenges the reigning high school girls' team to a series of games, ultimately raising enough funds to reinstate the local mammogram mobile unit and create a national media stir. In the process, each woman is transformed: the flighty, imperceptive housewife (Shields) embraces independence; the closeted lesbian (Hannah) comes out; the African-American image-conscious mayoral candidate (Sykes) lets loose. The film casts little person Mark Povinelli as the team's coach, making a bid to transcend stereotypes and reinforcing an overall theme that one should not judge based on appearances.

The Hot Flashes came to Seidelman's attention as a speculation script penned by unproduced writer Brad Hennig, whose day job was with a San Francisco marketing firm. Born in a small Texas town near Abilene, Hennig, having lost his mother to breast cancer, brainstormed the story during an annual pilgrimage to her gravesite, when he happened upon a group of women playing basketball (Archer 2013). Through a 'cold-call' email, Hennig queried Seidelman. Though she has agency representation, she notes that in the digital age her most viable material has come to her via unsolicited Internet correspondence.[12] Once she attached herself as director, the two pitched the script to studios. Seidelman remarks, 'We tried traditional routes but as soon as you said to executives the words, "movie about five middle-age women," you could see the light leaving their faces' (author interview). Seidelman and Hennig spent nearly four years putting together private financing, with the aid of producer (and former vice president of Black Entertainment Television's movie division) Nina Henderson Moore.

Eventually nineteen women and one man pooled together $4.5 million to form The Hot Flashes, LLC. They were Silicon Valley-based angel investors (many of whom were cultivated through Hennig's professional connections) with demonstrated philanthropic interests in women's sports and/or breast cancer prevention (Robinson 2013). Seidelman explains, 'We made a concerted effort to think through the lens of story and character and we asked, "Who would be interested in seeing this film brought to the screen (author interview)?"'

The producers had compiled lists of potential funding or sponsorship targets, looking at sports team owners, health care organisations, cosmetic companies, and various individuals' personal donation track records. Seidelman attributes their triumphant fundraising measures to Hennig and Moore's savvy ability to adapt different proposals for individual parties who held discrete and not always overlapping interests. Women's media networking connections paid off as well: Seidelman came into contact with then Women's National Basketball Association (WNBA) president Donna Orender, who began to champion the film. All told, twenty corporations and non-profits, including the American Cancer Society, signed on as sponsors, an enormous number given the film's budget and scale (author interview).

One of the greatest assets of *The Hot Flashes* was its cast; many of the leading actresses were once- or still-powerful Hollywood names. Now in their late forties and early fifties, they were likely to attract women audiences who had 'grown up' with them. Likewise, these actresses had 'grown up' knowing who Seidelman was; her early attachment to the project gave it legitimacy, offering one example of how her 'indie-auteur' origins provided a boost (author interview). Many of the actresses worked on a reduced salary. They apparently trusted that Seidelman would not make a spectacle out of middle-aged womanhood. And, given the paucity of Hollywood roles for women over forty, they jumped at the chance to play an active role, rather than 'somebody's mother,' or 'somebody's grandmother,' according to Seidelman (author interview; see also Archer). On the set, Shields told an interviewer, 'I've never been in a movie with this many women, and with so many women in primary roles and directing' (Halley 2013).

During production, costs were kept down in a number of ways. Producers took advantage of tax incentives by filming on location in New Orleans, and specifically in areas damaged by Hurricane Katrina (Sheffield 2013). Without such credits, the budget would have been $6 million. Seidelman shot *The Hot Flashes* digitally, having left her 35 mm filming days behind due to prohibitive costs (author interview).

Throughout production and distribution, sponsors participated in vigorous social media campaigns, tweeting and posting updates. In an example of inclusive marketing, Shields purportedly placed a cold phone call to a Canadian winery asking if they might donate bottles of their signature (and unrelated) product 'Hot Flash' for a cast party ('Brooke Shields' 2012). She recorded a no-budget 'thank you' video for the company to exploit in its own marketing, which was also posted to YouTube to promote the film. Additional publicity came from a cameo appearance by ABC morning show anchor (and former college basketball player and breast cancer survivor) Robin Roberts.

Some pre-financing was obtained from the distributor Lightning Entertainment in exchange for international theatrical rights and home entertainment/Video on Demand (VOD) licensing. By early 2013, the newly formed distributor Vertical Entertainment (which launched a year prior) signed on for US theatrical rights, VOD, and digital platforms. *The Hot Flashes* was only Vertical's second project, in a projected slate of twenty-four pictures a year. In July 2013, after several festival dates, the film enjoyed a limited platform release in twelve markets, including New York, Los Angeles, San Francisco, and Miami. It was simultaneously distributed via streaming by broadcast and cable companies. The following month saw the release of DVDs in such retail outlets as Walmart and Target. In October 2013, *The Hot Flashes* became available on Netflix.

At each step, social media sites were used to build long-term audience interest and drive traffic to digital exhibition platforms. On Facebook, viewers were solicited to write user reviews on the Netflix site in exchange for grab bags (which might include a logo T-shirt, prop, or part of a costume) (The Hot Flashes, Facebook page). Those who uploaded a photo of themselves holding the DVD could obtain a free DVD for a friend. Short video interviews with individual cast members were leaked gradually. As individual theatrical premieres or joint cancer fundraisers occurred, they were announced on Facebook and Twitter. One campaign in particular helped give the film added momentum: a group of inspired women from West Virginia formed their own 'Hot Flashes' basketball team and played a series of games to assist the homeless in their community (Bone 2014). The movie's Facebook page regularly updated the West Virginia scores.

The case of *The Hot Flashes* illuminates how traditional dichotomies separating pre-production from marketing, director from platform, and film from viewer have broken down (to the extent that such dichotomies ever truly did exist in practice). An indie-crossover film can succeed or fail long before its release, based on its efforts to include potential audiences as participants, crowdfund, and advance market via social media networks. These activities breed a sense of community and, in ideal cases, loyalty among potential viewers. The 'exclusive film rights' model has given way to one of audience involvement, or at least perceived involvement. This discursive shift towards inclusion and interactivity corresponds with a cultural move away from celebrity-fan and content-viewer hierarchies.

In the midst of so much change, the question arises: What counts as a success? In a way, *The Hot Flashes* signals a victory. It was produced, distributed, and energised a female audience subset. It can be held up, as I do here, as a model of feminist entrepreneurialism and savvy. Yet, in the unsettled environment where indie features intersect with emergent media trends, there is no effective way to tabulate its proceeds outside of theatrical box office figures, which comprise the least of its profits.

As platforms multiply, and consumer habits change, statistics are increasingly difficult to obtain. With Amazon and iTunes (and some on-demand or pay-per-view outlets), quantification is made a bit easier: individual titles are sold or rented in discrete units. But with viewer subscription packages and distributor bundling of titles, producers and directors often have limited ability to track website clicks or gauge profits, let alone acquire specific market research.

Netflix, for example, stockpiles massive information on its content and viewers, as aptly demonstrated in the 2013 *Atlantic* article, 'How Netflix Reverse Engineered Hollywood.' Yet the company rarely if ever discloses data to other corporations or media-makers (let alone consumers) (Madrigal 2014). The same is true for cost structuring of licensing rights, which are held close to the vest. The confusion over how to monetise contemporary film, television, and digital media is a widespread problem, exacerbated for outliers such as Seidelman. In her case, there are two specific fallouts: it hinders her ability to prove that her target audiences responded well to her film (as she predicted they would) and impedes her ability to, as she puts it, 'cycle through to budget, with an accurate forecast of its profits' (author interview).

Access to such information could arm women media-makers in significant ways, equipping them with evidence of their impact, as well as a language and a set of imaginative strategies for soliciting their anticipated viewers. The fact that so much industry and market data is concealed adds to the historically ingrained disadvantages they face. If certain obstacles are being removed with emergent technology and social media, it has not translated into notable progress for women. The 2015 Center for the Study of Women in Television and Film's Celluloid Ceiling report found that women made up only 17% of all above-the-line positions on the top 250 domestic grossing films, and only 6% of directors in that category. In 2013, the Celluloid Ceiling report had found they comprised 9%, leading *The New York Times* to proclaim, 'Female Directors Gain Ground, Slowly' (Rickey 2013). Yet Cathy Schulman, president of Women in Film Los Angeles, cautioned against overenthusiasm, explaining that for sixteen years, the number had fluctuated between 6–9%. In other words, 'it wasn't a deviation from the norm' (Sandler 2013).

The 'good faith efforts' by the Directors Guild of America (DGA) to increase diversity, initiated in the early 1980s, may have helped open doors for women, but progress has slowed to a glacial pace since the 1990s. A 2013 DGA initiative that grouped together women and ethnic minorities has come under scathing criticism by member Maria Giese, who makes the case that women face unique obstacles (that go unaddressed in the DGA's latest policy revisions) (Giese 2015). Though women may find a less hostile environment in the indie or quasi-independent realms, their employment numbers still fall well behind those of men. Women comprised 26% of above-the-line positions in independent films (Lauzen 2014). A benchmark 2013 research study (commissioned jointly by the Sundance Institute and Women in Film Los Angeles) surveyed women media-makers, concluding that limited access to financing, lack of mentoring, a 'male-dominated industry network,' and gender stereotyping were the top bars to professional success (Smith, Pieper and Choueiti).

One manifestation of these gaps in networking and mentoring is that women typically have trouble parlaying initial success into sustained independent careers. Consider Debra Granik who encountered much travail after directing her second feature, the two-million-dollar *Winter's Bone* (2010), which earned the Grand Jury Prize at Sundance and an Academy Award nomination while catapulting Jennifer Lawrence to stardom. She remarks, 'Each time [I tried to develop that third film] the project would become heavily compromised. I'd say, "I don't think she needs to be a prostitute to be interesting," or "I don't think she needs to be raped to be interesting." She posits, 'What do we have to do to change the cultural narrative?' (Stern 2014). Female producer Dori Sperko, speaking at an informal roundtable at Sundance in 2014, repeated the misogynist bias Granik has too often encountered, showing how vexing it can be, even for independents: 'I automatically passed on the movie with the woman producer attached. I just feel like you can't trust a woman you don't know. But you can trust a man. It is what it is' (Sandler).

Yet there is much to encourage women media-makers, younger and older, many of whom have been catalysed by the very research that signals their continued struggles. New organisations are being born, and established institutions are being renovated. The Sundance Institute Women Filmmakers Initiative began presenting fellowships and workshops in 2013. The women's film fund Gamechanger (examined in detail by Sarah Sinwell in this volume) was founded in 2014 by a 'new corps of investors' with the stated goal of radically altering the 'huge gender disparity' through equity financing. The first entity to exclusively support independent narrative features by women, Gamechanger gives unproduced and continuing filmmakers the opportunity to submit scripts for financing consideration. Next Gen Femmes, a New York- and Los Angeles-based women's networking organisation, launched in 2006. The most exciting, robust opportunities live in grassroots, collaborative, extremely low-budget spaces Feministing, the Feminist Media Collective, the Crunk Feminist Collective, and Fembot. They may suffer from uncertain economies, but they signal a vibrant next generation, energised by intersectional feminism and progressive youth movements.

Though the 1980s' indie wave ridden by Seidelman may live worlds apart from next-gen feminists, contemporary women practitioners have much to teach each other. Seidelman's endeavours offer a primary object lesson: even with remarkably rapid changes in technology and media trends, it is still the case that cultural barriers remain difficult to hurdle. No matter how quickly or radically the gadgetry turns over, the conditions for women stay relatively the same. This is why it is crucial to foreground women media-makers as mapmakers. Collectively, their best chances may reside outside of industry hierarchies, as they forge original passageways around existing powerbrokers. In an eloquent endorsement of the 'Trojan horse method,' Granik states, 'You have to stick to your vision, make it small, and then slowly let it detonate, slowly let them see that there's other content that could be interesting' (Stern).

Seidelman's contemporary films offer examples of these very strategies, shining a light on new paths for women in the age of digital film and media. Her move from 35 mm film to digital features has involved a much more profound shift – a professional realignment that spanned a range of choices, reactions, and chance encounters including self-distribution, bypassing traditional gatekeepers, crowdsourcing on the ground and on the web, crowd-funding, pre-financing, grassroots promotion, and use of social media. As feminist scholars endeavour to account for and reframe the work of indie women practitioners, these 'small' practices are well worth close analysis, especially when they occur in the shadows of low-budget male teen genre films, the more 'male-oriented' strains of mumblecore, and other cycles more heavily favoured by Indiewood. To advocate for structural, employment legal, and economic change – such as revised hiring guidelines or new industry initiatives – is absolutely essential. It is also vital to not only record but cast a feminist lens on the varied micro-strategies that indie women – a range of women from a host of positions and perspectives – are deploying in their efforts to take advantage of the cracks that have inevitably opened up within a marketplace system that has been at least temporarily upset by digital and emergent technologies.

Notes

1. I thank Vicki Callahan, Virginia Kuhn, Christine Holmlund, and Lisa Gottlieb for their valued insights into various drafts of this chapter. I thank Linda Badley, Claire Perkins and Michele Schreiber for conceiving this remarkable collection of feminist scholarship and inviting my participation. Ramon Enrique Febus and Ruth Reitan provided outstanding research assistance.
2. Nancy Savoca offers another example, self-distributing her microbudget feature *Union Square* (2011). Lisa Gottlieb has moved to web series while trying for years to get two feminist microbudget features funded.
3. For examples of utopian discourse surrounding networked societies and digital democracies, see Nelson 1965 and Anderson 2004.
4. This dynamic operates at the level of labour and manufacture as well, where women's work in developing countries – for 'export processing centers' owned by transnational corporations – is often elided.
5. Consider, for example *Catfish* (2010), *Paranormal Activity* (2007), *Primer* (2004) and *Saw* (2004).
6. A base for the funding pool was a $15,000 family inheritance (author interview).
7. Among other projects, Seidelman directed the 1993 short *The Dutchmaster*, nominated for an Academy Award. She directed the pilot episode of the *Sex and the City* (1998) television series.
8. 'Author interview' refers to information gleaned from three interviews I conducted with Seidelman between 2013 and 2015 (6 March 2013, 11 March 2015, 24 March 2015).
9. *Boynton Beach Club* is worthy of further feminist analysis. It prioritises female friendship even within a heterosexual romantic comedy framework and includes a rare moment of female frontal nudity by then sixty-eight-year-old Sally Kellerman (during a delicately handled sex scene).
10. One reason for the stagger was that it premiered the same week as the first *Hunger Games* (2012).
11. 'Hot Sheet: Take a Holiday Break'. *Advocate.com*, 21 December 2012, <http://www.advocate.com/arts-entertainment/hot-sheet/2012/12/21/hot-sheet-december-21-2012> (last accessed 1 March 2015).
12. Producer Jamin O'Brien, who has had involvement in the three films examined here, erroneously states that Seidelman does not have representation at all. She does have an agent, but rarely relies on him (author interview). O'Brien asserts, 'I have managers, talent agents I know who say, "Introduce me to her." I say, "She's not looking for representation." That's sort of being outside the system again. She's carved her own path, which is part of the reason she hasn't reached the highest echelons. She's not playing the game they want her to play' (Lamire 2013).

References

Anderson, Chris (2004), 'The Long Tail', *Wired*, April, <http://archive.wired.com/wired/archive/12.10/tail.html> (last accessed 31 March 2015).

Archer, Greg (2013), 'Camryn Manheim on *The Hot Flashes*', *Huffington Post*, 12 July 2012, <http://www.huffingtonpost.com/greg-archer/camryn-manheim-on-the-hot_b_3587300.html> (last accessed 10 March 2015).

Archerd, Army (2006), 'Post-Preem Participants', *Variety*, 9 August, <http://variety.com/2006/voices/columns/postpreem_parti-1200571469/> (last accessed 3 April 2015).

Balsamo, Anne (2011), *Designing Culture: The Technological Imagination at Work*, Durham, NC: Duke University Press.

Bone, Tom (2014), 'Pioneer Hoopsters to Play on Saturday', *Bluefield Daily Telegraph* (online), 14 April, <http://www.btdonline.com/sports/local_sports/pioneer-hoopsters-to-play-on-saturday/article_06c4bfa8-0137-5dca-896c-04ec14df7b14.html> (last accessed 10 March 2015).

Brody, Richard (2015), 'How Critics Have Failed Female Filmmakers', *The New Yorker*, 29 January, <http://www.newyorker.com/culture/cultural-comment/critics-failed-women-filmmakers> (last accessed 24 March 2015).

'Brooke Shields Has Twenty-four Hot Flashes' (2012), *Telegram* (online), 29 March, <http://www.thetelegram.com/News/Canada%20-%20World/Sports/2012-03-29/article-2943003/Brooke-Shields-has-24-Hot-Flashes-orders-wine-after-finishing-movie/1> (last accessed 3 April 2015).

Brooks, Brian (2012), 'Specialty Box Office: The Deep Blue Sea; Musical Chairs; The Raid Redemption', *Deadline*, 23 March, <http://deadline.com/2012/03/specialty-box-office-the-deep-blue-sea-musical-chairs-the-raid-redemption-444-last-day-on-earth-247533/> (last accessed 24 March 2015).

Callahan, Vicki (2010), 'The Future of the Archive: An Interview with Lynn Hershman Leeson', in Vicki Callaghan (ed.), *Reclaiming the Archive: Feminism and Film History* Detroit: Wayne State University Press, pp. 417–30.

Cole, Janis and Holly Dale (1993), *Calling the Shots: Profiles of Women Filmmakers*, Kingston, ON: Quarry Press.

Consoli, John (2013), 'Women Viewers Continue to Rule Broadcast Primetime,' *Broadcasting and Cable*, 17 April, <http://www.broadcastingcable.com/news/news-articles/women-viewers-continue-rule-broadcast-primetime/114370> (last accessed 24 March 2015).

Dargis, Manohla (2015), 'Lights, Camera, Taking Action: On Many Fronts Women are Fighting for Better Opportunity in Hollywood', *The New York Times*, 21 January, <http://www.nytimes.com/2015/01/25/movies/on-many-fronts-women-are-fighting-for-better-opportunity-in-hollywood.html> (last accessed 24 March 2015).

Facebook page for *The Hot Flashes* (2013), <https://www.facebook.com/TheHotFlashes> (last accessed 3 April 2015).

Foster, Gwendolyn Audrey (1995), *Women Filmmakers: An International Bio-Critical Dictionary*, Westport, CT: Greenwood Press.

Giese, Maria (2015), 'Women Directors: Not "Minorities"', *Women Directors in Hollywood blog* (online), 25 March, <http://www.womendirectorsinhollywood.com> (last accessed 3 April 2015).

Halley, Dana Moe (2012), 'Seidelman's Upcoming Film' *Shaping Youth* (online), 23 October, <http://www.shapingyouth.org/powerhouse-women-in-film-susan-seidelman-courts-an-all-star-cast/> (last accessed 3 April 2015).

Harris, Mark (2014), 'The Birdcage: How Hollywood's Toxic (and worsening) Addiction to Franchises Changed Movies Forever in 2014', *Grantland* (online), 16 December, <http://grantland.com/features/2014-hollywood-blockbusters-franchises-box-office/> (last accessed 24 March 2015).

'Hot Sheet: Take a Holiday Break' (2012), *Advocate* (online), 21 December, <http://www.advocate.com/arts-entertainment/hot-sheet/2012/12/21/hot-sheet-december-21-2012> (last accessed 1 March 2015).

Lamire, Christy (2013), 'Susan Seidelman, Survivor,' *Balder and Dash*, 12 July, <http://www.rogerebert.com/balder-and-dash/susan-seidelman-survivor> (last accessed 1 March 2015).

Lauzen, Martha M. (2008), 'Women @ the Box Office', *Center for the Study of Women in Television and Film*, CA: San Diego State University, <http://womenintvfilm.sdsu.

edu/files/Women%20@%20Box%20Office.pdf> (last accessed 24 February 2015).

Lauzen, Martha M. (2015), 'The Celluloid Ceiling: Behind the Scenes Employment of Women on the Top 250 Grossing Films of 2014', *Center for the Study of Women in Television and Film*, San Diego: San Diego State University, <http://womenintvfilm.sdsu.edu/files/2014_Celluloid_Ceiling_Report.pdf> (last accessed 24 February 2015).

Lauzen, Martha M. (2014), 'Independent Women: Behind the Scenes Employment on Festival Films 2013–2014', *Center for the Study of Women in Television and Film*. San Diego: San Diego State University, <http://womenintvfilm.sdsu.edu/files/2014_Independent_Women_Report.pdf> (last accessed 24 February 2015).

Madrigal, Alexis (2014), 'How Netflix Reverse Engineered Hollywood', *Atlantic*, 2 January, <http://www.theatlantic.com/technology/archive/2014/01/how-netflix-reverse-engineered-hollywood/282679/> (last accessed 10 March 2015).

Nelson, Theodor (1965), 'The Hypertext', *Congress of the International Federation for Documentation Abstracts*, Washington, DC: International Federation for Documentation Abstracts, p. 80.

Perren, Alisa (2012), *Indie, Inc.: Miramax and the Transformation of Hollywood in the 1990s*, Austin: University of Texas Press.

Rickey, Carrie (2013), 'Female Directors Gain Ground, Slowly', *The New York Times*, 11 January, <http://www.nytimes.com/2013/01/13/movies/female-film-directors-slowly-gain-ground.html> (last accessed 6 April 2015).

Robinson, James (2013), 'Women Take a Shot at Backing a Basketball Film', *San Francisco Chronicle*, 8 July, <http://www.sfchronicle.com/movies/article/Women-take-a-shot-at-backing-basketball-film-4652761.php?t=d9fdd86a6b> (last accessed 10 March 2015).

Sandler, Lauren (2013), 'Why Women in Hollywood Can't Get Financing', *Bloomberg* (online), 21 February, <http://www.bloomberg.com/bw/articles/2013-02-21/why-women-in-hollywood-cant-get-film-financing> (last accessed 24 March 2015).

Shatzman, Marci (2006), 'West Boynton Hits the Big Screen', *South Florida Sun Sentinel*, 10 December, <http://articles.sun-sentinel.com/2006-12-10/community/0612080221_1_movie-film-kellerman> (last accessed 3 April 2015).

Sheffield, Skip (2013), 'Susan Seidelman Has Hot Flashes', *Skip Sheffield's Flix Blog* (online), 4 July, <http://skipsheffield.blogspot.com/2013/07/susan-seidelman-has-hot-flashes.html> (last accessed 18 March 2015).

Sick, Jessica (2006), 'Sex and the Condo: From Manhattan to South Florida, Boynton Beach Club Director say the Story is Still All about Romance', *South Florida Sun Sentinel*, 18 March, <http://articles.sun-sentinel.com/2006-03-18/lifestyle/0603160911_1_boynton-beach-club-movie-idea-susan-seidelman> (last accessed 26 February 2015).

Smith, Stacy L., Katherine Pieper and Marc Choueiti (2013), 'Exploring the Barriers and Opportunities for Independent Women Filmmakers, Phase I and II', *Sundance Institute and Women in Film Los Angeles: Women Filmmakers Initiative*, Center for Media Diversity and Social Change. University of Southern California Annenberg School for Communication and Journalism, <http://www.sundance.org/pdf/press-releases/Exploring-The-Barriers.pdf> (last accessed 3 April 2015).

Stern, Marlowe (2014), 'Life After *Winter's Bone*: Debra Granik on Finding J-Law and the Plight of the Female Director', *Daily Beast* (online), 24 October, <http://www.thedailybeast.com/articles/2014/10/24/life-after-winter-s-bone-debra-granik-on-finding-j-law-and-the-plight-of-the-female-director.html> (last accessed 24 March 2015).

Tasker, Yvonne and Diane Negra (2007), 'Introduction: Feminist Politics and Postfeminist Culture', in Yvonne Tasker and Diane Negra (eds), *Interrogating Postfeminism: Gender and the Politics of Popular Culture*, Durham, NC: Duke University Press, pp. 1–26.

5. 'I'M ABSOLUTELY THE RIGHT PERSON FOR THIS JOB': ALLISON ANDERS AND MARY HARRON ON LIFETIME TELEVISION

Michele Schreiber

Allison Anders and Mary Harron are among a group of women directors that produced a substantial body of work in the thriving American independent cinema scene of the 1990s and 2000s. Anders, who rose to prominence in the Sundance Film Festival 'class of "92"', alongside Quentin Tarantino, Robert Rodriguez and Alexandre Rockwell, is known for her innovative interpretation of the women's film in *Gas Food Lodging* (1992), *Grace of My Heart* (1996) and *Things Behind the Sun* (2001). Harron's films *I Shot Andy Warhol* (1996), *American Psycho* (2000) and *The Notorious Bettie Page* (2005) offer indelible portrayals of larger-than-life characters that blur cultural, social, and gender boundaries.

Both women began to find steady work in television throughout the 1990s and 2000s, directing individual episodes of a broad range of broadcast and cable programmes. Harron's credits include *Oz* (1997–2003), *Six Feet Under* (2001–5), and *The L Word* (2004–9), and Anders' include *Sex and the City* (1998–2004), *The L Word* (2004–9), and *Orange is the New Black* (2013–). Both also directed biopics for Lifetime Television in 2013, with Anders making *Ring of Fire*, the life story of June Carter Cash, and Harron helming *Anna Nicole*, the life story of Anna Nicole Smith.

Unlike their predecessors in the 1970s and 1980s, directors such as Anders, Harron, Nicole Holofcener, Lisa Cholodenko and Lynn Shelton (among many others) have resisted the lure of commercial studio filmmaking. Their crossover into Hollywood has happened by way of television instead. In fact, this kind of transmedia movement has become a professional necessity for many women filmmakers (and independent filmmakers more generally) recently. With the proliferation of basic and premium cable programming over the last fifteen years, as well as the networks' desire to at least match the quality of their cable counterparts, it has become more common for television directing jobs to go to individuals with established indie film credentials.

By focusing on Anders' and Harron's work, this chapter will highlight the complications that arise when examining the industrial, aesthetic and authorial dynamics that accompany film directors' crossing over into TV. On one hand, by discussing Anders' and Harron's television texts alongside their films, I am implicitly arguing that their TV texts should be viewed as part of their oeuvres. However, in tandem, I will highlight how traditional definitions of authorship have profound limitations in this crossover context. In series television, a director is is often hired on a freelance basis to work with pre-existing content or a show's house style, and therefore their control over the finished product is limited. My study of Anders' and Harron's made-for-television films for Lifetime will allow us to circumvent the dead end that might arise if we were to focus solely on their series work. Yet, considering authorship in a trans-media context is only one of the many compelling aspects of these case studies. What is perhaps more revealing is the glimpse they offer into the economic and industrial significance of working in television and how it reflects on the beleaguered state of independent filmmaking today.

Film directors often work in television not necessarily because it is an extension of their personal artistry, but because they don't have the luxury of saying no to paid positions, especially if that job is on a high profile network or cable show. This reality is even more profound for women directors who are under-represented in all sectors of Hollywood and independent production. Consequently, this spotlight on Anders and Harron illuminates the position of many independent directors today, particularly those whose work has focused primarily on telling women's stories.

By considering Anders' *Ring of Fire* and Harron's *Anna Nicole*, both for Lifetime, we get a unique glimpse into the in-between space available for directors in television. They are 'directors for hire' but maintain some degree of artistic control over these films. They can implement a vision that is consistent with their previous work, but, of necessity, their brand merges with the Lifetime brand, which throughout its history has also occupied an in-between space amid respectability and disdain or even outright ridicule.

Both *Ring of Fire* and *Anna Nicole* are notable contributions to the biopic genre; both look into the lives of women (June Carter Cash and Anna Nicole Smith, respectively) who, true to the Lifetime tradition, are torn between worlds themselves, having to balance their private selves with their public, professional personas. Both women might be perceived as being inconsequential historically, either because they were overshadowed by the men in their lives (in the case of

June Carter Cash) or because they were famous for challenging the standards of cultural acceptability and good taste (in the case of Anna Nicole Smith). These films therefore fit within and are representative of the two directors' oeuvres *and* the Lifetime brand. For the latter, the films continue the network's tradition of relating stories of women who are frequently overlooked or devalued. In this way, Anders' and Harron's move to Lifetime may not be either a major departure from the indie film world or a strange curiosity that such a move might initially seem, but instead may speak to a broader sense of in-betweenness that is explored in each director's larger body of work. To be sure, their move to television is something more than just a shift in medium, and their work on Lifetime is something more than just an anomaly: these shifts reveal many truths about the necessity of telling women's stories in the contemporary media landscape, even in unexpected industrial and production contexts.

The Case of the Missing Television Director

The television director has been largely overlooked in discussions of television for many reasons. Like film, television production is a highly collaborative medium; therefore giving a single person credit as the author of any type of show is just as fraught with problems as it is in the film industry. If credit is bestowed on a single individual in contemporary television series production, it is generally the writer-showrunner who is often also the show's creator and serves as an executive producer. With the pilot episode and subsequent few episodes usually directed by one of the show's creators and/or executive producers, its house style is set early on and later directors generally adhere to this style. As Jason Mittell states, 'Since most programs' managerial oversight typically comes from a writer, the writing process is seen as more central to a series's creative vision than is the contribution of directors, who are often hired as rotating freelancers rather than permanent members of the production team' (Mittell 2015: 90).

A show's head writer will often assume the role of director. For instance, in addition to executive producing *Girls* (2012–), Lena Dunham also writes and directs many of its episodes. Also typical is a show like *House of Cards* (2013–) that brought in executive producer David Fincher to direct the first two episodes of the show, thereby establishing its visual mood. A broad range of other directors has helmed its subsequent episodes, including highly regarded independent filmmakers John Dahl and Carl Franklin. However, television critics or scholars rarely if ever discuss the contribution made by the director of individual episodes of a series, like Dahl or Franklin, even if they are known quantities for their work in other media. As Mittell notes about the popular AMC show *Breaking Bad* (2008–2013), it 'features a distinctive visual sensibility, performance style, and pacing – all facets typically controlled more by directors than by writers – its staffing patterns suggest that such vision comes more from the ongoing writing and production team than from the rotating crew of directors, a balance typical for most contemporary fictional television' (Mittell 2015: 90).

These industrial realities mean that traditional notions of authorship break down when we attempt to discuss the contributions that directors make to individual episodes of series television shows. While a good television director can establish a strong sense of pacing or help build tension or suspense through framing and *mise-en-scène*, it is difficult to relate these choices back to their film work because the directors are serving both the show's house style and the episode's narrative, rather than applying their own aesthetic signature.

It is even problematic to claim that Anders and Harron are chosen as directors on series with a tone or subject matter that is similar to their films – for instance, Anders as a woman directing women-oriented TV shows like *Sex and the City* and *Orange is the New Black*, or Harron as a cult, noir-ish director working on dark shows like *Oz* and *Six Feet Under*. These assertions can easily be discounted through counter examples. For instance, Anders directed episodes of the WB series *Grosse Pointe* (2000–1), a short-lived behind-the-scenes parody of a teen television show, and Harron directed episodes of the also fleeting night-time soap operas *Pasadena* (2001–2) and *Six Degrees* (2006–7). The content of these shows is quite different from what one would expect based on the film profiles of both women, but is evidence of how the willingness to be flexible and invisible is integral to the role of the television director.

Anders' and Harron's more recent films have received limited distribution and little critical acclaim. Therefore, as previously noted, their moves into television are not necessarily out of a newfound interest in dabbling in the medium but because they need the work. In a 2013 interview with *Indiewire*, Anders discussed how directing television has provided a key source of income for her while trying to finance independent film projects. She says, 'Needless to say, it's been an interesting time with indie film. I haven't *not* wanted to make movies – I've had a few things out there that were close to getting made. The very first TV show I ever directed was *Sex and the City*, and thank fucking God I did, because it continues to take care of me in residuals. You cannot make that kind of money in indie films' (Willmore 2013). In short, there is often a trade-off made by these filmmakers between authorial visibility and gainful employment.

Ring of Fire and *Anna Nicole* make fascinating case studies in this regard because the films capitalise on Anders' and Harron's off-beat indie authorship but do so in the context of a network whose brand identity is derided as lowest-common-denominator, 'trash' programming. Regardless, the films portended a chance for Anders and Harron to tell women's stories, an opportunity that has become increasingly uncommon in independent cinema but is the stated mission of Lifetime Television.

Lifetime and the Made-for-television Biopic

The made-for-television movie was a significant source of profits for the major networks during the 1970s and 1980s. As Douglas Gomery writes in the early 1980s, 'The made-for-TV movie has formed its own genre since 1966. This form seems to have fulfilled a particular cultural need: topical entertainment reaffirming basic values and beliefs' (Gomery 1987: 206). He goes on to further define the ingredients for a successful film: 'TV movies have excelled in telling small stories . . . The more familiar the "story concept," the better chance it has to sell. Appropriately, for its *Movies-of-the-Week* ABC sought seventy-five-minute tales that could be comprehended in thirty seconds . . . and effectively be promoted in thirty-second commercials' (ibid. pp. 207 and 208). The decreased popularity of the genre as a network product resulted from the burgeoning programming options made available by premium and broadcast cable television throughout the 1990s but the basic precepts of the made-for-TV film that Gomery outlines still remain pertinent to the made-for-cable films produced in the contemporary period.

In today's television landscape, cable networks are the primary producers of original television films, attracting a significant number of high profile Indiewood directors to the genre. For instance, premium cable channel HBO alone attracted Todd Haynes to direct the miniseries *Mildred Pierce* (2011), Stephen Soderbergh to direct *Behind the Candelabra* (2013), Lisa Cholodenko to direct the miniseries *Olive Kitteridge* (2014), and Dee Rees to direct *Bessie* (2015). Of course, over the last twenty years, HBO has taken the lead on creative, artist-centred quality programming that has inspired other networks, including Showtime, AMC, and more recently, Netflix and Amazon, to produce content that rivals (and often surpasses) the complex storytelling and high production values found in feature films. As Gary Edgerton puts it, HBO 'is an idea or identity brand' and '[b]y the late 1990s [it] had emerged as the equivalent of a designer label' (Edgerton 2008:9).

The Lifetime network, which at one time added but then later dropped 'Television for Women' in its name, is in a different and far less prestigious category than HBO and these other networks and streaming services. Known for specialising in sensationalised, 'ripped from the headlines' original movies with B- and C-level actors, Lifetime has historically been more of a punchline than a trendsetter. Unlike many of its aforementioned competitors, which offer shows or movies without commercial interruption, Lifetime's brand is intertwined with advertising targeted towards its primary demographic: women. Since the network's formation in 1994, it has struggled to develop programming that continues to appeal to this core audience while also widening its appeal to men, in addition to targeting desired economic and age-related demographics.

The original, made-for-television movie has been an integral part of Lifetime's efforts to attract a diverse group of viewers, and the importance of these made-for-television movies to Lifetime is made clear by the number of times it has rebranded its original films. Lifetime's first original films, produced in 1990, were called 'Original Lifetime World Premiere Movies' (Hundley 2002: 176); in 1995 they became simply 'Lifetime Original Films' (Meehan, Byars 2000: 44). In 1995 the network recognised the popularity of its films and committed to air one original movie per month (Hundley 2002: 178). According to Heather Hundley, Lifetime's head of programming at the time, Dawn Tarnofsky-Ostroff, claimed that female viewers in their focus groups frequently cited the pleasure they find in these films, and that female viewers 'identify with drama. The [heroines] are women who overcome obstacles, and I think women love to see women triumph.' (McAdams quoted in Hundley 2002: 180). Hundley offers a slightly less upbeat interpretation by citing the labelling of Lifetime by critics as '"the victim's network"' because its original movies frequently featured a storyline in which the female lead is terrorized, abused, or threatened' (Hundley 2002: 179–80).

The biopic has been a significant sub-genre of Lifetime original films because the form generally depicts its subjects successfully prevailing over hardships. In fact, the various types of biopics that the network has made throughout its history offer a peek into its often-conflicting programming priorities. On one hand, Lifetime has struggled to tell stories that represent the complex social and political issues facing women, but on the other, stories 'ripped from the headlines' that border on the salacious are often aired. Indeed, showing how women triumph over obstacles and the nature of those obstacles provides varied entertainment for a broad swathe of viewers. In their article 'Telefeminism: How Lifetime Got Its Groove 1984–97,' Eileen Meehan and Jackie Byars present case studies of two Lifetime biopics made in the mid-1990s that illustrate this tension. The first is *Choices of the Heart: The Margaret Sanger Story*, about the American women's health rights pioneer (Meehan, Byars 2000: 44). Under the supervision of then CEO Douglas McCormick, Lifetime established partnerships with the Ms. Foundation for Women and NOW (National Organization for Women), bringing some historical and political heft to the 'women triumph' formula found in the Sanger story. As Meehan and Byars point out, despite the fact that the film emphasised 'relationships' rather than the controversial topic of women's health, it was the worst-rated film of any original film aired during this period, earning a 1.8 rating (ibid. p. 45).

Lifetime's second biopic of significance in the mid-1990s was *Almost Golden: The Jessica Savitch Story*, which focused on well-known news anchorwoman Savitch. According to Meehan and Byars' description, Savitch 'threw violent temper tantrums during commercial breaks, only to resume her calm demeanour on cue', and her 'self-interest and self-destructiveness clearly marked her as no crusader for women's rights' (ibid. p. 45). The film received a 7.9 rating, which was a 'benchmark event for Lifetime' (ibid.). The contrast between the reception of these two movies is a telling indicator of the contradictions inherent in the network's programming. Historically, it has appealed to both a wide audience through highly dramatic but not necessarily progressive stories about women, and also fulfilled a smaller and decidedly less popular niche with topical and historically significant portraits of politically engaged female figures.

Under the supervision of current President and CEO of A&E Networks Nancy Dubuc, Lifetime has produced a number of high-profile biopics that fall somewhere between these two extremes, including *Liz & Dick* (about the tumultuous relationship between Elizabeth Taylor and Richard Burton) in 2012 and *Bonnie and Clyde* in 2013. This new slate of original films signals a new era for the network, which has made a concerted effort over the last seven years to produce and acquire 'buzz-worthy' shows. It acquired the very popular reality television fashion show *Project Runway* from Bravo in 2009, and launched numerous new reality and original series, including the critically acclaimed *Unreal* (2015–), and the fashion and pop culture talk show *Fashionably Late with Rachel Zoe* (2015–) (Johns 2014).

This recent programming has broadened Lifetime's reach, particularly to a much younger demographic than it had attracted in the past. In a 2013 profile of A&E and Lifetime executive Vice President and General Manager Robert Sharenow, he stated, 'One of our nights of reality programming this year was 28 years old in a median age [sic]. I don't think we expected Lifetime to be that young that quickly' (Johns). Sharenow continued, 'One of the things that has really been the secret sauce for us is taking subjects that are really in the pop culture zeitgeist and bringing fresh elements that are the leading edge of creative' (Johns).

Lifetime's effort to create biopics about June Carter Cash and Anna Nicole Smith and to employ Anders and Harron to helm these films seem slightly less incongruous when viewed through the lens of Sharenow's comments and an overview of the network's history with the biopic genre. Anders has summed up the eccentric pairing perfectly. In reference to her choice to work on *Ring of Fire*, she states, 'I would normally not say I'm the right person for this job, but I'm absolutely the right person for this job' (Willmore). Indeed, Lifetime provides an unconventional home for these women artists to tell female stories and in Sharenow's words, to invite 'an audience that doesn't always tune in to Lifetime, but is just an audience that is hungry for great writing and exceptional performances' (Johns). As I will discuss, while *Ring of Fire* and *Anna Nicole* aren't necessarily a full realisation of the quality television paradigm to which Sharenow aspires, the Lifetime brand in concert with the authorial style of these two filmmakers does create a vision of the lives of June Carter Cash and Anna Nicole Smith, which might not have been realised in any other form of media.

ANDERS AND *RING OF FIRE*

There are several reasons why *Ring of Fire* does indeed feel like the right film for Anders. Its tone and subject matter have a great deal in common with Anders' *Grace of My Heart* (1996), which focuses on a female singer's journey of self-discovery that is very loosely inspired by the life of Carole King. The *Grace of My Heart* protagonist Denise Waverly (who changes her name from Edna Buxton) is an aspiring singer who starts as a songwriter for other artists in New York in the 1960s, and emerges as a solo singer-songwriter on the West Coast in the 1970s. Denise's professional trajectory mirrors King's but veers away from King's story in its depiction of the character's romantic life. Therefore, *Grace of My Heart* is not truly a biopic but does follow a biopic narrative model by portraying Denise's evolution from a naïve, deferential young woman who is comfortable remaining out of the spotlight to one who finds her voice, both literally and figuratively.

The film is as invested in telling Denise's story as it is in chronicling the changing social and cultural times in which she lives. Its style is glossy, and as Janet Maslin's review for *The New York Times* argued, 'more scrapbook than story' (Maslin 1996), without the sort of gritty realism of *Gas Food Lodging* and *Things Behind the Sun*. This scrapbook style, with its setting in the music industry, in addition to the exploration of the life of a woman artist whose career is sometimes problematically intertwined with the men who surround her, introduces a fluidity from *Grace of My Heart* to *Ring of Fire*. The similarities between the two films also demonstrate that Anders' signature style might not be so associated with the indie, low-key, gritty realism of *Gas Food Lodging* as one might have presumed.

Ring of Fire does have all of the earmarks of a Lifetime made-for-television movie, and Anders makes the best out of the lower budget and B- and C-list actors that are hallmarks of this terrain. In fact, Anders was honoured for her work on the film with an Emmy nomination for outstanding directing for a mini-series, movie or dramatic special, a rare feat for a Lifetime production. While they are not household names, two of *Ring of Fire*'s primary cast members have quality TV associations, having starred in two of HBO's most successful shows of the late 1990s and early 2000s. Matt Ross from *Big Love* (2006–11) plays Johnny Cash and Frances Conroy from *Six Feet Under* (2001–5) plays June's mother Maybelle Carter.

June Carter Cash is played by music star Jewel Kilcher, better known by her stage name Jewel, who, unlike her castmates, has a background in singing, not acting. She is able to pull off the vocal aspects of the role with great expertise but has difficulty conveying the complexity of Carter Cash. Therefore, the emotional depth of the film remains fairly surface-level, with the portrayal of the singer failing to go much beyond the idea of Carter as a chipper comediansongstress. Richard Friedenberg does his best in his screenplay to bring some depth to the story, but the fact that the source material with which he worked is a biography of Carter Cash written by her son John Cash, results in a film that feels sanitised and fails to communicate fully the emotional range of a woman who would write the eponymous song 'Ring of Fire' about her burgeoning feelings for a married Johnny Cash.

The film follows a basic biopic formula, beginning with historical photographs of the Carter family in casual and professional settings playing against the opening credits. Then the narrative opens with scenes of June as a young girl learning of her family's plans to launch itself on a professional singing career, and continues through to the family's subsequent success and June's later solo career as both a singer and comic vaudeville-type performer. It chronicles her first two marriages but does so very briefly and in broad strokes, without conveying to the audience much about the two husbands, other than that they stayed largely in the background as she pursued her musical profession.

The film progresses rather hastily in some of its early parts, but the momentum slows down once June's romantic relationship with Johnny Cash begins. It is the ups and downs of this relationship, including his ongoing battle with alcohol and drug addiction, which comprises the bulk of the film's narrative. June's relationship with her son John is also in the foreground, while their other children (from previous marriages) are given scant attention. The film follows June's life until the production of her last album, *Wildwood Flower*, produced by John Jr, which she recorded when she was seventy-four years old in the Cash family home. The film concludes in 2003, the year of June's death.

Ring of Fire's narrative limitations are augmented by the commercial interruptions that are part of basic cable production. The pacing and structure of the film revolve around these breaks. Frequently, scenes of heightened drama wrap up prematurely, just in time for a commercial break, and then, to the film's detriment, the conflict isn't reintroduced after that break. When the film is broadcast with commercials, a flow is created where conflicts introduced before the break circulate into the advertising for various products and other Lifetime shows. When the film is broadcast sans commercials, the breaks feel distinctly like interruptions, rather than pauses, creating a sense of fragmentation rather than continuity.

My discussion of *Ring of Fire* thus far has focused a great deal on its limitations, many of which are contingent upon its production context. To say that the film is akin to the 'quality television' output of films made by other cable networks would be disingenuous. However, to limit the discussion of the film to merely a 'good' versus 'bad' dynamic would not account for what the film does accomplish, which is to tell the story of a famous couple from the woman's perspective, rather than the man's.

Ring of Fire is obviously a counter to 2005's large-screen *Walk the Line* (Mangold), a feature-length Academy Award-winning Johnny Cash biopic that details the complexity of the Carter-Cash relationship from Johnny's point-of-view. The differences between the two films go beyond the gender of the lead character to the broader industry truths that the gender difference reveals. Specifically, *Walk the Line* is a big-budget, Oscar-calibre film based on two Cash autobiographies (*Man in Black* and *Cash: The Autobiography*), which therefore focuses on Johnny Cash first and June Carter Cash second (although it is Reese Witherspoon's performance as June, which garnered the film's only Oscar win). Historically speaking, stories of great and/or flawed men are significantly more likely to attract large budgets and esteemed Hollywood production personnel, whereas stories of significant and/or imperfect women tend to get treated in lower budget films or television, as these Lifetime case studies evince.

Therefore, Anders' efforts to bring June Carter Cash's story to life were already subject to a great many industry factors that predetermine the scale and approach to telling women's stories in the contemporary entertainment industry. Anders has spoken about the challenges that arose for her in trying to convey the point of view of a woman who is discussed most often in relationship to Johnny Cash, the 'great' man in her life. Unlike *Grace of My Heart* that Anders both wrote and directed, in *Ring of Fire* Anders was working with another writer's script and therefore was forced to convey June's point of view and agency visually. She says, . . . she was married to someone so phenomenally iconic, the problem was not to have her in the shadow of Johnny Cash. He's a powerful image, as powerful as Elvis. How do you constantly steer it back to her point of view? Believe it or not, it's really tough. We had to do it every step of the way: this is her point of view. I've never done this before . . . Usually when I write my own stuff, it's [the female point of view] just there' (Willmore).

Anders is speaking here about the challenge of remaining true to her own vision, which is intertwined with remaining true to Carter Cash's vision in the context of a story (that of Cash and Carter) and entertainment landscape that favours male stories. That the film is filtered through the Lifetime brand and its attendant production issues is less consequential than the fact that the film was made at all. For a director like Anders to have the opportunity to present an overlooked female artist's point of view on a channel focused on appealing to female audiences and telling women's stories is a significant accomplishment in itself. As a case study, it may prompt a reconsideration of whether the 'quality' versus 'non-quality' debate is even relevant in this context. By looking at Mary Harron's more experimental *Anna Nicole*, this question is even more acute.

Harron and *Anna Nicole*

Recalling Anders' earlier statement about *Ring of Fire* being both an odd and perfect fit for her, we can certainly say the same strange alchemy is also present for Mary Harron in directing *Anna Nicole*. Just as there are natural affinities between *Grace of My Heart* and *Ring of Fire* for Anders, *Anna Nicole* shares a great deal in common with Harron's *The Notorious Bettie Page* (and to a lesser degree, *I Shot Andy Warhol*).

Harron is no stranger to the biopic genre and the importance of her contributions to it cannot be underestimated since she makes biopics not only about women but women on the historical and cultural margins. Both *Page* and *I Shot Andy Warhol* are remarkable films in that they succeeded in telling stories of women who attempted to gain relevancy and acceptance in their lifetime but remained outcasts from mainstream culture. *The Notorious Bettie Page* may seem like the more obvious companion piece to *Anna Nicole* because both films focus on women who received attention and notoriety due to their adherence to conventional conceptions of beauty and sexual attractiveness. As I have written in other work, *The Notorious Bettie Page* doesn't just tell Page's life story, it explores the complexities that ensue when a woman becomes famous (or infamous) because of her sexualised image. By using a number of visual formats – 8 mm and 35 mm film, colour and black-and-white – Harron explores one of the central questions asked by feminist visual culture studies: can a woman like Page who is known for being a sexual object, also be in control of her own image (Schreiber 2012)?

Anna Nicole explores similar questions about sexuality and fame, but its tone is quite different than that of *Page*. This difference is due primarily to the fact that Smith's story does not benefit from the same degree of historical hindsight (and nostalgia) as Page's. After all, a 2013 audience was still very much immersed in the tabloid-centric, reality TV-obsessed, 'Girls Gone Wild' cultural environment that saw Anna Nicole Smith rise to fame. The film almost anticipates that its viewers may question whether she 'deserves' a biopic at all.

These questions about who deserves a film about their life and how much industry clout and money should be used to produce such a film were raised in the *Ring of Fire* example, but here they are even more relevant. In the case of *Anna Nicole*, gender *and* respectability are called into question. The story's attendant difficulties make Lifetime's choice of Harron as director so inspired. She crafts the film not just about Smith as an individual but as an examination of the nature of fame itself, particularly as it relates to women who push our collective buttons and whose actions fall outside the boundaries of 'acceptable' behaviour. In this regard, as a woman who gained notoriety for unconventional reasons, Smith is more likely to be paired and compared with *I Shot Andy Warhol*'s Valerie Solanas.

Harron seems very aware of the tabloid and sensationalistic nature of the Anna Nicole Smith narrative and the audience's potential difficulty in taking Smith seriously, let alone feeling sympathetic towards her. Harron employs several compelling techniques in the delivery of Anna Nicole's story, along with recognisable actors such as Martin Landau, Virginia Madsen, Adam Goldberg and Cary Elwes, which together instil in the film hints of the quality television model of which Sharenow speaks. The film follows the same type of conventional biopic formula as *Ring of Fire*: young Vickie Lynn Hogan (Agnes Bruckner) transforms herself from a neglected child of a single mother in Texas to someone who becomes a single mother herself in her early twenties, and then develops into Anna Nicole Smith, a successful stripper who becomes a model, the wife of an elderly billionaire, and then reality television star. The film also resembles *Ring of Fire* in its sympathetic representation of Smith as a mother. It doesn't hesitate to portray how Smith's ambition and vices prevent her from focusing on motherhood, but it always returns to her efforts to be a good parent. She is loving and selfless at the same time as she is narcissistic and ambitious, part of the broader duality of her persona that Harron is clearly invested in exploring. In an interview with the website HitFix, Harron spoke about the complex nature of Smith's story,

> . . . [T]he story itself is so kind of lurid that you didn't have to add anything – her life was made for this melodramatic story, full of incredible, outrageous highs and lows, working at this fried chicken place and becoming a world-class model. But one thing that Lifetime does because it's very female-centric is, you know, you can do a sympathetic take on Anna. It would be very much Anna's point of view, a woman's point of view, and I thought that was very important for this – for it to be her story. (Gilchrist 2014)

Here Harron echoes Ander's earlier comments about the importance of representing her female subject's point of view. In an effort to capture the complicated nature of Smith's life, Harron introduces multiple visual tropes that convey Smith's highs and lows and the duality of a woman who is both sympathetic and relatable but also campy and melodramatic. Many of these techniques call to mind Harron's other work that blurs boundaries between fantasy and reality, and by extension, the entertainment industrial complex and those who exploit, and are exploited by it.

The first shots of *Anna Nicole* show her filming a segment that we later find out to be part of her appearance on CNN's *The Larry King Show*. She takes the camera crew to several different locations in her hometown of Mexia, Texas. The camera crew films Anna Nicole as she shows them the town's welcome sign and the fried chicken restaurant where she met her first husband (the father of her son). The scene moves back and forth between a long shot that shows the production set up with the camera filming her and the image of Anna as seen in the monitor of the camera as she is being filmed. The latter shots are clearly marked by a REC (record) indicator in the upper right-hand corner of the frame, a battery life indicator on the upper left-hand corner, and time stamp on the bottom.

This visual choice immediately calls to mind *The Notorious Bettie Page* in illustrating the act of a woman being filmed, as well as how she performs a particular role in front of the camera: it bears traces of her authentic self but is also necessarily removed from that self. The distinction between private and public seems considerably more blurred here than it does in *Bettie Page*. Smith is being herself in so far as she is revealing her own history for a talk show on which she is featured, rather than playing a fictional role in a film. However, there are no discernible differences between the self that she is off-camera versus on-camera, which is demonstrated by the visual similarities between the framing we see through the camera lens and the framing of *Anna Nicole*. The montage that follows, which features flash-forwards to various scenes of Smith at the height of her fame, with both colour and black-and-white images, similarly points to the performative qualities that lie at the heart of Anna Nicole's persona.

After this opening sequence of flash-forward scenes (that also include a brief scene showing Smith in a morgue after her death), the film's main narrative begins with a few brief scenes depicting Smith's childhood in Mexia. Smith, at this point still named Vickie Lynn Hogan, is a child of a single mother who, as Smith's voiceover tells us, marries four inappropriate and often abusive men. A young Vickie finds one of her stepfather's *Playboy* magazines featuring Marilyn Monroe on the cover, beneath his bed, while she overhears him sexually pursue her young aunt. The voiceover suggests that if her aunt didn't live with them, she (Vickie Lynn herself) would have been the victim of her stepfather's attacks.

Vickie Lynn turns her attention back to the *Playboy* and the soundtrack swells while she moves her fingers over Marilyn's face and body. Her voiceover states, 'I always felt like if I hadn't met Marilyn, I never would have become Anna.' The scene cuts to her mother kicking her stepfather out of the house, with Vickie Lynn cowering behind the bed. She hears a voice calling to her, and she looks up to see a future vision of herself as Anna Nicole, made up in the image of Marilyn Monroe, in her dressing table mirror. She is wearing a red dress with a plunging neckline and a large, sparkling diamond necklace and earrings, and like a beauty pageant contestant she waves to her younger self. When Vickie Lynn asks the image who she is, the image replies, 'Anna Nicole' and then continues, 'You're so pretty. When you grow up, you're going to get earrings just like mine.' The image is both a representation of Vickie Lynn's

Figure 5.1 Agnes Bruckner in *Anna Nicole* (Mary Harron, 2013).

future and what she aspires to be, as well as a clear reference to the past, with Monroe cited multiple times throughout the film as Smith's role model and inspiration. The visual trope of the mirror appears several times throughout the first half of the film to remind the viewer of Anna's aspirations to become like Marilyn Monroe. Even though the real Monroe had her share of vices, here she functions as the classy, old-school sexual icon that Smith wants to emulate but can't because her (Smith's) lower-class background and addiction to drugs and alcohol prevent her from playing the role appropriately. (The film also uses retro 1950s era font for the opening credit sequence and inter-titles, as if to remind the viewer of how heavily Anna Nicole's perceptions of 1950s culture figure in her fantasies.)

In addition to introducing the mirror trope that will recur throughout the film, this early sequence is notable for how it establishes an association between Vickie Lynn's fascination with Marilyn and her negative association with her stepfather's inappropriate sexual behaviour. This early connection establishes the curious dynamic that emerges in the telling of Anna Nicole's story. The figure of 'Anna Nicole' is inseparable from her performance of sexual availability but, with a few exceptions, the film hesitates to represent her as an interested and willing sexual subject. Her longest lasting relationships with J. Howard Marshall (whom she calls 'Papa') and Howard K. Stern are seemingly non-sexual. This emphasises even further the inseparability of the young Vickie Lynn who looks in the mirror and the Anna-as-Marilyn who looks back.

From the moment the film shows Anna getting a breast enhancement in order to increase her income as a stripper, it presents her body as growing increasingly abject. There is just too much of her: her breasts are too large, her hair too poofy, her clothes too tight or too garish, and her behaviour too outlandish. And, because she can't be contained, she becomes a prime target of the tabloid culture and increasing social media in the late 1990s and early 2000s. As the film goes on to chronicle Anna Nicole's rise to and then fall from fame, it is clear that whatever semblance of a private, authentic self she once had completely disappears. Her respectable role as a model and spokeswoman for GUESS, in which the ads show her (usually in black and white) as a more classically attractive Marilyn doppelgänger, gives way to public displays of drunkenness and sexual innuendo. Any time she engages in behaviour that is too much like lower class Vickie Lynn and not enough like Marilyn, she is seen and shamed by those around her. Even when Anna marries Marshall, his money can only buy her the earmarks of wealth but not the good taste and propriety of the upper classes.

At a key point about three-quarters of the way through the film, when Anna Nicole is in the midst of filming her reality show, Harron notably reverses the Marilyn visual trope to show an older Anna Nicole seeing a young Vickie Lynn in the mirror. In this scene she is purging her food in the toilet and then is on the verge of taking drugs. She is distracted by the view of her younger self, which is hazy and fragmented in the mirror, with unsteady camera work reflecting Anna's disorientation. Here the film reflects on what becoming the woman in the mirror has cost her as well as the degree to which she can never rid herself of Vickie Lynn's youthful dreams or her lower-middle class inclinations.

The use of this technique in *Anna Nicole* calls to mind Harron's representation of other characters with complicated personas: think Patrick Bateman's murderous self and upstanding self in *American Psycho*, and Valerie Solanas's black-and-white SCUM manifesto rants and colour childhood home movie footage in *I Shot Andy Warhol*. Instead of simply demonstrating how the fantasy version of a character is at odds with the real or authentic version, Harron suggests that these boundaries are always blurred and fluctuate constantly. In other words, Anna Nicole is always Vickie Lynn and Vickie Lynn is always Anna Nicole. The mirror images harken back to the opening images of Anna Nicole being filmed in Mexia. They are visual reminders of what the film's narrative communicates about the melding of public and private space.

While *Ring of Fire*'s narrative flow was disrupted by Lifetime's advertising breaks, *Anna Nicole*'s commercial interruptions, and advertising geared towards women, not to mention Lifetime's own slate of female-targeted reality shows, support and augment the film's themes about the potentially toxic mixture of femininity and fame in contemporary media culture. While this reception context might seem to counteract or absorb the film's critique of the current landscape, the film would not have the same effect if it were shown on another network. Lifetime's own unique efforts to be both high- and lowbrow, to be taken seriously while simultaneously appealing to the broadest possible demographic, makes it the ideal place for Anna Nicole's story to be told.

In a sentiment almost identical to one expressed by Allison Anders earlier, Harron said of the opportunity to work on *Anna Nicole*:

> . . . it's hard to get a film made with a female central character – it's really hard. You can spend years trying to do it. And it was like, oh, good, this is just coming in, and it's about this very interesting, very complicated woman. She's got her good side and she's got her bad side. She's a lot of different things in one, so I was like, oh, this is a chance to tell an interesting female story – I don't get the chance to do that too often. (Gilchrist)

These case studies of Allison Anders and *Ring of Fire* and Mary Harron and *Anna Nicole* reveal many of the challenges that come with telling 'interesting female stories' in a media landscape that looks to bigger, flashier, quicker, and often, more masculine stories to attract an audience. These realities create a particularly difficult climate for independent women directors who are caught between their desire to make films with dynamic characters and their need to sustain themselves while these film projects come together, if they come together at all.

What *Ring of Fire* and *Anna Nicole* demonstrate is that sometimes you have to look in unexpected places to find compelling stories about women, which perhaps because of their production context don't get the same attention as their higher profile counterparts. Certainly, Lifetime is still removed from the 'quality television' model of the aforementioned channels and very far removed from the indie film world. It is probably not a place where most directors aspire to make films. However, it is revealing and important to move beyond preconceived ideas and learn from the 'in-between space' – between good and bad, and between the director and network as 'author' – of these made-for-television films, and others like them, to discover surprising portrayals of multifaceted female characters made by female artists.

References

Edgerton, Gary (2008), 'Introduction: A Brief History of HBO', in G. Edgerton and H. Jones (eds), *The Essential HBO Reader*, Lexington: The University Press of Kentucky, pp. 1–22.

Gilchrist, Todd (2014), '*American Psycho* Director Mary Harron talks *Anna Nicole*, *Hitfix* 20, Feb <http://www.hitfix.com/news/american-psycho-director-mary-harron-talks-anna-nicole> (last accessed 6 December 2015)

Gomery, Douglas (1987), '*Brian's Song*: The Movie Made for TV, in Horace Newcomb (ed.), *Television: The Critical View*, New York: Oxford University Press, pp. 197–220.

Hundley, Heather (2002), 'The Evolution of Gendercasting: The Lifetime Television Network – Television for Women', *Journal of Popular Film and Television*, 29: 4, Winter, pp. 175–81.

Johns, Nikara (2014), 'All in a Lifetime: Network once known as a hub for reruns evolves as a destination for fresh "original" content', *Variety*, 324: 12, 17 June, p. 66.

Maslin, Janet (1996), '*Grace of My Heart*: One Fine Day at the Brill Building', *The New York Times*, 13 September, <http://www.nytimes.com/movie/review?res=9802E5D9163AF930A2575AC0A960958260> (last accessed 6 December 2015).

Meehan Eileen R. and Jackie Byars (2000), 'Telefeminism: How Lifetime Got Its Groove, 1984–1987', *Television and New Media*, 1: 1, February, pp. 33–51.

Mittell, Jason (2015), *Complex TV: The Poetics of Contemporary Television Storytelling*, New York: New York University Press.

Schreiber, Michele (2013), 'Their Own Personal Velocity: Women Directors and Contemporary Independent Cinema', in G. King, C. Molloy and Y. Tzioumakis (eds), *American Independent Cinema: Indie, Indiewood and Beyond*, New York: Routledge, pp. 96–107.

Willmore, Alison (2013), 'Lifetime's *Ring of Fire* Director Allison Anders: How to be an Indie Filmmaker in a TV World', *Indiewire*, 24 May, <http://www.indiewire.com/article/television/allison-anders-lifetime-ring-of-fire> (last accessed 6 December 2015).

PART II

GENRES AND MODALITIES

6. GENDER, GENRE AND MORE GENERAL INDIE DIMENSIONS IN MEGAN GRIFFITHS' *THE OFF HOURS* AND *EDEN*

Geoff King

To what extent do the productions of independent women filmmakers display characteristics specific to constructions of gender identity, or ones that are better understood in keeping with broader indie traits – or some combination of the two? This rather large question will be initially addressed here through an examination of the textual qualities and production circumstances of *The Off Hours* (Megan Griffiths, 2011). Each aspect of this film can be interpreted as displaying a sensibility that is, in some respects, distinctly gendered *and* one that is more broadly characteristic of parts of the indie sector. How, then, should we understand the relationship between these two dimensions, and how might the specifics of gender be understood in such a case without recourse to any reductive forms of essentialism? These questions will further be explored through a comparison between *The Off Hours* and Griffiths' subsequent feature, *Eden* (2012), an example in which issues relating to the gender- and/or indie-specific are further complicated by the presence of aspects of the thriller genre, a format conventionally associated with male and/or more mainstream filmmakers.

At the textual level, *The Off Hours* employs a low-key realist approach in its slowly-paced tracing of a short period in the lives of several figures revolving around the central focus of an open-all-night diner. This is a style that could be seen as embodying a distinctly female approach, generally and in relation to some reference points from now-classic aspects of feminist film theory, but one that is also more widely familiar in the indie sector. The production of the film involved a strong element of communal focus, including support from other women filmmakers, another dimension that might appear distinctly – but far from exclusively – gendered. *Eden* combines its more heightened generic elements with some similar qualities and a more overtly gender-focused theme: of sexual slavery and imprisonment, a more extreme variety of the kind of social imprisonment that is implied to some extent by *The Off Hours*. What exactly we should conclude from these combinations of characteristics forms the core of this chapter, one that will argue that these particular qualities can be associated with gender in some cases but in a manner that is best understood in essentially relative and proximate terms.

A starting point for this argument is the view that certain aspects of film style *can*, in some important respects, be interpreted and located in relation to particular characteristics associated with aspects of gendered identity. This is not to suggest any essentialist notion of gendered style, male, female or otherwise, but to argue for the impact of the prevailing socio-cultural frameworks – including those of gender – within which we are all situated and socialised as part of our status as inhabitants of particular cultures. Prevailing gender frameworks are extremely powerful shapers of behaviour and attitudes towards the world, such that they are likely often to impact on the manner in which particular groups or individuals engage in any sphere of activity, including creative ones such as filmmaking or other forms of artistic expression. They create a substantial reality of their own, that is, as do such cultural constructs more generally, even if this ultimately remains proximate and open to challenge. As Bonnie Mann puts it, gender frameworks have real '"ontological weight" in the lived experience of the individual subject' (2014: 1). Films that can be seen as embodying a distinctly gendered aesthetic, at least to some extent, need not, therefore, be viewed as expressions of any absolute, universal or essential identity for this to remain a significant aspect of their status. In the case of independent women filmmakers such as Megan Griffiths, a number of characteristics can be identified that might fit with qualities associated with prevailing constructions of female gender identity – although, I would argue, it is important to see them as not entirely encompassed by this one dimension.

The Off Hours: Collective Narrative Drift and Collaborative Participation

The Off Hours is in many ways typical of a certain variety of low-key indie production, the dominant claims of which are to offer something approaching a realist portrait of a particular slice of contemporary American life.[1] The central character, Francine (Amy Seimetz), works the night shift in a twenty-four-hour diner, interacting with an ensemble of other primary characters. These include Ty (Bret Roberts), who appears to be the latest in a series of lovers; Oliver (Ross Partridge), a softly-spoken and educated former-banker-turned-truck-driver, to whom she is attracted; Corey (Scoot McNairy), the slobbish foster brother with whom it turns out she once had a sexual relationship; Stu (Tony Doupe), the alcoholic painter who owns the diner and is trying to retain contact with an estranged teenage daughter; and fellow waitress Jelena (Gergana Mellin). The style of the film is moody, low-lit atmospheric, evocative, gentle and slow-paced.

If these qualities typify a certain kind of indie feature production, they can also be read, to some extent, in gendered terms, along the lines of the socially-situated position outlined above. In very broad terms, a male-gendered form of narrative tends to be associated with more dynamic and assertive action, particularly on the part of one or more central heroic figures. To be the hero in these terms is, as Sue Thornham summarises this perspective in feminist film theory, 'to be subject, the maker of meaning, rather than its object', and structurally to be situated as male (even if enacted by a female character) (Thornham 2012: 11–12). The language employed by such accounts is often psychoanalytical, the medium through which such approaches were most often articulated in film studies, particularly from the 1970s, but such notions can also be interpreted in more socially-culturally specific terms, as I would use them here (this could clearly be the subject of much greater debate than space allows in this chapter). Francine does not really constitute a heroic figure in these terms, coming closer to the more complex figuration advocated by some feminist theorists (including Kuhn 1982 and Kaplan 1986, as cited below), although without offering the thoroughgoing deconstruction offered by more avant-garde or experimental approaches associated with feminist counter-cinema (for a useful summary of these issues, see Thornham: 12, 28–30).

The indie feature position (akin to that of some forms of art cinema) is one in which a middle option can be offered between the extremes of the most male/goal-oriented dominant forms and those of the experimental margins (the latter as manifested, for example, in readings of the work of Maya Deren or the direct links between theory and avant-garde production in films made by Laura Mulvey). Films such as those of Griffith remain within the realm of what prevailing feminist (and other ideologically focused) theory of the 1970s and 1980s would term the 'classic realist' text, a category that continues to be useful today. This is a variety of realism which, as Annette Kuhn puts it, 'rests on the credibility of texts which construct identifications for the spectator on the levels of character and narrative, within a fictional world constituted as coherent and internally coherent' (Kuhn 1982: 136). What is involved here is a modality in which the viewer may 'be drawn fairly readily into the identifications offered by the film', rather than being distanced through the use of the kinds of Brechtian alienation strategies employed in some more radical avant-garde approaches (whether this can be usefully read in the stronger terms of 'fixing' subject positions, implied or suggested in some psychoanalytically-oriented theory, is another matter).

Indie productions from filmmakers such as Griffiths share this broad position with those of the commercial mainstream. The same goes in Kuhn's account for examples of the 'new women's cinema' that appeared from the mid 1970s with films such as *Girlfriends* (1978, directed by Claudia Weill, independently produced and distributed by the studio Warner Bros.) and *Julia* (1977, directed by Fred Zinnemann, produced and distributed by Twentieth Century-Fox). The term is based on the primary focus of the films on strong central women characters, despite the fact that the majority of the examples cited are the products of male directors. These, Kuhn suggests, offer scope for departures from classical norms such as relatively open endings, characteristics similar to those often found in later films from the indie sector. The middle position offered by such work is ultimately to be condemned in the ideological judgement of Kuhn's kind of account, however. This is a characteristic response of much of the film theory of the time to work that offers a having-your-cake-and-eating-it compromise between dominant norms and departures, one outcome of which 'must be to buttress the textual and institutional operations of dominant cinema' (Kuhn 136). This seems an unduly dogmatic conclusion, even if we might agree that films of this kind – and many of those from the indie sector in general – are often limited in how far they go in challenging dominant norms.

What we find in *The Off Hours*, within a broadly conventional form of classical-type realism, is a prevailing impression of behaviour that *drifts* rather than being the outcome of decisive action. Francine is what would usually be termed a fairly 'strong' lead woman character, as measured in terms of traditional/patriarchal gender images; one who is generally in control of her destiny on an immediate level. She cuts a quite confident figure and is sexually free, although she also appears weary, somewhat glum and far from happy or fulfilled. The film holds out for some time the potential promise of a very mainstream/clichéd 'rescue' by the handsome Oliver, a figure who seems constructed to combine the appeal of the educated (books all over the cab of his truck) with the down-to-earth (having quit the world of banking to be his own boss, on the road). The various other character dynamics of the film are never reduced to the margins of this relationship as it grows, however, and it is not fulfilled at the end. After a strong tease that creates the impression that it will be (Francine is about to leave town and we see Oliver's truck draw up 'outside', but this only proves to be outside his family home, to which he is returning), Francine leaves in the cab of another, anonymous, truck, to a future that holds out no obvious promise of any great change or progression. The final images are of her waking in the empty cab the following morning. The towers of a 'big city' beckon in the distance, but without any romantic impres-

Figure 6.1 Amy Seimetz in *The Off Hours* (2011).

sion, or any footage of her travelling to 'freedom' on the road; just a shot of her looking blank, followed by a cut to black and the end credits.

The overall impression is one of hesitancy and uncertainty rather than decisive central character action, despite the more conventional nature of the climactic 'leaving' trope. Francine might be read, that is, in the kind of terms advocated by Cora Kaplan, as a feminist alternative to the narrative of heroic progress, as part of what she terms more broadly 'a more complicated, less finished and less heroic psychic schema' (Kaplan 1986: 227; quoted by Thornham 2012: 12). The rest of the characters are also left in varying stages of non-progression, few expressing and none seeming to have achieved any 'goals' in the course of the film (the strongest expression of desire comes from Stu, who comes somewhat closer to his daughter at one point but ends up with the prospect of losing all contact after an incident in which he allows her to drive because he has been drinking). The position of Francine within this wider group of characters again seems characteristic of the strategies employed by the film as a whole, in terms of how it can be understood in relation to more mainstream/conventional/male-oriented narrative approaches. She does offer a central organising ground for the film, one to which the others are all related. This is an important aspect of the dynamic, as opposed to the film offering a series of more tangential character/plot lines. But the overall effect is not one of subordinating all else to this end, as might be expected of a more Hollywood-classical narrative structure. If part of what makes *The Off Hours* most obviously an example of women's independent production is the fact that it fits largely into a category of films 'by and about women' – to use a phrase employed by the independent collective Women Make Movies – one element that gives it some of these particular and at least partially gendered resonances is the fact that it is not solely *about* any single individual character (and not only women) but involves the evocation of a somewhat wider milieu.

If the traits outlined above can all be read at least partly in relation to figurations associated with particular gender positions (or the particular aspects of these on which I have focused above), how then might we square this with their broader prevalence in the indie sector? Low-key, unheroic and somewhat decentred narrative approaches of this kind are found much more widely in indie films, including the work of many male filmmakers (for more on this, see King 2005). It would be a mistake, that being the case, to view them as in any way *essentially* gendered, as part of an understanding of a distinct aesthetic to be associated exclusively with the work of women. Other types of indie films can also be viewed as expressing qualities more likely to be associated with a more assertive 'male' style, however, when this concept is also located as a matter of prevailing cultural construction rather than any essence. This would be likely to include certain types of traditionally male-oriented genre films, including some of the thriller/noir-inflected work of figures such as Quentin Tarantino and the Coen brothers. Some of the assertively stylised features of work of this kind might be seen as embodying, for example, some of the specifically masculine aesthetic qualities attributed to 'men's cinema' by Stella Bruzzi (2013), particularly here in the case of Tarantino (who, for Bruzzi, draws on a tradition rooted in the films of Sergio Leone and Sam Peckinpah).

Writing about indie films distributed (but not only produced) in the United States between 1980 and 2001, E. Deidre Pribram (2002) suggests that productions from women tended overall to be 'less aesthetically experimental than much male-originated work', although no suggestion is made here that the more formally innovative might be a gendered quantity in itself. (Pribram's point is that the absence of more alternative approaches might be one factor behind the general under-representation of films by women among those that gained distribution.) We might also include as (in some way, or sometimes or to some degree) male gendered the more broadly ironic distance characteristic of the tradition of 'smart' cinema identified by Jeffrey Sconce (2002), or the archly stylised approach of a figure such as Wes Anderson. In the latter case, any gender connotations might be less obvious, and certainly less obviously coded as masculine than the kinds of styles examined by Bruzzi. The films of Anderson, such as *The Grand Budapest Hotel* (2014), might be said to manifest a camp aesthetic, one that is not traditionally masculine but the rigidly controlled nature of which might still be considered to exhibit some similarly gendered facets. What remains to the fore in the work of many such figures is a focus on issues relating to male identity and performance, to which other textual qualities might be related. The type of indie that positions itself, or is positioned by others, as 'cool' and 'hip' might also fit into this general territory in some respects, although we should be wary of making any such assertions in too sweeping a manner.

Any equation of the indie- and female gender-specific is only likely to be partial, therefore, and to apply in particular types of production. But this still requires explanation. The simplest way to understand this might be in the context of a recent/contemporary Hollywood that is so heavily driven or shaped by approaches that are strongly in tune with dominant, male-oriented tropes (whatever else they might be or whatever other roots they might also have). Some films that effectively rebel against the Hollywood model in general, in their choices of indie-alternative approaches, might then find themselves employing forms that can be associated with other gendered positions without that needing to be either at all conscious (in gendered terms) or involving the occupation of any particular gender identity on the part of the filmmakers concerned. To turn away from some aspects of Hollywood might, then, effectively be to turn away from some of its own gendered tropes, as a result, without this itself being the conscious point of departure. If we understand the gendered dimension of approaches to film (or anything else) to be socially grounded and often deeply sedimented within particular practices, we can also understand these to exist as broader cultural repertoires available not exclusively to any particular social identities, gendered or otherwise. They might, in some cases, be adopted more deliberately or consciously, or more implicitly, as a result of the gender positioning of the creative artist, or associated more directly with this. But they are likely to have a saliency such that they can also transcend such limits, as seems to be the case in the aspects of indie film style examined here.

Some similar parallels might be drawn between the aspects of *The Off Hours* examined above and the circumstances of its production, one that entailed a collaborative dimension that might also be related to both gendered and more broadly indie status. The film is quite strongly rooted in the specific individual experiences of Griffiths (another not uncommon indie trait), being inspired by her own experiences of working the night shift in a diner (this and the following detail, unless otherwise stated, is from Dawson 2011). But the writer-director also puts much emphasis on the collaborative nature of the process through which it was developed after the writing of the script, an emphasis that differs from the focus on individual male auteurs that is widespread in many of the more high-profile parts of the indie sector. Initially, she reports, she went into development with three women she had met in the industry, Lacey Leavitt, Joy Saez and Mischa Jakupcak, who formed a business plan and sought to set the film up together on a traditional indie basis. Eventually, however, after seven years of trying, amid the financial collapse of the late 2000s, they decided to go ahead with the production themselves, a process for which much of the credit is given to the filmmaking community in her home city of Seattle. 'There is so much community support', she suggests, 'from the film office and incentive program, from vendors, from locations, and most of all from fellow filmmakers and crews' (quoted by Dawson).

Collaborative approaches to filmmaking, or other such activities, might suggest another aspect of the film that could be interpreted in what are often understood – from sometimes contrasting perspectives – in broadly female-gendered terms. The notion that women are essentially more cooperative and collaborative than men is a conventional patriarchal construct, usually likely to be associated with gender divisions in areas such as child-care and/or 'nurturing' more generally (for one example that derives an explanation of such a difference biologically, from testosterone levels, see Wright *et al* 2012). That the status of any such general characterisation might be questioned does not prevent it having a real impact on lived social existence, along the general lines suggested at the start of this chapter. But collaborative and/or collective approaches have also played a more specific, active and political part in the history of women's art practice (and within feminist activism more generally), especially from the 1970s onwards, including feminist film production. Such approaches are often positioned as a conscious rejection of patriarchal formations of individualism (see, for example, Kuhn 184–5).

This is another dimension in which an overlap can be found between that associated with some areas of women's filmmaking and the wider indie sector. Collaboration as a mode of production can also be found in other parts of the indie sector, regardless of gender identity, and as another basis on which it can mark a difference from the approaches usually characteristic of its mainstream other (Kuhn makes a similar point about more radical independent feminist filmmaking in the 1970s). Some of the connections made by Griffiths, for example, correspond with the myriad links found among the filmmakers grouped with what became known as the 'mumblecore' movement of the mid-2000s, itself a tendency primarily viewed as male-oriented, in both the identity of its most prominent figures and some aspects of their output (the latter applied in particular to the films of Joe Swanberg; for more on this, see King 2014). She was, for instance, one of the producers of Todd Rohal's *The Catechism Cataclysm* (2011) and was introduced to her lead, Amy Seimetz, by a personal friend, Lynn Shelton, the latter a filmmaker associated with mumblecore (*Humpday*, 2009; *Your Sister's Sister*, 2011) who was consulting producer of *The Off Hours* and in the cast.

Griffiths had herself performed numerous roles in other films (as cinematographer, editor, producer and assistant director, the latter a role in which she worked on more than a dozen productions while trying to get *The Off Hours* off the ground), including Shelton's *Humpday*, which she describes as a source of inspiration (Dawson; Baltus 2013). Any gender ascription of particular textual qualities can also be complicated when we consider other collaborators within a production such as *The Off Hours*. Griffiths credits 'a huge part in the film's overall feel' – the texture and atmospherics that contribute to what was above suggested to include some potentially female-specific qualities – to the contributions of the cinematography (by Ben Kasulke) and music (by Joshua Morrison and Jeramy Koepping), the work of male collaborators. That none of this can be reduced to any simple and clear-cut correlations – gender with certain narrative or other approaches, or with certain forms of collaboration – does not mean that no such factors might usefully be identified and given particular associations on a more proximate and relative basis.

Eden: Adding Genre to the Mix

What happens, then, when a filmmaker such as Griffiths moves into genre territory more often associated, within prevailing gendered conventions, with a culturally male sensibility? The answer is that a number of similar correlations and distinctions can be made, again on the grounds of both gender and the more indie specific, including characteristic indie uses of genre frameworks. *Eden* adopts a thriller format to a significant extent, in its dramatisation of the experiences of Hjun Jae (Jamie Chung), a young woman kidnapped and forced into the sex trade. Central thriller components structure the film, including the general threat posed throughout to the protagonist, renamed Eden by her captors, and tension about the likely outcome (implicit questions are posed, including: will she be able to escape, will her oppressors be discovered by the police, and so on). The generic dynamics loom over the entire film, creating a heightened context marked by a situation beyond the sphere of anything like 'ordinary everyday' life (the kind of milieu evoked in *The Off Hours*). They are far from entirely dominating the tone of the piece, however, which retains some of the brooding, atmospheric, downplayed and realist qualities of its predecessor.

The territory is heightened, in a manner that entails certain thriller-generic dimensions, but in a way that also makes claims to the depiction of an impression of everyday 'ordinariness' of texture. This is another strategy typical of many low-key indie ventures into genre territory, the effect of which can be to blur the lines between the distinct worlds of film genres – as places marked off by familiar routines and expectations – and those that appear to bear a closer relationship to the world of everyday lived reality (for more examples, see King 2005). *Eden* moves into a distinctly generic mode on numerous occasions of heightened action. These include the initial moment of kidnap and other incidents, such as one point at which the central character seeks to escape, being chased from the garden of a 'client' to whom she has been taken.

Other generic components are added to the mix at various points. A dramatic early sequence features a corrupt marshall (Beau Bridges) shooting a deputy and another witness to the finding of the body of a girl who had escaped from the traffickers. An element of 'investigation' is added when, much later, he is quizzed by a detective about his presence in the area at the time. The marshal is subsequently beaten to death by the younger Vaughan (Matt O'Leary), the member of the gang with whom Jae sometimes works closely. In between, however, much is articulated in a far more implicit and throwaway manner, one that owes more to an 'everyday' realistic approach, even given the horrible circumstances faced by the victims. That Jae and the many other young girl captives are sex slaves is never spelled out explicitly, just witnessed through various incidents. There is no moment of big protest, no melodramatic proclamation to the effect that 'you can't do this', as might be expected in a Hollywood treatment of such material. Once the situation is established, it is presented as an implacable reality faced by its victims. When a title 'one year later' follows the aftermath of Jae's attempted escape, the effect is flatly matter-of-fact, and all the more shocking as a result, is its swift acknowledgment of the passing of so substantial a period of time during which there is no hope of escape. The world of the film is not presented as one that is extraordinary, in the sense of involving 'crazed' kidnappers, or any such exaggerated trope, but as a matter of well-run, if odious, business enterprise; the banality of such evil is more shocking than any more strident treatment.

The sense of employing but also downplaying key generic elements persists to the end of the film. Jae escapes, through taking brave and resourceful direct action, but only eventually and after being forced into a kind of complicity with her captors. In order to survive – and not be killed because she is older than the target age group sought by the trafficking gang – she takes on the role of helper, particularly to Vaughan. This entails an act of betrayal – itself handled in an oblique way, without being shown directly – in which she appears to give away the location of two other girls who escape from a party. She gains what is at least a partially trusted position, to the extent to which she is present during the disposal of the bodies of fellow victims, another event that is entirely downplayed, just presented as a matter-of-fact part of her existence (the actual activity, as with many others, is not depicted, but lurks at the edges of the frame). In one of the most heightened moments of drama, Vaughan pushes her to the point where she is about to prove her 'loyalty' by following an order to shoot another girl in the head. The film ends with her escaping and rescuing a friend who became pregnant and whose baby has been sold. This last action is a 'heroic' move in which she puts herself back in danger instead of taking the chance to get away.

The viewer is offered, then, the single most important aspect of any possible 'happy' or heroic ending, although this seems qualified in several ways. We close with Jae making phone contact with her mother but only briefly, rather than any more sustained emotional high (a cut to black is followed by a lengthy landscape travelling shot over the credits, implying some sense of freedom/movement but not explicitly anchored to any perspective). The fate of the other victims remains uncertain, as is the psychological state in which Jae might be left. The gang is about to move the entire operation overseas, the factor that finally impels Jae to take action. What effect resulted from the earlier involvement of the detective is uncertain (probably nothing, given the marshal's death). A direct connection is made to a heightened earlier moment in which Jae, as a trustee, is given phone duty and answers a question from a caller about the cost of the service – something she is told would not be asked by clients and would be the likely marker of a call from the police. A gang member subsequently killed for having worn a wire is identified as the one who had acted upon the call, but this kind of material remains underplayed and largely in the background. The predominant focus is on the realities faced by Jae, the film showing little interest in following through any such generic 'procedural' routines or offering any broader resolution at this level. This is another dimension that might also, conventionally, be situated in at least partially gendered terms, as involving the activities of what are usually male-dominated social institutions, here displaced to the margins of the diegesis. Jae is without doubt an heroic figure of a conventional type in a stronger sense than is Francine in *The Off Hours*, both in facing a more clear-cut, heightened and dreadful situation and in eventually taking decisive action. But her status is also complicated by the compromises into which she has been forced and the fact that her action does not appear to have the 'transcendent' status often implied of that found in more mainstream films, in which it creates an impression of resolving a broader conflict or situation.

In its more heightened generic moments, *Eden* adopts a style that seems to owe something to the thriller terrain, but again in a restrained manner. No great stylish flourishes are used to offer aesthetic pleasure to the viewer in its own right. Instead, we find brief, economical touches, stylised in their way but in a low key: a rapid cut to black, for example, at the instant of Jae's capture, when she tries to run and its stopped; bright flashlight beams in the darkened back of a van, evoking a subsequent moment shortly afterwards; darkly atmospheric tones at some points in the soundtrack. If the sustained, fetishised, overtly stylised approach found in the work of some other filmmakers – Tarantino again being the most obvious example in the indie or Indiewood sectors – can be understood as in some ways expressing a masculine aesthetic, as Bruzzi argues, then this is much more nuanced. Whether that itself equals something differently gendered seems far from clearly the case, but it can be understood as at least a relatively different positioning within the available scale, with gender as one potential resonance that might be in play. There is also no effort here to use film style itself to elevate the action of the protagonist to any kind of heroic pitch, or to give any such resonances to any of the other action that occurs during the narrative. *Eden* offers some points of clearly marked genre *frisson* of its own, but these are both underplayed and strongly balanced by a great deal of material that is presented in a more quotidian manner.

Eden can more clearly be read as displaying a gender position at the level of its subject matter: an extreme version of the exploitation of women as sexual objects. The world of the film beyond the bland surroundings of the storage facility where the women are confined is one in which the availability of young women for such dubious services seems unquestioned. Whether or not the various male 'clients' understand the status of the girls as kidnap victims is not made clear; that it seems not to matter, or to be marked as an issue, seems itself to make its own point about the broader gender landscape in which such operations are able to thrive. This gives the film a sharper feminist dimension, as far as the subject matter is concerned, than is the case with *The Off Hours*. What appears to be another clear gender marker here is the manner in which all sexual activity is depicted, which is to say: as little as possible. A careful effort has been made for the film not to risk offering any of the kinds of 'thrills' or pleasures associated with the 'exploitation' film tradition (one on which some indie films draw, to varying extents), in the representation of sex acts or the victims in states of undress. This is a strong marker of the particular part of indie territory to which the film belongs, one that makes claims to the presentation of harsh realities without seeking any compromise that involves an incidental – or otherwise – process of trading in its own representational sexual currency.

Sequences involving clients and one during the shooting of pornography are minimal, and oblique where they are found, mostly inhabiting the implied off-screen space that plays a central role in the film more generally. It seems unlikely to be possible for anyone to watch 'against the grain', as it were, to seek to take enjoyment from the sexual exploitation of Jae or other young women characters. A persistent risk in any treatment of such material is that it can end up being vulnerable to such appropriation, unless this is carefully avoided (that this was a deliberate aim is suggested by the comments of Griffiths in Silverstein 2014). For any male viewer who might use such 'services', this film also offers food for thought about the damning conditions in which they are produced, all of which can be interpreted as a distinctly feminist perspective on both the material and the manner in which it is treated.

As far as its own production process was concerned, *Eden* appears to have followed a somewhat more conventional path than its predecessor, although one that also included some personal connections. The project, based on a true story, was brought to Griffiths from the outside, rather than being rooted in her own experience. She was given a copy of the script, she reports, on her way home from taking *The Off Hours* to the Sundance Film Festival. It came from one of *Eden*'s producers, Colin Plank, who, somewhat unusually, had worked on *The Off Hours* in a voluntary capacity without Griffiths being aware that he appeared to be 'sort of scouting' her for the job (quoted in Tully 2014). She signed on, initially to do a rewrite and eventually to direct the film.

If we might want to look for aspects of these two films by Griffiths that can be related, variously, to the gender- or indie- specific, these should not be seen as the only parameters within which they might usefully be viewed. As far as broadly political dimensions are concerned, they are also notable for their green credentials, as productions rather than in relation to their subject matter. *The Off Hours* was the first feature to receive a stamp of approval from the Sustainable Style Foundation, for its use of a number of environmentally-friendly production processes such as shooting digitally, buying locally, recycling and making use of second-hand items for props and clothing (for details, see *The Off Hours* 2011). The same was achieved by *Eden*. This is another dimension to which more relatively low-budget indie films are particularly well-suited more generally, both in their tendency to be relatively lower users of resources – largely, often, as a result of lack of funds – and in the greater likelihood of their makers to be alive to such issues than those involved in more industrialised forms of production. Whether the latter also includes the gender of the filmmaker specifically is, perhaps, less likely to be a subject on which agreement might be found.

Note

1. *The Off Hours* is Griffiths' second feature. Her first, *First Aid for Choking* (2003), gained little wider attention even within indie circles and was not available on DVD or elsewhere to my knowledge at the time of writing.

References

Baltus, Leah (2013), 'Life in Pictures', *City Arts* (online), Seattle, 26 April, <http://www.cityartsonline.com/issues/seattle/2013/05/life-pictures> (last accessed 10 October 2014).

Bruzzi, Stella (2013), *Men's Cinema: Masculinity and Mise-en-scène in Hollywood*, Edinburgh: Edinburgh University Press.

Dawson, Nick (2011), '"The Off Hours" director Megan Griffiths', *Filmmaker*, January 2011, <http://filmmakermagazine.com/18883-the-off-hours-director-megan-griffiths/> (last accessed 10 October 2014).

Kaplan, Cora (1986), *Sea Changes: Culture and Feminism*, London: Verso.

King, Geoff (2005), *American Independent Cinema*, London: I. B. Tauris.

King, Geoff (2014), *Indie 2.0: Change and Continuity in Contemporary American Indie Film*, London: I. B. Tauris.

Kuhn, Annette (1982), *Women's Pictures: Feminism and Cinema*, London: Routledge.

Mann, Bonnie (2014), *Sovereign Masculinity: Gender Lessons from the War on Terror*, Oxford: Oxford University Press.

Off Hours, The (2011), 'Shooting Sustainably' page of website of *The Off Hours*, <http://www.theoffhoursfilm.com/p/shoot-it-green.html> (last accessed 12 October 2014).

Pribram, E. Deidre (2002), *Cinema and Culture: Independent Film in the United States, 1980–2001*, New York: Peter Lang.

Sconce, Jeffrey (2002), 'Irony, nihilism and the new American "smart" film', *Screen*, 43:4.

Silverstein, Melissa (2014), 'Interview with Megan Griffiths – Director of SXSW Audience Winner Eden', *Women and Hollywood* (online), <http://blogs.indiewire.com/womenandhollywood/interview-with-megan-griffiths-director-of-sxsw-audience-winner-eden> (last accessed 12 October 2014).

Thornham, Sue (2012), *What If I had Been the Hero? Investigating Women's Cinema*, London: BFI.

Tully, Michael (2014), 'A Conversation with Megan Griffiths (LUCKY THEM)', *Hammer to Nail* (online), 4 June, <http://www.hammertonail.com/interviews/a-conversation-with-megan-griffiths-lucky-them/> (last accessed 10 October 2014).

Women Make Movies (n. d.), 'About Women Make Movies', in 'General Information' at website of Women Make Movies, <http://www.wmm.com/about/general_info.shtml> (last accessed 10 October 2014).

Wright, Nicholas, Bahador Bahrami, Emily Johnson, Gina Di Malta, Geraint Rees, Christopher D. Frith and Raymond J. Dolan (2012), 'Testosterone disrupts human collaboration by increasing egocentric choices', *Proceedings of the Royal Society*, 279, <http://rspb.royalsocietypublishing.org/content/early/2012/01/27/rspb.2011.2523.full.pdf+html> (last accessed 18 June 2015).

7. DOWN TO THE BONE: NEO-NEOREALISM AND GENRE IN CONTEMPORARY WOMEN'S INDIES

Linda Badley

Social realism, whether in documentaries or features or experimental blends of both, was once a distinguished, if not the definitive, tradition in American women's independent cinema that included pioneers such as Barbara Kopple, Shirley Clarke, Julia Reichert, Su Friedrich and Allison Anders. In the Miramax-Sundance era, it struggled to survive through non-profit producer-distributors such as Women Make Movies and women's and gender studies festivals, conferences, and exhibitions. But with the attenuation of the Indiewood sector (detailed by James Lyons and others in this volume), the last decade or so has witnessed a resurgence in both women's independent documentary (by Liz Garbus, Laura Poitras, Ava DuVernay, Lauren Greenfield, and Heidi Ewing) and documentary-style social realist features by and about, and ostensibly for, women that have found not only critical acclaim and mainstream awards[1] but modest commercial success.[2] I am interested in the latter trend, one including (among several others) Karen Moncrieff's *The Dead Girl* (2006), Courtney Hunt's *Frozen River* (2008), Debra Granik's *Down to the Bone* (2004) and *Winter's Bone* (2010), Megan Griffiths' *The Off Hours* (2011) and *Eden* (2012), Ava DuVernay's *Middle of Nowhere* (2012), and Kelly Reichardt's films through *Meek's Cutoff* (2011).

These films feature middle and lower-class female protagonists who find a limited agency within a meticulously rendered web of intersectional circumstances in which they are embedded. Thus they eschew the hyper-stylisation and choreographed action sequences of what Stella Bruzzi deems contemporary Hollywood 'men's cinema' in the sense that the latter is 'grounded in the relationship between masculinity – its ideology as well as its representation – and aesthetics' (2014: 6).[3] In contrast to 'smart' and mumblecore indies about (and largely by) solipsistic white male urban sophisticates (which constitute another kind of 'men's cinema') they are unironic and deliberately 'uncool'. This choice is political as well as aesthetic and, for many female/feminist practitioners, it represents a significant, low-budget and relatively sustainable, alternative in recent years.

In juxtaposition with 'men's cinema' in all these senses, this group of films might seem to support the widespread assumption, noted by Geoff King in the previous chapter, that women's films tend to be representational, low key, and concerned with the day-to-day routines of ordinary life. But I am not arguing for a 'feminine aesthetic' in any all-embracing sense;[4] if anything, the reverse, in that most of these films emerged from a specific – often post-2008 – social-historical context. What is more, most of the 'neo-neorealistic' films I discuss have appealed to festival and mainstream-indie audiences of both genders. Also, if their austere aesthetic makes a socioeconomic statement, it does so by borrowing from movements such as Italian neorealism that are associated primarily with male directors and critics. Finally, as I contend later in this chapter, they often transmit their political 'messages' through a nuanced use of melodrama and Hollywood genre tropes in ways that support Claire Johnston's argument, in 'Women's Cinema as Counter-Cinema' (1973), that feminist filmmakers should work within the mainstream of cinema as entertainment even while exploring alternatives to it. Politically, aesthetically and institutionally, their cinematic discourse thus represents another example of women's independent cinema that has emerged within the space of the 'in-between'.

Women's Neo-neorealism

In her recent book *Not Hollywood: Independent Film at the Twilight of the American Dream* (2013), cultural anthropologist Sherry Ortner analyses the 'dark' (pessimistic and political) disclosures of recent independent movies, especially women's indies that have registered the negative effects of neoliberal capitalism on women, children and communities.[5] Ortner's indie 'Film Feminism' does not fit Laura Mulvey's prescription for a counter-cinema that formally exposes Hollywood-style sexism nor, in what is often called a postfeminist era, does it even call itself 'feminist' (Ortner 2013: 179–85). Simply in being grounded in the material concerns of at risk and 'downwardly mobile' women, however, these films offer an alternative not only from (male) Indiewood fare but from the postfeminist 'chick flick' that descends from the privileged consumerist perspective of *Sex and the City* (1998–2004), to achieve an authenticity rare in contemporary American indies, much less Hollywood. And as Ortner claims, they have struck a nerve with middle-class audiences with similar, if less extreme, economic concerns in the second decade of the twenty-first century (Ortner 2013: 189–98).[6]

These films by and about women may be approached more broadly as part of a widespread post-postmodern return to realism in world cinema and the 'rehabilitation' of realism in global film and media theory since the late 1990s. This rehabilitation has occurred through movements including Dogme95, the 'New Sincerity', the Iranian New Wave, and 'slow cinema' – known for minimalist, on-location shooting, indigenous, non-professional or relatively unknown actors, and a *cinéma vérité* effect. More precisely, they may be situated in relation to a tendency noted by Roget Ebert (2009), Manohla Dargis (2008, 2011) and A. O. Scott and dubbed 'neo- neo realism' by the latter. 'What Kind of Movies do we need now?', Scott asked rhetorically in 2009, pleading for 'an escape from [Hollywood] escapism' that he had found in films by Reichardt, Ramin Bahrani, So Yong Kim, and the early David Gordon Green (Scott 2009).[7] Scott's extension of the term 'neorealism' is useful in the cases of Granik and Reichardt, who are articulate about intentions and international influences. After studying at NYU under Latvian neorealist filmmaker Boris Fruman, who taught her to see beauty in 'imperfections', Granik adopted a similar aesthetic in both fictional features and documentaries (Stern 2014). Discussing *Wendy and Lucy*, Reichardt mentions 'revisiting' the Italian neorealists, New German cinema, and British kitchen sink dramas 'rooted in class and whose heroes are confronted with difficult situations that often seem beyond their control' (quoted in Sholis 2008).[8] In contrast, DuVernay mentions Asghar Farhadi's Iranian social realist family drama *A Separation* (*Jodaelye Nadere az Siimin*, 2011) as a film she admires. In an apropos self-referential moment in *Middle of Nowhere* a young bus driver (David Oyelowo) invites the protagonist Ruby (Emayatzy Corinealdi) to the movies, and when she responds warily that she watches only 'indies' and 'foreign' films, he rejoinders, 'You mean a brotha's got to read?' The film's answer to this rhetorical question is implicit in its 'slowness' and nuanced minimalism, which DuVernay describes as riveted on 'the interior movement of [a black woman's] heart' (Hornaday 2012) – and its lesson might be applied to this group of women's films in general. This cinema forces spectators to immerse themselves in the monotony, oppression, and hazard experienced by ordinary yet diverse women in specific environments and to contemplate what is not simply on the surface.

To this end, they are usually filmed on location with long takes and/or an unobtrusively 'documentary' style, often with non-professionals or lesser-known actors in key roles. Granik's first feature *Down to the Bone* is a case study of a harried grocery-store checkout clerk and mother (a then little-known Vera Farmiga) whose cocaine addiction allows her to function in her mechanical job in which speed and accuracy are requisite – until she is unable to support her accelerating habit. The film's title, particularly the word 'bone', repeated in the title of Granik's second feature *Winter's Bone*, evokes both films' stylistic austerity, bleak and isolated winter setting and class concerns. In fact, it could be a touchstone for this entire group of films, with their insistence on scarcity, desperation, and women's daily grind, whether struggling through the slough of rehab, serving breakfast in the darkness of 4:30 a.m., riding the bus to and from work, or walking behind covered wagons in the desert; whether checking out a line of customers at the Dollar store or shooting and cleaning a mess of squirrels to supplant the meagre food supply. In *Winter's Bone*, set in the impoverished back country of the Ozarks, Granik filmed within and surrounding the homes of local families many of whose members joined the cast or crew, for example, the protagonist Ree Dolly's younger sister Ashlee Thompson,[9] whose family's toys, trampoline and abandoned vehicles are integral. Other key roles played by locals and partly improvised included Ree's younger brother (Isaiah Stone), the army recruiter (Russell Schalk), folk singer Maredith Sisco, and Thump Milton, played by Ron 'Stray Dog' Hall, a local Vietnam veteran and biker. (Hall's real life became the subject of Granik's next film *Stray Dog* (2014)), which likewise treads a 'thin line between narrative and documentary forms' (Gills 2014)). *Winter's Bone* became a breakthrough for current it-girl Jennifer Lawrence, then an unknown twenty-year-old from Louisville, Kentucky. Similarly, other than the late Misty Upham, a young, little known Blackfoot actress, *Frozen River*'s Native American cast consisted of indigenous non-actors, with many of the extras from the local St Regis Mohawk Reservation adjacent to the Akwesasne territory straddling the US and Canada on the banks of the St Lawrence River.

A thread throughout this group of films is the threat of dispossession and, specifically, homelessness by the already marginalised, who are constricted within isolated and often hostile communities. In a notable example, *Frozen River*'s Lila Littlewolf (Upham) and Ray Eddy (Melissa Leo) survive day-to-day in drafty trailers in northeastern New York on the Canadian border, and 'home' comes to mean the claustrophobia and agoraphobia of poverty. As dispossession leads to homelessness, several of these films turn at key points into road movies about border crossing, marginal or intersectional spaces, and getting lost. While the visual irony of *Frozen River* is that its uniformly white landscape makes natural borders invisible, the film is about what Klaus Dodds terms a 'biopolitical present' (Dodds 2013: 562) involving the St Regis Indian Nation, a white working-class community in Massena, New York, and illegal immigrants 'working with and against the legal geographical order of two nation-states who share a common border' (Dodds 2013: 562). This border constitutes 'a complex space of alienation, containment, dispossession, and incorporation' (ibid.) and reflects both the effects of neoliberal capitalism and post–9/11 xenophobia. Wendy (Michelle Williams) of *Wendy and Lucy*,

Figure 7.1 Isaiah Stone, Jennifer Lawrence and Ashlee Thomson in *Winter's Bone* (Debra Granik, 2010).

a college dropout destitute after some unnamed catastrophe and hoping to find work in Alaska, is another casualty of the economy in what Reichardt has called (in the loosest of senses) a 'post-Katrina story' (Hoberman 2008). She lives with her dog Lucy in her car until it breaks down and she runs out of money – and Lucy gets lost. Shot in what Reichardt describes as the 'ugly America' of malls, store-fronts, railroad tracks, and parking lots, it is an overcast, 'beige film, full of flat, anonymous walls', and 'generic spaces' (Sholis 2008). At one time 'this kind of character would seem heroic' Reichardt comments, but now that '[i]t's all about the middle class and their houses and God and families' (quoted in Sholis 2008), Wendy is a merely a very human casualty of the economy. The film ends as Wendy finds Lucy, who has been adopted by a man with a home and a yard, in a scene that highlights the extent to which Wendy is dispossessed and lost. *Meek's Cutoff*, set in the 1840s in Oregon and based on a true story, could function as *Wendy and Lucy*'s prequel: focusing on the women's perspective, it follows three emigrant families living in wagons with dwindling food and water, who are shedding furniture and belongings. Having been persuaded by the blowhard trapper and guide Stephen Meek (Bruce Greenwood), a probable reference to George W. Bush, they have diverged from the main party to follow a shortcut across the desert and have become hopelessly lost.

Technically the 'slowest' of this group of films, all of which repeat, plod, circle, or stall rather than progress inevitably to a conclusion, *Meek's Cutoff* focuses on laborious, repetitive processes, with silences, stalled conversations, muted and/or sparse dialogue amidst ambient sounds from lumbering oxen hooves, jostling objects in the wagons and squeaking wheels. Time is spatialised in long takes of arid stretches of desert and in the relentless alternation of blinding sun and dense black nights. With the landscape framed in a square academic ratio to represent the pioneer women's restricted peripheral vision from under a bonnet, this feminist neorealist western offers a (paradoxically) claustrophobic alternative to the widescreen expanse that once conveyed mastery, Manifest Destiny and the American Dream. The film's aesthetic, an extreme, historicised variation on the 'beige' minimalism of *Wendy and Lucy*, was also a response to (or a metaphor for) the 'harsh economic and ideological realities' in the US just before and during the time the film was made, the neo-liberal 'imperatives' of the Bush and post-Bush era that 'insist that citizens do less with less', as Elena Gorfinkel puts it (2015: 124). Whereas sex trafficking and sexualised violence are prominent in Moncrieff's *The Dead Girl* and Griffiths' *Eden*, in most of these films the issue is passive aggressive ('trickle-down') socioeconomic violence against women and children. Granik, Hunt and Reichardt in fact rigorously desexualise their protagonists, who have dependents and/or day-to-day survival on their minds.[10]

While most neo-neorealist narratives emphasise how characters are determined by their environments, DuVernay's *Middle of Nowhere* internalises its realism, focusing directly on Ruby's strategies for emotional survival. When her husband Derek (Omari Hardwick) begins an eight-year sentence for armed robbery, Ruby gives up medical school to work as a nurse on the night shift. Witholding information to reflect Derek's withdrawal into the incriminating routines of prison life, the film closely follows *her* rituals of ironing a dress and riding the bus to work for four hours each weekend to the prison where he is incarcerated. Yet while the film dwells in quotidian existence, it is not self-consciously naturalistic. DuVernay uses sustained close-ups and moments of stillness to immerse spectators in Ruby's emotional interiors. In contrast to Hunt, Granik, Moncrieff, and Griffiths, and (in direct opposition to the black male 'hood' film) DuVernay does not place Ruby in an impoverished or neglected environment. Instead, a mark of Ruby's coming into her own is her modest but pristine middle-class home, which is paid for even as she teeters on the edge of respectability, as revealed in a scene in which she has to beg for $750 from her mother to help pay the $1,500 demanded by the lawyer for Derek's parole defence. Echoing Charles Burnett and the plays of August Wilson (Turan 2012), DuVernay contrasts her deft, nuanced realism (for which she won Sundance's directing award for 2011) with Behn Zeitlin's *Beasts of the Southern Wild* (2012), whose fantastic 'stunts' (Adams 2012) and exoticised images of a young black girl in extreme poverty (Hornaday 2012) made it a hit with indie audiences.[11] Simply in focusing on the everyday interior life of a young black woman, *Middle of Nowhere* is experimental and quietly political.

Neorealism, Melodrama and Genre

Although their social realism and neo-neorealistic modality has received the most attention, these films frame social and ethical issues through twists on tropes from classical Hollywood, specifically male, genres commonly associated with spectacle, action and adventure.[12] This strategy has proved essential for breaching the commercial-independent mainstream. Adapting motifs and characters from genres such as the crime thriller, road/buddy/outlaw movie, prison drama and Western, while grounding genre in female-centred social context and related issues, these films offer a modest but important alternative to current genre trends, whether extravagant postmodern pastiches or chick flick clichés. The most overtly artful in this respect, Reichardt adapts a distinctively American cinematic idiom to a global slow cinema aesthetic associated with the work of Abbas Kiarostami, Béla Tarr, Carlos Reygadas, or Tsai Ming-liang; yet, as Gorfinkel notes, her work takes elements from classical film form, shot structure, and character subjectivity (2015: 125), and lies between the radical end of the slow cinematic spectrum and a Hollywood norm (King 2013: 22). One might describe Reichardt's feminist western as a blend of Chantal Akerman's *Jeanne Dielman* (1975) with Kiarostami's *Bad ma ra khabad bord/The Wind Will Carry Us* (1999) and John Ford's *The Searchers* (1956).

This gender bending/genre blending strategy has undoubtedly helped female practitioners breach the commercial-independent mainstream. But if *Meek's Cutoff* has attracted the most academic attention as a feminist adaptation of a male genre, it was not a box office success. At the other extreme, *Winter's Bone* generated a popular controversy over whether its 'hillbilly noir', drug culture and crime genre elements compromise its authenticity, with Ozark residents chiming in (usually positively) via blogs and message boards.[13] *Down to the Bone*, *Frozen River*, *Eden* and *The Dead Girl* similarly threaten to compromise their realism by drawing on suspense and thriller genres (drug, crime/noir, sex trade and serial killer) commonly associated, like the Western, with 'men's cinema'. I argue however that their use of genre tropes and melodrama, in the sense in which the latter term refers to a modality,[14] have been as essential to the articulation of their female-oriented social and political commentary as to their critical success and popular appeal.

To be sure, and to return to the original term, Italian neorealism was never 'pure' in the Bazinian sense, having developed out of Fascist and popular cinema and melodrama.[15] Moreover, melodrama 'reinvests with moral urgency what is liable to appear random or insignificant in a secularised world', as Frank Kelleter and Ruth Mayer explain (2007: 9) and Louis Bayman explores in 'Melodrama as Neorealism in Italian Cinema' (2013). Hence Luchino Visconti's *Obsessione/Obsession* (1942), which took an anthropological perspective featuring long takes of street scenes and socioeconomic analysis, was either the first neorealist film or a key precursor but is equally exemplary as film noir. Based on James M. Cain's *The Postman Always Rings Twice*, about a cheating couple who plot to murder the woman's husband, it exudes melodrama in the heated sensuality of the sweaty realism of the couple's scenes together (Bayman 2013: 50). *La terra trema/The Earth Trembles* (Visconti, 1948), set among the poor fishing villages of Acci Trezza, Sicily, is one of the most self-consciously neorealist films, one that foregrounds environmental determinism in long shots featuring women in a group against the seascape, shots that are equally melodramatic in their expressivity. In fact, 'neorealist revelation occurs frequently through the excessively melodramatic impact of social reality', as when in *Roma, città aperta/Rome, Open City* (Roberto Rossellini, 1945), Pina (Anna Magnani) is shot to death in the street on her wedding day (Bayman 2013: 56).

The films I discuss are similarly inflected. Their 'neo- neorealism' consists of finely tuned negotiations between two modalities – neorealism and melodrama, one 'objective' and analytically distanced, the other expressionistically heightened and affective. Beyond this, however, they are nuanced with idioms from popular Hollywood genres. In several examples, their adaptations of male genres within minutely represented socioeconomic contexts expose how the desperation stemming from poverty leads to crime while generating suspense about the outcome. In the Italian touchstones of the 1940s, poverty often thrust naïvely honest people into crime, rendered as often as not as noir or with melodramatic affect – as in *Obsessione* and even in Vittorio De Sica's *Ladri di biciclette/Bicycle Thieves* (1948). Similarly in recent women's neo-neorealist films, crime is shown to result from poverty and indicates underlying socioeconomic causes, blending social realism with the crime thriller. Short on money to feed her only friend and dependent, her dog Lucy, Wendy is caught stealing dog food and is subsequently detained at the police station for hours. Lucy, who is tied up outside, gets loose and gets lost, and Wendy wanders for much of the rest of the film looking for her. Without Lucy to alert her, Wendy is attacked by a man while sleeping in a park. However, this film is not ultimately about crime or molestation, and all this is played out in a meticulously low-key style. More obviously a road movie (typically about two male buddies on a quest for discovery and adventure), the film is neorealistically truncated and also extended in Wendy's increasingly random drift.

In a more conventional manner, *Frozen River* and *Winter's Bone* marshal repetition and complication to build suspense and lend noir-style foreshadowing, yet while depicting crime as a consequence of the environment, including a meticulously delineated network of socioeconomic causal connections. Between pay checks, and saving to make a down payment on a double-wide trailer, *Frozen River*'s Ray feeds her children on popcorn and

Tang. As Christmas approaches, her fourteen-year-old son scams an old Native American woman for $25 to buy his four-year-old brother an action toy advertised on television, and Lila, a young Mohawk woman, persuades Ray, whose racist contempt seethes throughout the first half of the film, to smuggle immigrants across the Canadian border (the frozen St Lawrence River) in Ray's battered (but in this context, privileged) car. The strength of *Frozen River*'s blend of social realism with film noir lies in its gradual exposure, through mundane particulars and connections, of a web of intersectional (socioeconomic and interracial) conditions in which the characters are trapped. Ray's husband (conspicuously absent throughout the film) is addicted to gambling at the reservation's casino, and has absconded with the money Ray intended for her dream trailer with a jacuzzi. The same casinos are the only source of income for the tribe's people unless, like Lila, they engage in illegal activities. The gangsters who run the smuggling ring charge enormous fees that the immigrants must spend years in indentured servitude to pay off. Similarly, Ray works at the Yankee Dollar store, yet she and her kids are regulated through TV advertising and credit card companies to lease a large flat-screen television set and furniture, leaving them in another kind of indentured servitude. By midpoint, the conventional concept of crime is undermined by the film's complex intersectional perspective. Because of ageism and liberal capitalist economics, Ray can get only short-term, minimum-wage employment at the Dollar store although she has worked there for years. In thus questioning Ray's 'legitimate' employment, as Mark Berrettini notes, the film 'blurs distinctions between lawful enterprise and criminal activity . . . a narrative feature' common in gangster, heist, and drug trafficking film narratives that 'indict business ventures and capitalist institutions' (2015: 57). Here, however, the issue is tellingly highlighted. Even more tellingly, as Lila points out, for most Mohawks, smuggling is not a crime; it is regarded as free trade between nations within Mohawk borders.

Winter's Bone similarly heightens tension as Ree's quest exposes the socioeconomics, kinship relations, and other antagonisms that have entangled the Ozark mountain people in a cycle of abject poverty, meth cooking, addiction, secrecy, and revenge in which 'snitching' is a cardinal crime. With a mother who has reverted, via prescription medication, to a childlike state, and a meth-cooking dad who gets caught, puts their house and land up for bond and suddenly disappears, the film becomes a quest narrative as Ree searches for him or his body (without which she and her two younger siblings will be homeless). After running a gauntlet of hostile and dangerous distant relations in a wintry landscape, the sequence in which Ree is escorted by Merab (Dale Dickey) and her sister to her father's underwater corpse and forced to cut off his hands with a chainsaw (to provide evidence of his death) would have been effective in a horror film and is her archetypal quest hero's 'descent into hell'. Represented within the context of the code of the hills, however, it becomes simply the thing (however difficult) that she has to do.

Reframing Male Genres

In these examples, neorealism merges with melodrama and intersects with classical Hollywood cinematic rhetoric and genre tropes, especially noir, at key moments, with allegorical and specifically feminist resonances and purposes – thus to expose issues rather than simply to create suspense or heighten emotion. In *Winter's Bone*, *Frozen River* and *Meek's Cutoff*, Granik, Hunt and Reichardt draw on the gender codes of the crime thriller and western respectively to highlight a patriarchal homosocial kinship structure: men are aligned with the law or the unwritten code of the community, the discourse within which the women must find their own way and negotiate with each other – until the protagonist breaks the rule of female silence. Suspense mounts as Ree approaches the local patriarchs in ascending rank, first negotiating with the womenfolk who guard their lairs, until a cadre of the latter, led by Merab, stop her in her tracks by brutally beating her up. Subsequently they offer her a compromise that includes assistance in locating her father's corpse. In *Frozen River*, tension mounts as Ray is visited by repossession men and encounters a police officer (who is suspicious and concerned in a white, heteropatriarchal way about her association with Lila) until the ending in which Mohawk law offers a surprisingly matriarchal compromise. *Meek's Cutoff* also, if differently, features an ambiguous bond between the female protagonist and an American Indian man formed against white male authority. Initially the film restricts the spectator to the women's blinkered point of view as they do 'women's work' in groups, cooking in the pitch darkness of early morning or evening, gathering scattered, paltry pieces of firewood or standing together near the wagons, watching the men. Meanwhile the men cluster and talk in the distance in muffled, inaudible tones, perhaps arguing or else deciding the party's next move – until the turning point in which Meek draws his gun on the Cayuse tribesman (Rod Rondeaux) he has captured (and who may or may not be leading his abductors to water) and Emily Tetherow (Michelle Williams) aims a rifle at Meek, initiating a Mexican standoff. Meek finally relents, but not without a quip directed at Emily's husband), 'Looks like your woman's got some Indian blood in her'. Replacing Meek, the morally questionable outlaw antihero as guide, the marginalised 'Mrs Tetherow' and the Cayuse henceforth take the (however) tenuous lead to what may or may not be water.

Frozen River is also, if less obviously, an inverted western from a marginalised character's (female and non-white) point of view. Yet the tense austerity of Melissa Leo's (award winning) acting style may have been inspired by Hunt's suggestion that she look no farther than John Wayne: at 'how much his lack of expression was really full of emotion', as Hunt put it while comparing her film to the classic American tale of venturing into the lawless territory of the border (Silverstein 2009). Hunt readily admits to using genre to get a broader audience: 'If suspense keeps me viable then that's good. The next generation of men are totally comfortable seeing a woman protagonist as long as she's doing something . . . A woman engaged in fascinating action is just as interesting as a guy . . . since we've seen guys pretty much do everything' (quoted in Silverstein 2009). But the exclusively-trained lethal assassin so popular in contemporary action cinema (by Tarantino, for instance) is nowhere to be seen. Instead, as in Ray's case (or that of Reichardt's Cozy (Lisa Bowman) in *River of Grass* (1994) or Emily in *Meek's Cutoff*) she is a rank amateur who may resort to violence out of a complicated intersectional mix of motivations. Moreover, '[r]eal violence is small' in contrast to 'big', choreographed Hollywood violence. 'It's messy and inaccurate. People try to shoot somebody and wind up shooting their own ear off'. She staged the initial fight between Ray and Lila, a scene that is weighted with racism and desperation born of poverty, in 'a spastic, awkwardly angled way' in which 'Lila whacks Ray in the head, and Ray's head is bleeding, and she's like, "Bitch!" That's what fighting is, in my mind' (Hunt, quoted in Schoemer 2008). No one wins, and no lone hero rides off into the sunset. Instead, Lila and Ray find ways to collaborate to improve their respective situations within the socioeconomic context in which they are inextricably embedded.

If *Meek's Cutoff* and *Frozen River* are (however differently) inverted Westerns, Griffiths' *The Off Hours*, a film about women working at a truck-stop diner and based on her own experience (Dawson 2007), is a road movie from a 'reverse angle' focusing 'on those who stay behind', as Ronnie Scheib observes. This focus is sustained in its critically acclaimed cinematography: 'whenever one character moves away from another, Griffiths keeps the camera bracketed on the person left in the frame, adding to the atmosphere of stasis and stagnation that hangs over the film' (Scheib 2007). With similar intentions but taking on more obvious risks, Moncrieff's *The Dead Girl* challenges the serial killer genre, turning its gender codes inside out, omitting the police investigation, the fascination with the killer, and the murder scene itself. With five episodes, the film examines what the genre typically short-shrifts, the collaterally damaged women: a lonely caregiver (Toni Colette) oppressed by her bedridden mother who finds the body; a forensic graduate student (Rose Byrne) with a sister who is a missing person statistic, who examines the body; the religious housewife married to the killer; the dead girl's estranged, guilt-ridden, middle-class mother Melora (Marcia Gay Hardin); and the dead girl herself, Krista (Brittany Murphy), a junkie prostitute on the last day of her life, who is on the road to take her three-year-old daughter a birthday present. In the most telling segment, the killer's wife (Mary Beth Hurt), left alone for days at a time, discovers her husband's blood-encrusted trophies and, rather than initiate the trauma of change into the numb routine of their shared life, burns them, finally stripping and burning her own DNA-contaminated clothes. Yet the emphasis is not on the fact that the killer lives on to kill again. If the case remains unsolved, the ending of the film emphasises small openings achieved in each of these 'minor key' stories about wounded and closed-off lives. Collateral damage is similarly the subject of *Middle of Nowhere*, a prison film in reverse. DuVernay, who began by making acclaimed black music documentaries,[16] and is best known for her understated historical-biographical drama *Selma* (2014), has said that she was interested in exploring the rarely depicted lives of the wives of incarcerated black men. Interrogating the stereotype of the 'strong black woman', the film focuses narrowly on Ruby's internment in the role of the 'prison wife' until she grows into her own life. The film refuses audiences the prison film they are primed for and whose tropes – the prison setting (except for the exterior and the waiting room) and routines, gang activities, outbreaks of violence, and escape attempts – are all left off screen, referred to only as Derek, with increasing sullenness as he adapts to (and is corrupted by) life in prison, discloses the truth.

Notably, several of these films evoke, whether consciously or not, the classical era 'woman's picture' that, made by men for a female audience, reinforced heteronormative roles, hence constituting another kind of men's cinema. Exceptions include films by Douglas Sirk or the recent postmodern homages of Todd Haynes (*Far from Heaven*, 2002, *Mildred Pierce*, 2013) who have turned the genre to gender-conscious social realist ends. *Frozen River* nevertheless resonates with women's melodramas such as *Stella Dallas* (King Vidor, 1937), *Mildred Pierce* (Michael Curtiz, 1945) and *Now Voyager* (Irving Rapper, 1942) and their weepy 'spectacles' of a woman guiltily and/or self-sacrificially 'consumed by maternal zeal' (Haskell 1987: 169). In the most extreme example, *The Dead Girl*'s penultimate segment is a showpiece for Hardin as the dead girl's mother when she discovers that Krista left home after her partner sexually abused her, then uncovers the existence of Krista's child, whom she 'rescues' from an impoverished Mexican caretaker. *Frozen River*'s racist protagonists eventually and pointedly bond, not through their mutual need for money but through their common motherhood, in a poignant scene involving their belated rescue of a Pakistani couple's baby (after Ray, fearing terrorism, has forced the couple to leave the conspicuous bundle they are carrying out on the ice). The film ends in what Lila interprets as rebirth or resurrection, attributing the baby's return to warmth and consciousness to 'the Creator' appropriately on Christmas. When Ray and Lila are caught, they work out an agreement in which Ray goes to prison, enabling Lila to recover her own baby from her mother-in-law, move into Ray's trailer and take care of Ray's kids in the interim. The film ends bittersweetly with Ray serving time as the women's pooled resources enable the newly blended family to acquire a new single-wide trailer. *Frozen River*'s ending transcends the typical maternal melodrama, however, in several respects. As Berrettini usefully points out, Ray and Lila show their ability to 'negotiate the legal authority of their respective states' and economic systems (2015: 59); and their collaboration allows Lila to leave behind her former status as a woman shunned within the Mohawk community and unworthy to be a mother. In the process, the film 'sidestep[s] the nuclear family model' and the demand for a 'heteronormative narrative closure' (Berrettini 2015: 59). *Winter's Bone* ends more understatedly, with Ree cast as a teenaged stepmother giving up a career (in the army) for the sake of her younger siblings (anticipating Katniss Everdeen in *The Hunger Games*) – and closing with Ree's words of maternal comfort crossed with sibling camaraderie, 'I'd be lost without you kids on my back'. Notably, these films appeal to the culturally 'universal' and usually far more sentimentalised concern for mothers and children to facilitate their exploration of the complexities of gender roles within class and regional contexts. Conversely in omitting children and motherhood from the picture, *Meek's Cutoff* and *Middle of Nowhere* can afford less compromise, as Reichardt's and DuVernay's quietly assertive protagonists, discovering their resources from within, become understated heroines.

Exploring the textures of these various, 'collaterally damaged' women's lives, these films utilise, invert, contextualise, and 'reframe' genre for women. Through 'neo-neorealism' – through narratives in which the monotony, oppression, and hazard experienced by ordinary women in specific environments make a stark impression – they situate melodrama and genre within a meticulously depicted social reality. In so doing, they restore a few indie moments from irony and convention to authenticity and to social and political resonance. Their austere aesthetic is political on several levels. In addition to making specific points about the socioeconomic fallout of the Bush and post-Bush era and the history that led to it, this minimalistic, anti-blockbuster aesthetic is also the face of an often collaborative, 'green', sustainable filmmaking practice, as Geoff King suggests in reference to Megan Griffiths in this volume. As a feminist negotiation of genre film, melodrama and neo-neorealism, this trend offers an alternative – an 'escape' from the escapist extremes that have all but taken over American screens yet, far more than that, a form of resistance to them that constitutes an intervention within current filmmaking practice.

Notes

1. *Frozen River* and *Winter's Bone* each won the Sundance Grand Jury Prize and Best Actress as well as multiple nominations and/or awards by the Golden Globes, Independent Spirit Awards, and various critics' groups. With five acclaimed films to her credit, Kelly Reichardt is one of a very small group of women filmmakers who is regarded as an auteur, and her films have won an array of festival awards. *Middle of*

Nowhere won the Best Director award at Sundance, and the Gotham Breakthrough Award, and swept the various African-American film critics' awards. *The Dead Girl* was nominated for three Independent Spirit Awards: Best Picture, Director, and Best Supporting Female (Mary Beth Hurt). *The Off Hours* was nominated for an Independent Spirit Award for Best Cinematography, and *Eden* won several film festival awards.

2. With a $2,000,000 budget, *Winter's Bone* made $13,831,503 worldwide; with a $1,000,000 budget, *Frozen River* made $6,030,129 worldwide; with a $200,000 budget, *Wendy and Lucy* made $1,416, 046; *Meek's Cutoff* had a $2,000,000 budget and barely covered its costs.
3. For a somewhat more extensive definition see Claire Perkins' chapter in this volume.
4. After Laura Mulvey's 'Visual Pleasure and Narrative Cinema' (1975), women's cinema was defined largely as an avant-garde or 'counter-cinema' intended to expose and destroy male/Hollywood 'visual pleasure' and limited more or less to feminist audiences. In one exception, Bruzzi (2014: 6, 11–12) cites Silvia Bovenschen's essay 'Is there a feminine aesthetic' (1976) as an attempt to propose an aesthetic of 'women's cinema' from a second-wave feminist perspective.
5. In a parallel trend that Ortner notes in Chapter 8, a number of successful political documentaries have taken on capitalism directly – *Enron: The Smartest Guys in the Room* (Alex Gibney, 2005), *Walmart: The High Cost of Low Prices* (Robert Greenwald, 2005), *Inside Job* (Charles Ferguson, 2010) – in sober, fact-based treatments with cumulative affect rather than Michael Moore-style polemics (*Capitalism: A Love Story*, 2009) (Ortner 229–58).
6. At the same time, mainstream indie audiences have responded to films like Nicole Holofcener's *Friends with Money* (2006) and *Please Give* (2010), about white upper-middle class characters' anxieties and guilt over their participation in neoliberal capitalist culture.
7. In *Indie 2.0* (2014), which updates his 2005 book *American Independent Cinema*, Geoff King features the new 'Social Realism and Art Cinema' of Reichardt and Ramin Bahrani along with mumblecore, digital video, Internet and new social media ventures, as an important twenty-first-century trend.
8. Many critics including J. Hoberman have recognised the neorealist influence: 'Reichardt has choreographed one of the most stripped-down existential quests since Vittorio De Sica sent his unemployed worker wandering through the streets of Rome searching for his purloined bicycle, and as heartbreaking a dog story as De Sica's *Umberto D.*' (2010).
9. Ashlee Thompson, who lived in one of the houses used for filming, 'wasn't really acting', remembers Shelly Waggoner, who played Ree's neighbour, Sonya. 'She was basically living her real life on screen – playing with her own toys and her own dogs' (Swain 2011).
10. In *Winter's Bone*, for instance, Granik keeps the film's focus on Ree's present socioeconomic and domestic crisis, excising Ree's sexual experimentation with her best friend Gail and her history of rape by a distant older relative, both of which are highlighted in flashbacks in Woodruff's novel.
11. Ann Hornaday notes that DuVernay is among a 'growing cadre of filmmakers of color – including Barry Jenkins ("Medicine for Melancholy"), Dee Rees ("Pariah"), Tanya Hamilton ("Night Catches Us") and Andrew Dosunmu ("Restless City") who are creating a new vernacular for black cinema, one that owes as much to the white independent tradition of John Cassavetes, John Sayles and Richard Linklater as to such African-American pioneers as Charles Burnett, Haile Gerima, John Singleton and Spike Lee' (Hornaday 2012).

12. Bruzzi (2014:13) and Thomas Elsaesser (1985: 176) are two of a number of critics who define 'male' genres in these terms. Bruzzi applies and goes beyond Elsaesser however in suggesting a commonality between the classical Hollywood 'family' or 'woman's' melodrama and men's genres in their expressive uses of style and *mise-en-scène* to create emotional identification and convey ideas.
13. See, for example, Pruitt 2010 and Styron 2010.
14. See Brooks (1976), who redefined melodrama as a 'mode of excess' (xiii) and Linda Williams, who argued that melodrama should be seen as the predominant mode in American cinema (1998: 42) and a 'cultural mode driving the articulation of particular genres' (2001: 17). Also, although they treat melodrama primarily as a 'woman's' genre noted for externalising emotion and ideas through style and *mise-en-scène*, Elsaesser (1985: 176) and Bruzzi (2014: 12–17) in particular suggest that a similar expressionism is sustained in more typically 'masculine' Hollywood genres.
15. Italian neorealism, the style of filmmaking associated with Roberto Rossellini, Luchino Visconti, and Vittorio De Sica among others working with writers such as Cesare Zavattini, dealt with the 'ravages of fascism' on national identity and communities, and showed people 'suffering various forms of material and spiritual poverty and oppression' (Gottlieb, 2004: 32). Providing a 'continuing critique of the conditions, institutions, and individual predilections that cause violence, poverty, isolation, and spiritual distress', neorealism also represented resistance (Gottlieb, 2004: 32).
16. Examples are *This is the Life* (2008), *TV One Night Only: Live from the Essence Music Festiva*l (2010), and *My Mic Sounds Nice: The Truth about Women in Hip Hop* (2011).

References

Adams, Sam (2012), 'Middle of Nowhere', *A. V. Club*, 11 October, <http://www.avclub.com/review/middle-of-nowhere-86517> (last accessed 15 June 2015).

Bayman, Louis (2013), 'Melodrama as Realism in Italian Neorealism', in Lucia Nagib and Cecilia Mello (eds), *Realism and the Audiovisual Media*, New York: Palgrave Macmillan, pp. 47–62. Originally published in 2009.

Berrettini, Mark (2015), '*Frozen River* (2008): Mobility and Uncertain Boundaries', in Claire Perkins and Constantine Verevis (eds), *US Independent Film After 1989: Possible Films*, Edinburgh: Edinburgh University Press, pp. 53–61.

Brooks, Peter (1995), *The Melodramatic Imagination: Balzac, Henry James, Melodrama the Mode of Excess*, New Haven: Yale University Press. Originally published in 1976.

Bruzzi, Stella (2014), *Men's Cinema: Masculinity and Mise-en-scène in Hollywood*, Edinburgh: Edinburgh University Press.

Dargis, Manohla (2008), 'New American Realism Emerges Amid Grousing and Hummers', *The New York Times*, 29 January, <http://www.nytimes.com/2008/01/25/movies/25sund.html?_r=0> (last accessed 12 June 2015).

Dargis, Manohla and A. O. Scott (2011), 'In Defense of the Slow and Boring', *The New York Times*, 5 June 2011 (last accessed 2 August 2013).

Dawson, Nick (2011), '"The Off Hours" director Megan Griffiths', *Filmmaker*, January 2011, <http://filmmakermagazine.com/18883-the-off-hours-director-megan-griffiths/> (last accessed 2 June 2015).

Dodds, Klaus (2013), '"I'm Still Not Crossing That": Borders, Dispossession, and Sovereignty in *Frozen River*', *Geopolitics*, 18:3, 560–83.

Ebert, Roger (2009), 'The Great American Director', *Roger Ebert's Journal*, *Roger.*

ebert.com, 22 March, <http://www.rogerebert.com/rogers-journal/the-new-great-american-director> (last accessed 12 June 2015).

Elsaesser, Thomas (1985), 'Tales of Sound and Fury: Observations of the French Family Melodrama', in Bill Nichols, *Movies and Methods II*, Berkeley and Los Angeles: University of California Press, pp. 165–89.

Gills, Melina (2014), 'Debra Granik on Following Up 'Winter's Bone' With a Documentary and Possibly Reuniting With Jennifer Lawrence', *Indiewire*, 6 August 2014, <http://www.indiewire.com/article/debra-granik-on-following-up-winters-bone-with-a-documentary-and-possibly-reuniting-with-jennifer-lawrence-20140806> (last accessed 18 June 2015).

Gorfinkel, Elena (2015), 'Exhausted Drift: Austerity, Labor and the Politics of Slow in Kelly Reichardt's *Meek's Cutoff*', in Tiago de Luca and Nuno Barradas Jorge (eds), *Slow Cinema*, Edinburgh: Edinburgh University Press, pp. 123–36.

Gottlieb, Sidney (2004), 'Rossellini, Open City, and Neorealism', in *Roberto Rossellini's Rome Open City*, Cambridge: Cambridge University Press, pp. 31–42.

Haskell, Molly (1987), *From Reverence to Rape: The Treatment of Women in the Movies*, 1973, 2nd edn, Chicago: University of Chicago Press.

Hoberman, J (2008), '*Wendy and Lucy*', *Village Voice*, 10 December, <http://www.villagevoice.com/film/wendy-and-lucy-6392311> (last accessed 13 June 2015).

Hornaday, Ann (2012), '*Middle of Nowhere*'s director helping to redefine black indie films, *Washington Post*, 12 October, <http://www.washingtonpost.com/entertainment/movies/middle-of-nowheres-director-helping-to-redefine-black-indie-films/2012/10/12/2a97b442-13b4-11e2-ba83-a7a396e6b2a7_story.html> (last accessed 15 June 2015).

Johnston, Claire ([1973]/1999), 'Women's Cinema as Counter-Cinema', in Claire Johnston (ed.), *Notes on Women's Cinema*, London: Society for Education in Film and Television, reprinted in Sue Thornham (ed.), *Feminist Film Theory: A Reader*, Edinburgh University Press, pp. 31–40.

Kelleter, Frank, and Ruth Mayer (2007), 'The Melodramatic Mode Revisited', in Frank Kelleter, Barbara Krah and Ruth Mayer (eds), *Melodrama! The Mode of Excess from Early America to Hollywood*, Heidelberg: Universitätsverlag, pp. 7–18.

King, Geoff (2013), 'Indie's Continuities: The Persistence of American Independent Tradition in Kelly Reichardt's *Meek's Cutoff*, *Revue Francaise de'Etudes Americaines*, 136, pp. 15–27.

King, Geoff (2014), *Indie 2.0: Change and Continuity in Contemporary American Indie Film*, London: I. B. Tauris.

Mulvey, Laura (1975), 'Visual Pleasure and Narrative Cinema', *Screen*, 16: 3, pp. 6–18.

Ortner, Sherry B. (2013), Not *Hollywood: Independent Film at the Twilight of the American Dream*, Durham, NC and London: Duke University Press.

Pruitt, Lisa R. (2010), 'All the hype about "Winter's Bone" has me a bit worried . . .', *Legal Ruralism* (blog), 11 June, <http://legalruralism.blogspot.com/2010/06/all-hype-has-me-bit-worried-about.html> (last accessed 15 June 2015).

Scheib, Ronnie (2011), *The Off Hours, Variety*, 22 January 2011, <http://variety.com/2011/film/reviews/the-off-hours-1117944303/> (last accessed 15 June 2015).

Schoemer, Karen (2008), 'Little Miss Darkness: Courtney Hunt's first film won Sundance, but it's hardly cute', *New York Magazine, 24 March*, <http://nymag.com/movies/profiles/45293/> (last accessed 17 June 2015).

Scott, A. O. (2009), 'Neo-Neo Realism', *The New York Times Magazine*, 17 March, pp. 38–43, <http://www.nytimes.com/2009/03/22/magazine/22neorealism-t.html?pagewanted=all> (last accessed 12 June 2015).

Sholis, Brian (2008), 'Interview with Kelly Reichardt', *Artforum*, October, <http://

www.briansholis.com/category/publications/artforum-dot-com/> (last accessed 7 February 2013).

Silverstein, Melissa (2009), 'Interview with *Frozen River* Director Courtney Hunt', *WowOWow: The Women on the Web*, 2 February, <http//www.wowowow.com> (last accessed 5 December 2009).

Stern, Marlow (2014), 'Life After "Winter's Bone": Debra Granik on Finding J. Law and the Plight of the Female Director', the *Daily Beast*, 24 October, <http://www.thedailybeast.com/articles/2014/10/24/life-after-winter-s-bone-debra-granik-on-finding-j-law-and-the-plight-of-the-female-director.html> (last accessed 12 June 2015).

Styron, Harry (2010), '"Winter's Bone" and the Image of the Ozarks', *Ozarks Law and Economy* (blog), 11 June, <http://styronblog.com/2010/06/11/winters-bone-and-the-image-of-the-ozarks/> (last accessed 15 June 2015).

Swain, Kim (2011), '*Winter's Bone*: The Little Movie That Could', *417 Magazine*, <http://www.417mag.com/417-Magazine/February-2011/Winter-039s-Bone-The-Little-Movie-that-Could/?cparticle=3&siarticle=2#sthash.y7jiThn3.dpuf> (last accessed 16 June 2015).

Turan, Kenneth (2012), 'Deft *Middle of Nowhere* is Moving and Complex', *Los Angeles Times*, 11 October, <http://articles.latimes.com/2012/oct/11/entertainment/la-et-mn-middle-of-nowhere-review-20121012> (last accessed 15 July 2015).

White, Patricia (2015), *Women's Cinema, World Cinema: Projecting Contemporary Feminisms*, Durham, NC and London: Duke University Press.

Williams, Linda (1998), 'Melodrama Revised', in Nick Browne (ed.), *Refiguring American Genres*, Berkeley: University of California Press, pp. 42–88.

Williams, Linda (2001), *Playing the Race Card: Melodramas of Black and White from Uncle Tom to O. J. Simpson*, Princeton: Princeton University Press.

8. MY EFFORTLESS BRILLIANCE: WOMEN'S MUMBLECORE

Claire Perkins

In 2009, while Lynn Shelton's third feature *Humpday* was touring the US festival circuit, an interview appeared in *The New York Times* with the headline 'She's a Director Who's Just Another Dude' (Orange 2009). Like Shelton's previous feature *My Effortless Brilliance* (2008), *Humpday* features two male friends tensely reuniting a decade or so after college. The later film is distinguished by its specifically high concept premise, though, where the men attempt to counter their respective anomie by proposing to have sex with each other on camera – in an 'art project' destined for Seattle's famous amateur porn festival HUMP! *The New York Times* piece went to some lengths to detail the complex themes that ground this arresting plot. But the enduring effect of the article is the way its headline captures just one sentiment: the comment from *Humpday* performer and mumblecore regular Mark Duplass that the success of its improvised style was enabled by Shelton's 'greater affinity for men'. 'You know those girls that are closer with dudes, in general?' he posed, 'She's got a bit of that going on, so obviously that plays into it'. Duplass's remark – and its take-up in the article's headline – is striking for its causal summary of a position that is central to indie discourse: namely, that the visibility and success of female directors in the sphere of independent filmmaking depends upon their capacity to align with a sensibility and brand that has been gendered as masculine. In this chapter I will examine how the niche indie mode of mumblecore has been constructed in this way, and can subsequently be understood as a form of what Stella Bruzzi has called 'men's cinema'. I will then consider how the work of some of the women whose work is linked to the mode – namely,

Shelton, So Yong Kim and Desiree Akhavan – 'reframe' the broad parameters of mumblecore syntactics to open up to feminist, queer and racial perspectives in their content and style.

Mumblecore as Men's Cinema

Mumblecore was the first bona fide 'subgenre' of the post–1989 Indiewood era. As the high period of the production and discourse on these ultra low-budget, largely improvised, self-consciously 'amateur' films occurred between roughly 2005 and 2010, the films and practitioners associated with this mode form a point of transition between the first 'Sundance-Miramax' generation and the practical and discursive changes that digital technologies have enabled in the subsequent period. Geoff King has temporalised these latter years as 'Indie 2.0' (King 2014). As a contested critical category, mumblecore also serves as a synecdoche for the way in which the broader field of indie discourse operates. While the filmmakers involved have rejected the label and its unifying imperative,[1] critics and audiences alike have cultivated a taste culture that values notions of 'reality' and 'authenticity' against the perceived formulas and confections of Hollywood, grounding this in a loose set of lo-fi formal characteristics, and a group of acclaimed practitioners whose visions are seen to defiantly refuse mainstream conventions of narrative, style and characterisation. These supporters typically discuss the contribution of mumblecore in terms of three points of invention and Maria San Filippo has summarised these as: the viability of digital distribution, the rejuvenation of US art cinema's commercial appeal, and the honest and thoughtful consideration of contemporary American sexual mores (San Filippo 2011: 2). For King, mumblecore is a distinct example of 'Indie 2.0', showcasing familiar indie tendencies in a millennial world: 'ultra-cheap DV aesthetics and a quite narrow focus on the everyday relationship foibles and inarticulacies of a "twenty-something" post-college generation in the era of the text message, email and YouTube' (King 2014: 122–3).

These lines point to how mumblecore is valued as an intervention into the mainstreaming of contemporary American independent cinema, but also to how the films transpose some of the principal themes of this realm into a different key. Most notably, the mode amplifies the indie imperative for realism – as broadly represented in ordinary or 'small' character-driven stories –into a defining aesthetic and thematic focus that manifests in typically 'low' production values and micro-plots centring on minor human interaction. In this, mumblecore maintains indie cinema's knowing interest in the anxious and verbose emotionalism of the white middle class, but figures this in looser and less sardonic terms, and brings the favoured theme of arrested development into almost singular focus. The tonal result is a group of films that transpose the sharp play between irony and sincerity that anchors indie cinema's structure of feeling into a signature, diffident murmur of emotions.

Another key distinction, which is of particular relevance to this volume, is the manner in which gender politics figure in both the subject matter and the critical take-up of these films. While gender is an area that has been largely sidelined in discussions of the broader sphere of indie cinema, it is a central theme in criticism on mumblecore, with evaluations frequently commenting upon the fact that almost all the directors who have achieved prominence within the cycle are straight, white and male (see, for instance, Alberti 2013; Lim 2007; Taubin 2007). The trope of the maverick male auteur is a defining feature of indie culture (as it is for almost all other historical cycles or waves), but this fact attracts greater comment in association with mumblecore directors like Andrew Bujalski, Joe Swanberg and Aaron Katz than it does with Indiewood figures like Wes Anderson, Charlie Kaufman and Whit Stillman. This is substantially influenced by the way that most of the prominent mumblecore films foreground male identity politics in their slight narratives. A key example is *The Puffy Chair* (Mark and Jay Duplass, 2005), where the titular chair bought online by Josh (Mark Duplass) for his father's birthday present serves as an obstinate metaphor for both Josh and his brother Rhett's (Rhett Wilkins) emotional childishness in their relationships. Another is *Dance Party: USA* (Aaron Katz, 2006), which provides a study of teen protagonist Gus' (Cole Pensinger) diffident sexual behaviour that John Alberti calls 'a version of the coming-of-age teen high school movie that foregrounds genre performativity through an examination of the pathology/obsolescence of the conventional genres of male centrality' (Alberti 2013: 54).

In this way, mumblecore has dominantly been constructed as what Stella Bruzzi calls 'men's cinema' – a mode of filmmaking in which thematic, aesthetic and discursive tropes all encourage the spectator's engagement and identification with a certain vision of men and masculinity. Admittedly, the style and sensibility of the films associated with mumblecore bear little resemblance to the structured *mise-en-scène* that Bruzzi identifies as upholding the hegemony of white, heterosexual masculinity in spectacular genres like the Western and the action film (Bruzzi 2014: 68–95). While following the basic conditions of mainstream continuity style, the defining characteristic of mumblecore is its impression of the immediacy of real life – an antithesis to filmmaking models where on-screen events are clearly the result of careful arrangement. This approach actively resists the arch, ironic style that I have elsewhere argued constitutes a masculine aesthetic in the niche indie realm of the 'smart' film (Perkins 2014). Following Bruzzi, though, the mumblecore style can be understood to *convey* – and not just represent – a particular version of masculinity. Bruzzi argues that the emotions impelled by men's cinema are the result not simply of identification with a figure of idealised masculinity on screen but are also 'responses – less intellectual, more instinctive, physical, visceral –

shaped by a noticeable conjunction of stylistic elements' (Bruzzi 2014: 5). In mumblecore, the 'excitement and camaraderie' with which the kinetic style of the action film conveys a robust sense of masculine identity is replaced by the uncertain diffidence of a millennial *crisis* of masculinity, which emanates from a shaky sense of verisimilitude.

An instructive resource in understanding mumblecore as men's cinema is Alberti's theorisation of the mode as a 'genre of gender'. Arguing for its status as a neorealist reaction to the Hollywood bromance, Alberti suggests that mumblecore is defined by awareness and anxiety over the growing obsolescence of conventional cinematic genres of masculine performance (Alberti 2013: 52). Claiming that 'postness' is the defining existential condition of the characters – 'they are postgraduate, postpatriarchy, postnarrative, and postgender, not in the sense that they have transcended these categories, but that these categories only exist in a state of flux' (Alberti 2013: 52) – Alberti's characterisation offers a millennial version of the 'strain' of masculinity that Bruzzi identifies in the melodramas and film noir of classical Hollywood cinema. Across all cycles, 'the determining male "anxiety" is not that masculinity is foolish or easily mocked, but that, having thought it was the identity position against which its "Others" were defined, it discovers, in fact, that it is the most precarious and unstable of identity positions' (Bruzzi 2014: 50).

The majority of films nominated as mumblecore products present quiet dramatisations of this anxiety in scenarios where male characters fail to live up to the social and romantic expectations of those around them. The lo-fi ideology is also substantially supported by mumblecore's identity as an indie 'scene'. While this is an ironic result, perhaps, for a group of filmmakers who rejected both the label and the concept that their films had anything in common, the discursive construct undeniably brought visibility to the individuals involved. Both positive and negative commentary on the group of works created a legible – and legitimating – framework for their 'minor' or 'mundane' concerns, identifying a shared aesthetic and philosophy as well as a group of recurrent and interconnected directors, writers and performers who work on and appear in one another's films. As James Lyons has described, the concept of mumblecore is in this way underpinned by a 'constellation of practitioners' – a cluster of networked individuals who became readable through intertextual and paratextual connections (Lyons 2013: 165). By drawing attention to such connections, the brand of mumblecore has provided a platform for the career of a figure like Mark Duplass. Several years after the supposed 'death' of the cycle, Duplass based his keynote address at the 2015 SXSW festival on its highly recognisable philosophy, mobilising ideas of digital utopianism around the premise that inherent value lies in small scale, personal observations and interactions – and specifically in autobiography over 'bigger' issues and questions (Duplass 2015).

The discursive construction of mumblecore in this way both contributes to and exemplifies the formation of an indie canon, where, as Constantine Verevis and I have described elsewhere, a relatively small group of figures are regularly attended to by commentators and scholars – not because their work is valued as 'great', but because it is representative of indie as a legible cultural formation (Perkins and Verevis 2015: 2). In mumblecore, as elsewhere in the indie sector, this canonisation has occurred to the significant exclusion of female practitioners. Rather than being associated with a historically 'pure' form of mumblecore that provides context and authority for their later work (as has happened for Duplass, Swanberg, Bujalski and Katz), female directors – when mentioned – are tangentially associated with a diluted or hybridised version of the sensibility. Hence Shelton's recent films have been called 'studio mumblecore', So Yong Kim gives 'nods to mumblecore' (Rayns 2013) and Desiree Akhavan's work contains 'a dash of mumblecore' (Emblidge 2015). As mobilised in these instances, the term presents not an orienting philosophy but a puzzle that critics often struggle to come to terms with. And this is a fact that many of the contributors to this volume note in reference to the way female practitioners working in the zone between Indiewood, the mainstream chick flick and feminist counter-cinema all struggle to attain credible indie visibility because their work is not ironic, popular or political enough to be readily absorbed into any pre-existing categories.

In the remainder of this chapter I will consider how these 'hybrid' characterisations can be repurposed to demonstrate the way women filmmakers reframe the dominant tone and sensibility of mumblecore, which remains best characterised by the terms Dennis Lim used in an early *New York Times* article, where he noted that this work constitutes a 'state of mind' that focuses on the 'in-between years', understanding that these drifting periods '[mask] quietly seismic shifts that are apparent only in hindsight' (Lim 2007). As identified above, this perspective demonstrates an exaggeration of the familiar indie orientation towards loosely plotted stories, but combines this with a neo-realist drive to capture life 'as it is', and makes indie cinema's preoccupation with interpersonal dynamics and politics a singular focus. As Lim writes, the narratives 'hinge less on plot points than on the tipping points in interpersonal relationships' (Lim 2007). In the cycle's narrative image, this manifests as the formation, wavering or breakdown of a white, middle-class, heterosexual relationship where, even if the protagonists are women, identification with the anxious perspective of the male characters is encouraged. In the films by female writers and directors that are linked to mumblecore, the focus on both 'in-betweenness' and the 'tipping points' of interpersonal relationships takes a range of different forms that all, in varying ways, depart from this paradigm by orienting their narratives and perspectives in terms of different racial, cultural and queer female subjectivitities.

Lynn Shelton: Not Just a Female Judd Apatow

Within the context of mumblecore that has been sketched above, the Seattle-based Shelton has a profile that is unusual for an indie female practitioner, insofar as her six features are regularly discussed in popular round-ups of the cycle, which means that she is closely aligned with its brand. Significantly, though, her profile was built on the back of *Humpday*, which in 2009 marked the breakout success of mumblecore by earning more than $500,000 in theatrical release – more than any film linked to the mode had to date (San Filippo 2011: 6). In the large amount of critical attention that *Humpday*'s premise provoked, and following on from the similar relationship dynamics of *My Effortless Brilliance*, Shelton was framed as a director with a flair for the politics of male identity. Both films were described in terms of their 'subtle, almost anthropological scrutiny of the male of the species' (Orange 2009), with Alberti taking *Humpday* up as an exemplary instance of the mumblecore anxious bromance; a film that posits an indie counterpart to Judd Apatow's work in demonstrating the gender crises of contemporary American comedy (Alberti 2013: 52). In interviews, Shelton's success was framed in more pragmatic terms, with prominent male 'mumblecorps' like Duplass and Swanberg positioned as the friends and mentors who gave her the 'confidence' and 'inspiration' to pursue her own projects (Orange 2009; Alter 2012). While demonstrating the ethos of collaboration that underpins the production processes of these films, these descriptions quite pointedly position the female director as a mentee, not a maverick.

Both textually and contextually, then, Shelton's name was constructed in masculine terms, and for this reason readily absorbed into mumblecore's 'men's cinema' brand. I argue that it is this image that has shaped the decidedly cool critical reception of Shelton's last three films and simultaneously obscured the feminist dimensions of this work that give a blunt and funny perspective on female subjectivity, relationships, desires and ambitions. The three films revolve around female protagonists who are all 'stuck' in some way. In *Your Sister's Sister* (2011), Hannah (Rosemarie DeWitt) is just out of a long-term lesbian relationship and, away for a weekend in the San Juan islands, has a sexual encounter with her sister's best friend Jack (Mark Duplass) in an attempt to get pregnant; in *Touchy Feely* (2013), the spiritual massage therapist Abby (again, DeWitt) is suddenly repelled by human skin and can no longer do her job, while her uptight dentist brother Paul (Josh Pais) simultaneously acquires a mysterious healing touch; and in *Laggies* (2014), 28-year-old Megan (Keira Knightley) retreats from her adult responsibilities into the company of a sixteen-year-old girl.

These features have gradually moved away from what Shelton calls the 'upside-down' mode of filmmaking in which she made her early films, where the screenplays were crafted primarily through the actors' contributions (Silverstein 2009). While maintaining the distinctive mumblecore tendencies towards 'in-between' periods of down-time and lengthy, inchoate conversations, the newer films merge structured improvisation with varying levels of scripting, and also include the presence of indie stars like DeWitt, Alison Janney and Ellen Page. *Laggies* is also the first film that Shelton has directed but not written. On the whole, these films have received far less acclaim than the decidedly rougher *Humpday*. They have been called 'disjointed', 'inconsequential' and 'curious' (Myers 2013; Scott 2014), with one critic drawing on the new-age theme of *Touchy Feely* to proclaim that Shelton's newer work needs its chakras aligned – saying it 'can't get a grip on tone' in the way it moves between broad comedy, quiet character-driven study and moments of serious gravitas (Perez 2013). While an unpredictable tone and movement between diverse generic and emotional terrain is celebrated as the very core of 'indie-ness' in the work of a director like Wes Anderson or Charlie Kaufman, in Shelton's filmmaking it presents a puzzle whith which critics struggle to come to terms.

Another way to read the hybrid quality of Shelton's recent work is to understand it as a transformation of the received categories of both popular and indie US cinema. Here, it fits into the emerging development of the 'smart chick flick' – films by female practitioners that bring the textual qualities and taste dynamics of 'smart' cinema to narratives that centre on female characters and experience.[2] I have argued elsewhere that a central innovation of such work is its capacity to present a knowing assessment of the white middle class in everyday terms that do not broach the quirky or deadpan style of more popular, male-directed smart and indie films (Perkins 2014). In Shelton's case this everydayness is readable in terms of her links to mumblecore. She brings to her female-centric films a sensibility and shooting style derived from improvisation – a freedom and permissiveness that means the interaction between her characters is grounded in ordinary human rhythms and speech. Crucially, though, this interaction also moves substantially away from the space of the heterosexual relationship that defines both mumblecore and the chick flick. The key relationship of each film is instead between two siblings, centring on Dewitt's sister characters in *Your Sister's Sister* and *Touchy Feely*, and Knightley and Chloe Grace Moretz's 'pseudo' sisters in *Laggies*.

The sibling relationship is a key trope in indie cinema, where it often functions as an index of a troubled or dysfunctional family history. In the smart image that has been popularised by directors like Wes Anderson, Noah Baumbach and Todd Solondz, this is typically figured in arch, highly-strung terms – the sibling relationship is carried by careful dialogue and precise stylisation that renders the individuals and their personalities in archetypal terms. In Shelton's films, the absurd, whimsical or vicious effects that arise from these strategies are transposed into something looser and more everyday, and the relationship becomes the focal point for the narrative's state of 'in-betweenness'. This is reflected in the way the bond between Hannah (DeWitt) and Iris (Emily Blunt) in *Your Sister's Sister* is conveyed not by scripting but by the body language of the two performers as they engage in long, halting, intimate conversations where they explore and judge each other's emotions and behaviour. Their shared history and respective roles are not spelled out, but are palpable in their manner with one another – which is, by turn, easy and prickly – in the push-pull way that all siblings interact. As a chamber drama that for all but its first scene contains just three characters, the peculiar romance of the sibling relationship here is crucial to the film's dramatic intrigue, and is forcefully evoked through the idiolects that each performer brings to their semi-improvised role – with the taut but volatile personas of DeWitt and Blunt aligning against the shaggy, relaxed image of Duplass. Mumblecore directors famously prefer to work out a backstory for their characters in lieu of a set script, and what Shelton does here is connect this strategy with an inspired deployment of indie star power.

The female protagonists of *Touchy Feely* and *Laggies* are more literally 'stuck' at intersections in their romantic and professional lives, and the sibling relationships of each function as a conduit for a transfer of energy that represents and reacts to this. In *Touchy Feely*, the energy of an initially animated Abby (DeWitt) visibly drains to her 'wan' and 'depleted' brother as she falters in her commitment to her partner and job, before leaking into the texture of the film itself when – via the plot device of a drug trip - Abby rediscovers the vitality of her environment in a series of fluid, dialogue-free scenes shot in macro close-up from her perspective. The week-long 'timeout' that Megan (Knightley) takes with Annika (Moretz) in *Laggies* functions similarly, with the unusual maturity and poise of the younger woman renewing the older's perspective on her life and enabling the forward movement that ends her state of 'arrested development *in extremis*' (Myers 2014). In this way, all three films focus the interlude that structures their narrative around the subjectivity of the female protagonist and her 'sibling', charging this relationship with an unpredictable dynamic of intimacy and exchange in which she constantly evaluates, competes and judges. This focalisation represents a transformation of the dominant paradigms of both mumblecore and the chick flick by making the sibling relationship more important than the eventual heterosexual dyad, and resonates with feminist scholarship on this topic by proposing sibling love with its 'ambivalences' and 'oxymoronic bittersweet connotations' as 'an alternative to patriarchal law and its concomitant heterosexuality' (Mills 1997: 49).

So Yong Kim: In the In-between

If Shelton was readily absorbed into the mumblecore 'scene', So Yong Kim is – paradoxically – most famous within this discourse for being excluded from it. The Korean-American writer, director and producer was evoked by Amy Taubin in her well-known critique of the cycle in a 2007 issue of *Film Comment*, where the constructed identity of mumblecore – already 'yesterday's programming ploy' for Taubin – was labelled '[an] indie movement that was never more than a flurry of festival hype and blogosphere branding' (Taubin 2007). More pointedly, Taubin identified the distance between mumblecore works and former no-budget, 'talkie' indies such as *Go Fish* (Rose Troche and Guinevere Turner, 1994) to lie in the newer films' homogeneity, stating bluntly that 'the directors are all male, middle-class Caucasians, and they make movies exclusively about young adults who are involved in heterosexual relationships and who have jobs (when they have them) in workplaces populated almost exclusively by SWMs and SWFs'. Directly supporting her point, Taubin here raised Kim's first feature *In Between Days* (2006) as a film that fits the mumblecore parameters but didn't register for the scene's taste-makers on account of the female, Korean identity of both director and protagonist.

In Between Days resonates with the mumblecore style and sensibility with its rough production values, faltering communication and low-key, frustrated romantic relationship. Teen Aimie (Jiseon Kim) obliquely yearns for her friend Tran (Taegu Andy Kang), with whom she kills time in the video game arcades and fast food restaurants of a snowy Toronto, where she has recently immigrated with her single mother. *Treeless Mountain* (2008), Kim's second feature, is quite different in tone and style. Shot entirely around Seoul and the rural district of Hunghae, the Korean language film makes two young sisters – six-year-old Jin (Hee-yeon Kim) and four-year-old Bin (Song-hee Kim) – its guarded and hesitant communicators, with slower, more fluid and polished camerawork which captures the siblings' watchful interaction with the distantly known relatives their mother leaves them with when she sets off to – ostensibly – find their absent father. The third feature, *For Ellen* (2012), is a stylistic hybrid of the earlier works, focusing on Paul Dano's clichéd rock musician Joby Taylor as 'an overgrown boy, deeply solipsistic and emotionally clueless' (Rayns 2013) who makes a frozen trip upstate to see his five-year-old daughter Ellen before giving away his custody rights to her.

With its recognisably arrested and 'troubled' male protagonist, its links to the road movie and alternative music cultures and its blankly registered shots of small town America, only *For Ellen* has been received as a 'resolutely American indie film' (Rayns 2013). Taken as a trilogy though, the three films together can be understood to transform this tradition and, more specifically, expand the mumblecore terms with which the first and third have been explicitly associated. The films form an 'absent father' trilogy, with each – like Shelton's – putting its key relationship into terms other than the heterosexual romance. In place of Shelton's siblings, though, Kim focuses attention on the link between young girls and their estranged fathers. Together with the films she has produced with husband Bradley Rust Gray for the couple's soandbrad label – *Salt* (2003), *The Exploding Girl* (2009) and *Jack and Diane* (2012) – the group of works provide a subtle and complex commentary on the dynamics and anxieties of girls and girlhood. Kim has described how the specific iteration of this theme in her work is inspired by her own life and experiences, when, initially, she was left as a young child in Pusan on her grandparents' rice farm while her single mother immigrated to America to find a better life for her family, and later as a teenager growing up in a suburb of Los Angeles where, in her words, a lack of discussion around the topics of love and sex created a 'persistent tension' among her Korean immigrant friends which obscured their ability to express their feelings (soandbrad.com).

In *In Between Days* and *Treeless Mountain*, the figure of the father is a structuring absence for these inchoate emotions; the former film iis punctuated by Aimie's internal monologues to him about her new life in Canada and the latter is focused around the father as a symbolic 'tipping point' who, once located, will mean both the return of the young girls' mother and a more secure and prosperous life. The third film manifests the father as a figure who is continuously present onscreen, but still palpably absent from his daughter Ellen's ongoing life – framing the brief hours they spend together over the course of the narrative as a tentative in-between interlude before he signs away his rights to any future contact with her. Each film showcases mumblecore's temporal drift, its autobiographical imperative and its signature struggle with the expression of difficult emotion. But the trilogy also pushes beyond the level of personal interaction to make the structuring father-daughter relationship a site for social commentary. In *In Between Days*, Aimee's imagined communication with her father is also a record of her experience as a Korean immigrant, where the lies she tells – 'I've made a lot of friends, Dad. Mom's working hard. Don't worry about us' – highlight her desire to assimilate and the sense of loss that attends her difficulty in doing so. Similarly, the two later films also show how the emotions and behaviour of the characters issue from their material circumstances rather than from the more typical mumblecore context of middle-class anomie – the mother in *Treeless Mountain* has to finally admit she doesn't have the means to look after her daughters, and Joby in *For Ellen* is ultimately more tempted by his financial share of his ex-wife's house settlement than by an ongoing relationship with his daughter.

This powerful dimension of Kim's work demonstrates how she is also transforming and hybridising received 'genres' of indie film. While critically linked to mumblecore by Taubin and others, Kim was also linked to the now widely cited category of 'neo-neorealism' that Linda Badley examines in detail in this volume. Within this context, A. O. Scott locates *Treeless Mountain* alongside the works of Ramin Bahrani and Kelly Reichardt (whose films, like Kim's, are released through Adam Yauch's Oscilloscope label) as evidence of a realist 'antidote' to 'Hollywood wish-fulfilment tales' and 'faux independent' dramas of adversity and redemption (Scott 2009). While mumblecore can and has been understood as a similarly realist 'backlash' against mainstream US film-making, this description does not typically encompass the social and political aspects of *neo*-realism - and, indeed, mumblecore has been critiqued by figures like Taubin for its singularly *apolitical* sensibility. Against this critical backdrop, Kim's trilogy not only restores the place of women and girls to mumblecore, but it also forges a mid-point between these two millennial brands of US-realism that is as concerned with social conditions as it is with emotion.

Desiree Akhavan: Inappropriate Behaviour

The third example of this female-centric and politicised mumblecore sensibility that I will discuss belongs to the work of Desiree Akhavan who, upon the release of her first feature *Appropriate Behavior* (2014), became best known in popular indie discourse as the 'not Lena Dunham'. This characterisation reflects how the two women were endlessly compared in initial media interviews and profiles around the film, a critical tic sparked by their shared taste for semi-autobiographical, sexually frank portraits of forthright, creative young women figuring out their post-collegiate existence in knowingly hip Brooklyn neighbourhoods. Supported by the tangible link of Akhavan's appearance as a fellow graduate writing student in the fourth season of Dunham's HBO series *Girls* (2012–), these comparisons always carried the caveat of Akhavan's intersectional identity as an Iranian-American bisexual. Quickly, though – and encouragingly – this discursive trend itself became an object for comment, with pieces on Akhavan skewing towards observations on how the media presents female practitioners. In *The Guardian*, for instance, Hadley Freeman commented that 'there's something very odd about how the media will find ways in which a young woman is different (Iranian! bisexual!) while at the same time insisting she is exactly like someone else (the new Dunham!)' (Freeman 2015), while Akhavan herself noted that 'it's the idea that there's room for only one funny woman whose work can be monetised. It happens with any young female film-maker with humour in their work . . . but no one ever looks at [indie director] Alex Ross Perry and says: "Oh, another Noah Baumbach!"' (quoted in Freeman 2015).

As many reviews of *Appropriate Behavior* noted, Akhavan's work is only superficially similar to Dunham's and, while the similarities can be discussed in terms of a broadly shared mumblecore ethos – collaborative, low-budget production, states of arrested development, a focus on the conversation as set piece and a preoccupation with difficult relationships – the more interesting analyses arise from the diverse ways in which the women filmmakers reinvent these familiar tropes.[3] In Akhavan's work, the most compelling example of this process lies with how *Appropriate Behavior*, alongside her two-season web series *The Slope*, function to queer the non-teleological sensibility of mumblecore. As discussed above, the films associated with this mode are dominantly characterised by their attempt to capture the rhythm of everyday life, where the emotions and interaction of the present moment are more pressing than how they connect to a broader story. This quality makes San Fillipo's suggestion that the concept of 'slow film' comes closest to the mode and mood of mumblecore (San Filippo 2011: 15) especially instructive for, while she is primarily mobilising the term to evoke the 'sustenance and simplicity' of these films, the description 'slow' also taps into issues of cultural value that can productively illuminate their operation and impact.

While radically different in style, mumblecore work is as susceptible as the global art films of the discursive slow cinema to the critique that 'nothing happens' and that the films are therefore 'wasteful' of their spectators' time and energy.[4] In scholarship on slow cinema, this debate is taken up to argue that the cycle is, at its core, about the question of productive human labour, asking 'what is a worthy "thing" of representation in film' (Lim 2014: 18). Karl Schoonover has astutely extended this logic to the realm of queer studies, suggesting that the debates over slow cinema are ultimately about 'the question of queerness, or what it means to live queerly' because of the way that critics and supporters of slow film in turn valorise and condemn the 'ordinary, everyday notions of temporality – including linear narrative, teleology, reproduction, progress [and] history' that anything named 'queer' works against (Schoonover 2012: 74–5).

In Akhavan's work, these issues are focalised within the diegesis. The fractured narrative of *Appropriate Behavior* moves non-chronologically between vignettes of the life of protagonist Shirin (Akhavan) before and after her break-up with girlfriend Maxine (Rebecca Henderson). In each, the titular concern with appropriateness registers as Shirin's struggle to be productive and 'correct' in terms of the social expectations that shape each part of her intersectional identity. For most of the film she hides her relationship from her Persian parents and brother, who disapprove of her drifting Brooklyn lifestyle and 'wasted' MA in Journalism. When, in a seemingly tender moment, her austere mother Nasrin (Anh Duong) attends to a burn that Shirin has sustained in a fire ritual at a large family party and the daughter admits she is 'a little bit gay', the mother gently but firmly retorts that 'no. No you're not'. The topic is not raised again. Meanwhile, in the flashbacks of their relationship Maxine encourages Shirin to be *more* queer, plying her with literature and sulking over the family she

Figure 8.1 Maxine (Rebecca Henderson) and Shirin (Desiree Akhavan) in *Appropriate Behavior* (Desiree Akhavan, 2014).

perceives to be overbearing, having voluntarily 'orphaned' herself from hers many years ago on account of her own sexuality. In some of the post break-up scenes, Shirin forcefully embraces her self-proclaimed bisexual identity, pursuing an awkwardly performed encounter with an OkCupid date and later, in the film's most striking scene, a threesome with a straight couple who pick her up in a bar. Here, Shirin and the male partner's mutual discomfort with their sudden, blunt intimacy and the females' obvious preference for each another is conveyed entirely through their gauche body language and the blocking of the performers' bodies in a silent, unflinchingly extended sequence.

Upon being questioned about the extent to which she identifies her own work with the mumblecore label, Akhavan has described how Swanberg's depiction of 'young, normal people having sex' definitely influenced how she wanted to shoot sex scenes (Alcamo 2014), and the frank nature of this sequence clearly betrays that imperative. Beyond this, though, the scene also indexes the ways in which Akhavan's work is powerfully distinctive. It transposes the emotional awkwardness of mumblecore from the terms of male anxiety and egotism to those of a queer female subjectivity, where the in-between sensibility manifests as a commentary on the difficulty – and undesirability – of 'achieving' the social and temporal expectations of a range of intersecting identities. Akhavan mobilises the 'slow' dimension of the mumblecore ethos to reframe the question of what counts as 'productive' to what counts as 'appropriate', and in doing so illuminates a range of 'alternate forms of living' (Schoonover 2012: 74) that extend substantially beyond the typical mumblecore spectrum.

Women's Mumblecore

These discussions of the films of Shelton, Kim and Akhavan support Alison Butler's identification of women's filmmaking as a 'minor cinema' that 'is not "at home" in any of the host cinematic or national discourses it inhabits' (Butler 2002: 2). Butler's conception of minority as a position that is neither included within nor excluded from cultural traditions offers a precise description of the place of women filmmakers in the indie realm. Here, in what Thomas Schatz has identified as the second and third tiers of the millennial Hollywood system (Schatz 2009: 25–9), women are better represented than they are in the first, tentpole-oriented tier, but remain marginal in terms of their visibility and recognition within the 'maverick' male-driven indie narrative. The subgenre of mumblecore provides a contained and instructive example of how this occurs by showing the way male indie practitioners possess a 'cohesive collective identity' (Butler 2002: 22) that women do not – an effect that is substantially impacted by the mode's character as 'men's cinema'. Discussing the work of female practitioners linked to the mode is thereby not, or not *only*, a strategy of genre revisionism; it aims to expand the popular understanding of what 'indie' is. Identifying Shelton, Kim and Akhavan's affinity with mumblecore subscribes them to a taste culture that claims legitimacy for their films and audiences over and against the commodity ethos of the mainstream. Beyond this, though, it also opens the way to considering how the work forges feminist perspectives by transposing the mumblecore ethos to a range of different subjectivities and experiences. The innovation – and intervention – of these women filmmakers is here to transform the white, masculine, heterosexual image that has been popularised by the prominent male directors and put the diffident manner of the cycle into new configurations. The resulting films may not give rise to an easily marketable image or 'scene', but their specific strategies of observation play an important role in restoring women's contributions and perspectives to the male-driven narrative of contemporary indie cinema. It is ultimately a sign of the value of this work that it is *not* readily absorbed into any of the existing niches of this realm, and instead contributes to a new type of 'arrested' image that focuses on female experience, and puts some key themes of indie film into different terms.

Notes

1. For some examples of how mumblecore is understood as a 'non movement' by filmmakers see comments from Andrew Bujalski in Gilbey (2013) and Lynn Shelton in Alter (2012).
2. This concept is addressed in my essay 'Beyond Indiewood: The Everyday Ethics of Nicole Holofcener' (Perkins 2014), and by both Linda Badley and Hilary Radner in their chapters in *U.S. Independent Film After 1989: Possible Films* (Perkins and Verevis 2015).

3. Corinn Columpar's essay in this volume gives a compelling reading of how Dunham 'reframes' the mumblecore strategy of collaboration.
4. Some of the key pieces of popular writing in this debate include Kent Jones's editorial in *Sight & Sound* 20: 4 (2010), Steven Shaviro's blog-post 'Slow Cinema Vs Fast Films' (2010) and Harry Tuttle's 'Slow Films, Easy Life' (2010).

References

Alberti, John (2013), *Masculinity in the Contemporary Romantic Comedy: Gender as Genre*, New York: Routledge.

Alcamo, Jess (2014), 'Appropriate Behavior – An Interview with Writer/Director Desiree Akhavan, *4.3 Film*, 15 June, <http://fourthreefilm.com/2014/06/appropriate-behavior-an-interview-with-writerdirector-desiree-akhavan/> (last accessed 25 June 2015).

Alter, Ethan (2012), 'Sisterly Rivalry', *Film Journal International*, 115:6, 14–17.

Bruzzi, Stella (2013), *Men's Cinema: Masculinity and Mise-en-scene in Hollywood*, Edinburgh: Edinburgh University Press.

Butler, Alison (2002), *Women's Cinema: The Contested Screen*, London: Wallflower.

Duplass, Mark (2015), '2015 SXSW Film Keynote', 17 March, <http://www.sxsw.com/film/news/2015/watch-sxsw-video-2015-sxsw-film-keynote-mark-duplass> (last accessed 21 April 2015).

Emblidge, Wesley (2015), Review of *Appropriate Behavior*, *Entertainment Monthly*, 22 January, <http://emertainmentmonthly.com/2015/01/22/review-appropriate-behavior-reveals-desiree-akhavans-unique-voice/> (last accessed 25 June 2015).

Freeman, Hadley (2015), 'Desiree Akhavan on Appropriate Behavior and not being the "Iranian bisexual Lena Dunham"', *The Guardian*, 6 March, <http://www.theguardian.com/film/2015/mar/05/desiree-akhavan-appropriate-behaviour-not-being-iranian-bisexual-lena-dunham> (last accessed 25 June 2015).

Gilbey, Ryan (2013), 'Mumblecore: It was never a unified movement. There was no manifesto', *The Guardian*, 8 November, <http://www.theguardian.com/film/2013/nov/07/mumblecore-andrew-bujalski-computer-chess> (last accessed 20 April 2015).

Jones, Kent (2010), Editorial, *Sight & Sound*, 20: 4.

King, Geoff (2013), *Indie 2.0: Change and Continuity in Contemporary American Indie Film*, London: I. B. Tauris.

Lim, Dennis (2007), 'A Generation Finds Its Mumble', *The New York Times*, 19 August <http://www.nytimes.com/2007/08/19/movies/19lim.html?pagewanted=all&_r=0> (last accessed 20 April 2015).

Lim, Song Hwee (2014), *Tsai Ming-liang and a Cinema of Slowness*, Honolulu: University of Hawaii Press.

Lyons, James (2013), 'Low-flying stars: Cult Stardom in Mumblecore', in K. Egan and S. Thomas (eds), *Cult Film Stardom: Offbeat Attractions and Processes of Cultification*, Basingstoke: Palgrave Macmillan, pp. 163–78.

Mills, Jane (1997), 'There never were such devoted sisters', *Refractory Girl*, 52, pp. 47–9.

Myers, Emma (2013), Review of *Touchy Feely*, *Film Comment*, 49: 5, pp. 73.

Myers, Emma (2014), Review of *Laggies*, *Indiewire*, 18 January, <http://www.indiewire.com/article/sundance-review-kiera-knightley-and-sam-rockwell-charm-in-lynn-sheltons-laggies> (last accessed 21 April 2015).

Orange, Michelle (2009), 'She's a director who's just another dude', *The New York Times*, 2 July, <http://www.nytimes.com/2009/07/05/movies/05oran.html?pagewanted=all&_r=0> (last accessed 11 February 2015).

Perez, Rodrigo (2013), Review of *Touchy Feely*, *Indiewire*, 6 September, <http://blogs.indiewire.com/theplaylist/review-lynn-sheltons-touchy-feely-starring-rosemarie-dewitt-ellen-page-josh-pais-20130905> (last accessed 26 February 2015).

Perkins, Claire (2014), 'Beyond Indiewood: The Everyday Ethics of Nicole Holofcener', *Camera Obscura*, 85, pp.136–59.

Perkins, Claire and Constantine Verevis (2015), 'Introduction: Possible Films', in C. Perkins and C. Verevis (eds), *US Independent Film After 1989: Possible Films*, Edinburgh: Edinburgh University Press, pp. 1–14.

Rayns, Tony (2013), Review of *For Ellen*, *Sight & Sound*, 23: 3, p. 95.

San Filippo, Maria (2011), 'A cinema of recession: micro-budgeting, micro-drama, and the 'Mumblecore' movement', *Cineaction*, 85.

Scott, A. O. (2014), Review of *Laggies*, *The New York Times*, 23 October, <http://www.nytimes.com/2014/10/24/movies/laggies-stars-keira-knightley-embracing-immaturity.html> (last accessed 19 April 2015).

Scott, A. O. (2009), 'Neo-neo realism', *The New York Times*, 17 March, <http://www.nytimes.com/2009/03/22/magazine/22neorealism-t.html?pagewanted=all> (last accessed 21 April 2015).

Schatz, Thomas (2009), 'New Hollywood, New Millennium', in W. Buckland ed., *Film Theory and Contemporary Hollywood Movies*, Hoboken, Taylor and Francis, pp. 19–46.

Schoonover, Karl (2012), 'Wastrels of Time: Slow Cinema's Laboring Body, the Political Spectator, and the Queer', *Framework*, 53: 1, 65–78.

Shaviro, Steven (2010), 'Slow Cinema vs. Fast Films', *The Pinocchio Theory*, 12 May, <http://www.shaviro.com/Blog/?p=891> (last accessed 13 April 2015).

Silverstein, Melissa (2009), 'Interview with Lynn Shelton, Director of *Humpday*', *The Huffington Post*, 8 August, <http://www.huffingtonpost.com/melissa-silverstein/interview-with-lynn-shelt_b_227673.html> (last accessed 15 April 2015).

Taubin, Amy (2007), 'Mumblecore: All talk?' *Film Comment*, November/December, <http://www.filmcomment.com/article/all-talk-mumblecore> (last accessed 4 March 2015).

Tuttle, Harry (2010), 'Slow Films, Easy Life', *Unspoken Cinema*, 12 May, <http://unspokencinema.blogspot.com/2010/05/slow-films-easy-life-sight.html> (last accessed 13 April 2015).

9. BLACK WOMEN, ROMANCE AND THE INDIEWOOD ROM COMS OF SANAA HAMRI

Shelley Cobb

> I very clearly stated that my colleague had challenged every form of filmmaking because she was a Black woman standing behind the camera and she put Black women in front of it! That combination alone defied every form.
>
> Carmen Coustaut (1998: 140)

> Images of romantic love on film tend to reduce Black women to sex objects and male adornment – in other words, he looks good if she looks good hanging off his arm. But I always want to know who she is.
>
> Carmen Coustaut (1998: 141)

Black Women Directors in Contemporary American Cinema

In 2014, Ava DuVernay became the first black woman director to be nominated for the Golden Globe's Best Director award. An important first, this was quickly followed by the Academy Awards' Best Picture nomination for her film *Selma*, the first film by a black woman director to be nominated for that prestigious category. Widespread critical praise for *Selma* and for its star David Oyelowo, who plays Martin Luther King, Jr, increased the public profile of both DuVernay and Oyelowo. However, controversy swirled around the conspicuous lack of nominations for DuVernay's directing from the Academy and the Directors' Guild, and the fact that the Academy and the BAFTAs did not recognise Oyelowo's performance with nominations. The mixed recognition by awards institutions for a widely praised film featuring African Americans both behind and on the screen gave rise to many opinion pieces about the representation of black Americans in film, the lack of diversity among members of the various awarding bodies, the low numbers of women directing feature films in Hollywood, and, most importantly, the even lower numbers and rarer occurrence of black women directing Hollywood films or feature films at all. DuVernay, however, is not the first black woman to direct a Hollywood feature film; she is the third. The first was French filmmaker Euzhan Palcy who directed Marlon Brando in the 1989 film adaptation *A Dry White Season*. The second was Darnell Martin who wrote and directed the 1994 romantic comedy *I Like It Like That*. The twenty years between Martin's first feature (which made her the first black American woman to direct a Hollywood film) and DuVernay's Golden Globe nomination for her first studio film should surely be read as a symptom of Hollywood's systemic discrimination against black women filmmakers.

Compared to Hollywood, the independent film scene in America has been a more productive, if not welcoming, place for black women filmmakers. This arena has allowed these women to make shorts, documentaries and features, the significance of which has been articulated and analysed by critics such as Jacqueline Bobo and Gloria J. Gibson, who show that black women's filmmaking in America has a long history. During the 1990s evolution of American independent cinema (with major studios entering into the sector) three independent feature films by African-American women achieved both critical and box-office success, to varying degrees; all have become key films for scholarship on contemporary women's cinema and African-American cinema. Julie Dash's *Daughters of the Dust* (1991), financed by the National Endowment for the Arts, Women Make Movies and other grants, and then distributed by Kino International, was the first full-length feature film with general theatrical release made by an African-American woman.[2] Miramax distributed Leslie Harris' *Just Another Girl on the I.R.T.* (1992), which won the Special Jury Prize at the Sundance Film Festival. And Kasi Lemmons' *Eve's Bayou* was the highest grossing independent film of 1997. Dash's and Harris' feature films appear during what Paula Masood describes as the early 90s rise and fade of Black City Cinema by black filmmakers, which includes films such as *Boyz N the Hood* (John Singleton, 1991), *Menace II Society* (Allen and Albert Hughes, 1993), and *Set It Off* (F. Gary Gray, 1996) (Masood 2003: 176). Their films also appeared at a time when women filmmakers such as Nancy Savoca and Allison Anders were, as Christina Lane puts it, on 'the verge of an indie explosion' (Lane 2005: 196).

Although the early 90s are seen by some as a renaissance of black cinema in America, the numbers of black women involved were actually very low. Of the fifteen black directors who released feature films in 1991, Julie Dash was the only woman.[3] In 'Black Women's Films: Genesis of a Tradition', Bobo situates the indie films discussed above within the history of black women filmmakers throughout the twentieth century, arguing that 'centering Black women as subjects recognisable as human beings is paramount in Black women's films' (1998: 8). And in her article 'Black Women's Independent Cinema', Gloria Gibson considers three films from the 1980s and shows that '[films by black women] provide narratives that relate to historical occurrences and conditions, beliefs and values that are germane to black women. Consequently, their cinematic frames challenge decades of "structural silence" levied against African-American women' (Gibson 2002: 314). Carmen Coustaut in her chapter 'Love on My Mind: Creating Black Women's Love Stories' from Jacqueline Bobo's 1998 edited collection *Black Women Film & Video Artists* argues that black women filmmakers challenge that structural silence by virtue of their very existence.

The first epigraph above is Coustaut's summation of her response, while on a panel of black women filmmakers, to a white woman who critiqued a black woman's documentary for not challenging the form at all. As Coustaut implies with her retort, the white woman's critique is informed by her own racial privilege in the ways that it disregards the marginalisation of black women throughout cinema history and the fact that black women's films about black women, no matter the form, can be understood as both political and aesthetic challenges to that history. The white woman's emphasis on form also may have been a product of the historical times in which feminist film studies privileged the avant-garde text and its ability to 'destroy . . . the satisfaction, pleasure and privilege' of the masculine gaze as argued in Laura Mulvey's seminal article 'Visual Pleasure and Narrative Cinema' (Mulvey 1999: 69). The ability of the avant-garde to challenge the dominant whiteness and patriarchy of cinema has also been championed by bell hooks in her work on African-American filmmakers: 'If we long to transform the culture . . . then we have to embrace the avant-garde/the experimental' (hooks 1996: 107). At the same time, however, hooks admires Julie Dash's narrative short film *Illusions* – the story of an African-American woman passing as white in the 1940s film industry - for the ways that it uses Hollywood conventions and 'offers the black female spectator representations that challenge stereotypical notions that place us outside the realm of filmic discursive practices'. She also suggests the film is potentially problematic because the ending leaves open the possibility that Mignon could just as easily be co-opted into the system as work to change it (hooks 1996: 211).

Taking all these thoughts together, the complex mix of socio-cultural historical factors which include racism, sexism, the historical domination of Hollywood cinema, the politics of form (both popular and alternative) and the cultural politics of black women's authorship cannot easily be teased apart, nor should they be. In this chapter, my focus on the independent romantic comedies of Sanaa Hamri raises all these issues because they are films by a black woman about black women that largely draw on mainstream aesthetics, both in form and narrative, and consequently have politically problematic elements, as hooks says of Dash's *Illusions*. However, as a feminist film scholar, I hold the view that because the number of women directing films remains so low and is clearly a product of a sexist industry and culture, the study of women's film authorship is inherently political, even if the films are not necessarily progressive. As a white woman, I recognise that this is doubly true for the study of black women filmmakers whose films are regularly left out of women's film studies and, more generally, film history. Hamri's films have been largely overlooked in studies of both contemporary black cinema and contemporary women's cinema.

This chapter seeks to begin to redress that absence, in the space available, by showing how Hamri and her films 'challenge all forms' by being films about black women by a black woman. Born in Morocco to a Muslim Moroccan father and a Jewish-American mother, Hamri moved to the United States to study theatre at Sarah Lawrence College where she received a scholarship. She began her directing career making music videos for the likes of Mariah Carey, Prince and Christina Aguilera, among others – a typical beginning on the path toward feature filmmaking for many male directors, but much less common for women. Hamri has directed three feature films, *Something New* (2006), *The Sisterhood of the Traveling Pants 2* (2008) and *Just Wright* (2010). She also directs television, including multiple episodes of *Nashville* (2012–), *Elementary* (2012–) and *Shameless* (the US version) (2011–). Hamri is not a writer, which consequently makes it difficult to label her an auteur. Her films also all fall in the broad chick-flick category, which is largely a culturally disparaged genre.

Hamri's films are independent by virtue of their production and distribution. Homegrown Pictures along with the mini-major Gramercy produced *Something New*, and Focus Features, the art-house division of NBCUniversal, distributed it. *Just Wright* was produced by Flavor Unit Entertainment with Fox Searchlight Pictures who also distributed the film. Both are aesthetically mainstream romantic comedies, making it harder to claim that Hamri's films raise 'questions of resistance and social oppression' (Bobo 1998: 14) or that they 'stem . . . from black feminism' (Gibson 2002: 314) in the same ways as do the films that Bobo and Gibson consider. However, they do centre black women as subjects and, consequently, they challenge the 'structural silence' imposed on black women. Consequently, I want to suggest that they do offer alternative representations of black women that productively engage with and even challenge the usual stereotypes, even as they use and conform to mainstream cinematic conventions. As such, it is possible to see them as inverting Martin L. Patrick's claim that Hollywood's 'usurp[ation] of new strategies in independent film ... continues to halt the progress of African-American cinema' through the ways that Hamri's films contribute to the development of African-American independent cinema by usurping Hollywood's aesthetic strategies (Patrick 2010: 45).[4]

Cinematic Romance and the Postfeminist Politics of the Black Lady

Hamri's *Something New*, produced by Stephanie Allain (Homegrown Pictures), written by Kriss Turner (who has previously written for the television shows *Living Single* (1993–8) and *Everybody Hates Chris* (2005–9)) and starring Sanaa Lathan, is a rare thing: a feature film about black women, written, directed and produced by black women. This fact in itself makes the film a challenge to the systematic silencing and marginalisation of black women in American cinema. In an interview, Hamri describes her film in terms of the productive potential Coustaut gestures towards in the epigraphs of this chapter:

> that it's produced, directed, written and starring all women of color. It's never happened as a major studio release in Hollywood and that's amazing ... In this film, not only do we have an African American lead as a woman, but we are looking at the film from her perspective as a human being versus a gratuitous moment in somebody else's movie. (Morales 2006)

One of the key ways in which Hamri's *Something New* (2006) and *Just Wright* (2010) both use and disrupt Hollywood cinema is through their romantic plots: in *Something New*, Kenya McQueen (Lathan), an 'uptight' accountant, falls for Brian (Simon Baker), her white landscape gardener, of whom Kenya's upper-middle class family disapprove; in *Just Wright*, Queen Latifah's Leslie Wright is a physical therapist who falls for pro basketball player Scott McKnight (Common) while helping him recover from a career-threatening injury. As Donald Bogle has shown, American cinema has an ongoing inability to portray black women as anything other than mammies, jezebels and tragic mulattos (Bogle 2004). And as Coustaut says in the second epigraph to this chapter, the black woman is often on the margins of the romantic plot, as the sex-object, or the adornment for the male hero. In making the case for her own film, Coustaut argues '[Stories about love] can be constructive, political projects. There are few films from Black women's perspectives about romance' (Coustaut 1998: 140).

The politics of Hamri's films I consider here are simple but clear: they are by a black woman and are about black women and love. Furthermore, as I will show, as romance films they also challenge the conventions of what Michele Schreiber calls 'the postfeminist romance', film that encompasses a range of genres, from romantic comedies to dramas and art films. Schreiber articulates the key tenet of the postfeminist romance as 'choice', a choice usually between love and career:

> The most significant of these is the age-old choice between career versus love and family, but such dilemmas also include the choice between sexual expression, and self-absorption and community investment, amongst others. (Schreiber 2014: 2–3)

Hamri's films do structure the plot around these kinds of choices, but their outcomes are, as I will show, different from postfeminist romance films about white women's search for the postfeminist cliché of 'having it all'. That the two films in this chapter fall within the historical period that many feminist media critics and scholars have labelled postfeminist is indisputable. How representations of black women and films by black women relate to postfeminist media culture, which all the key critics of postfeminist media (Rosalind Gill, Angela McRobbie, Diane Negra, and Yvonne Tasker, among others) have suggested is insistently white is complicated, and I will outline some of the issues below.[5] My claim in this chapter is that Hamri's films are, in Coustaut's words, productive political projects that challenge the history of American cinema's form as well as complicate the whiteness of postfeminism when it comes to the representation of black women.

As romance naratives, these films are sites of resistance to cinema's dominant whiteness through their casting of the black woman in the marriage plot. The traditional stereotypes of black women – the jezebel, the sapphire, the mammy – exist as binaries of the cult of true womanhood, which have idealised white women as pious, pure, submissive and domestic, and therefore deserving of marriage. Despite the long history of diverse and complex scholarship on nineteenth-century novels like Charlotte Brontë's *Jane Eyre* or the earlier novels of Jane Austen, for contemporary popular culture they epitomise the romance plot as a bildungsroman for women. This continues through the myriad film, television and new media adaptations of the novels, as well as the ways they are used as templates and sources for contemporary postfeminist romance novels and films, such as *Bridget Jones's Diary* and the *Twilight* saga, about young, white women who discover their worth through the process of finding/choosing the right man. The jezebel's wanton sexuality, the sapphire's angry dominance over black men, and the mammy's loyalty to her white slaves (which is grounded in the idea of her as sexless and superstitious), all function to exclude the black woman from the feminine bildungsroman narrative that portrays successful heterosexual coupledom as the climax of the coming of age plot for white women.

Those traditional stereotypes underpin the contemporary stereotypes of black women as the welfare queen, the angry black woman, the black bitch, and the black American princess. The latter two are the lower-class and the upper-class versions of the contemporary sapphire whose independence is a threat to black masculinity. Most relevant for the discussion at hand is the black American princess or the independent black woman who has her own money and does not need a man to take care of her and is therefore represented as domineering and unmarriable. The news media perpetuate this stereotype outside of fictional representations by reporting and re-reporting the statistics that of all women, black women are the least likely to be married, that black women are less likely to be married than black men, and that black women are less likely to be a part of the trend in assortative mating (marrying one's peer in educational status) because black women are much more likely to have higher education degrees than black men.[6]

In her book, *Beyond the Black Lady: Sexuality and the New African American Middle Class*, Lisa B. Thompson discusses the turn-of-the-century trend for 'feel-good films targeted at the black community' (Thompson 2009: 74), which are exemplified by 'romantic comedies [that] provide some of the most visible and enduring images of middle-class blacks' (ibid. p. 75). Thompson argues that these films are particularly pernicious in the ways they stereotype the black woman as a contemporary, middle-class sapphire:

> Popular African American romantic comedies like *The Best Man* and *Soul Food* consistently reward women who pursue traditional female roles. They present the desperate social circumstances of professional black women as the result of misplaced priorities and aggressive personalities. In essence, these films uphold and further the cultural stereotype of the black lady as cold, prim, passionless. They also, in light of bleak marriage rates for black professional women, send an alarmingly conservative message and signal a blacklash against the recent academic and professional successes the women have enjoyed. (Ibid. p. 76).

The two films by Hamri in this chapter are part of this trend for 'feel-good' films that focus on middle-class blacks.[7] Moreover, they all employ romance film conventions. However, Hamri's films refuse the stereotype of 'the black lady as professionally exceptional but personally doomed', allowing their protagonists to achieve both romantic and career success (Thompson 2009: 75).

In millennial postfeminist media, the backlash discourse of the vilified career woman, exemplified by *Fatal Attraction* (Adrian Lyne, 1987), modified into the trope of 'retreatism', which became, as Diane Negra shows, 'a recognizable narrative trope ... both film and television have incorporated fantasies of hometown return in which a heroine gives up her life in the city to take up again the role of daughter, sister, wife or sweetheart in a hometown setting' (Negra, 2004). However, this return to the home and often the downsizing, if not giving up, of work, for the postfeminist woman draws on a long history of the imbrication of domesticity and the idealisation of the middle-class white woman. As Evelyn Brooks Higgenbottom has shown in her early work on the politics of respectability and the early twentieth-century Baptist church, and as Kimberly Springer has articulated for contemporary representations of 'the black lady', black women cannot give up work outside the home without risking their respectability: 'black professional women must adhere to the role of the black lady, a role designed to counter accusations of black female licentiousness and one that can accommodate the ascension to middle-class status through work outside the home' (Springer 2007: 258). Springer goes on to show that:

> Films featuring black women protagonists also portray retreatism, but filmmakers attempt to make their departure points and destinations seem racially authentic. The black female heroine goes in one of two directions: she either returns to her family and the black community she has neglected or she turns to a tight network of sister-friends. (Ibid. p. 269)

Retreatist plots for black women, then, are partly predicated on the 'implication ... that when a black female protagonist has it all she becomes a snob and is in danger of no longer being authentically black' (ibid. p. 272). The films by Hamri complicate these issues to some extent. Both protagonists are working women, but they also have complicated relationships with their stay-at-home middle-class mothers who act as foils for the protagonists' more authentic blackness. This is signified through their decisions to 'remain true to themselves' by refusing retreatism to varying degrees, as well as by finding both love and career success rather than by following their mothers' paths.

Sanaa Hamri's Romantic Comedies

When there are so few black women filmmakers and so many stereotypes of black women on screen, Thompson's stance is an important one:

> Although few opportunities exist for African American women to direct feature films, filmmakers such as Cheryle Dunye, Darnell Martin, Leslie Harris, and Sanaa Hamri have joined Lemmons and Dash with complex

Figure 9.1 Kenya (Sanaa Lathan) and single-sister friends in *Something New* (2006).

narratives that allow for a broader range of African American characters. They continue to prioritize compelling, realistic, and nuanced depictions of black women who have sexual agency' (Thompson 2009: 94)

Hamri's films in particular situate their prioritisation of black women within the mainstream narrative and aesthetic style of the romantic comedy, a genre largely associated with white, straight women and the contemporary postfeminist politics of gender. By making the black woman the centre of this universe, the mainstream tropes of both the romantic comedy and postfeminist media culture are troubled and exposed, even as they, in many ways, remain intact.

Both films signal their genre early on. *Something New* begins with Kenya waking from a nightmare in which her wedding abruptly ends with an air-raid siren that sends all the guests and her groom running. When she wakes, Kenya realises it is Valentine's Day. While at work that day, her engaged colleague and friend bombards her with photos of wedding dresses and then promises to set her up on a blind date. At the end of her workday, Kenya has a message on her phone from an ex who is calling to invite her to his wedding. When she meets her single sister-friends for a drink that night, they all tell her that she is too uptight (signified by her slicked back hair, her suit, her fastidiousness, and her beige painted house) and needs to let go in order to find a man. Kenya's abject singleness and the film's focus on her point of view are quickly established within the first ten minutes of the film. In *Just Wright*, the first images of Leslie are of her working as a physical therapist with her patients, but within a minute, her co-worker asks her what time her blind date is. The blind date seems like a dream with Leslie and Mark (Laz Alonzo) hitting it off over dinner as they talk about work, future kids and food, and joke about getting 'toasted'. In the end, although Mark says he had a great time, he wants to be 'just friends' and gives Leslie a hug. As she tells her thin, conventionally sexy, husband-hunting, god-sister Morgan (Paula Patton), Mark thought she would 'make the perfect homegirl'. Leslie's abject singleness is signalled through her easy-going personality and down-to-earth style – she drives a broken down Mustang inherited from her grandfather; she's up for getting 'toasted' on a date; she's an unapologetic New Jersey Nets fan, who is appalled by Morgan going to the game to find a man rather than to watch the game. By putting Leslie, who is played by Queen Latifah, in opposition to Morgan, the film also implies, through comments made by Leslie's mother (Pam Grier) and the attention Morgan receives from men, that Leslie's weight is also a reason she is single.

All these tropes align Hamri's two romantic comedies with mainstream films with white protagonists that privilege their point of view, while presenting their singleness as abject – from *My Best Friend's Wedding* (P. J. Hogan, 1997), to *Bridget Jones's Diary* (Sharon Maguire, 2001) to *27 Dresses* (Anne Fletcher, 2008). They also appear to participate in the postfeminist obsession with consumption (Tasker and Negra 2007: 4). Schreiber argues that 'class plays a largely unspoken but significant role in the postfeminist romance film, as the wealth and upward mobility of the female characters undergird their personal dilemmas, but also enable a pleasurably commodified backdrop for their love affairs (Schreiber 2014: 15). Leslie comes from a middle-class family and Kenya from an upper-middle class family, and both films display wealth prominently in their *mise-en-scène*. Neither of their mothers appear to work, and each impresses on their daughter the need to dress in an appropriately feminine fashion. Both protagonists have recently bought homes that need a bit of fixing up, and both go to events where they must wear fashionable dresses – the Cotillion ball ('the black high-society event of the year') in *Something New*, and the birthday party for NBA star Scott McKnight in *Just Wright*. The films' settings in the black middle-class, rather than urban working-class, neighbourhoods, distinguish Hamri's comedies from the 'hood' films of the 1990s. They also set themselves apart from Hollywood's insistent habit of ignoring the black middle classes and stereotyping African Americans as unemployed, drug addicts, gangsters, and prostitutes. In Hamri's films class and upward mobility come into play in more complex ways than in most mainstream white romantic comedies.

Both Leslie's and Kenya's mothers' stay-at-home status appears to contradict Springer's claim that the black lady must work to retain respectability. Within the conventions of the romantic comedy though, both mothers are made out to be ridiculous if not abject. Leslie's mother clearly favours her god-daughter over her own daughter, regularly pointing out to Leslie that Morgan knows how to perform her femininity properly through her dress, physique and flirtatious ways. Before the two god-sisters head off to McKnight's birthday party, Leslie's mother brings her own mother's diamond earrings into the room where the two are getting dressed, thus setting up our assumption that she will give them to Leslie to wear. Instead she gives them to her god-daughter because, as she says, 'I know Leslie that you don't like the "splashy style"'. Though the line is followed with a joke about Leslie's preference for trousers over dresses, it is a painful moment: one that makes clear that this is not the kind of black lady that Leslie wants to be or ever will be. When she is married to (the very wealthy) Scott in the end, not only does she still have a job, but she also has her dream job as a trainer for the New Jersey Nets. Though she attained this new position because she was able to get Scott through his recovery from a torn ACL, it is still her skill and commitment to success that is on display throughout the film in scenes that parallel the display of Scott's skills and commitment to success on the court. In the very last scene, Leslie sits with the other NBA wives (and Morgan, whom she has invited) in the stands. But as a trainer for the team and super fan of the Nets, she still wears her jersey and trousers and shouts louder than anyone around her, in direct opposition to and in defiance of the upper-class femininity of the other wives and girlfriends around her. The opposition between Leslie's 'homegirl-ness' and other women has constructed her as more authentically black throughout the film; as such, and in distinction to Springer's argument above, her narrative successes – marriage, professional fulfilment, reconciliation with her god-sister – culminate in the film's happy ending and 'having it all' without being a snob.

Diane Negra shows how postfeminist media culture, and postfeminist chick flicks in particular, negotiate contemporary anxieties about women and work either by putting the protagonists in retreatist plots, in which they quit work or downsize their careers, or by 'celebrating female protagonists whose work places them in a clearly subordinate role and for whom any display of ambition would be out of character' (Negra, 2008: 87). Neither Leslie nor Kenya fulfils either of these postfeminist archetypes. Both have careers that require years of training (physical therapy and accountancy) and skill, and both display ambition. Kenya is in line to be made partner in her firm, and she relishes the possibility. Like Leslie, her fulfilment of the working requirements of the black lady is countered by her mother's presentation of another kind of abject type of black lady. For a brief period, after breaking up with Brian, Kenya dates successful tax lawyer Mark Harper, played by Blair Underwood. In a scene reminiscent of Bridget Jones's relationship with her mother, Mark incites an over-the-top reaction from Kenya's mother when he smugly says, 'Who knows what we'll be celebrating in six months', with his arm draped around a clearly-uncomfortable Kenya: the implication being that they might be getting engaged soon. With a silver coffee pot in her hand, Joyce McQueen (played by Alfre Woodard) cannot hold herself still. She gently bounces up and down on her feet while saying 'Oh my god' in a high register, and choking slightly on her impending tears when she says 'Let's just forget the coffee and pop some champagne', much to Kenya's horror. Back at Mark's house, after the evening with her parents, Kenya tells him their relationship is over, that he is 'too perfect'.

Her rejection of Mark and her eventual return to Brian together function as Kenya's rejection of her mother's expectations. Even more provocatively, it functions as the film's rejection of assortative mating and the expectation that such a match is the only kind that would cement her black lady status. At the earlier Valentine's dinner with her sister-friends – who are a judge, a banker and a paediatrician – one brings up the reports that '42.4% of black women have never been married' and that the 'problem is most acute amongst African-American women who are educated professionals'. In choosing Brian, Kenya defies these odds. Though Brian has a degree and used to work in advertising, his 'downgrading' to landscape architecture and working with his hands suggests, on the surface, that Kenya has rejected the perfect assortative match, which was Mark, for the more intuitive and emotional match that she finds with Brian.[8] Her marriage to Brian is not a retreatist choice either. Before they get back together and in a dramatic denouement, in which Kenya runs out of the Cotillion to the sounds of midnight chimes like Cinderella, Kenya wins her promotion to partner based on her skill and integrity with a difficult client. The wedding is held in her own backyard, in a nod to Brian's landscaping and the ways that he has loosened her up over the course of the narrative. This is another sign that Kenya rejects the uptight black lady type of her mother. Of course, it is also important that Brian is white. He has in the first half of the film, problematically, helped her to be more 'authentic' by encouraging her to get rid of her weave, to embrace colour in her clothes and house, and to choose love over racial compatibility. In its conclusion, though, the film uses some of the standard tropes of a rom com ending (the denouement and the wedding) and others uncommon in mainstream, white, versions of the genre (interracial romance and female career success) in a combination, like that in *Just Wright*, which exposes the limitations of scholarship on postfeminism to take into account representations of women of colour.[9]

In reference to Geoff King's claim that independent cinema's distinction from cinema rests largely on its 'avant-garde', 'art', or 'quality' style, Yannis Tzioumakis argues that

> the eclectic mixture of conventions from all these modes of filmmaking has created a distinct type of (generally low-budget) film that has been

> labelled independent primarily because of its difference from mainstream American cinema (special effects-driven blockbusters and expensive genre/star vehicles) and very often regardless of whether the film has been financed, produced and/or distributed by an independent company, a classics division, a major independent or even a major company. (Tzioumakis 2006: 248)

Hamri's films and my analysis of their relationship to both mainstream and black independent cinema suggests that there are other types of independent films that further complicate this loose distinction between the independent and the mainstream by virtue of their racial identities. In other words, my contention is that the dominant whiteness of mainstream cinema and the dominant whiteness of independent cinema mean that Hamri's films trouble the idea of independence as a style or 'mode of filmmaking' because they use mainstream conventions but would be very unlikely to be produced and financed by a major studio because of their focus on African-American women. That they also trouble the whiteness of the romantic comedy genre and the politics of postfeminist media means that they do much more interesting work than the lack of scholarship on them implies.

Notes

1. My focus in this chapter is on feature films but it is important to note that black women directors have made numerous independent short and video films. In another kind of chapter, we might also expand black women filmmakers to include those who work in other roles behind the camera such as producing. See Heyde and Bobo.
2. The first feature film directed by a black woman is Kathleen Collins' *Losing Ground* (1982). Though critically acclaimed it aired only on PBS and was never released in theatres. Dash is, of course, a part of the L. A. Rebellion of black filmmakers, and her first (and to date only) feature as well as her previous shorts are key films of that movement. See Diawara.
3. See Edward Byrne, 'Followin' Spike's X-Ample', *The Cresset: A Review of Literature, the Arts, and Public Affairs*, LVI: 3, pp. 28–31, <http://thecresset.org/FilmArchive/1993/Byrne_January%201993.html> (last accessed 22 May 2015).
4. Another important black American woman filmmaker whose independent films also function in this manner is Gina Prince-Bythewood.
5. For a more detailed articulation of the whiteness of postfeminism and the need to rethink the racialised politics of postfeminism, see Jess Butler, 'For White Girls Only? Postfeminism and the Politics of Inclusion', *Feminist Formations*, 25: 1, Spring 2013, pp. 35–58.
6. See 'Marriage in Black America', BlackDemographics.com, <http://blackdemographics.com/households/marriage-in-black-america> (last accessed 18 June 2015); and Gillian B. White, 'Marrying Your Peer, a Tougher Prospect for Black Women', *The Atlantic*, <http://www.theatlantic.com/business/archive/2015/04/marrying-your-peer-a-tougher-prospect-for-black-women/391586> (last accessed 18 June 2015); see also, for a refutation of these statistics, Nadra Kareem Nittle, 'Four Myths About Black Marriage', RaceRelations.com, <http://racerelations.about.com/od/

diversitymatters/a/Four-Myths-About-Black-Marriage.htm> (last accessed 18 June 2015).

7. An earlier film by a black woman director about the black middle classes is Kathleen Collins' *Losing Ground* (1982). See Gloria J. Gibson (2002), 'Black Women's Independent Cinema', in *Experimental Cinema: The Film Reader*, in Winston Wheeler Dixon (ed.), London: Routledge.
8. Brian's 'earthiness' works in opposition to Kenya's uptightness, and she eventually, and literally, lets down her hair, learns to love colour, and even dirt. The politics of black women's hair on display are complex in this film.
9. For a more detailed analysis of the politics of racism and interracial romance in *Something New*, see Tru Leverette, 'Guess Who's Welcome to Dinner: Contemporary Interracial Romance and the New Racism', reconstruction: studies in contemporary culture, 8.4 (2008) <http://reconstruction.eserver.org/Issues/084/leverette.shtml> (last accessed 7 December 2015).

References

Bobo, Jacqueline (1998), 'Black Women's Films: Genesis of a Tradition', in Jacqueline Bobo (ed.), *Black Women Film & Video Artists*, New York: Routledge, pp. 3–20.

Bogle, Donald (1994), *Toms, Coons, Mulattos, Mammies and Bucks: An Interpretive History of Blacks in American Films*, Oxford: Roundhouse.

Coustaut, Carmen (1998), 'Love on My mind: Creating Black Women's Love Stories', in Jacqueline Bobo (ed.), *Black Women Film & Video Artists*, New York: Routledge, pp. 139–52.

Diawara, Manthia (1993), *Black American Cinema*, New York: Routledge.

Gibson, Gloria J. (2002), 'Black Women's Independent Cinema', in Winston Wheeler Dixon (ed.), *Experimental Cinema: The Film Reader*, London: Routledge.

Gibson-Hudson, Gloria J., 'The Ties That Bind: Cinematic Representations by Black Women Filmmakers', in Jacqueline Bobo (ed.), *Black Women Film & Video Artists*, New York: Routledge, pp. 43–66.

Heyde, Paul (2006), 'Black Women Filmmakers Forum: An Alternative Aesthetic and Vision', *Black Camera*, 21:1, Spring/Summer, p. 15.

hooks, bell (1996), *Reel to Real: Race, Sex and Class at the Movies*, New York: Routledge.

Lane, Christina (2005), 'Just Another Girl Outside the Neo-Indie', in Chris Holmlund and Justin Wyatt (eds), *Contemporary American Independent Film*, New York, Routledge, pp. 193–209

Mask, Mia (2012), 'Introduction', *Contemporary Black American Cinema: Race, Gender and Sexuality at the Movies*, New York: Routledge, pp. 1–13.

Massood, Paula J. (2003), *Black City Cinema: African American Urban Experiences in Film*, Philadelphia: Temple University Press.

Morales, Winston (2006), 'Something New: an interview with Sanaa Hamri', blackfilm.com, <http://www.blackfilm.com/20060127/features/sanaahamri.shtml> (last accessed 15 July 2015).

Mulvey, Laura (1999), 'Visual Pleasure and Narrative Cinema', in Sue Thornham (ed.), *Feminist Film Theory: A Reader*, Edinburgh: Edinburgh University Press, pp. 58–69.

Negra, Diane (2004), 'Quality Postfeminism? Sex and the Single Girl on HBO', *Genders Online Journal*, 39, <http://www.genders.org/g39/g39_negra.html> (last accessed 15 July 2015).

Negra, Diane (2008), *What a Girl Wants: Fantasizing the Reclamation of Self in Postfeminism*, London: Routledge.

Patrick, Martin L. (2010), 'African-American Cinema', in John Berra (ed.), *American Independent*, Bristol: Intellect, pp. 42–5.
Schreiber, Michele (2014), *American Postfeminist Cinema: Women, Romance and Contemporary Culture*, Edinburgh: Edinburgh University Press.
Springer, Kimberly (2007), 'Divas, Evil Black Bitches, and Bitter Black Women: African American Women in Postfeminist and Post-Civil-Rights Popular Culture', in Yvonne Tasker and Diane Negra (eds), *Interrogating Postfeminism: Gender and the Politics of Popular Culture*, London: Duke University Press.
Tasker, Yvonne and Diane Negra (2007), *Interrogating Postfeminism: Gender and the Politics of Popular Culture*, London: Duke University Press.
Thompson, Lisa B. (2009), *Beyond the Black Lady: Sexuality and the New African American Middle Class*, Urbana: University of Illinois Press.
Tzioumakis, Yannis (2006), *American Independent Cinema: An Introduction*, Edinburgh: Edinburgh University Press.

PART III

IDENTITIES

10. FROM DOCUMENTARY TO FICTIONAL REALISM: MIRA NAIR'S DOCUMENTARY ROOTS, FICTIONAL HOME AND PRODUCTION POLITICS

Sarah Projansky and Kent A. Ono

The 1988 release of Mira Nair's film *Salaam Bombay!* immediately signalled her international significance as a director when the film earned an Oscar nomination and won numerous international festival awards, including two at Cannes. While this was her first fictional film, she had been making documentaries for nearly a decade, gaining recognition on the festival circuit with films such as *India Cabaret* (1985), which won several awards including one at the Athens International Film Festival. Although Nair has primarily made fictional films since 1988, to date she has directed one additional documentary, *Laughing Club of India* (2001), and she periodically makes biographically informed films, including *11'9'01* (2002) and *Amelia* (2009). Moreover, critics have noted the 'realistic' quality of her fictional films (e.g., Foster, 1997). And topically she has entertained global political events, such as Idi Amin's expulsion of Asian Indians from Uganda in 1972 (*Mississippi Masala* (1991)) and the 1980 Cuban boat lift (*The Perez Family* (1995)); and she has confronted matters relating to health and social justice, including the spread of HIV/AIDS (*Migration* (2008)) and women's rights within marriage (*How Can It Be* (2008)).

Despite her success with both fictional and documentary films and her concern with stories of real people and global political events, those who have studied her emphasise the fictional nature of her feature films. For instance, two reviewers address romance and class in her fictional films, even as they identify different feature films as relevant. In discussions of *The Namesake* (2006), Philip Kemp (2007) sees the film as the third in a trilogy that begins with *Mississippi Masala* and follows with *Monsoon Wedding* (2001); whereas Elizabeth Heffelfinger and Laura Wright view *The Namesake* as part of a different trilogy beginning with *Vanity Fair* (2004), followed by *The Namesake* and ending with *Amelia* (2011: 142). By focusing in this way primarily on recent fictional feature films, both Kemp and Heffelfinger and Wright miss an opportunity to draw connections, for example, among the documentary *So Far From India* (1983), the biopic *My Own Country* (1998) and *The Namesake*, all three of which explore an ethnically Indian man confronting his relationship to India and/or his identity as a resident (and, in *The Namesake*, citizen) of the United States. We suggest therefore that an approach to Nair as solely a fictional feature filmmaker – which is not limited to Kemp and Heffelfinger and Wright – restricts the scholarly understanding of her work.

In contrast, we argue that it is important to attend to all of Nair's films, as well as to her political efforts, in order to understand the larger cultural and political import of her work. We think more can be said about her fictional feature films, knowing what her documentaries and political work do and attending to the specific global political issues that many of her short films address. We also suggest that it is important to acknowledge that Nair engages the film industry as a transnational, independent filmmaker, working not only out of New York, but also out of India and Uganda. Thus, we emphasise that as an independent filmmaker she has her own production company, Mirabai films, and she often collaborates with another New York-based producer, Lydia Dean Pilcher, who has worked with Nair on nine films (since 2002, through her production company, Cine Mosaic). Additionally, Nair has two non-profit organisations, one supporting children in need and training them in film and other artistic practices (Salaam Baalak Trust, in India) and the other providing free film education in East Africa (Maisha). These aspects of Nair's career go beyond the films themselves, but nevertheless suggest a pattern of activism in film that in turn informs her film work. Thus, in this chapter we trace connections among all of her films – regardless of genre, intended audience, or funding source – as well as her approach to production and her involvement in social activist education.

As of 2014,[1] Nair has directed five documentaries, eleven full-length fictional films, and six fictional shorts (most of which are part of compilation films). Her films have been entirely independent (e.g., *Jama Masjid: Street Journal* (1979)), internationally funded (e.g., *The Reluctant Fundamentalist* (2012)), and occasionally entirely Hollywood funded (e.g., *Amelia*). They have shown on the festival circuit and then gone direct to video/DVD/digital release (e.g., *So Far From India*), and they have had both a rolled-out release (e.g., *Monsoon Wedding*) and a nation-wide release in the United States and the United Kingdom (e.g., *Vanity Fair*). They have aired on US television (e.g., *My Own Country*), Canadian television (*Children of a Desired Sex* (1987)) and UK television (*The Laughing Club of India*). They have featured unknown actors (e.g., *Salaam Bombay!*) as well as celebrities in both India (e.g., Irrfan Khan in *The Namesake*) and the United States (e.g., Denzel Washington in *Mississippi Masala*). They have been predominantly about people of Indian descent (e.g., *Monsoon Wedding*), Cuban descent (e.g., *The Perez Family*), and European descent (e.g., *Hysterical Blindness* (2002)). They have featured interracial relationships (e.g., *New York, I Love You* (2008)), and monoracial relationships (e.g., *Kama Sutra: A Tale of Love* (1996)). They have dealt with migration within nations (e.g., *Migration*) and between nations (e.g., *Mississippi Masala*), and they have dealt with life in a particular locale (e.g., *India Cabaret*). They have taken place predominantly in the United States (e.g., *New York, I Love You*), India (e.g., *Migration*), South Africa (e.g., *The Day the Mercedes Became a Hat* (1993)), England (*Vanity Fair*) and Pakistan (e.g., *The Reluctant Fundamentalist*). And they have been political (e.g., *11'9'01*), educational (e.g., *How Can It Be*), and entertaining (e.g., *Amelia*).

In short, Nair does not have one approach to filmmaking; nor does she seek to reach one particular kind of audience. This complex and diverse approach parallels her identity as a transnational (including US American) independent filmmaker. Thus, we argue that her films maintain an independent sensibility, even when she is working within the context of the Hollywood-conglomerate-controlled industry (e.g., *The Perez Family* with Samuel Goldwyn and *Amelia* with Fox Searchlight) and with major US celebrities (e.g., Reese Witherspoon in *Vanity Fair* and Natalie Portman in *New York, I Love You*). Furthermore, we would emphasise that Nair did not move from the documentary festival circuit to independent features to Hollywood; rather, she continuously moves among and across these modes of production. Similarly, she did not move from India to the United States to Uganda, taking her work with her; rather, she and her films continuously crisscross these locations. Thus, because of this continuous back and forth movement, we argue that there are traces of all three modes of production and all three locations in nearly all of her films.

It is important to acknowledge that many critics challenge Nair and her work on several levels. For instance, while ultimately sympathetic, Heffelfinger and Wright critique *Mississippi Masala*, *Monsoon Wedding* and *Amelia* for their collective classism, conventional romantic narrative outcomes, limitation of women's options and western-style frontier narratives. And Prateeti Punja Ballal (1998) is critical of *Mississippi Masala* for constructing a western (progressive)/postcolonial (backward) dialectic, as well as for representing only a middle-class diasporic identity and thereby masking the difficult economic histories of multiple diasporic subjects. Further, Jenny Sharpe is critical of gender, nation, and globalisation in *Monsoon Wedding* (2005: 73), and Jigna Desai (2004) is critical of that same film's heteronormativity.

Our goal is not to contradict these scholars; in fact, our own scholarly approach would likely lead us to similar conclusions were it not for our study of Nair's work as a whole. But, here, we place more emphasis on the possibilities we see in Nair's work, arguing that collectively her work engages social activism, maintains an educational impulse, attends to everyday experiences and forwards a postcolonial, diasporic, feminist, class, and cultural critique. To support this argument, we organise our analysis into three broad sections that stand out thematically in a review of her work: migration and everyday life, education and feminist critique. We conclude by suggesting that Nair's work illustrates a career-long independent sensibility that engages the institutionalised film industry and gestures towards global political effectivity.

Migration and the Everyday

Nair's work emphasises people in everyday life situations who are caught within the contexts of migration and its relationship to globalised economies; social strictures; class and caste relations; racial, gender, and immigrant intolerance; and events and circumstances of the day. Her films imagine individuals within social life, bringing out nuances in situations and locations. And her work explores larger social questions at the level of the local, the individual, and the relational. This familial, interpersonal, and community focus humanises – draws out human idiosyncrasies and individual conditions – in relation to social organisations and circumstances of migration.

The theme of migration runs through nearly every film Nair has directed, from her first documentary, *Jama Masjid: Street Journal*, in which she reflects on her difference from her subjects and implicitly acknowledges that she is a migrant, producing this film as a project for her degree from Harvard; to the recent *The Reluctant Fundamentalist*, in which Changez (Riz Ahmed) moves from Pakistan to the United States and back again. Even Nair's films about one particular place – such as *India Cabaret*'s look at a group of exotic dancers who live and work in one area or *How Can It Be*, which takes place entirely within one apartment and the street out in front – deal with migration, as both films end with a woman deciding to leave an untenable situation in order to make a better life for herself.

Given that the theme of migration emerges in nearly all of Nair's films and that her films are so diverse, what her films say about migration is not fixed or singular. For example, while her films repeatedly use the trope of a child looking out of the back of a car window as the car takes her or him away from home, this means different things each time we see it. In *Salaam Bombay!*, Solasaal (Chanda Sharma) is leaving one prison for another; the man who bought her as a virgin drives her away in his car as she watches her friend Krishna (Shafiq Syed) through the window. This movement is a continuation of Solasaal's difficult life as sexual property. Alternatively, in *The Day the Mercedes Became a Hat* when a white South African boy watches a black South African boy, with whom he has struck up a friendship of sorts, from the back of the car window as his parents drive away from their home (they are fleeing the country on the day of the funeral of assassinated black South African activist Chris Hani) the white boy is moving from a privileged position to (likely) another privileged position.

Nair's films also often depict cultural interaction, often through romance, as part of migration. For example, in *The Reluctant Fundamentalist* and *The Namesake* a Pakistani and Indian man, respectively, make sense of the United States in part through their romantic relationships with white women. But the interactions develop differently in each film. In *The Reluctant Fundamentalist* Changez loses Erica (Kate Hudson) because she cannot understand his hurt and anger over her exploitive and racist photographs of him, which she displays in an art exhibit for everyone to see, and because he cannot forgive her for her actions or for her inability to understand. Alternatively, in *The Namesake*, it is his father's death that helps Gogol (Kal Penn) realise that he does not want to be the Americanised person he performs when he is with his white girlfriend, Maxine (Jacinda Barrett). While he had assumed there was no cultural clash for him, that he simply was an 'American', losing his father throws him back into his Indian culture, forcing him to come to terms with his father's legacy and his relationship with his family.

Nair's films not only explore migration through narrative trajectories, as in the above examples, but they also address the physicality of place in relation to migration. For example, many of Nair's films include landscape shots, often taken from vehicles in which characters are moving from place to place. Here, locations, places, settings, and conditions give a sense of 'where' people are, of the beauty and feel of their surroundings, offering a distinctive sense of what life must be like for them. For example, in *Mississippi Masala* we see images of the Ugandan countryside as the Asian Indian family – father, mother, and young daughter – travels away from their home, forced to leave the country by Idi Amin. Thus, in this instance, the film explores exile, the experience of forced migration, and then what people go through when living in a new place, in this case Mississippi. Later in the film we see images of the Mississippi countryside as the daughter, now grown, willingly has a rendezvous with her African American lover. Both sets of images depict the landscape as beautiful – open, colourful, peaceful – regardless of whether the characters travel in despair and grief for a lost past or in joy towards a hopeful future. In both cases, place matters.

In other films street scenes locate characters in specific places. Nair's first documentary, *Jama Masjid: Street Journal*, is built entirely around shots of people in the streets of Jama Masjid, and the camera depicts not only the people but also the locations through which they move, including street markets. Additionally, the image of street children in *Salaam Bombay!* has become iconic of children's homelessness globally; images of homeless children in the streets, sometimes playing in flooding rainwater, appear in such films as *Three Seasons* (1999), *Slumdog Millionaire* (2008), and Nair's own *Monsoon Wedding*. While this image arguably has become trite more recently, rather than using homeless children's experience simply as a signifier of third world conditions, *Salaam Bombay!*'s original rendition explores those experiences in depth, including the details of hiding money and anything of emotional value behind a loose brick and of having to sleep on dirty concrete.

Additionally, Nair's films often contrast two characters' experiences, emphasising the differences in their lives in relation to the same everyday circumstances. For example, the documentary *So Far From India* contrasts the lives of husband and wife. The film depicts Ashok's life in New York, far from his pregnant wife, Hansa, and then later in the narrative far from Hansa and their new baby. We see Ashok working at a newspaper stand, eating a meal with a friend, and talking with an interviewer about how often he writes to Hansa (rarely) and why he has not sent for her yet. The film also spends time in India with Hansa, showing her cooking for her husband's family, singing to her child, and talking to an interviewer about her life. Thus, while the title of the film references Ashok's experience of being far from home, the film is equally interested in Hansa's life in India, which emphasises the complexity of family within conditions of diaspora.

The Perez Family also tells two different stories, in this case about members of the same family dealing with very different relationships that are affected by migration to the United States. The film is about two sets of Cuban immigrants living in Florida: first, a well-to-do mother, Carmela (Anjelica Huston), her grown daughter, and her overprotective brother; and, second, Juan Raul (Alfred Molina), her husband who has been in a Cuban prison for twenty years and has only now managed to immigrate to Florida; he forms a bond with Dottie (Marisa Tomei), a woman who is also immigrating. While Juan Raul searches for Carmela he also begins to fall in love with Dottie; meanwhile, Carmela admits to herself (it turns out in error), that Juan Raul will never come back, and so begins to allow herself to fall in love with someone else. These stories are parallel, in that they are about letting go of a fantasy past in order to find a connection with someone in the present, but they are also dramatically different in that Juan Raul is a refugee who sells flowers on the street to make a living while Carmela lives in a well-appointed home. While *The Perez Family* offers idyllic (doubled) heterosexual romance as a happy ending, the same/different narrative structure emphasises the specificity and diversity of immigrants' experiences.

Education

Arguably, the comparison of Carmela's and Juan Raul's very different experiences of migration, couched within romantic narratives, offers a gentle education for the audience, teaching us about migration and asking us to reflect on the challenges Cubans and Cuban Americans faced in 1980s Florida. Not all of Nair's films – or certainly her larger approach to film work – educate quite so gently, however. Much of her work, we argue, is overtly educational.

First, because Nair works across so many types of films, she is able to bring the politicised themes we discuss here to many different types of audiences. Her early documentaries, as well as *Salaam Bombay!*, played on the festival circuit, bringing the specificity of various different aspects of Indian culture and society to a global festival audience. Then, *Mississippi Masala* and *The Perez Family* reached a predominantly US audience, addressing the specificity of racialised experiences in the United States. *Kama Sutra: A Tale of Love* challenged audiences in India by explicitly depicting women's sexuality, and *Monsoon Wedding* became a global entertainment hit, while at almost the same time *My Own Country* taught US television audiences about the history of AIDS. And *Vanity Fair* and *Amelia* used big name stars, Reese Witherspoon and Hilary Swank, respectively, to reach out to a mainstream US audience, teaching about British colonial history and the story of Amelia Earhart in the process.

In addition to reaching these large and specific audiences, starting in 2002 many of Nair's short films (most released as segments of compilation films) grappled with political issues in a specifically educational way. For example, in the fictionalised *11'9'01* (a segment of *September 11*) we learn about a real person, Salman Hamdani (Suleman Din), a Pakistani American man who went missing on 9/11. As the film develops we learn that while he was accused of terrorism (an accusation the government investigated), he died in fact in an act of heroism, trying to rescue people from the burning twin towers. Towards the end of the film, Hamdani's mother speaks as if to her son, at his funeral:

> Perhaps if your name had been Jesus or David, it would have been a different story. They tell me I should be proud to raise such a noble son. First they called you a terrorist and now they call you a hero. You just went to help fellow human beings in need. You are a hero. But then I think, what does that mean? If I had raised you with wrong values, at least you would have been alive. Is this the price you pay for raising a compassionate human being? . . .

This film, then, teaches not only about Hamdani's death and life, but also – through his mother's words – about a resistant relationship to hegemonic narratives of 9/11 heroism, one that centres a mother's ambivalent relationship to sacrifice.

Migration, a segment of *AIDS Jaago*, is perhaps the most didactically educational of Nair's films. It tells a fictional story of Birju (Irrfan Khan), an Indian man who travels from the countryside to the city to find work. There he has a brief sexual encounter with a middle-class housewife, who unknowingly passes HIV to him. She, we assume, has acquired the virus from her husband, who is having an affair with a man. Birju then travels back home and unwittingly gives the virus to his wife, who becomes pregnant and passes the virus to their child. This narrative trajectory teaches the audience about how AIDS spreads, and the film teaches about HIV/AIDS in other ways as well. For example, Birju observes a street scene in which a performer dances with a giant blow-up penis (with a face), and talks to and jokes with his audience about AIDS. The hand-held camera is down in the street with the performer and the people, placing the audience there as well. The performance is funny and fun, but also serious. The performer asks: 'Are you scared? My brother, when you feel the urge then not even the Lord of Death can stop you'. When a man in the crowd yells 'Could you stop yourself!?' the performer continues: 'Why should I stop? Am I not a man? I'll eat the whole chocolate and lick my fingers after! But! I have a trick I use to save myself. I always wear this', as he points to a condom blown-up like a balloon and attached to his chest. Here, performance and play not only teach the characters within the film but also, hopefully, the audience. At the end, the film offers a direct and directive address to the audience. After a grim scene of Birju in the hospital with his wife and newborn baby as he learns that he has passed HIV to them, the film offers two intertitles on a black screen: 'Protect those you love' and 'Wear a condom'.

This is not the only film Nair has made about AIDS. *My Own Country* is based on Dr Abraham Verghese's (Naveen Andrews) memoir about working in the mid-1980s as an infectious disease doctor in Johnson City, Tennessee, as AIDS spread to that small community. The film depicts the complexity of the lives of AIDS patients, from the deep love between Chester (Sean Hewitt) and Langdon (William Webster) as they face Chester's death; to Vicky's (Glenne Headly) fury at her husband Clyde (Oliver Becker), who is dying of AIDS and has passed HIV to her; to Gordon's (Adam Tomei) return home to his loving family to die, a family he had left because he could not tell them he was gay; to husband and wife Lloyd (Hal Holbrook) and Hope (Swoosie Kurtz), who finally make the decision to tell their family that Lloyd is dying and Hope will eventually die from AIDS, a disease Lloyd acquired from a heart transplant that took place only months before hospitals started testing donated blood and organs for AIDS. Emphasising the specificity and diversity of the people who are living with and dying from AIDS, the film insists on the humanity of all the characters, taking particular care to show how deeply Chester and Langdon love each other – Dr Verghese's nurse watches the couple interact and comments: 'Lord, I'd die for a man to love me like that' – while also documenting the pain of discrimination when at the hospital Chester's brother makes the decision to keep Chester on life support, even though Langdon, Chester's life-partner, knows and says that Chester asked to be let to die in peace.

Other Nair films teach history. For example, *Vanity Fair* takes place in England in the 1800s. Although the film follows the novel on which it is based by focusing on Becky Sharp's life in England, it also spends time documenting colonisation by depicting the English characters consuming Indian foods and textiles as a form of privilege and pleasure. In addition, the film ends with an extended scene of Becky's move to India, where she presumably will make her life anew. While this scene is a passing thought for Becky in the novel, in the film it becomes both the narrative's conclusion and a window into Becky's future. As Nair puts it, 'I wanted to weave in India, because all the men were making their fortunes there in the story and each one had a relationship to it. I took that skein of what was already given in the novel and just flew away with it' (Lamborn 2004).

Many of Nair's films encourage the audience to reflect critically, for example by repeatedly drawing attention to film's constructed nature and thereby encouraging the audience to think about film as film rather than just as story. For example, in *Jama Masjid: Street Journal* Nair's voiceover comments on whoever looks at her camera as she shoots in the streets – men, boys, and unveiled women – and on who does not look, just as we see veiled women pull their burkas further up to cover their entire faces as they turn away from the camera. Nair's narration notes this and reflects upon it, refusing to offer a definitive interpretation and thus cautioning her audience to reflect deeply on what they see. She says,

> Is it possible that these women are happy with their veiled existences? It seems un-liberated to me, but then perhaps it is the most effective way of maintaining some private space in this extraordinary public community. Why then are some women so obviously resentful about what I represent? I don't think it's because they feel I'm intruding into their privacy, for in Jama Masjid as in many older parts of India the concept of individual privacy really doesn't exist.

Nair offers education above and beyond her films, as well. Her non-profit film school, Maisha, located in Kampala, Uganda, opened in 2005 with a screenwriting lab and now also offers courses in directing, producing, cinematography, editing, sound recording, acting, and documentary, as well as running a film festival (Emslie 2010). When opening the school, Nair said: 'My goal is, in five years, to be able to present to the world a locally told story made in

Uganda or Tanzania, but with the highest of international standards' (quoted in Kamin 2004). Articles about Maisha often quote Nair saying something such as: 'It is wrong to let other people speak for us. We should tell our own stories' (Ssejjengo 2013). Nair links this need to 'tell our own stories' directly to colonialism: 'The cruelest impact of colonialism was the belief that we are incapable of representing ourselves, our cultures being akin to a child or sick person who needs a guardian to serve as an intermediary . . . We must put this crisis of self-confidence behind us' ('Mira Nair debuts' 2005). Thus, Maisha combines the act of education with some of the political investment we read in and across her films, in this case grappling with the continuing impact of colonialism by reaching the filmmakers as opposed to the audience.

In 1988, Nair used earnings from *Salaam Bombay!* to found Salaam Baalak Trust, run by her mother Praveen Nair, which provides shelters for homeless children, collaborates with other NGOs, and helps to remove children from forced or exploitive labour conditions ('22 kids' 2014). While Salaam Baalak Trust is not solely an educational organisation, it does contain many educational components. For example, the Trust runs the Salaam Baalak City Walk, 'a walking tour of the city's Paharganj and New Delhi Railway Station areas aimed at sensitising others about street life and street children' ('From Paharganj Streets' 2010). It also participates in seminars to educate the public both in India and abroad about the lives of street children ('NGOs organize' 2012), and it helps to educate children about health issues such as HIV/AIDS ('Child-friendly' 2006). Furthermore, the children who live in the shelters have access both to general education and to education in the digital and performing arts (Gupta 2014). Sanjoy Roy, a founding trustee, explains: 'Drama and arts classes play a cathartic and therapeutic role, providing traumatized young people with a way to express and explore the pain, insecurity, and broken dreams' (quoted in Gupta 2014). Based on this work, in 2014 Salaam Baalak Trust won the National Arts and Humanities Youth Program Awards 'in recognition of SBT's use of the creative and performing arts to bring change in the lives of disadvantaged children' (Gupta 2014).

In short, Nair's educational impulse works at multiple levels, from seeking to impact individuals' health in relation to HIV/AIDS (*Migration*, Salaam Baalak Trust), to redefining how people live with AIDS (*My Own Country*), to challenging post-9/11 racism (*11'9'01*), to articulating the complexity of gender politics in everyday life (*Jama Masjid*), to offering a revisionist history of 1800s English/Indian colonial interaction (*Vanity Fair*), to producing new ways of understanding for both audiences and filmmakers (Maisha). Thus, we are suggesting that Nair's film work is deeply invested in education as a vehicle for social change for audiences, for filmmakers, and for everyday children.

Feminist Critique

Many of the examples we have discussed thus far implicitly illustrate a feminist perspective on issues of migration, the everyday and education. From the inclusion of the wife's perspective on her husband's migration in *So Far From India*, to Nair's narration on the complexity of Muslim women's relationship to the burka on the streets of Jama Masjid, to *Salaam Bombay!*'s depiction of forced child prostitution, to the privileging of mothers' perspectives on HIV/AIDS and a son's tragic heroic death in *Migration* and *11'9'01*, respectively, Nair's films persistently consider women's perspectives even when the narratives are ostensibly about men.

In fact, a great deal of the scholarship on Nair defines her as a feminist filmmaker. For example, in her comparison of Thackeray's and Nair's version of *Vanity Fair*, Ana Moya (2010) points out that in Thackeray's novel Becky is awkward and masculinised; and, because of her ambition and intellect, she is othered within Victorian society. In Nair's version, however, Moya argues, 'Becky undergoes a process of feminisation and is rescued by Nair from Thackeray's construction of her as a monstrous female masculine' (2010: 84). Thus, Moya reads the film as revealing the constructedness of gender and highlighting the postcolonial dimensions of Thackeray's novel. Here, we continue this attention to Nair's films' feminism by focusing on how the films use aesthetics and characterisation within relationships to centre women's experiences and humanity.

Monsoon Wedding is one of the more intriguing examples of an explicitly feminist narrative because, as Nair articulates,

> I wanted to make a commercial movie. Weddings often figure in popular movies in India. . . . I wanted to reach the same people who go to those blockbuster movies, but I wanted to incorporate social comment . . . It's very nice to not lose your own tone, your own voice, and still reach millions of people. (Badt 2004)

The social commentary to which she refers includes a narrative about sexual abuse in the family. This story develops slowly, first in a way that only those attuned to issues of sexual violence likely would recognise, but by the end of the film in such an explicit way that any audience could understand.

When Tej (Rajat Kapoor) arrives at the family home for the wedding, close-ups of Ria (Shefali Shetty), the bride's cousin, show her visibly distraught: she is crowded in the frame, often moving backward and away from the group, and constantly looking off frame. Point of view shots show Tej as the troubling object of her gaze. When he greets her warmly, she responds coldly, and when he offers to pay for her graduate education she appears even more distraught.

Figure 10.1 *Monsoon Wedding* (2001): Ria (Shefali Shetty) confronts her attacker as her uncle looks on.

Having established for some spectators that Tej had previously abused Ria, the film then insists that this is not just a bad memory but a very real present-day threat, not only because Ria's peace is disrupted but also because Tej begins to approach another young girl, Aliya (Kemaya Kidwai). And, again, the film establishes this danger through Ria's perspective, depicting her watching Tej and Aliya together in the kitchen such that Tej's kiss on the top of Aliya's head appears not fatherly (as an uncle's kiss on a child's head might) but ominous. After the kiss, Ria enters the kitchen and glowers at Tej, who shows that he knows why she is upset when he immediately leaves the room. Later, when Tej offers to take the sleepy Aliya home and the girls' mother does not yet know of a reason to say no, Ria has no choice but to speak of Tej's abuse explicitly – to the family and to the audience. Putting her body in front of Tej's car as he tries to pull away, she confronts him: 'What did you get out of it!? I didn't even have breasts. Seven afternoons. "This is how grownups kiss. Open your mouth Ria." Now you're doing it all over again to Aliya'.

By moving through these three stages of attention to Ria's experience – her private pain, her protection of Aliya, and her public declaration of Tej's violation – the film insists that the audience take Ria's perspective seriously. But it does not stop there. After speaking of her childhood experience of abuse, Ria flees the family. When her uncle, the bride's father, begs her to come back – 'the wedding cannot happen without you' – she reluctantly agrees. At first her uncle maintains a traditional understanding of the meaning of family, overlooking and downplaying the sexual assault in favour of keeping his family together. But he cannot tolerate his own pain over Ria's experience, and thus he shifts to a modern understanding of family, expelling the sexual offender from the family and thereby making it possible for Ria to maintain her sense of family. In this way, *Monsoon Wedding* tells a feminist story of sexual assault, one that requires both Ria's uncle and the audience to give up any thoughts of tolerance or dismissal in relation to men's sexual assault of young girls in their families.

Unlike *Monsoon Wedding*, *How Can It Be* is specifically marketed as a feminist segment of *8*, a film that addresses the United Nation's Millennium Development Goals through eight shorts directed by eight different directors. Marketing connects Nair's segment to the goal 'to promote gender equality' ('Short films' competition "8. Time is short"' 2011). Specifically, Nair's segment teaches about a woman's life when caught between a man with whom she has fallen in love and a loveless marriage that nevertheless includes a dearly loved son. Told entirely within Zainab's (Konkona Sen Sharma) apartment – until she puts on her veil and leaves the house to join the man she loves – we learn that she has no choice but to leave. Zainab's voiceover explains to her son, in a video letter she leaves for him: 'There will be no little hands where I'm going. No little words to wear in my heart. No one to call me Munna Sona. But there will be other big words, Babu, that I hope will mean something to you one day. Like integrity, like courage, and perhaps, forgive me, adventure. A belief in something you start'. While Zainab does not achieve gender equality – she must leave her son – she moves towards it, making the choice to leave her marriage and thereby to maintain her integrity, her humanity.

Nair's films often address women's humanity in relation, in particular, to their sexuality. *Kama Sutra: A Tale of Love*, of course, is famous for its explicit representation of women's sexuality, having been censored in India when it was first released. What is important for us here is the specific way the film depicts women's bodies and sexuality. Certainly, this film offers images of women's bodies in erotic situations, and thus as potential objects of the gaze; yet, the narrative positions the women's bodies in the context of a story about a woman's relationship to her own sexuality. Thus, when Maya (Indira Varma) has sex for the first time, giving herself willingly to the King (Naveen Andrews), although she is slightly apprehensive, she makes the decision to approach him and expresses pleasure during their love-making. As in most of the sex scenes in Nair's films, the bodies move slowly and sensually, together. The camera is close to the bodies and, while this fragments those bodies, it does so in a way not that objectifies but that draws attention to a woman's pleasure, for example, as she moves her foot against her own leg or against her partner's foot.

When a woman in a Nair film is uninterested in sex, however, the scene is quite different. For example, in *The Perez Family* when Dottie moves from wanting to have sex with Steve (Bill Sage), a good-looking but (she discovers) racist guard at the makeshift refugee camp where she is living, to not wanting to have sex with him, the camera is overhead and at a distance as he roughly turns her over onto her stomach just before she extracts herself from the situation. While her body is on display throughout much of the film and she engages in erotic interaction with Juan Raul in several scenes (much as in *Kama Sutra*), in the scene with Steve the position of the camera and Dottie's actions protect her body from the spectator's view. Thus, in Nair's films the woman's body is available to the spectator only when the character herself is sexually or erotically engaged. In this way, when spectators gaze at her body, they simultaneously gaze at a woman making her own choices, engaging in her own sexuality and pursuing her own pleasures.

Women in Nair's films pursue not only their own erotic interests but also their emotional and relational interests through unyielding emotional connections with others. Nair's segment in *New York, I Love You* is perhaps the most dramatic example of this. In this film, an Indian Jain man, Mansukhbhai (Irrfan Khan), and a white Hasidic woman, Rifka (Natalie Portman), interact in a work context as she buys diamonds from him. At first glance they have nothing in common, and yet as they talk they find that they share an ironic attitude towards their respective religions' rules about which foods one cannot eat, and they laugh and agree over the joke, 'That's why there are no Christians in the diamond market. How can you trust a person who will eat anything?' While a counter separates them during much of their scene together, when Rifka reveals to Mansukhbhai that she has shaved her head in preparation for her wedding the next day and is wearing a wig, he comes around the counter and approaches her. He tells her (and perhaps teaches the audience) that the hair in her wig might have come from a temple in India, and then she takes off her wig, revealing her shaved head. In a moment of deep connection, a close-up shows him putting his lips to her shaved head and kissing her gently, and another shows her face as she closes her eyes, perhaps in pleasure, perhaps in peace. While their religions and cultures are quite different, by talking openly with each other they have found a connection that persists for each of them in fantasy, even as the film shows that Rifka has gone ahead with her marriage.

This kind of deep connection exists between two women in several films, as well. For example, in *Hysterical Blindness*, even as best friends Beth (Juliette Lewis) and Deb (Uma Thurman) avoid and critique each other at times, and even as Deb ditches Beth in order to spend time with a man who is clearly using her for sex, the two women love each other deeply and seem to function as each other's life partner. The film ends with the two sitting on the stoop, watching Beth's daughter play and reminiscing about the past. This emotional connection is so strong in Nair's films that it can emerge even for women who never actually meet. In *The Perez Family*, as Carmela starts to let go of the dream of her husband Juan Raul returning she begins a relationship with John (Chazz Palminteri) and agrees to go dancing with him at a club. Simultaneously, Dottie is negotiating her relationship with Steve while dancing at the same club. The camera shows both couples on the dance floor, close together but unaware of each other. In a passing moment Carmela and Dottie bump into each other and for an instant grasp hands. Fleetingly, their hands appear clasped together in close-up, and then each woman returns to the process of making sense of her feelings about her romantic relationship. Carmela and Dottie do not know that the brief image of their clasped hands represents a family connection in that they are both connected to Juan Raul, that it represents a narrative connection in that they are both working to come to terms with their relationships to love, and that it represents the unfulfilled possibility that they could be good friends; but spectators (might) know these things. For those who have watched many of Nair's films, a close-up of the clasped hands of two women reminds us of women's humanity, and of how they pursue their own choices, not for others but for themselves.

Conclusion

It becomes clear when looking across all of Nair's films, as well as her non-profit work, that she is not satisfied with an analysis of globalisation that centres the positive nature of transnationalism. Indeed, her take on globalisation includes a devotion and commitment to exploring, unearthing, and bringing to light the experiences of ordinary people. Thus, Nair's films remind us that one of the foremost effects of globalisation is autonomisation, anonymity, and the reduction of the subject to function, and ultimately the construction of the subject as 'bare life' (Agamben 1998). It is in response to the way politics is distributed 'biopolitically' (Foucault 1997), with some deemed worthy of life and others deemed worthy of death, that we can understand Nair's films. To counter the dehumanising effects of globalisation which tend to reduce subjects and their subjectivity to the particular role or mechanism they play within capitalist processes, one must humanise and breathe life into characters within narratives. It is not odd, then, that Nair emphasises the individuality, the uniqueness, of her subjects; in her film work – including her fictional films, documentaries, and social activism – she foregrounds the social experiences and realities of everyday people. Thus, as a transnational independent filmmaker, Nair demonstrates that simply knowing about changing social conditions does not erase the 'living within' conditions that subjects must experience. In this way, one can see Nair's approach as a critique of the social critique that sees subjects as merely the passive effects of power and not as subjects with agency, affect, bodies, and experiences within their lived conditions, that is, their lives.

NOTE

1. Unfortunately, as of this writing, *Words with Gods* (2014), which includes a segment directed by Nair, has not been released on DVD or in digital distribution; and we have not been able to attend any of the festivals at which it has played. Thus, in this essay we are able to address Nair's films only up to *The Reluctant Fundamentalist* (2012). In addition, we have been unable to locate a copy of *Children of a Desired Sex* (1987).

REFERENCES

'22 kids found in east Delhi sweatshops' (2014), *The Times of India* (online), 13 June.

'Abu Dhabi Film Commission announces summer camp with Maisha Film Lab' (2009), *Emirates News Agency*, 9 May.

Agamben, Giorgio (1998), *Homo Sacer: Sovereign Power and Bare Life*, trans. Daniel Heller Roazen, Stanford: Stanford University Press.

Badt, Karin Luisa (2004), '"I want my films to explode with life": An interview with Mira Nair', *Cineaste*, Winter, pp. 10–15.

Ballal, Prateeti Punja (1998), 'Illiberal Masala: The diasporic distortions of Mira Nair and Dinesh D'Souza', *Weber: The Contemporary West*, 15: 1, n.p.

'Child-friendly HIV, AIDS awareness communication materials launched' (2006), *The Hindustan Times*, 30 March.

Desai, Jignai (2004), *Beyond Bollywood: The Cultural Politics of South Asian Diasporic Film*, New York: Routledge.

Emslie, Rowan (2010), 'Reclaiming national culture', *The Independent* (Kampala), 1 September.

Foster, Gwendolyn Audrey (1997), *Women Filmmakers of the African and Asian Diaspora: Decolonizing the Gaze, Locating Subjectivity*, Carbondale: Southern Illinois University Press.

Foucault, Michel (1997), 'Society must be defended', in Mauro Bertani and Alessandro Fontana (eds), *Lectures at the Collège de France, 1975–76*, trans. David Macey, New York: Picador.

'From Paharganj streets to Atlanta: A love story' (2010), *Indian Express*, 10 July.

Gupta, Gargi (2014), '$10,000 international award for Salaam Baalak Trust', *Daily News and Analysis* (Mumbai), 12 November.

Heffelfinger, Elizabeth and Laura Wright (2011), *Visual* difference: *Postcolonial Studies and Intercultural Cinema*, New York: Peter Lang.

Kamin, Debra (2004), 'Nair unspools film lab for Africans, Asians', *Variety*, 8 July, p. 8.

Kemp, Philip (2007), '*The Namesake*', *Sight & Sound*, April, pp. 74–5.

Lamborn, Karyn Kubo (2004), 'Director Mira Nair adds Indian flair to *Vanity Fair*', *International Examiner*, 1 September, p. 15.

'Mira Nair debuts movie lab' (2005), *India Abroad*, 2 September, p. A5.

Moya, Ana (2010), 'The politics of re-presenting *Vanity Fair*: Mira Nair's Becky Sharp', *Atlantis: Journal of the Spanish Association of Anglo-American Studies*, 32: 2, pp. 73–87.

'NGOs organize seminar' (2012), *NGO Daily News*, 18 December.

Rivera, Raynald C. (2013), '17 participate in Maisha filmmaking lab', *The Peninsula* (Doha), 22 January.

Sharpe, Jenny (2005), 'Gender, nation, and globalization in *Monsoon Wedding* and *Dilwale Dulhania Le Jayenge*', *Meridians: Feminism, Race, Transnationalism*, 6: 1, pp. 58–81.

'Short films' competition "8. Time is short": Awards ceremony' (2011), *ACTED* 28 January, <http://www.acted.org/en/short-films-competition-8-time-short-awards-ceremony> (last accessed 30 November 2015).
Ssejjengo, Emmanuel (2013), 'The return of Mira Nair', *The New Vision* (Kampala), 16 August.

11. HAVING ITS CAKE AND EATING IT TOO: CONTEMPORARY AMERICAN 'INDIE' CINEMA AND *MY BIG FAT GREEK WEDDING* REFRAMED

Yannis Tzioumakis and Lydia Papadimitriou

An industrial 'rags to riches' story, the phenomenal box office success of *My Big Fat Greek Wedding* (Joel Zwick, 2002), a small ethnic romantic comedy with an unusual production and distribution history, has rendered it an anomaly in the context of American indie film. Written by and starring Greek-American Nia Vardalos, who prior to this film had only a handful of acting credits, primarily in television, and no writing or other credits in film, *My Big Fat Greek Wedding* attracted significant producing power in the form of two well-capitalised independent companies, Gold Circle and Playtone. With only partial finance by HBO for a negative cost of just $5 million, and a theatrical release by niche film distributor IFC Films, the film nonetheless connected with a huge theatrical audience in the North American market. Released on 19 April 2002 in just 108 theatrers, *My Big Fat Greek Wedding* played for fifty-one weeks (until 13 April 2003), with forty-three of these weeks featuring in the list of the Top 20 films in the North American Box Office chart. Its final theatrical domestic gross was $241.4 million, placing it in the Top 5 films for 2002, and its worldwide gross was $368.7 million in total.

This remarkable performance places *My Big Fat Greek Wedding* in a very small group of similarly low-budget films that for a number of different reasons defied industry expectations and performed disproportionately well in the marketplace. *The Blair Witch Project* (Daniel Myrick and Eduardo Sanchez, 1999), *Fahrenheit 9/11* (Michael Moore, 2004), *The Passion of the Christ* (Mel Gibson, 2004), *Juno* (Jason Reitman, 2007) and *Slumdog Millionaire* (Danny Boyle, 2008), among a few others, have had a similar trajectory in terms of connecting to a vastly larger audience than that anticipated by their producers and distributors, while also attracting wide media and other attention.[1] However, partly because of their extraordinary commercial success, all these films have also faced strong criticism, with some even becoming the subject of a backlash, especially with regard to their status as independent.[2] With discourses of low-budget quality cinema dominating in the construction of 'independence' in American cinema (Tzioumakis 2011a and 2011b), it is perhaps not surprising that films which perform like blockbusters at the box office attract often dismissive critical scrutiny. For films that reach a wide audience seem to radically counter Emanuel Levy's often cited definition: 'ideally, an indie is a fresh, low-budget movie with a gritty style and offbeat subject matter that expresses the filmmaker's personal vision' (1999: 2). It is for such reasons that scholarship on American independent cinema has either ignored *My Big Fat Greek Wedding* or dismissed it as a film with no aesthetic value and a surprise hit with nothing to contribute to the understanding of this field. J. J. Murphy, for example, has called it 'pseudo independent', and its politics 'pure Hollywood hokum' (2007: 4–5), while Geoff King (2005: 163 and 166) and John Berra (2008: 17 and 25) have stressed the film's conventionality and kinship to Hollywood, respectively. In this chapter, we argue that there is another implicit reason for the film's critical dismissal, and that is its perceived authorship, which in contemporary American independent cinema traditionally lies with a film's director – in this case Joel Zwick. A veteran television director with dozens of credits, especially in American television sitcoms and with just one film credit before directing *My Big Fat Greek Wedding*,[3] Zwick's contribution as director was often critically regarded by reviews following the film's theatrical release. With his television background constantly highlighted, reviewers often compared the film to a feature length sitcom, dismissing it as the product of a sitcom director and failing to identify any redeeming features. For instance, a review in *The New York Times* complains about the film's 'pedestrian direction', linking it to 'television veteran Joel Zwick' (Kehr 2002), while *Variety* labelled the film 'familiar and sitcom broad' thanks to a 'visually uninspired, workmanlike competency that doesn't transcend helmer Joel Zwick's TV roots' (Harvey 2002).

Such focus on the director's contribution, however, shifted attention away from Vardalos' involvement with the production of the film, especially with regard to its creative and aesthetic dimensions. Besides writing the screenplay and starring in the film, Vardalos was also involved at all stages of its production and promotion, and has been credited widely for bringing this small project to fruition and for its unlikely global success. However, despite being considered the 'architect' behind *My Big Fat Greek Wedding*, this perception rarely extended to questions of film authorship per se. As a result, narrative, aesthetic and other textual dimensions of the film have rarely been discussed as Vardalos' creative choices. For most critics, such matters were attributed to director Joel Zwick, whose training and long career in television marked the film as banal, pedestrian and sitcom-like and as such not worthy of sustained discussion and inclusion in the canon of quality American independent cinema.

This chapter reframes *My Big Fat Greek Wedding* as a film predominantly authored by Nia Vardalos and, in doing so, repositions it in the context of contemporary American indie cinema. Taking as a starting point King's tripartite definition of independence in American cinema as a concept that can be approached in terms of a film's industrial location, the aesthetic strategies it adopts and its 'relationship to the broader social, cultural, political or ideological landscape' (2005: 1–2), we highlight a number of industrial, textual and ideological complexities that point to closer ties to indie cinema than normally assumed. Key to understanding them all is the film's unusual focus on an ethnic Greek female, played by Vardalos herself, and the narrative and aesthetic emphasis placed on her cultural identity. Industrially, the difficulty in anticipating the potential market for the film and its crossover appeal complicated the film's distribution; textually, the romantic comedy generic conventions were adapted to incorporate the spectacle of ethnic difference; while ideologically, the drive to assimilation and conformity is complicated by an acceptance and celebration of otherness. Our chapter therefore argues for *My Big Fat Greek Wedding* as a limit case indie film, and as a film authored by its Greek female writer-star, whose vision and sensibility, and arguably progressive politics, permeate the film. For such an approach to bear fruit, however, one needs to scratch beyond the surface and transcend traditionally constructed authorship models.

Testing the Boundaries of Production and Distribution in the Independent Film Sector

The industrial history of the film's making and release is particularly relevant in trying to assess the location of *My Big Fat Greek Wedding* in relation to concepts of independence in American cinema. Relevant to this is also the extent to which Vardalos successfully resisted pressures to make key changes to the film that were deemed to render it more saleable. In her detailed and highly illuminating article on the film's independent status, Alisa Perren (2004) foregrounds a number of distinguishing characteristics, arguing for its status as a mainstream Hollywood film. While reviewing the same field, we offer here a counterargument. We demonstrate first that the film's production history was much more typical of the indie scene of the early 2000s than is often assumed; and, secondly, that the initial difficulty in securing theatrical distribution rights in the US was partly due to uncertainty about how to market a film deemed thematically marginal, as it was situated within an ethnic community rarely represented in American cinema. In the process of the discussion that follows, Vardalos' crucial decision-making role at key stages in the film's production also becomes evident.

For a small independent film, *My Big Fat Greek Wedding* had the financial, production and institutional support of strong industry players. Based on a play under the same title written and performed by Nia Vardalos, initially in a six-week run at the Hudson Backstage Theatre in Los Angeles in 1997 (*10 Things*), the writer-actor quickly sold film rights to her play to MPH Entertainment, a company specialising primarily in television series, for $60,000 (Grace, 2003). However, Vardalos also received interest from Greek-American actress Rita Wilson and Playtone, a recently established independent production company co-owned by Wilson's husband Tom Hanks, which at that time had a finance deal with HBO and was prepared to co-produce the film. Furthermore, another recently established independent production company, Gold Circle Films, set up by billionaire Norm Waitt and specialising in genre films, especially romance and horror, also approached Vardalos. Noticing the high calibre of these companies, MPH Entertainment sold the rights to Playtone and Gold Circle for a percentage of profits and a co-producer credit, and the two production outfits co-financed the picture for $5 million (ibid.). With Vardalos retaining writing and acting credits and with the rest of the above-the-line credits filled in by inexpensive talent primarily known from television (with *Sex and the City*'s John Corbett being the most recognisable participant), it was clear that the film was conceived as a small production. Indeed, its main selling point seemed to be the romantic comedy genre, with the ethnic Greek-American community expected to provide a sizeable enough core audience for a small profit. While such emphasis on genre and advance considerations of marketing potential may seem to contradict concepts of independence, it should be stressed that since the 1990s elements that could attract what Annette Insdorf had called 'commercial money' (1981: 58) had become commonplace in the indie scene (Tzioumakis 2012: 8). The film's commercial orientation, therefore, cannot in itself act as an argument against its indie status, since it represents a much wider direction in the field.

To keep costs down, the production was relocated to Canada, with only some exteriors shot in Chicago, where the story is set (Fleischer 2008). With the production process streamlined under a tight budget, the film's producers turned their attention to distribution and marketing. Just like many independent films, *My Big Fat Greek Wedding* had been put into production without a theatrical distribution deal in place. However, by 2001 this was becoming increasingly rare, especially for films supported by significant production muscle, as the American independent film sector was entering its Indiewood phase, which was characterised by higher budgets, bigger stars, and stronger genre and institutional frameworks (Tzioumakis 2015: 292). In this climate, the absence of a theatrical distributor for a film with the commercial appeal of *My Big Fat Greek Wedding* was indeed something of an anomaly, and Perren provides some good explanations for this. First, she highlights that, given the film's co-finance by HBO, it could have been optioned by any of the three theatrical distributors operating under Time Warner (HBO's parent company): Warner Bros., New Line Cinema or Fine Line Features. She stresses, however, that the film's subject matter and style did not suit any of these companies as each specialised in different types of film (2004: 21). A further obstacle was the fact that the producers had already pre-sold other distribution rights for the film – for instance, in exchange for putting up half of the film's budget, HBO had secured both home video and cable television rights in the US. Furthermore, Gold Circle had acquired the film's theatrical distribution rights outside the North American market as part of the co-finance and co-production deal with Playtone (Perren 2004: 20). Any distributor interested in acquiring the film's theatrical rights would therefore have to take a high risk, as the exponential rise of the costs of a theatrical release since the late 1980s meant that by the early 2000s it was very difficult for a distributor to recoup their investment without access to ancillary markets.

On the other hand, the producers needed a theatrical release both in order to recoup costs and to maintain prestige. For this reason, they approached a theatrical distribution company with a view to making a service deal. Such deals usually involve the producers paying the distributor an upfront fee and a percentage of box office returns in order to get the film into theatres, while the cost of publicity and advertising lies with the producers rather than the distributor. While service deals were 'once considered a mark of shame, a last resort for films', as production increased exponentially since the 2000s service deals have become more common (Goldstein 2010).

Playtone and Gold Circle approached IFC Films for such a deal. Set up in 2000 as a theatrical distribution spin-off company from the Independent Film Channel (IFC) – itself a subsidiary of Rainbow Media Holdings, which was a joint venture by Cablevision Systems Corporation, NBC/General Electric and MGM (Perren 2004: 22) – IFC Films was not a standalone/independent company but a specialty film division established to trade in the independent film market. However, although Perren uses the company's strong corporate links to major entertainment conglomerates to argue against the independent status of the film (ibid.), we would like to argue instead that this need not be the case. For IFC Films was no different to other specialty film divisions established in the late 1990s to early 2000s, in the wake of Indiewood. As both King and Tzioumakis acknowledge, specialty-oriented distributors and/or producers owned by the major studio companies were central to the independent film industrial landscape of these years.[4] Suggesting that IFC Films is not an independent film distributor because of its corporate links to a conglomerate is therefore inconsistent with understandings of the indie and Indiewood scene of the period. Indeed, this company's profile was both distinctive and in tune with such trends. While in many ways similar to the 1999-established USA Films, unlike this short-lived company's focus on easily marketable films, IFC Films prioritised less commercially obvious films akin to early 1990s indie films, as well as non-English language fare (thus resembling the 1992 established Sony Pictures Classics). It is also worth noting that within IFC Films, the marketing campaign for *My Big Fat Greek Wedding* was largely decided by Bob Berney, one of the most well-known independent film marketers (Kilday 2013), which further underlines the film's independent status.

The service deal between the producers of *My Big Fat Greek Wedding* and IFC Films was unusual. According to reports, IFC Films did not receive a percentage of the film's box office gross, agreeing instead to distribute the film for a flat fee of $300,000 paid by the film's producers – which eventually went to 'seven figures' following a bonus payment after the film's incredible theatrical success (Broderick, quoted in Rebort 2005). Indeed, the deal was so unusual that IFC Films' competitor Sony Pictures Classics' president Tom Bernard called it 'the best deal any producer ha[d] made in the history of movies' (quoted in Susman 2002). However, despite the hefty remuneration for all producing partners in the film, the film's marketing campaign had cost substantially, dramatically even, for an independent film. Perren describes how the film's producers had invested close to $20 million in marketing costs by September 2002, and uses this as further evidence in arguing against popular and industry press discourses that considered the film small and independent (2004: 28). It should be stressed, however, that by the early 2000s, several small budgeted indie films (such as *The Blair Witch Project* and many Miramax acquired films) were aggressively and expensively marketed with very positive financial returns.

In this deal Vardalos also played a significant role. Given that the film's original P&A budget was set at a very low level (approximately $1 million (Seiler 2002)), the film's writer and star was identified and became the key focal point in IFC Films' early grassroots marketing efforts to position *My Big Fat Greek Wedding* in the US market. These efforts involved Vardalos 'travelling town to town and making appearances at Greek organisations and bridal shows' (Susman 2002), spreading the word to and mobilising the film's two core demographics, Greek-Americans and adult women. Once these practices showed very promising results, the film's producers immediately upped the ante and committed the necessary funds required to make the film competitive in the national marketplace. As we have argued elsewhere, the film's marketing campaign focused strongly on a stereotypical representation of Greek-American ethnicity in the generic context of a romantic comedy aiming to appeal to two core audiences, the Greek-American community and adult women (Tzioumakis and Papadimitriou 2015: 39), but it soon became clear that the film was embraced by a host of other demographics, which helped make it a box office smash.

Although the film's marketing emphasis on ethnic stereotype and generic features suggests conventionality akin to Hollywood and a distance from the independent film sector, in the next section we will argue for a more nuanced understanding of the film's textual and ideological qualities. Taking our cue from the other two elements in King's definition of American independent cinema, we will claim that the film is permeated by both progressive politics and some uncommon aesthetic choices, which arguably can be attributed to its writer-star Nia Vardalos and the ways in which she conceptualised – and celebrated – otherness as ethnic difference in a story about a female Greek-American's effort to marry outside her ethnic group. Furthermore we will explore its generic construction arguing that, like many other indie films of the time, *My Big Fat Greek Wedding* undermines several of the conventions associated with its genre, in this case the romantic comedy.

Having its (Wedding) Cake and Eating it Too: Gender, Narration and Ethnic Politics in *My Big Fat Greek Wedding*

The first major distinguishing point from the perspective of the film's politics is its focus on an ethnic group rarely depicted in American cinema, mainstream or independent: Greek-Americans. Despite its sizeable number (approximately three million people or 1% of the US population (US Department of State 2012)), Greek-Americans have enjoyed much less cinematic exposure than similar ethnic groups originating from the European mass migration to the US in the late nineteenth and early twentieth centuries – especially Italian Americans, Irish Americans and Jewish Americans. And while certain high profile Hollywood films such as *The Postman Always Rings Twice* (Tay Garnett, 1941 and Bob Rafelson, 1981), *The Exorcist* (William Friedkin, 1973) and *Charlie Wilson's War* (Mike Nichols, 2007), have featured American characters of Greek descent, these have tended to be supporting roles with little or no emphasis given to the characters' ethnicity. Indeed, one has to go back almost twenty years to before the release of *My Big Fat Greek Wedding* to find a film that puts a Greek-American at the centre of the narrative, Paul Mazursky's *The Tempest* (1982), starring John Cassavetes, and another twenty years before that for a film that focuses squarely on the Greek-American experience, Elia Kazan's *America, America* (1963).

As such, the release of a film with a Greek American character – a female one for that – at its centre was almost unprecedented, pointing to its novelty and departure from American cinema norms. Vardalos has been quoted several times stating that she had other proposals to adapt her one-woman play into a film, but most requested that the ethnic context would be changed to the more commercially appealing Italian– or Hispanic–American. Indeed, her decision to accept the Playtone/HBO-Gold Circle arrangement had a lot to do with their guarantee that that they would respect the 'integrity' of her play and screenplay, which were built around the peculiarities and particularities of Greek-American ethnicity (Strickler 2002), especially in relation to women. The fact that Vardalos successfully resisted pressures to homogenise ethnic American representations and further commercialise her film by adapting it for a larger demographic, indicates not only the extent to which she managed to maintain control over the film's content, but also – and as a consequence – the film's strong independent status. For, as Peter Krämer has demonstrated, control of form and content by a film's key creative authors when working within commercial structures constitutes a crucial marker of a film's independence (2012: 154).

However, giving a voice to an ethnic minority and representing it from a female perspective do not necessarily result in progressive politics. In fact, in the context of independent cinema, progressive politics tend to be associated with edgy representations questioning the status quo, combined with character-driven complex narratives supported by a distinctive visual style. But while these are often markers of political radicalism and critical success, the majority of films made in the margins of the independent film sector do not necessarily conform to this 'ideal', in Levy's term (1999: 2). Countering the critical consensus on *My Big Fat Greek Wedding* that saw the film as 'conventionally assembled . . . but with an ethnic spin' (King 2005: 163; 166), or fitting 'into the Hollywood production mould' and permeated by a 'conservatism' that 'strives for novelty value that will distinguish an independent film from a studio film but at the same time does not wish to alienate or offend any potential ticket-buying demographic' (Berra 2008: 17; 25), we will argue that the film is more complex and less conservative than such observations suggest. This is primarily because of the ways in which the film openly celebrates Greek-Americaness as an ethnic identity and takes a very unusual, even radical, position when it comes to questions of ethnic assimilation. In this respect, it is clear that the film's authorship rests with its 'creative *nous*', Nia Vardalos.

It should be acknowledged that, at first sight, *My Big Fat Greek Wedding* does indeed appear conventional. Its romantic comedy attributes are registered early in the story, while it adheres to many, though not all, key generic qualities identified by Jeffers McDonald (2007): in terms of 'visual characteristics', it takes place in an urban location, its iconography revolves around a wedding, while all its stock characters are present, including a host of unsuitable partner characters that are presented in an entertaining montage sequence (2007: 11). In terms of 'narrative patterns', the film employs the 'meet cute' trope (2007: 12) which foreshadows the couple's later union, though here the union takes place early in the film, immediately after Toula (Vardalos) and Ian's (John Corbett) second meeting (a first less cute meeting at the very beginning of the film acts as an early indicator), and there is no initial hating of each other, a trope that many romantic comedy couples start with. On the other hand, however, the couple never splits (the boy does not lose the girl and so does not need to find her again), despite efforts on the part of the couple's families to convince them that they are unsuitable for each other. No one tries to derail the wedding – at least not consciously – and there is no masquerading and no public humiliation 'to prove that love is more important than dignity' (2007: 13) – even though, as we will explore in more detail later, Ian's Greek Orthodox baptism might qualify as humiliation.

Arguably the strongest narrative trope in the film is one that romantic comedy shares with other genres: the makeover. When we first see Toula Portokalos, she is a thirty-year-old woman with a full, rounded figure, wearing big glasses, ordinary clothes, with no make-up and un-styled hair. She has 'no life', as she confesses to her mother when questioned about her constant presence in the family's restaurant business. Her father tells her openly that she looks 'old' and that she needs to 'marry soon', implying that if she does not she will stay 'on the shelf'. However, Toula sees her family's obsession with her getting married (and having children) as a strong register of her ethnic background about which she has been feeling ambivalent all her life. Toula wants to assimilate, to be more like the non-ethnic (blonde, slight-figured, white) girls she went to school with, of which, we are led to believe, no matrimonial and procreational demands are made by their families and surrounding communities.

Putting her 'frump phase' behind her, while also escaping her ethnically determined fate, become one and the same narrative goal for Toula. We see her gradually paying increasing attention to her looks while also, and despite her family's initial disapproval, registering in the local college to gain professional qualifications and seek a job different from restaurant seating hostess. These efforts pay off quickly as she is soon accepted by the blonde, slender women she now studies with, while her IT and tourism studies land her a job in her aunt's travel agency – still within the family fold but outside the direct purview of her oppressive parents. It is there that she meets Ian Miller, a WASP American from a wealthy family. Toula can now complete her assimilation and perform her gender role within a dominant, ethnic-free and thus (apparently) non-oppressive white environment, through her wedding with Ian.

As it turns out, then, Toula's problem is not with 'getting married and having babies' but doing these things within the cultural milieu of her strongly ethnic family and broader community. It is at this point that another key element of the romantic comedy genre emerges: ideology. While the genre endorses firmly the Western ideas of monogamy, stability and procreation, it also promotes the American Dream – that anyone can escape their background, can assimilate, can find happiness – as Toula's voiceover at the end of the film underlines: 'Sometimes I am afraid that it didn't happen! I am scared that I will wake up and still be battering up garlic bread, waiting for my life to start! But it did happen! It did!'

However, such a straightforward reading of the film does not take into account a number of narrative complications, some of which undermine its validity and support alternative interpretations. Principal among them is Toula's firm placement at the centre of a narrative that, as indicated before, diverges from some generic conventions – including the conventional use of omniscient narration in the genre. Instead, in *My Big Fat Greek Wedding* Toula is the spectator's guide to a narrative that is almost obsessively restricted to her own perspective. From the opening flashback sequences where she explains in voiceover the problems she has with her ethnic heritage, to the closing scenes where, again in voiceover, she confirms that she has found happiness, the narrative is filtered almost entirely through her viewpoint and her physical presence in the events depicted. Even when she is not initially present while other people talk about her future, she soon joins in and is therefore able to present these narrative events from her viewpoint too. Such a narrative choice, which clearly shows Vardalos' control over the ordering and structure of the narrative, makes Toula the spectator's only guide to the narrative world and thus a conduit through which the film can present certain complex and progressive political positions.

Arguably the most important, even radical, proposition that *My Big Fat Greek Wedding* makes via this strategy concerns the nature of Toula's assimilation. Despite her early rant about the backward-looking Greek American traditions, which are later accentuated through stereotypical depictions of Greek customs that are played for laughs (lamb on a spit, heavy ouzo drinking, lack of boundaries and privacy, spitting to take away the 'bad eye', etc.), Toula gradually realises that she does not really want to break away from her family and her ethnic background. In a key scene in the film, her brother Nikos tells her, 'Don't let your past dictate who you are but let it be part of who you will become', which introduces Toula to a world where cultural identity is flexible and controlled by individuals, through their ability to transform themselves with consumption and makeovers.

However, if this looks like a convenient way for Toula to escape an ethnically determined gender identity and partake in one in which the markers of ethnicity are all but erased, *My Big Fat Greek Wedding* surprises by the way it also reverses this strategy by taking Ian from the fold of the default whiteness that his WASP status suggests and providing him with an ethnic identity. In a rather unexpected turn in the narrative, and in order to make Toula and her family happy, Ian agrees to be baptised Christian Orthodox in the Greek Orthodox Church so that the wedding can take place in the Greek Church and according

Figure 11.1 'Love is more important than dignity': John Corbett, Anthony Kandiotis and Nia Vardalos in *My Big Fat Greek Wedding.*

to the Greek tradition and customs. In a scene that is played for laughs and borders on the kind of humiliation that Jeffers McDonald argues takes place 'to prove that love is more important than dignity', Ian in a pair of boxer shorts is christened in a huge inflatable pool in the middle of a church (Figure 11.1). As soon as he is dressed and meets Toula for the first time after his baptism, the first words he utters are 'I'm Greek now', which, however ironically uttered, also suggest that he has chosen to become part of Toula's ethnic group.

Ian's ritual assimilation is preceded by a scene, in which, for the first and only time, the narration breaks away completely from Toula's point of view and becomes omniscient.[5] While at work, Ian explains to his friend and colleague Mike that he cannot ask him to be Best Man in his wedding as, for the church ceremony, the Best Man needs to be Greek Orthodox. Mike understands but questions the extent to which Ian is prepared to compromise for the benefit of Toula and her family, stating, 'no offence, but this girl's family's got you by the short ones. They say "jump" and you pull out the trampoline', to which Ian makes a playful 'jump' gesture to show that he is indeed ready to do whatever it takes, including becoming a member of an ethnic minority group by adopting their religion, in order to make Toula happy.

Ian's casual admittance that he is ready to 'jump' is particularly interesting because it is uttered away from Toula's knowledge. At this point he could have said anything: that he is doing it for ease rather than because he wants to, that it does not mean anything, that despite the perceived extremity of his action he is still 'in charge', or anything similar in order not to lose 'face' and credibility with his closest friend. But he does not. Instead, it becomes clear that Ian is ready to leave his WASP identity (and masculinity) aside and embrace the culture and customs of an ethnic minority group. Furthermore, the choice in this particular scene of omniscient narration in a film that is otherwise organised through restricted narration allows for this unusual political position to be presented as 'natural' rather than filtered by the film's main narrative agency, that is, Toula.

Irrespective of how it is communicated, such a position also aligns with female-driven politics that once again betray who the film's author is, while at the same time highlighting *My Big Fat Greek Wedding*'s independent credentials given that such politics are rarely seen in a patriarchal institution such as Hollywood cinema. Writing on *Groundhog Day* (Harold Ramis, 1993), Kristin Thompson noted how 'certainly unusual . . . for a Hollywood film' it was that, after a while, the film's main male character's narrative goal was to 'become the ideal of a modern, liberated woman' (1999: 147). And while in *Groundhog Day* this means that the character played by Bill Murray becomes a kind and much nicer person than the egocentric careerist we experienced at the start, identity pillars such as class, ethnicity and sexuality are certainly not touched. But in *My Big Fat Greek Wedding*, they are.

Indeed the kinds of representations that the film offers are extremely rare. After all, Toula decides not to assimilate and instead converts Ian to the minority to which she belongs, a proposition that ideologically places the film firmly away from most of Hollywood cinema and next to films that challenge the status quo. Furthermore, the fact that this representation is found in a film released in the early months of 2002, within a socio-political climate of intense suspicion of ethnic minorities following the 9/11 attacks, makes its presence in the film and its spectacular embrace by such a wide audience unprecedented and almost radical. As *The New York Times* reported, 'since the attacks, people who look[ed] Middle Eastern and Muslim, whatever their religion or nation of origin, ha[d] been singled out for harassment, threats and assaults' (Goodstein and Lewin 2002), often condoned by the US government's initiatives and laws that, despite aiming to stop terrorism, also enabled practices of 'stereotyping and scapegoating' (Bakalian and Bozorgmehr 2009: 2). And even though Greek-Americans as an ethnic group were not Muslims and modern Greece has belonged historically to the Western political and cultural sphere, its geographical position in the Balkans amongst nations with significant Muslim populations, its close proximity to the Middle East, and the Greeks' darker skin colour compared to other 'whiter ethnic groups' certainly made inclusion in this stereotyping and scapegoating possible.[6]

This is especially relevant as the film does not shy away from many of these characteristics but often juxtaposes them with non-ethnic whiteness setting up binary oppositions and underlining the cultural difference of the Greek-Americans. As mentioned before, at the beginning of the film, Toula is depicted twice as a dark-coloured ethnic girl and later as a woman who is 'different' from the others in terms of her looks and her food. Later on, Toula and her family are joined by her *yaya*, a stereotypically clad-in-black-clothes-and-head-scarf grandmother, who unable to cope easily with life in her culturally alien surroundings, often wanders into other people's gardens and is delivered back home in disdain by non-ethnic neighbours such as 'Mrs White'. Arguably the most interesting such juxtaposition is the one between Toula's Greek-American and Ian's WASP family. With the latter also stereotypically presented as quiet, emotionally reserved, culturally refined and with a very US-centric view of the world in which Greece, Armenia and Guatemala are interchangeable, Toula's family, in contrast, appears even louder, with no understanding of boundaries and with suspect customs such as roasting a whole lamb on a spit in the front yard. 'They look at us and they think we are from the zoo', Toula's father proclaims after their first encounter, while also being quick to label Ian's family 'dry as toast'.

Clearly, the film made few – if any – concessions in terms of glamorising the 'ethnic other' or removing sensitive marks of ethnicity that could have rendered Greek-Americans vulnerable in the immediate post–9/11 climate. Under these circumstances, Ian's complete espousal of such cultural identity is even more astonishing as, according to Benshoff and Griffin, 'the most common designation of whiteness in the United States is the term WASP', an identity from which Ian flees, and that 'people of non-Anglo Saxon European ancestry have historically had to negotiate their relation to whiteness' (2004: 53), including of course the Greek-Americans who become Ian's people.

Conclusion

Despite its apparent conventionality, *My Big Fat Greek Wedding* is industrially less mainstream, textually more complex, and ideologically more challenging than previously assumed. For these reasons, we have argued that it deserves to be considered as part of an inclusive canon of American independent cinema, alongside many other films produced and circulated during the indie and Indiewood years of American independent cinema that may – or may not – be explicitly sophisticated in form and oppositional in content. We have also demonstrated the decisive role that *My Big Fat Greek Wedding*'s writer-star has played in informing its subject matter, aesthetic sensibilities and cultural priorities. Indeed, while almost all accounts of the film were quick to construct Vardalos as the film's author in terms of the *process* of bringing it to the screen and creating a global smash from a one-woman play, they nonetheless steered clear of extending this authorship to the film's formal and stylistic elements, opting instead to dismiss them on account of the film director's TV background. In reframing American independent film, therefore, it is not only necessary to address gender prejudices but also to question the automatic privileging of a film's director as its sole author. For, as our discussion of *My Big Fat Greek Wedding* has shown, creative control and cultural influence can be exercised from other positions too.

Notes

1. For instance, for *The Blair Witch Project* see Caro 1999, while for *My Big Fat Greek Wedding* see Lyman 2002 as well as Kostaki 2002 and Susman 2002.
2. See for instance the discussion of the strong backlash against *Juno* in Newman 2011: 240–5.
3. Among the many TV shows for which Zwick directed episodes, one could find *Perfect Strangers* (1986–93) and *Full House* (1987–95), both with Greek interest due to particular characters' and/or actors' ethnic background, which might have helped Zwick land the director's job in *My Big Fat Greek Wedding*.
4. The term *Indiewood* has been used in slightly different ways by scholars. For King, 'Indiewood' (with a capital *I*) is an industrial/institutional phenomenon of the 1990s and 2000s that has produced a number of films with particular textual qualities that stem both from the mainstream and the independent sector (2009: 1–4). For Tzioumakis, 'Indiewood' (with lower case *i*) is a period in the history of contemporary American independent cinema that starts from the mid-/late–1990s in which the dominant expression of filmmaking is characterised by many of the elements identified by King (2012: 10–12). With the exception of direct quotations from King, here we use Tzioumakis' approach to Indiewood.
5. There are two other scenes that are arguably also coded as omniscient moments and both involve a short discussion between Ian and Toula's brother. In the first of these Nikos teases Ian that he would 'kill him' if he makes his sister unhappy while in the second Nikos plays a prank on Ian by asking him to use Greek swear words. But despite the absence of other people in these two short scenes, they both take place in geographical proximity to Toula and can, therefore, easily be missed or misunderstood as being filtered through her perspective.
6. For an excellent discussion of the stereotyping and representation of ethnic groups of European origin in American cinema see Benshoff and Griffin 2004: 54–73.

References

10 Things You Never Knew About 'My Big Fat Greek Wedding', <http://screen.answers.com/movies/10-things-you-never-knew-about-quot-my-big-fat-greek-wedding-quot> (last accessed 15 April 2015).

Bakalian, Anny, and Medhi Bozorgmehr (2009), *Backlash 9/11: Middle Eastern and Muslim Americans Respond*, Berkeley: University of California Press.

Benshoff, Harry, and Sean Griffin (2004), *America on Film: Representing Race, Class, Gender, and Sexuality in the Movies*, Malden, MA: Blackwell.

Berra, John (2008), *Declarations of Independence: American Cinema and the Partiality of Independent Production*, Bristol: Intellect.

Caro, Mark (1999), 'Frightfully, Frightfully, Frightfully Real: The Bewitching Story Behind The "Blair Witch Project"', *Chicago Tribune*, 14 July, <http://articles.chi

cagotribune.com/1999-07-14/features/9907140115_1_daniel-myrick-myrick-and-sanchez-blair-witch-project> (last accessed 15 April 2015).

Eller, Claudia and Lorenza Munoz (2003), '"Wedding" Party Leaves Some Behind', *Los Angeles Times*, 23 March, <http://articles.latimes.com/2003/mar/23/business/fi-greekmess23> (last accessed 15 April 2015).

Fleischer, Dave (2008), 'Reel Toronto: *My Big Fat Greek Wedding*', *Torontoist*, 23 September, <http://torontoist.com/2008/09/reel_toronto_my_big_fat_greek_weddi/> (last accessed 15 April 2015).

Goldstein, Gregg (2010), 'Service Deals Becoming a Hit at Sundance', *Hollywood Reporter*, 26 January, <http://www.hollywoodreporter.com/news/service-deals-becoming-hit-sundance-19985> (last accessed 15 April 2015).

Goodstein, Laurie and Tamar Lewin (2001), 'A Nation Challenged: Violence and Harassment', *The New York Times*, 19 September, <http://www.nytimes.com/2001/09/19/us/nation-challenged-violence-harassment-victims-mistaken-identity-sikhs-pay-price.html> (last accessed 15 April 2015).

Grace, Francie (2003), '"Big Fat Greek Wedding" Lawsuit', *CBS News*, 2 July, <http://www.cbsnews.com/news/big-fat-greek-wedding-lawsuit/> (last accessed 15 April 2015).

Harvey, Dennis (2002), 'Review: *My Big Fat Greek Wedding*', *Variety*, 15 April (online), <http://variety.com/2002/film/awards/my-big-fat-greek-wedding-3-1200550281/> (last accessed 16 July 2015).

Insdorf, Annette (1981), 'Ordinary People, European Style: How to Spot an Independent Feature' in *American Film*, 6:10, pp. 57–60.

Jeffers McDonald, Tamar (2007), *Romantic Comedy: Boy Meets Girl*, New York: Wallflower.

Kehr, Dave (2002), 'Film in Review: *My Big Fat Greek Wedding*', *The New York Times*, 19 April, <http://www.nytimes.com/movie/review?res=9D03E7D9153FF93AA2575 7C0A9649C8B6> (last accessed 16 July 2015).

Kilday, Gregg (2013), 'Bob Berney Relaunching Picturehouse, Signs Output Deal with Netflix', *Hollywood Reporter*, 15 January (online), <http://www.hollywoodreporter.com/news/bob-berney-relaunching-picturehouse-signs-412732> (last accessed 15 April 2015).

King, Geoff (2005), *American Independent Cinema*, London: I. B. Tauris.

King, Geoff (2009), *Indiewood USA: Where Hollywood Meets Independent Cinema*, London: I. B. Tauris.

Kostaki, Maria (2002), 'Nia, Rita and Tom too: Nia Vardalos & Her Big Fat Greek Wedding', *Odyssey*, May/June, pp. 43–5.

Krämer, Peter (2012), 'The Limits of Autonomy: Stanley Kubrick, Hollywood and Independent Filmmaking, 1950–53', in G. King, C. Molloy and Y. Tzioumakis (eds), *American Independent Cinema: Indie, Indiewood and Beyond*, London: Routledge, pp. 153–64.

Levy, Emanuel (1999), *Cinema of Outsiders: The Rise of American Independent Film*, New York and London: New York University Press.

Lyman, Rick (2002), 'A Big Fat (And Profitable) Cinderella Story; "Greek Wedding" Courts A Prince Named Oscar', *The New York Times*, 28 November, <http://www.nytimes.com/2002/11/28/movies/big-fat-profitable-cinderella-story-greek-wedding-courts-prince-named-oscar.html> (last accessed 15 April 2015).

Murphy, J. J. (2007), *Me and You and Memento and Fargo: How Independent Screenplays Work*, New York: Continuum.

Newman, Michael Z. (2011), *Indie: An American Film Culture*, New York: Columbia University Press.

Perren, Alisa (2004), 'A Big Fat Indie Success Story? Press Discourses Surrounding the

Making and Marketing of a Hollywood Movie', *Journal of Film and Video*, 56: 2, pp. 18–31.

Rebort (2005), 'Rethinking Film Distribution', *iofilm*, 15 November, <http://www.iofilm.co.uk/io/mit/001/film_distribution_20051115.php> (last accessed 15 April 2015).

Seiler, Andy (2002), 'Their Big Fat Success Story', *USA Today*, 28 August, <http://usatoday30.usatoday.com/life/movies/2002-08-27-big-fat-story_x.htm> (last accessed 17 July 2015).

Strickler, Jeff (2002), 'Truth Sillier than Fiction for Film's Writer', *Star Tribune*, 9 May, <http://www.startribune.com/lifestyle/11473461.html> (last accessed 15 April 2015).

Susman, Geoff (2002), 'My Big Fat Greek Wallet', *The Guardian*, 29 November, <http://www.theguardian.com/culture/2002/nov/29/artsfeatures> (last accessed 15 April 2015).

Thompson, Kristin (1999), *Storytelling in the New Hollywood: Understanding Classical Narrative Technique*, Cambridge, MA: Harvard University Press.

Tzioumakis, Yannis (2011a), 'Academic Discourses and American Independent Cinema: In Search of A Field of Studies, Part 1 – From the Beginnings to the 1980s', *New Review of Film and Television Studies*, 9: 2, July, pp. 105–31.

Tzioumakis, Yannis (2011b), 'Academic Discourses and American Independent Cinema: In Search of A Field of Studies, Part 2 – The 1990s and beyond', in *New Review of Film and Television Studies*, 9: 3, September, pp. 311–40.

Tzioumakis, Yannis (2012), *Hollywood's Indies: Classics Divisions, Specialty Labels and the American Film Market*, Edinburgh: Edinburgh University Press.

Tzioumakis, Yannis (2015), 'Between Indiewood and Nowherewood: American Independent Cinema in the 21st Century', *International Journal of Media and Cultural Politics*, 10: 3, pp. 285–300.

Tzioumakis, Yannis, and Lydia Papadimitriou (2015), 'Marketing Greekness: Aspects of Greek Identity in the Marketing Strategies for *My Big Fat Greek Wedding* (2002) and *My Life in Ruins*' (2009), in Nolwenn, Mingant, Cecilia Tirtaine and Joël Augros, eds, *Film Marketing into the 21st Century*, London: BFI, pp. 36–46.

US Department of State (2012), 'US Relations with Greece', 2 October 2012, <http://www.state.gov/r/pa/ei/bgn/3395.htm> (last accessed 15 April 2015).

12. NOT JUST INDIE: A LOOK AT FILMS BY DEE REES, AVA DUVERNAY AND KASI LEMMONS

Cynthia Baron

Indiewood directors Dee Rees, Ava DuVernay, and Kasi Lemmons aim to 'tell stories that are universal' (Prince-Bythewood 2014). They also sustain and enrich the Black Nationalist project of reclaiming and recasting African-American culture and identity (Larkin 1988: 158). Yet familiar characterisations of Indiewood (1995 onwards) tend to reflect the views of dominant culture, overlooking the presence of alternative voices, including those of African-American artists. With ideas about Indiewood often failing to square with the tangible achievements of directors like Rees, DuVernay, and Lemmons, a look at their films can bring perceptions into closer alignment with actual developments. Inspired by work such as Valerie Smith's *Not Just Race, Not Just Gender*, I approach films by Rees, DuVernay, and Lemmons through a lens that makes visible the intersectionality of race, class, gender, and sexuality in Indiewood cinema.[1] Their films are also a keen reminder that accounts of Indiewood and American independent cinema as a whole should consider that work by African-American filmmakers constitutes America's first and perhaps most politically significant 'independent cinema', past and present.

A focus on Indiewood's mainstream business and aesthetic practices leads the creative labour of women and other 'minorities' to be marginalised. With man-children and torn T-shirt outsiders more visible in easily marketed indie-chic films, accounts of Indiewood sometimes give little attention to the kind of filmmaking once associated with 1980s independent cinema, when 'the ethos of public service broadcasting became a defining factor . . . for the articulation of the new independent cinema' (Tzioumakis 2006: 208–9). Yet the films of Rees, DuVernay, and Lemmons prompt a rethinking of assumed divisions between Indiewood and the 1980s, when 'American independent feature film-making became widely perceived as a vehicle for the articulation of alternative voices and political positions' (ibid. p. 209). Among the 'countless films . . . significant to indie culture' that do not overtly exemplify 'the indie "brand"', films by Rees, DuVernay, and Lemmons reveal that American independent cinema remains 'a space for the critique of social structures of class, race, gender and sexuality' (Perkins and Verevis 2015: 3, 8).

One might expect descriptions of Indiewood to acknowledge the fact that African-American directors, actors, cinematographers, editors, composers, and other craftspeople working above and below the line belong to a generation of African-American artists, sports figures, and other professionals who have transformed American culture. For example, whereas musicians in earlier generations had to fit themselves 'into an allotted image reserved for Black performers', in the 1990s dominant white society changed and embraced hip hop culture (Boyd 2002: 46). The fact that billionaire media mogul Oprah Winfrey and Cheryl Boone Isaacs, the first African-American woman to head the Academy of Motion Picture Arts and Sciences, hold highly visible positions of power is a reminder that 'black intellectuals, filmmakers, musicians, choreographers, playwrights, and novelists are profoundly shaping the imagination of American culture' in the late twentieth and early twenty-first century (Gray 2005: 13; see Boyd 2008).

The current understanding, on the part of artists, audiences, and critics, is that artistic expression by African Americans is now integral to mainstream American culture. Yet this perception does not generally carry over into discussions of Indiewood, despite observers' awareness that mainstream and outsider cinema are interdependent. Individual articles about New York University film school grad Dee Rees, former West Coast film publicist Ava DuVernay, and actress-writer-director Kasi Lemmons indicate that they are part of Indiewood. Yet as in various high profile media representations where 'black women's experiences have been rendered almost uniformly invisible', the implications of black women filmmakers generating bodies of work are not part of narratives about Indiewood, so that critical accounts lag behind industrial practices and audience expectations (Gray 2005: 24).

The careers of Lemmons, Rees, and DuVernay reflect Indiewood trends. Lemmons became an Indiewood director to watch when her first feature, *Eve's Bayou* (1997), won the Independent Spirit Award for Best First Feature, *and* the film's domestic box office reached $14,842,388, making it the highest grossing independent film of the year (Alexander 2003: 253; Berry 2001: 261–3). Dee Rees transformed her short film *Pariah* (2007) into her first feature *Pariah* (2011) with mentorship from the Sundance Institute and director-turned-producer Spike Lee, and it was released by Indiewood distributor

Focus Features. Highlighting the Indiewood era link between film and television, Rees' second feature *Bessie* (HBO 6 May 2015) became a marketable commodity and critical accomplishment with the participation of the film's star Queen Latifah and her production company 'Flavor Unit Entertainment' (Sahagian 2015). DuVernay's well-orchestrated career has combined critical acclaim as an independent – she is the first African-American woman to win the Sundance Film Festival US Directing Award: Dramatic for *Middle of Nowhere* (2012) – and mainstream recognition (Wilson 2015). After directing two small but acclaimed films, she was tapped to direct the $20 million Paramount Pictures release of *Selma* (2014), and with its impeccable production qualities and Oprah Winfrey's powerful on- and off-screen participation, the film garnered many accolades, including Oscar and Golden Globe nominations, and a number of NAACP Image Awards (Outstanding Motion Picture, Actor in a Motion Picture, Supporting Actor in a Motion Picture, and Supporting Actress in a Motion Picture).

The films directed by Rees, DuVernay, and Lemmons also reveal their distinctive but complementary voices. There is the rich, cacophonous audiovisual sampling in Rees' coming-of-age story *Pariah* (2011) and multi-layered biopic *Bessie* (2015), while DuVernay's elegant, almost minimalist naturalism distinguishes her woman's pictures *I Will Follow* (2011), *Middle of Nowhere* (2012) and historical epic *Selma* (2014). Lemmons' films, *Eve's Bayou* (1997), *The Caveman's Valentine* (2001), *Talk to Me* (2007), and *Black Nativity* (2013), feature stylistic constants woven into productions where formal choices convey each film's unique exploration of the psychic, cultural, and spiritual dimensions of African-American identity. The work of these filmmakers, together with their distinctively Indiewood careers, demonstrates the importance of female African-American practitioners within contemporary American independent cinema.

Black/American Independent Cinema and the New Black Aesthetic

Studies sometimes suggest divisions between American independent and Black independent cinema. Geoff Andrews' *Stranger than Paradise: Maverick Filmmakers in Recent American Cinema* (1999) has chapters on individual male directors, with its chapters on Spike Lee and Wayne Wang perhaps balancing its emphasis on white filmmakers. Emanuel Levy's *Cinema of Outsiders: The Rise of American Independent Film* (1999) gives priority to film practice by and for straight white men, with closing chapters that briefly discuss Hispanic and Asian films, women's cinema, African-American cinema, and queer cinema. Greg Merritt's *Celluloid Mavericks: A History of American Independent Film* (2000) considers African-American filmmakers throughout its expansive chronological study, but it casts American independent cinema as a white endeavour by identifying *Birth of a Nation* (D. W. Griffith, 1915) as 'America's first major independent film' (2000: 3). Geoff King's *American Independent Cinema* (2005) takes an in-depth look at industry, narrative, form, and genre, then finally turns to a ghettoised chapter on work by African-American filmmakers, female, queer and left-leaning filmmakers.

With American independent cinema discussed in segregated terms, investigations of African Americans' contributions are found in a line of work initiated by volumes like *Black Cinema Aesthetics: Issues in Independent Black Filmmaking* (1982) and *Black Frames: Critical Perspectives on Black Independent Cinema* (1988). Subsequent work includes Mark Reid's discussions of films that focus on 'the Afro-American community, [are] written, directed, and produced by Afro-Americans and people of African ancestry who reside in the United States [and are productions] not distributed by major American film companies' (1993: 4). Tommy Lott analyses films that support 'black people as a group engaged in a protracted struggle for social equality' (1997: 93). Gladstone Yearwood examines films that challenge 'traditional cinema and the social understanding on which it was based', and explore 'black experience [to offer] a vantage-point from which special insights on society and the human condition' emerge (2000: 54). He finds these films do not present 'a frozen moment in black history as the defining black experience', but instead address 'the core problem of the constitution of power in society and the sexual and racial positions it prescribes' (ibid. pp. 183 and 246).

Scholarship such as this is vitally important to studies of American independent cinema, because American film history is inextricably linked to filmmaking and movie-going practices shaped by the legacy of slavery. James Snead astutely notes that 'separate but equal' African-American cinema became 'inevitable' in 1896, when the Edison Company replaced kinescopes with film projection the same year that the US Supreme Court provided legal sanction for segregation in its 'Plessy versus Ferguson' decision (1994: 108). Recognising that black films are a response to white society's 'remorselessly negative images', he also emphasises that Black independent cinema arose directly from the collision between the new, communal experience of movie-going and 'the Supreme Court's division of this potential communality into black and white segments' (ibid.). 'Separate but equal' productions date back to *The Railroad Porter* (William Foster, 1910); the Lincoln Motion Picture Company started in 1916 and Oscar Micheaux directed his first film in 1918. By the 1920s, the exhibition circuit for this separate cinema had some 700 theatres; the system 'designed to stop blacks from taking part in the new white dominated ritual of movie-going helped create the market for films featuring blacks', and gave rise to America's most significant and politically charged independent film movement (Yearwood 2000: 33).

In the mid-twentieth century, film and the legacy of slavery would again intersect. The US Supreme Court's 1954 decision in *Brown* v. *Board of Education* overturned '*Plessy* v. *Ferguson*' and led to the Black Nationalist phase of Black independent cinema in the 1960s (Snead 1994: 114). Independent filmmaking took on a new urgency as 'the black nationalist movement undertook a major thrust to redefine and reclaim black history, culture and identity' (Yearwood 2000: 46). The era's 'activist aesthetics ... influenced a new generation of blacks who were attending film school', and informed the drive for an 'Afrocentric aesthetic', which saw the (film) artist as 'an active participant in the struggle for racial dignity, cultural resonance, political empowerment and economic autonomy' (ibid. p. 49 and p. 47).

Dee Rees, Ava DuVernay and Kasi Lemmons build on this foundation. In 1969, Pearl Bowser organised the first Black Independent Film Festival in New York, and in 1980 curated a retrospective of Independent Black American Cinema, 1920–80 in Paris. Melvin Van Peebles' *Sweet Sweetback's Baadasssss Song* (1971) showed there was an audience for narratives that celebrated Black Nationalist values. The first conference of the Black Filmmakers Foundation convened in 1979, with L. A. Rebellion filmmakers Julie Dash and Alile Sharon Larkin participating (Snead 1994: 117). In 1980, the symposium on Black Cinema Aesthetics at Ohio University 'crystalized the impact of the new generation of black filmmakers and scholars', and Pearl Bowser's 'isolation of gender issues within black cultural expression signalled a critical moment for black film scholarship' (Yearwood 2000: 53). Her intervention also conveyed a break with white feminism, and gave expression to the 'womanist' perspective seen in the films of Rees, DuVernay, and Lemmons, which consistently explore 'the survival and wholeness of entire people, male and female' (Walker 1983: xi; see Reid 2005: 30–6, 86–90).

Films by the three Indiewood directors confirm Trey Ellis' insight that Black Nationalism 'continues to be one of the strongest forces in the black community' (2003: 196). Their work also suggests that the New Black Aesthetic, a term Ellis coined in 1989, is pertinent; for as he explains, New Black Aesthetic values are grounded in Black Nationalism *and* the middle-class experience of belonging to 'a multi-racial mix of cultures' (ibid. p. 189). Like other black urban professionals, these three filmmakers 'no longer need to deny or suppress any part of [their] complicated and sometimes contradictory cultural baggage to please either white people or black' (ibid). Their careers reflect a 'heightened sense of individual autonomy' *and* a drive to reclaim black culture and identity (Boyd 1997: 26). Their professional lives combine an ability to operate in the white world and an interest in transforming the public sphere by making black cultural expression a part of everyday life. Thus, scholarship on Black independent cinema and the New Black Aesthetic illuminates the career dynamics of Rees, DuVernay, and

Lemmons as Indiewood directors, and contributes to a better understanding of American independent cinema.

DEE REES AND AVA DUVERNAY: MAKING BLACK WOMEN'S LIVES PART OF AMERICAN CINEMA

Dee Rees' 2007 short *Pariah* brought her immediate recognition as a contributor to LGBT culture. The film won prizes at a number of festivals, including the Chicago Gay and Lesbian International Film Festival and the San Francisco International Lesbian and Gay Film Festival. Her 2011 feature *Pariah* received the year's Outstanding Film Award from GLAAD (Gay & Lesbian Alliance Against Defamation). In 2013, she was identified by *Ebony* magazine as one of America's black LGBT pioneers, recognition that put her in the company of artists like James Baldwin and Audre Lorde (Terrell 2013). Rees' fearless and insightful explorations of women's identities in her feature films, *Pariah* and *Bessie*, provide evidence that 'black independent cinema' is not simply oppositional but is, instead, on 'a search for a newly born cinema, one with its own discrete identity, evolving on its own axis' (Gabriel 1988: 72).

Her films build on a foundation created by independent black directors such as Yvonne Welbon, whose film *Sisters in the Life* (1993) dramatises and complicates 'a conventional reminiscence of "first love"', and Cheryl Dunye, whose work offers a 'model for minority self-representation'; starting with films like *She Don't Fade* (1991), which challenges the dismissive treatment of lesbian experience in *She's Gotta Have It* (Spike Lee, 1986), Dunye has created a body of alternative work that includes *The Watermelon Woman* (1996) and *Mommy is Coming* (2012) (Van Leer 1997: 174, 176). In addition, Rees has been compared to Tina Mabry, director of *Mississippi Damned* (2009), who also belongs to the 'cadre of emerging black filmmakers' known for their 'visually compelling cinema [about] the outliers at the edges of black culture in America' (Petrusich 2012).

Rees' feature *Pariah* centres on aspiring Brooklyn high school poet Alike (Adepero Oduye), 'a bashful young woman who is tentatively exploring her sense of self' and sexuality (Thomson 2011: 63). When Alike is with her close friends, 'she is out but not quite butch, wearing baggy pants and baseball caps. With her middle-class parents, she feminises her appearance just enough to pass as straight' (ibid.). She is 'like a chameleon', adapting to 'her environment', an idea that Rees conveys by having Oduye 'always bathed in the colours that surround her' (ibid.). There is 'a real tenderness to the film, especially as Alike navigates those first tentative moves at not just sex, but love' (Sharkey 2011). The story concludes with Alike focused on her future as an artist; in the final scene, for the first time in the film 'she is lit with pure sunlight . . . and the restless camera settles into a locked-down shot, the only one in the otherwise-handheld film' (Thomson 2011: 63).

The film 'carries with it [key] independent film legacies', most notably the 'century-long history of African American independent film culture and ... the more recent aesthetic and political challenges' first sparked by New Queer Cinema in the 1990s (White 2015: 133). *Pariah* also illustrates contemporary African-American artists' ability to explore 'sites of oppression ... to reinscribe their own empowered self-definitions erased from the official text of national history' (Ryan 2005: 89). Alike's journey, which leads to coming out *and* moving towards life as an artist, reflects the Black Nationalist drive for self-definition. Acknowledging this, the 2012 NAACP Image Awards gave the film its Outstanding Independent Motion Picture award. Recognising *Pariah*'s significance, the 2012 Independent Spirit Awards gave it the John Cassavetes Award for best film with a budget under $500,000. At Sundance, the film garnered the Excellence in Cinematography prize in the US Dramatic category for Bradford Young.

Rees' HBO feature *Bessie*, starring Queen Latifah as Bessie Smith, illustrates the point that 'one of the most important concerns shared by Black women filmmakers is a concern for the ways in which national history is constructed' (Ryan 2005: 87). By exploring the life and art of blues singer Bessie Smith, 'one of the most influential performers of the '20s and '30s', the film challenges Hollywood's tendency to avoid African-American biopics, an implicit policy that has been lifted on occasion but that has led observers to refer to 'the biopic [as] "the motion picture equivalent of the all-white neighbourhood"' (Sahagian 2015; Bingham 2010: 170). The film also illustrates Rees' interest in doing work that gives visibility to LGBT experiences, for it tells the story of Bessie Smith, who 'overcame all the obstacles of being black, a woman, poor, and bisexual' in a time when these were markers that would have kept someone out of the American public sphere (Sahagian 2015).

Ava DuVernay's first feature, *I Will Follow*, honours the life of a fictional black female musician whose identity did consign her to a life of invisibility. Flashbacks of Amanda (Beverly Todd) from the recent and distant past reveal that she had been a drummer who spent her entire life as 'a session musician – the mule of the music industry – renowned for her disco work while dreaming of being in a rock band' (Hardy 2011). Amanda's story serves as 'commentary on the limits imposed by race and gender, but the woman we see in flashback is someone who never let thwarted dreams lead to a stunted life' (ibid.). The film confirms Judylyn Ryan's insight that while black women filmmakers are examples of professional success, their films often do not depict black female characters in elite positions, but instead revisit fraught, even oppressive environments from the past, in this case prejudices shaping Amanda's career, as a way to generate new self-definition and 'empowerment' (2005: 4).

Set in the bucolic Topanga Canyon area of Los Angeles, it focuses on the day Amanda's niece Maye (Salli Richardson-Whitfield) packs up the house where Amanda has spent her final months after deciding not to be treated for breast cancer. The film suggests that 'interconnectedness' is a recurring theme in black women's films, for it conveys Maye's peace of mind knowing that, during the year she put her life on hold to care for Amanda, she had facilitated her aunt's quest to 'attain and preserve a righteous equilibrium of interdependent relationships' by dying on her terms (ibid. p. 2). By contrast, the film shows that Amanda's daughter (Michole White) struggles with her mother's death, for there is now no way to repair the distance that had existed between the two of them. The film was named Best Screenplay by the African-American Critics Association. Expressing a view found in a range of reviews, one IMDB user observes: 'It's rare that we get to see these slices of African-American life presented on screen . . . I really appreciate this film and what it represents historically for Black Cinema' (Shawnjames_2000: 2011).

DuVernay's second feature *Middle of Nowhere* garnered even more critical acclaim, with DuVernay becoming the first African-American woman to win a Directing Award at Sundance. The Independent Spirit Awards gave it the John Cassavetes Award; the African-American Film Critics gave it prizes for Best Independent Film, Screenplay, Actress, and Music; the Black Reel Awards awarded it the Best Director and Screenplay honours; and the Black Film Critics Circle named DuVernay Best Director. *Middle of Nowhere* makes interconnectedness a primary theme. The film follows the daily routines of Ruby (Emayatzy Corinealdi) as she works through the emotional and practical challenges of putting her life on pause to better support her partner Derek (Omari Hardwick), who is serving an eight-year sentence for dealing drugs, a choice he made to achieve upward mobility and support Ruby as she attended medical school. By examining the isolating pressures created when bourgeois aspirations combine with experiences faced disproportionately by African Americans (incarceration, family members in prison), the film illuminates challenges to the interconnectedness of African Americans and the culturally specific dimensions of New Black Aesthetic values and experiences.

As in *I Will Follow*, DuVernay places black women's subjectivities at the centre of the narrative. *Middle of Nowhere* allows audiences to discover Ruby's wistful recollections, stages of steely determination, and moments of surprise; pacing and composition make it possible to study her complex responses to the people around her, including her concerned but disapproving mother (Lorraine Toussaint), her caring but preoccupied sister (Edwina Findley), and Brian (David Oyelowo), a potential lover who has been touched by Ruby's quiet courage as she pushes through disappointment and loneliness during long bus rides to and from work. DuVernay's script and direction establish in Ruby a wholly individual character and, at the same time, make her story a window into the lives of the many African-American women who face having a family member imprisoned.

With the release of her third feature, *Selma*, DuVernay became the first female African-American director to be nominated for a Golden Globe and to have a film nominated for a Best Picture Oscar. She was given the Best Director award by the African-American Film Critics, the Black Film Critics, and the Black Reel Awards. 'Glory', written by hip hop artist Common, won an Oscar, Golden Globe, Black Reel, and African-American Film Critics award for Best Original Song. Common also received the Best Supporting Actor prize at the Independent Spirit Awards. The film swept the 2015 NAACP Image Awards; accepting the award for Outstanding Motion Picture, Oprah Winfrey captured the evening's abiding sentiment when she observed that *Selma* was 'more than a movie' (Elber 2015).

One would need to revisit *Malcolm X* (Spike Lee, 1992) to locate another film with comparable significance. As with *Malcolm X*, DuVernay's film was a moderate commercial success; with its smaller budget ($20 million versus $33 million), *Selma*'s domestic box office of $52 million represents a performance akin to the $94 million gross (adjusted for inflation) garnered by *Malcolm X*. DuVernay's film about Martin Luther King (David Oyelowo), voter applicant Annie Lee Cooper (Oprah Winfrey), Bloody Sunday on Selma's Edmund Pettus Bridge, the march from Selma to Montgomery, and the Voting Rights Act of 1965 moved into production only after false starts, with DuVernay the last in a series of directors attached to the project.

Paralleling *Malcolm X*, the release of DuVernay's film led to debates fuelled by struggles to control narratives about MLK, the civil rights movement, and US president Lyndon Johnson. Decades after the release of *Malcolm X*, observers continue to identify the racism behind the Motion Picture Academy's dismissal of the film, which received only two nominations, for Best Actor and Best Costume. Despite evidence of continuing racism, responses to *Selma* and the awards season reveal a change in American and African-American society. The 2015 NAACP Image Awards opened with 'a jab at the Academy Awards', which had not recognised David Oyelowo as a leading actor or Ava DuVernay as a director (ibid.). Giving voice to the Black Nationalist values that have transformed American popular culture, host Anthony Anderson explained: 'People are up in arms because they feel the other award shows have snubbed us. So what. We've got our own show, right?' (ibid.). He turned to a musical number that finished with the 'refrain, "Forget the Oscars, hallelujah," the Emmys and Golden Globes' (ibid.).

Discussing the film's legacy, *Ebony* writer Wendy Wilson notes that for 'those who are too young to remember the Civil Rights Movement, *Selma* is the kind of film that becomes a timeless reference' (2015). The film is another instance when work by an African-American woman artist involves 'a calculated return to sites of oppression from which, paradoxically, mechanisms of self-empowerment are retrieved' (Ryan 2005: 88). Describing the logic for this,

Selma producer Oprah Winfrey explains: 'One of the most important things that we can do as storytellers and filmmakers is to tell the story of who we are and who we've been [and] allow people to see this in such a way that they feel strengthened and inspired by it' (Wilson 2015). The film thus exemplifies the Black Nationalist orientation of DuVernay's work; 'particularly as a UCLA alumni', L. A. Rebellion filmmakers Haile Gerima, Charles Burnett, and Julie Dash are, as she explains, 'big, big influences and inspirations' (Cooper 2012).

Kasi Lemmons: A New Black Aesthetic Vision of American History

Lemmons' films have earned a good deal of critical attention since the late 1990s. *Eve's Bayou* was named one of the top black movies of all time by *Ebony* (November 1998), and Melvin Donalson calls it 'one of the most original films of the 1990s' (2003: 187). The film, which Donald Bogle describes as part 'coming-of-age story, part portrait of a family's secrets and evasions, and part melodrama with magical and mystical overtones', emerged from a screenplay Lemmons worked on for ten years, and *Dr. Hugo* (1996), a short she wrote and directed to show producer Caldecot Chubb she could lead a feature film production (2004: 388). Illuminating the Black Nationalist perspective found in films by many contemporary African-American women, the story returns to the past to envision 'Black women's agency as a basis for constructing future agency' (Ryan 2005: 88). The film suggests that an 'awareness of the nation's past is crucial for a proper understanding of race', for its story 'takes place entirely within the milieu of an all-black enclave in the United States – specifically, in a town that was "named after a slave" and whose residents are that slave's descendants' (Flory 2008: 226). Dan Flory sees *Eve's Bayou* exploring 'that quintessential American experience, blackness, to reveal its complexity [and] ambiguity' (ibid. p. 317).

Told entirely in flashback, the film follows ten-year-old Eve Batiste (Jurnee Smollett) as she tries to protect the women in her family from the threat posed by her philandering father, Dr Louis Batiste (Samuel L. Jackson), who seems to have also made advances on her older sister (Meagan Good). Grounded in noir's female gothic origins, the story transforms the family's home, 'a place of comfort and safety . . . into a place of mystery and danger by means of horrific revelations about one or more of the group's members' (ibid. p. 230). With 'low-key lighting, unbalanced compositions, voiceover narration, flashbacks, [and] detective-like investigation', the film resists ending with a return to simple 'moral equilibrium', but the heroine does 'attain a "new awareness of herself and her world"' (ibid. p. 228, p. 229 and p. 230).

Eve's Bayou shows audiences something consistently left out of noir films, 'namely, the employment of *noir* techniques for the purposes of centrally portraying concerns and outlooks of African-American women' (ibid. p. 232).

Figure 12.1 In *Eve's Bayou* (Kasi Lemmons, 1997), Aunt Mozelle (Debbi Morgan) shares a memory with her precocious niece Eve (Jurnee Smolett).

As Manthia Diawara and others show, black noir breaks with classic (white) noir, putting black characters at the narrative's centre and reversing the standard noir gaze where a white character looks out at a dark mysterious world. Diawara illustrates key aspects of black noir by referencing work by novelist Chester Himes. Whereas classic noir uses blackness as a metaphor 'for the white characters' moral transgressions', Himes employs noir techniques to illuminate 'a way of life that has been imposed on black people through social injustice' (1993: 262, 263). Himes subverts the typical view 'that blackness is a fall from whiteness' by showing that 'black people are living in hell and white people are in heaven not because the one colour is morally inferior to the other, but because black people are held captive' by values and institutions shaped by racial prejudice (ibid. p. 263). Noting that whiteness is the problem in black noir, Flory finds that the opening voiceover in *Eve's Bayou* plants the idea that Dr Batiste's license to philander has been 'inherited' from the unmitigated power that the institution of slavery afforded his white ancestor Jean-Paul Batiste (2008: 236).

Lemmons' second feature, *The Caveman's Valentine*, extends her exploration of black experience through the use of black noir strategies; Flory notes that the film 'looks and sounds much like *Eve's Bayou*, particularly in its *noirish* opening sequence, which uses distorted black-and-white imagery and sounds to make the audience feel anxious and uncertain' (ibid. p. 243). It is based on the novel and screenplay by George Dawes Green (who started 'The Moth' storytelling organisation). Having made a documentary in film school about homelessness in New York during the Reagan era, Lemmons was interested in directing a feature that could draw audiences into the life of someone whose status as a homeless person made them invisible. The film centres on former Juilliard Music School genius Romulus Ledbetter (Samuel L. Jackson), whose severe mental illness has separated him from his beloved wife and daughter, and led him to live in a cave in New York's Inwood Park. It depicts his subjective experiences and the detective investigation he undertakes 'to right what he perceives as the wrong done to the young homeless man he found early one Valentine's Day frozen to death in a tree outside his cave' (ibid. p. 242).

Like other iterations of black noir and ethnic crime fiction, in *The Caveman's Valentine* crime 'becomes a metaphor for all that is wrong with America', and the ongoing experiences of the black detective reveal 'injustices resulting in racial discrimination' (Goeller 2003: 175). His 'mental illness and circumstances betray overtones of the asymmetrical social pressures exerted on black men' (Flory 2008: 242). His drive to solve the immediate crime *and* the mystery of how to live in a society where one is 'invisible, or at the very least treated as [a] second-class citizen' makes black history and black experience visible (Goeller 2003: 177). Lemmons' film thus participates in the struggle for racial dignity and social empowerment found in Indiewood films inspired by the Black Nationalist movement.

Lemmons' third feature, *Talk to Me*, builds on her work in *Eve's Bayou* and *The Caveman's Valentine*, for in addition to being a film that illuminates the subjectivity, complexity, and full-fledged humanity of its black characters, *Talk to Me* uses the conventions of the biopic to demonstrate that Washington D.C. radio personality Ralph Waldo 'Petey' Greene, Jr (Don Cheadle) belongs in 'the traditional pantheon of American myth' (Bingham 2010: 190). As Willis notes, *Talk to Me* also 'tracks the development of African-American style and speech attending and responding to the emergence of black power, the Black Arts Movement, and blaxploitation cinema' (2015: 163). For her work on the film, Lemmons received the NAACP Image Award for Outstanding Directing in a Motion Picture (Theatrical or Television) and was named Best Director by the African-American Film Critics Association.

While covering Greene's career as a disc jockey and TV show host from the mid-1960s to the mid-1980s, *Talk to Me* achieves dramatic force by focusing on key events from the late 1960s: first, Greene's meteoric transition from prison disc jockey to host of the ground breaking call-in show, 'Rapping with Petey Greene', at AM radio station WOL, one of Washington D. C.'s top black music stations; and second, Greene's memorable broadcasts when he led the call for calm, mourning, and transformative action during the riots that erupted in Washington D. C. in 1968 following the news that Martin Luther King had been assassinated.

Scenes presenting Greene's gutsy entrance into the American public sphere depict his close personal relationships, first with his audacious girlfriend Vernell Washington (Taraji P. Henson) and later with Dewey Hughes (Chiwetel Ejiofor), the straight laced program director at WOL who becomes Greene's admirer and personal manager. Translating the screenplay by Michael Genet (Hughes' son) and Rick Famuyiwa with adroit pacing and bold choices about characters' hair, clothing, and body language, Lemmons uses Cheadle's vivid portrayal of Greene's wit, determination, and self-doubt as a window into the period when the civil rights and black power movements changed America. Taking audiences through another range of emotions in the scenes showing Greene, the WOL staff and Washington, DC in crisis following MLK's assassination, Lemmons combines the communicative power of the actors' intimate portrayals with her facility for staging scenes that convey the scale of historic events. Giving expression to the Black Nationalist values of New Black Aesthetic projects, *Talk to Me*, set in the nation's capital, illustrates that King's assassination is a tragedy for African Americans and America, and that Petey Greene is an African-American and American hero.

Continuing the epic scale and Black Nationalist perspective of *Talk to Me*, Lemmons' fourth feature film, *Black Nativity*, preserves Langston Hughes' Gospel Song-Play for future generations of African Americans, sustaining the tradition of stage productions mounted in cities throughout the US since the 1960s. The story follows fifteen-year-old Langston Cobbs (Jacob Latimore), who finds himself exploring and then solving the mystery that led Langston and his mother (Jennifer Hudson) to become estranged from his father (Tyrese Gibson) and his maternal grandparents (Forest Whitaker and Angela Bassett). Echoing strategies found in *The Caveman's Valentine*, the film uses dream sequences to communicate Langston's subjective experiences; following the use of locale in *Eve's Bayou*, this story is set in Harlem, 'the cultural heart of Black America', with important sequences set in the grandparents' 'lushly furnished brownstone', which Langston sees as a museum for black people, and in the massive church led by his grandfather, a respected minister who was a colleague of Martin Luther King (Seitz 2013). With the family's reconciliation celebrated by the congregation gathered to participate in the church's annual 'Black Nativity' production, the rebirth of Langston's family suggests that a sustained focus on community is what is needed for the rebirth 'of Harlem, and by extension America' (ibid.). The happy ending made possible by caring family and supportive congregation members reveals another theme in black women's cinema, by suggesting that a consciousness of 'life-force' sustains African Americans as individuals and members of a community (Ryan 2005: 2).

An *Ebony* article describes *Black Nativity* as one of many 2013 films showing the importance of Black independent cinema, and it applauds Fox Searchlight, the Weinstein Company, and Universal Pictures for 'backing this new wave' (Anonymous 2013). Illustrating an observation by Kasi Lemmons that 'a full spectrum of films' would be 'an indicator of success' for African-American filmmakers, the article highlights the 2013 release of *12 Years a Slave* (Steve McQueen), *Baggage Claim* (David E. Talbert), *Battle of the Year* (Benson Lee), *The Best Man Holiday* (Malcolm Lee), *Fruitvale Station* (Ryan Coogler), *Lee Daniel's The Butler* (Lee Daniels), *Mandela: Long Walk to Freedom* (Justin Chadwick), and *Tyler Perry's A Madea Christmas* (Tyler Perry). A piece on National Public Radio describes *Black Nativity* as one of several films with 'African-American casts and themes' backed by Zola Mashariki, Searchlight's senior vice president of production (Del Barco 2013). Discussing Searchlight's commitment to independent black films, NPR highlights Mashariki's involvement in *The Secret Life of Bees* (Gina Prince-Bythewood, 2008), *Notorious* (George Tillman, Jr, 2009), *Just Wright* (Sanaa Hamri, 2010), and *Belle* (Amma Asante, 2013). It also notes Black independent releases by Universal, the Weinstein Company, and Lions Gate Films, the distributor of films such as *Precious* (Lee Daniels, 2009), *Dear White People* (Justin Simien and Adriana Serrano, 2014), and Tyler Perry's productions from 2008 to 2014.

Future Research

The films of Rees, DuVernay, and Lemmons contribute to Indiewood cinema and the body of work created by the African-American artists who are shaping contemporary American culture. This chapter is merely a snapshot of their careers that highlights their participation in the ongoing Black Nationalist project to regain control of black images, one that indicates how much future research is to be done. The African-American Film Festival Releasing Movement, established by DuVernay, could be studied. The relationship between black women's Indiewood film and television merits investigation. Debbie Allen and Neema Barnette have substantial careers in television, as do film directors Darnell Martin, Angela Robinson, Millicent Shelton, Euzhan Palcy and Yvonne Welbon. Also worthy of study is the work of filmmakers with whom Rees, DuVernay, and Lemmons have collaborated: Bradford Young shot *Pariah*, *Middle of Nowhere*, and *Selma*; Amy Vincent shot *Eve's Bayou* and *The Caveman's Valentine*; Lemmons' films have been edited by Terilyn A. Shropshire and have scores composed by Terrence Blanchard. Research on Indiewood could compare films such as *Woman Thou Art Loosed* (Michael Schultz, 2004) or *Not Easily Broken* (Bill Duke, 2009) by established male directors, with *Night Catches Us* (Tanya Hamilton, 2010) or *Peeples* (Tina Gordon Chism, 2013) by emerging women directors. Studies could compare black women's films released during the Indiewood period with early independent films, such as discussed in *Spirits of Rebellion: Black Film at*

UCLA (Zeinabu Irene Davis, 2011) or productions screened at the 2015 series at Lincoln Center, 'Tell it like it is: Black Independents in New York, 1968-1986', which featured *Losing Ground* (Kathleen Collins, 1982), *Ganja and Hess* (Bill Gunn, 1973), and *Suzanne* (Camille Billops and James Hatch, 1982) (Brody 2015; Scott 2015).

Together with this chapter, the work to be done should explore how, during the Indiewood period, more 'black women directors [have gotten] the opportunity to work' because of the pioneering films by women and black male directors in earlier iterations of American independent cinema, the visibility of authors such as Toni Morrison and Maya Angelou, and the increased production opportunities in television (Donaldson 2003: 174). This volume illustrates the need to reframe American independent cinema so that accounts of it reflect the contributions of women's creative labour. This chapter aims to support that project by suggesting the need for research at the intersection of Black and American independent cinemas.

Note

1. Valerie Smith notes that her analysis of intersectionality builds on the work of Kimberle Crenshaw, who coined the term in her 1989 article, 'Demarginalizing the Intersection of Race and Sex' (Smith 1998: xiv, 139).

References

Alexander, George (2003), *Why We Make Movies: Black Filmmakers Talk About the Magic of Cinema*, New York: Harlem Moon.

Andrew, Geoff (1999), *Stranger than Paradise: Maverick Film-makers in Recent American Cinema*, New York: Limelight Editions.

Anonymous (2013), 'Coming to Your Theater Soon: Black is Apparently Back – In Terms of Movies, That Is', *Ebony*, 1 July, <http://www.ebony.com/entertainment-culture/coming-to-your-theater-soon> (last accessed 20 April 2015).

Berry, S. Torriano with Venise T. Berry (2001), *The 50 Most Influential Black Films: A Celebration of African-American Talent, Determination, and Creativity*, New York: Citadel Press.

Bingham, Dennis (2010), *Whose Lives Are They Anyway? The Biopic as Contemporary Film Genre*, New Brunswick, NJ: Rutgers University Press.

Bogle, Donald (2004), *Toms, Coons, Mulattoes, Mammies & Bucks: An Interpretive History of Blacks in American Films*, 4th edn, New York: Continuum.

Boyd, Todd (1997), *Am I Black Enough for You? Popular Culture from the Hood and Beyond*, Bloomington: Indiana University Press.

Boyd, Todd (2002), *The New H.N.I.C. (Head Nigger in Charge): The Death of Civil Rights and the Reign of Hip Hop*, New York: New York University Press.

Boyd, Todd (2008), 'Introduction', in Todd Boyd (ed.), *African Americans and Popular Culture: Volume 1: Theater, Film, and Television*, Westport, CT: Praeger, pp. vii–xii.

Brody, Richard (2015), 'Lost and Found: Kathleen Collins's 1982 Feature Gets Its First Release at Film Society of Lincoln Center', *The New Yorker*, 9 February, <http://www.newyorker.com/magazine/2015/02/09/lost-found> (last accessed 7 April 2015).

Cooper, Nekisa (2012), 'Love on the Outside', *Filmmaker Magazine*, 1 November, <http://filmmakermagazine.com/57145-love-on-the-outside/#.VHP814vF8rU> (last accessed 2 May 2015).

Crenshaw, Kimberle (1989), 'Demarginalizing the Intersection of Race and Sex: A Black Feminist Critique of Antidiscrimination Doctrine, Feminist Theory and Antiracist Politics', *The University of Chicago Legal Form*, pp. 139–67.

Del Barco, Mandalit (2013), 'How "Black Nativity" Made Its Way to the Big Screen', *National Public Radio*, 5 December, <http://www.npr.org/blogs/codeswitch/2013/12/06/247504610/how-black-nativity-made-its-way-to-the-big-screen> (last accessed 18 April 2014).

Diawara, Manthia (1993), 'Noir by Noirs: Toward a New Black Realism', in Joan Copec (ed.), *Shades of Noir: A Reader*, New York: Verso, pp. 261–78.

Donalson, Melvin (2003), *Black Directors in Hollywood*, Austin: University of Texas Press.

Elber, Lynn (2015), '*Selma* Wins Big at NAACP Awards', *Huffington Post*, 9 February, <http://www.huffingtonpost.com/2015/02/09/selma-blackish-among-big-_n_6645032.html> (last accessed 24 April 2015).

Ellis, Trey (2003), *Platitudes and 'The New Black Aesthetic'*, Boston: Northeastern University Press.

Flory, Dan (2008), *Philosophy, Black Film, Film Noir*, University Park, PA: the Pennsylvania State University Press.

Gabriel, Teshome H. (1988), 'Thoughts on Nomadic Aesthetics and the Black Independent Cinema: Traces of a Journey', in Mbye B. Cham and Claire Andrade-Watkins (eds), *Black Frames: Critical Perspectives on Black Independent Cinema*, Cambridge, MA: MIT Press, pp. 62–79.

Goeller, Alison D. (2003), 'The Mystery of Identity: The Private Eye (I) in the Detective Fiction of Walter Moseley and Tony Hillerman', in Dorothea Fischer-Hornung and Monika Mueller (eds), *Sleuthing Ethnicity: The Detective in Multiethnic Crime Fiction*, Cranbury, NJ: Associated University Presses, pp. 175–86.

Gray, Herman S. (2005), *Cultural Moves: African Americans and the Politics of Representation*, Berkeley: University of California Press.

Hardy, Ernest (2011), '*I Will Follow*', *LA Weekly*, 10 March, <http://www.laweekly.com/film/i-will-follow-2169472> (last accessed 5 April 2015).

King, Geoff (2005), *American Independent Cinema*, Bloomington: Indiana University Press.

Larkin, Alile Sharon (1988), 'Black Women Film-makers Defining Ourselves: Feminism in Our Own Voice', in E. Deidre Pribram (ed.), *Female Spectators: Looking at Film and Television*, New York: Verso, pp. 157–3.

Levy, Emanuel (1999), *Cinema of Outsiders: The Rise of American Independent Film*, New York: New York University Press.

Lott, Tommy L. (1997), 'A No-Theory Theory of Contemporary Black Cinema', in Valerie Smith (ed.), *Representing Blackness: Issues in Film and Video*, New Brunswick, NJ: Rutgers University Press, pp. 83–96.

Merritt, Greg (2000), *Celluloid Mavericks: A History of American Independent Film*, New York: Thunder's Mouth Press.

Perkins, Claire and Constantine Verevis (2015), 'Introduction: Possible Films', in Claire Perkins and Constantine Verevis (eds), *US Independent Film After 1989: Possible Films*, Edinburgh: Edinburgh University Press, pp. 1–14.

Petrusich, Amanda (2012), 'He's Just a "Custodian of the Moment"', *The New York Times*, 16 May, <http://www.nytimes.com/2012/05/20/movies/bradford-young-cinematographer> (last accessed 5 April 2015).

Prince-Bythewood, Gina (2014), 'It's Time to Obliterate the Term Black Film', *National*

Public Radio, 14 November, <http://mtpr.org/post/director-gina-prince-bythewood-its-time-obliterate-term-black-film> (last accessed 6 April 2015).

Reid, Mark A. (1993), *Redefining Black Film*, Berkeley: University of California Press.

Reid, Mark A. (2005), 'Black Female-Centered Film', in Mark A. Reid, *Black Lenses, Black Voices: African American Film Now*, New York: Rowman and Littlefield, pp. 79–104.

Ryan, Judylyn S. (2005), *Spirituality as Ideology in Black Women's Film and Literature*, Charlottesville: University of Virginia Press.

Sahagian, Jacqueline (2015), 'HBO's "Bessie", With Queen Latifah, Is Ideal Awards Bait', *Entertainment Check Sheet*, 12 April, <http://www.cheatsheet.com/entertainment/hbos-bessie-with-queen-latifah-is-ideal-awards-bait.html/?> (last accessed 21 April 2015).

Scott, A. O. (2015), 'Peeling Back the Layers of Black Indie Film', *The New York Times*, 5 February, <http://www.nytimes.com/2015/02/06/movies/tell-it-like-it-is-a-chapter-of-new-york-from-1968-to-86> (last accessed 6 February 2015).

Seitz, Matt Zoller (2013), '*Black Nativity*', *Roger Ebert.com*, 27 November, <http://www.rogerebert.com/reviews/black-nativity-2013> (last accessed 18 April 2014).

Sharkey, Betsy (2011), '*Pariah*', *Los Angeles Times*, 28 December, <http://www.focusfeatures.com/pariah/reviews> (last accessed 4 April 2015).

Shawnjames_2000 (2011), '*I Will Follow:* One of the Best African-American Films of 2011', *Internet Movie Database*, 10 September, <http://www.imdb.com/title/tt1624426/reviews?ref_=tt_urv> (last accessed 5 April 2015).

Smith, Valerie (1998), *Not Just Race, Not Just Gender: Black Feminist Readings*, New York: Routledge.

Snead, James (1994), *White Screens-Black Images*, Colin MacCabe and Cornel West (eds), New York: Routledge.

Terrell, Kellee (2013), 'Celebrating Black LGBT Pioneers', *Ebony*, 24 June, <http://www.ebony.com/photos/news-views/celebrating-black-LGBT/pioneers/photos-506> (last accessed 21 April 2015).

Thomson, Patricia (2011), 'Sundance 2011: Spirited Images: *Pariah*', *American Cinematographer*, April, pp. 63–4.

Tzioumakis, Yannis (2006), *American Independent Cinema: An Introduction*, New Brunswick, NJ: Rutgers University Press.

Van Leer, David (1997), 'Visible Silence: Spectatorship in Black Gay and Lesbian Film', in Valerie Smith (ed.), *Representing Blackness: Issues in Film and Video*, New Brunswick, NJ: Rutgers University Press, pp. 157–82.

White, Patricia (2015), '*Pariah* (2011): Coming Out in the Middle', in Claire Perkins and Constantine Verevis (eds), *US Independent Film After 1989: Possible Films*, Edinburgh: Edinburgh University Press, pp. 133–43.

Willis, Sharon (2015), 'Black Authenticity and the Ambivalent Icon: Keeping It Real in *Talk to Me*', in Sharon Willis, *The Poitier Effect: Racial Melodrama and Fantasies of Reconciliation*, Minneapolis: University of Minnesota Press, pp. 161–99.

Wilson, Wendy L. (2015), 'From Selma, To Hollywood, With Love', *Ebony*, 25 March, <http://www.ebony.com/entertainment-culture/from-selma-to-hollywood-with-love-639#axzz3YYVwEIeD> (last accessed 27 April 2015).

Yearwood, Gladstone L. (ed.) (1982), *Black Cinema Aesthetics*, Athens, OH: Ohio University Center for Afro-American Studies.

Yearwood, Gladstone L. (2000), *Black Film as a Signifying Practice: Cinema, Narration and the African-American Aesthetic Tradition*, Trenton, NJ: Africa World Press.

13. SEXUAL IN-BETWEENER/INDUSTRY IN-BETWEENER: THE CAREER AND FILMS OF LISA CHOLODENKO

Maria San Filippo

> I've always been interested in what makes people attracted to each other. How do people negotiate their needs? And where do sexual attraction and power and intimacy come into the mix for better and not better?
>
> Lisa Cholodenko (Spines 2010: 42)

With her debut feature *High Art* (1998), Lisa Cholodenko achieved art-house notoriety that portended a new wave of women filmmakers who were aiming to provoke both in their dark, sexually-charged subject matter and in their troubling of industrial and critical designations such as 'indie', 'feminist film', and 'gay cinema'. Lesbian independent filmmaking in the wake of New Queer Cinema had ventured little beyond the romantic comedies popularised by *Go Fish* (1994), but *High Art* departs radically from that film's Do-It-Yourself aesthetic, positive images, and identity politics with its lushly-filmed yet grittily-depicted portrait of an ill-fated affair between an ambitious aspiring art critic and a heroin-addicted has-been photographer. Cholodenko's subsequent feature, *Laurel Canyon* (2002), is less bleak and less identifiably queer, though it too focuses on a professionally driven young woman who experiences personal – and sexual – awakening in her encounter with an older, accomplished, but (self-)destructive woman. The arrival in 2010 of Cholodenko's third feature, gay-themed crossover hit *The Kids Are All Right*, caused a stir as clamorous as had *Philadelphia* (Jonathan Demme, 1993) and *Brokeback Mountain* (Ang Lee, 2005) before it, and its comparable commercial and critical success was hailed as evident of strides in mainstream gay visibility and acceptance. The narrative, in which partners Nic (Annette Bening) and Jules (Julianne Moore) and their two teenage children find their tenuous domestic harmony threatened after meeting their sperm donor Paul (Mark Ruffalo), is autobiographically informed by Cholodenko's mothering of a child with longtime partner Wendy Melvoin, one-half of the Wendy and Lisa duo from the musical act Prince and the Revolution. Yet Cholodenko's collaboration on the screenplay with Stuart Blumberg, known for scripting conventional Hollywood romcoms (and a straight man, no less), raised eyebrows. Also perceived by some as a betrayal of her queer/indie roots was the film's ostensibly homonormative promotion of bourgeois values and allegedly phallocentric sex scenes, which sparked a much-read blog-post critique by queer scholar Jack Halberstam titled 'The Kids Aren't Alright!' (Halberstam 2010).

In revisiting these alternately adulatory and divisive responses to *High Art* and *The Kids Are All Right*, in addition to considering the underdiscussed *Laurel Canyon* and Cholodenko's recent television work, I identify an 'in-betweener' space and approach that characterises Cholodenko's career and films. In the context of identity formations around gender and sexuality, 'in-betweener' signifies a position and/or movement between binary constructions that serves to disrupt and resist such binaries. In addition to demonstrating how Cholodenko's politics of representation generate a body of work defiantly in-betweener in its troubling of sexual binaries alongside the binary of gay versus straight/mainstream cinema, I also locate Cholodenko's oeuvre as staking out an in-betweener position that negotiates and resists additional entertainment industry categorisations. Thinking specifically of those industrial categorisations regulating notions of 'art versus commerce' and 'film versus television', and reinforcing notions of 'gay cinema' and 'women's cinema', Cholodenko's career constitutes a disruption of boundaries established by an industrially and ideologically heteropatriarchal hierarchy, and thus valuably models an in-betweener route for women practitioners in the contemporary US indie sphere. So too, I argue, do Cholodenko's individual works reflexively stage negotiations resonant of her extra-diegetic concerns as a sexual/industry in-betweener, focusing specifically on the politics of queer representation (*High Art*), on the mediation between art and commerce (*Laurel Canyon*), and on personal/artistic engagement with sociopolitical issues (*The Kids Are All Right*). With characters who resist sexual categorisation as much as she herself resists ideological and industrial categorisation, Cholodenko's work to date probes the fluidity of desire and the complexities of identity while traversing the dividing lines of American filmmaking to establish a site of in-betweenness on all counts.

Highs and Lows

For a fifty-two-year-old commercial director whose debut feature appeared in 1998, Cholodenko's output is relatively diminutive; in addition to (co-)writing and directing the three aforementioned features, over the past eighteen years she has directed a handful of television episodes (*Hung* (2009–11), *Homicide: Life on the Street* (1993–9), *The L Word* (2004–9), *Six Feet Under* (2001–5)) and three projects adapted for American television: 2004 Showtime film *Cavedweller*, based on a Dorothy Allison novel and starring and produced by Kyra Sedgwick; 2014 HBO mini-series *Olive Kitteridge*, based on Elizabeth Strout's Pulitzer Prize-winning novel and featuring Cholodenko's second collaboration with performer Frances McDormand, who stars in *Laurel Canyon*; and 2015 NBC mini-series *The Slap*, an ensemble drama adapted from a best-selling novel and preceded by an Australian mini-series before its US importation by executive producer Cholodenko, who directed the first episode. Cholodenko admits to the intermittency of her directorial yield in tones that suggest it was anything but self-chosen: 'I've had years that have been horribly depressing and scary and I've been *that close* to applying to work at Whole Foods', she confesses (Spines 2010: 43). It is testament to the vicissitudes of American low-budget filmmaking after the 1990s indie boom that a director whose first feature won the Waldo Salt Screenwriting Award at the Sundance Film Festival and whose subsequent efforts have continued to garner awards and (however relatively modest) profits would need to contemplate such a professional demotion. Certainly other American indie directors (Gregg Araki, Cheryl Dunye, Tom Kalin, Rose Troche) with whom Cholodenko shared the New Queer Cinema spotlight cast by critic B. Ruby Rich's heralding of an emergent movement (in a 1992 *Sight & Sound* piece) have faced career lags, with only Todd Haynes and Gus Van Sant mustering consistently active careers (Rich 1992: 30–4). Haynes and Van Sant provide interesting counterpoints to Cholodenko for the way all three have reshaped queer cinema's contours towards more commercially and sexually expansive ends, though we might speculate that the former two filmmakers' greater productivity stems from the white male privilege that still affords (even gay) men disproportionate access to directing both within Hollywood and on its margins. Alongside Cholodenko's out lesbian status as a determinant of her erratic employment and tempered recognition in the industry, what also seems causative is Cholodenko's resistance to being professionally as well as sexually 'pigeonholed', a term uttered by both female protagonists, with similar inflection, in *High Art*.

Cholodenko's debut feature is a feminist *bildungsroman*, which chronicles a focused young woman's professional rise and congratulatory emergence upon editing a spread for eminent photography magazine *Frame*. From its opening sequence of Syd (Radha Mitchell) assiduously working after hours as an assistant editor who is nonetheless expected to run demeaning errands for her higher-ups, *High Art* proves attuned to how women's labour is devalued and exploited even in the ostensibly nurturing, non-corporate art world. When Syd reports to editor Harry (David Thornton) that she knows of a photographer whose work should be considered for the magazine, he tellingly replies, 'What's his name'? Moreover, *High Art* challenges feminism's frequently hollow exhortations that female solidarity is the route to women's professional success by tainting relations amongst on-the-rise Syd, *Frame*'s imperious executive director Dominique (Anh Duong), and Lucy Berliner (Ally Sheedy), Syd's upstairs neighbour and a once-famous photographer who will take Syd as her editor, muse, and lover before succumbing to a fatal overdose. In so doing, Cholodenko inaugurates within *High Art* a narrative framework that will importantly inform each of her feature films: women's navigation of a post-feminist professional landscape in which their success is nominally encouraged but beset by external and internal modes of containment that prompt them to explore alternative forms of fulfilment, artistic and otherwise.

That *High Art* is intent on scrutinising the gendered contours of careerism and female self-fulfilment is signalled by the casting of Sheedy, known for her youthful career as one of the 'Brat Pack', who retreated from Hollywood prematurely because, as she describes, 'I just needed to get out. I was really unhappy. I needed to find something different for myself" (Rich 1998: 46). Her comeback role in *High Art*, for which she won a National Society of Film Critics Award, dovetails with the self-exiled character she plays, in one of several reflexive layers in the film. In an intimate discussion with Syd in the creative refuge of her darkroom, Lucy rationalises her spiral into burnout obscurity by claiming to have felt 'pigeonholed' by the art world in the initial flush of attention she received at the start of her career. 'There just stopped being a line between me and work. People were glomming on to something I was doing then, and I just got trapped'. Dominique pushes Syd to use her influence with Lucy to solicit a new piece, but pronounces dissatisfaction with Lucy's initial offering of stylised underwater portraits of girlfriend Greta (Patricia Clarkson). Pushing Lucy to 'revisit some of your older themes . . . an examination of your friends and your life', Dominique and Harry decree that the 'cultural currency' of Lucy's work resides in the 'rigor' and 'realism' that characterised her early focus on 'the intimacy and desolation of her subjects'. That early work, which featured druggy, sexually-debauched depictions echoing Nan Goldin's *The Ballad of Sexual Dependency* and other controversial chronicles of New York's heroin-chic, No Wave downtown scene, first caught Syd's discerning eye when she saw it hanging in Lucy's apartment. Though Syd's superiors veil their demands in euphemism, it's evident that Lucy once more risks being pigeonholed as an imagist of explicitly queer eroticism. The underwater portraits, though featuring Lucy's lover Greta, are denounced by Dominique for having 'no context';

she scoffs at Syd's defence of their beauty and quality, saying 'Lucy Berliner has been invisible for ten years. The public has a five year memory and that's it'. Echoing her, Harry says, 'If a best-selling crime writer disappeared for ten years and came back peddling love poems, how do you think it would do? It's a business, Syd'. Noting Cholodenko's allusion to R. W. Fassbinder's high-camp lesbian ménage in *The Bitter Tears of Petra von Kant* (1972), Lee Wallace sees *High Art*'s Sapphic triangle as a stand-off between two artistic alternatives tethered to the old world and the new: German actress 'Greta's claim to the Fassbinder aesthetic, which ties together homosexuality, artistic intensity, and an unchecked impulse to self-destruction' versus the sober, industrious, American careerism Syd represents (Wallace 2009: 61). The in-betweener space that *High Art* occupies, unmistakably drawing on European art film but emerging from the grassroots 1990s US film movement that would by decade's end evolve into Indiewood, suggests a third way that, had she lived, Lucy would find through her productive, less compromised collaboration with Syd.

Syd's ultimate choice to turn over photographs Lucy takes during their weekend together constitutes a public (given her placement as cover model) coming out as a queer woman. Syd stands nervously by as Dominique examines the images, and then asks, with barely-contained elation at their scintillating potential, 'Are you her lover'? which, after a beat, Syd confirms. Having first clarified that she was not Lucy's sitter, Syd distinguishes here between artistic versus authentic performance; the photographs exhibit the truth of her lesbian desire. Lucy's urging of Syd to use these photographs defers to Syd's superiors' (and by extension the art world's) imperative that queer-identified artists such as Cholodenko make queerness explicitly visible in their work, preferably within established representational confines such as the *mise-en-scène* of erotic decadence suffusing Lucy's famous images. In comparison, Lucy's new piece for *Frame* reflects her less sensationalist, sober reality as Syd's lover; it still satisfies Dominique's (and the public's) desire to peer voyeuristically into explicitly queer spaces, but Lucy and Syd retain creative and editorial control and give clear-headed, full consent. The images they select for the spread highlight this reflexive gesture whereby Cholodenko connects and revises photographic and cinematic gazes. The first image shows Syd looking directly into the camera, confronting the viewer with the same knowingness she levelled at Lucy, at the point in the narrative when the photograph was taken, regarding her drug use. Also included are a series of shots in which Syd is seen sleeping, then groggily awakening to face the camera, then joined in the frame by Lucy, who (having set the self-timer) crosses the barrier to lie atop and nuzzle her as Syd continues to stare camera-wards. Collectively, the images are strikingly intimate yet resistant, by virtue of their reflexive techniques of direct address and author-as-subject, to allowing the viewer's immersion into a fantasy realm. Though offering up their sexual involvement for visual pleasure, Lucy and Syd

Figure 13.1 Radha Mitchell and Ally Sheedy in *High Art* (1998).

revise their queer self-representation by means of an in-betweener approach that seeks not to destroy that pleasure, but to actively engage the spectator in recognition of the sexual/visual economy that (re)produces queerness for financial profit and political containment.

Where Lucy seems to be Cholodenko's stand-in as embodiment of industrial in-betweenness, Syd signifies the sexual in-betweenness, if not of Cholodenko herself (who came out as lesbian at the age of 17), then of the logic of desire across Cholodenko's body of work. The impulse to read Syd as autobiographically inspired pertains to the industrial as well: as this was Cholodenko's first commercial directorial outing, she faced the challenge of entering a film industry affixed with the 'lesbian director' label and the expectations that would follow. Just as Cholodenko would confound those expectations by straying from the queer and narrow of gay filmmaking towards more mainstream projects, her characters – starting with Syd – defy what elsewhere I have called *compulsory monosexuality* to claim a sexual in-betweenness in keeping with the vicissitudes of desire (San Filippo 2013). In her confession to Dominique, Syd hasn't conformed to the coming out narrative that works to fix sexual identity as static, discursively bound, and thus politically containable; her admission remains in the realm of the behavioural, emotional, and fluid.

Unsurprisingly, in signalling the contingency of sexuality, Syd becomes vulnerable to aspersions that view her (unnamed as such) bisexuality in pejorative terms that ironically serve to disavow bisexuality as a viable identity – such as when Greta, in what surely is an intentional linguistic slip, judges Syd a 'psychophant' out to seduce Lucy as a means to attain professional access. But *High Art* itself views Syd more affirmatively, by figuring Syd's sexual desire as entangled with, but irreducible to, her professional desire. Responding to boyfriend James' (Gabriel Mann) similarly distrusting view, Syd proclaims her professional desire in terms that invite us to understand it through, though not to conflate it with, her analogous attraction to the queer world that Lucy represents:

> If you weren't so fixated on putting me in a box, on *pigeonholing* me . . . no matter what I do, you can't stop telling me it's wrong. I'm trying to get somewhere, all I get from you are these slurs about my job and the people that I've met and how pretentious and meaningless and idiotic it is, and – you know what? It's not meaningless to me. This is what I care about.

Yet Syd's attraction and ambition remain conflated by characters and critics alike, with Maria Pramaggiore positing 'The central theme of the art world's exploitation of artists is inextricably bound to Syd and to her bisexuality: Syd is the channel through which Lucy becomes vulnerable again to the expectations of commodified art making' (Pramaggiore 2002: 263). Here Pramaggiore views Syd rather more harshly than the film seems to, and overlooks the less exploitative industrial in-betweener position that I see Syd and (with her comeback) Lucy occupying. Pramaggiore goes on to note *High Art*'s affiliation between bisexuality and art: 'as an erotics of refusing distinctions, bisexuality acts as a metaphor . . . for the promiscuous blending of high art and low entertainment', an assessment I agree with but would add to that Cholodenko seems not simply to blend but to disidentify altogether with markers of high/low and straight/gay, a boundary-blurring that continues in her subsequent feature films (Pramaggiore 2002: 264).

California Dreamin'

Like *High Art*, Cholodenko's next two features *Laurel Canyon* and *The Kids Are All Right* can be read as industrial allegories of her negotiation of an in-betweener path between professional worlds – gay and straight/mainstream media – and between the expectations of compulsory monosexuality that those two worlds mandate. Jodi Brooks finds that Cholodenko's films ponder 'what it is to live and move – and to choose – between worlds', yet the female protagonists of *High Art* and *Laurel Canyon* are not forced to choose but rather navigate productive ways to inhabit both worlds and indeed reveal their porous overlaps (Brooks 2014: 113–14). After all, *Laurel Canyon*'s titular fantasy world of bohemian musicians and record producers is one of privilege, dependent on the commercial infrastructure of the music industry that supports it. Cholodenko's resistance to conjuring the queer spaces of her films in utopian terms, and indeed her willingness to confront the escapism they enable, suggests a similarly un-idealised vision of the space of queer cinema. Bohemian earthmother Jane (McDormand) admits to 'lik[ing] capitalism as much as the next guy', though she balances commerce and creativity with an ethical stance that mirrors the way she conducts her emotional life. Estranged son Sam (Christian Bale), in Los Angeles for his medical residency, works long hours while fiancée Alex (Kate Beckinsale), tasked with completing her dissertation, finds herself inexorably drawn to the studio where Jane and her significantly younger rocker boyfriend Ian (Alessandro Nivola) are themselves struggling to finish a record. Soliciting Alex for input, Jane describes her métier in terms suggestive both of Cholodenko's openness to working in more mainstream (popular) realms of the entertainment industry, as well as of Jane's fluid logic of desire: 'Anyone with instincts knows about popular music. That's why it's popular. You strike me as someone with strong instincts. Well, you know when you're repulsed and when you're turned on, right? That's all it is. Either it pulls you in or it leaves you cold'. The photographic legacy of her accomplished career that layer her home's walls, and which Alex pores over, establishes Jane as a kindred soul to *High Art*'s Lucy, but one who survives and flourishes by way of the more moderate means with which she keeps the bohemian spirit alive.

Jane manages her erotic life with a similarly open-minded but clear-eyed realism. Her bisexuality is presented in passing, almost as a given, when Sam inquires about an ex-girlfriend; 'Veronica and I stopped having sex after the third month', Jane replies in a foreshadowing of the 'lesbian bed death' cliché that angered critics of *The Kids Are All Right*. I find Jane's comment more objectionable here than in *Kids*, where the same-sex couple's near-celibacy seems attributed to long-term monogamy more than lesbianism. Otherwise, *Laurel Canyon*'s treatment of Jane's sexual fluidity resists heteronormativity ('Why do you want to spoil this with domesticity'? she asks Ian when he proposes moving in) while loosening associations of bisexuality with hedonistic amorality by having Jane ultimately abstain from a ménage-a-trois with Ian and her future daughter-in-law Alex. 'Sublimation', as Sam refers to it when fighting the urge to similarly act on his attraction to alluring co-worker Sara (Natascha McElhone), is sometimes necessary to avoid emotional casualty; in suggesting such a realistic but not moralistic view, Cholodenko again throws cold water on the voyeuristic expectations held by characters and viewers alike. As in *High Art*, Cholodenko seems at first to conform to 'lesploitation' convention, with amorous cavorting among Alex, Jane, and Ian in a swimming pool followed by a hotel room rendezvous recreating the heterophallic trope of a two girls-one guy threesome in which male pleasure is paramount. That Jane interrupts this scenario constitutes a cock-block of the straight male fantasy that Ian and the film's viewers anticipate.

As Jodi Brooks notes, 'Cholodenko's Laurel Canyon is a world that seems to be running according to its own clock and rhythms, and the film distils this alternate beat . . . through the ways it embodies the Canyon in its central character – Jane' (Brooks 2015: 94). Not unlike Jane's professional straddling of commerce and art, Cholodenko herself embodies in-betweenness with this, her second feature, which while hardly devoid of Hollywood wish fulfillment (its dreamy cast and setting, its romanticisation of the entertainment world) still clearly displays Cholodenko's alternative vision. That vision is exemplified by the character of Jane, who is exceptional for being a strong and sexy, grounded and flawed, middle-aged female protagonist. As with *High Art*, it is also possible to see shades of Cholodenko in *Laurel Canyon*'s younger female protagonist; like the filmmaker, Alex is an East Coast Ivy Leaguer who goes west to Hollywood and is caught up, for a time, in its seduction. Just as Syd establishes a middle way between Lucy's self-destructive path and Dominique's exploitative one, Alex by film's end acknowledges how the experience 'really opened me up' but appears back on track with her dissertation and relationship with Sam. While there's certainly something recuperative about *Laurel Canyon*'s getting its heterosexual, age-appropriate couple reunited at film's end, Cholodenko indicates how emotional commitment doesn't preclude sexual temptation but provides a worthwhile reason for sublimating. Thus I would challenge *Cineaste*'s view of the Cholodenko female protagonist as an 'interloper within a bohemian milieu with aspirations towards being an insider'; unlike *Kids*' Paul, whom lesbian mom Nic berates for having invaded her domestic sphere, Alex as well as *High Art*'s Syd seek to redefine themselves not by upsetting the balance of the queer space they enter but through unbalancing their own too rigidly conventional selves (Porton 2010: 14).

Yet the sexual fluidity that permeates Cholodenko's first two features arises again in *Kids* through an in-betweenness that acknowledges how emotional bonds (rather than normative values) are determinants of desire as well as, occasionally, reasons to sublimate those desires. Like Syd and Alex, Jules in *Kids* finds herself drawn by a complex skein of desire into an affair with her children's biological father. But just as *High Art* and *Laurel Canyon* resisted the conventional path of the coming-out narrative, *Kids* plays with but ultimately rejects Hollywood treatments of lesbianism undone by the arrival of a straight male interloper in films such as *The Fox* (Mark Rydell, 1967). Though Jules has enjoyable (far too enjoyable, to some critics) sex with Paul, she is not shown to doubt her sexual identity. When Nic, having learned of the affair, asks 'Are you straight now'? Jules responds with a defiant 'No! That has nothing to do with it', then tells Paul with equal vehemence, 'I'm gay'! – thereby pricking any fantasy Paul holds, as a straight man who 'loves lesbians', of lesbianism as always being susceptible to replacement by heterosexuality. While bisexuality again goes unspoken, Jules' affirmation of her lesbian identity seems less a knee-jerk endorsement of essentialism than a reclaiming of her uninterrupted impulse, and right, to so identify despite having had (enjoyable) sex with a man. Paradoxically, Jules' unwavering self-identification as lesbian – much like Cholodenko's own – testifies to the film's affirmation of sexual in-betweenness, wherein personal/political identity does not preclude erotic/emotional desire. In keeping with Cholodenko's aim to probe the rules of attraction, as the epigraph that starts this essay voices, this recognition of sexual fluidity valuably reveals how desire is often steered by circumstance and emotional need ('to be appreciated', as Jules tearfully tells Nic). Yet the sticky suggestion that Jules found herself irresistibly drawn to Paul specifically, in some primal urge prompted by seeing her kids' faces in his expressions, uncomfortably links female sexual attraction to mothering – one in a litany of criticisms aimed at the film.

Disciplining *Kids*

The unwieldy financing of Cholodenko's third feature led to a protracted development phase of five-plus years, such that she could not have foreseen that setting this film about lesbian partnership and parenting in present-day Los Angeles would make it ground zero when the anti-marriage-equality ballot Proposition 8 passed in the November 2008 California state elections. The would-be amendment was almost immediately appealed, and ultimately ruled unconstitutional by the California Supreme Court in 2010, the year of *Kids*' release. This degree of diegetic, if neither explicit nor didactic, political engagement is in keeping with Cholodenko's handling of controversy, courting it in her choice of subject matter at the same time that she disavows it through representational treatments that steer clear of the radical and with promotional statements such as this from the time of the film's release: 'Our intention wasn't overtly political. The subversion, as we saw it, was to be nonpolitical, and just to make this human story that was about a family that people could relate to, no matter what your identity or your sexual preferences were' (Austerlitz 2010). Yet as Fiona Cox perceptively notes, its 'ostensibly apolitical tone . . . is in fact its most political aspect' (Cox 2013: 255).

Kids is the film with which Cholodenko's status as an 'industry in-betweener' was consecrated. With a production budget of only $5 million, made possible by leads Bening and Moore working for scale, *Kids* is one of a dying breed of 'middle-class movies', so named by filmmaker Mark Duplass for their falling between the widening socioeconomic gap in American film production whereby the majority falls at either end of the financing spectrum: studio-backed blockbusters or micro-budgeted indies (Bakare 2015). This sweet spot that *Kids* occupies financially – not so big an investment as to risk losing creative control, but hardly hard-up, 'It felt a little like making *High Art* except we didn't exploit people', as Cholodenko puts it – parallels the in-betweener positioning that the film achieved by virtue of crossing over (Spines 2010: 43).

Kids' critical reception contributes to the extra-diegetic discourse that locates Cholodenko as an in-betweener vis-à-vis constructions of queer versus straight (that is, hetero- or homonormative) filmmaking. Much of the praise and criticism levelled at *Kids* echoed that which greeted *Brokeback Mountain*, as Suzanna Danuta Walters demonstrates in parsing how the public relations campaign and simpatico critics 'went down the well-worn universalist track' of emphasising the film's broadly identifiable characters, poignant storyline, and assimilationist gay family values, in order 'to have its homosexual difference and contain it too' (Walters 2012: 924). Given these (mostly straight white male) mainstream critics' apparent obliviousness to the film's objectionable aspects, it was apt and appreciated that so many feminist/queer voices rang in to oppose its widespread acclaim, though I would single out for criticism myself two blogged responses, by noted scholars Jack Halberstam and Lisa Duggan. Unsurprising given the solipsism that blogging encourages, their opining carried inflections of self-legitimating aimed at denouncing the film's own ostensible attempt to prove its lesbian bona fides. At its worst, these round-ups make *Kids* a whipping boy while voicing judgements about its lead actors' unglamorous styling (Halberstam terms Moore 'dowdy', lamenting that she 'loses her looks!') and one-upping their lesbian legitimacy with a show of insider knowledge (Halberstam questions why Nic, rather than Paul, isn't the BMW motorcycle enthusiast, 'classic beemers [being] a popular queer choice of motorcycle, in fact') (Halberstam 2010). Agreeing heartily with Halberstam, Duggan's response decries what she calls Cholodenko's 'absolutely vile' direction of a 'dyke-face minstrel show'; her comments are worth quoting at length for their similar fixation on visible markers of lesbianism:

> Annette Benning's [*sic*] Nic was a cartoon andro[gynous] dyke (they clearly didn't try for butch). Not just her scripted role as a priggish, controlling, condescending asshole, but . . . her gestures, her facial expressions and the way she held her mouth, her stance, her movements. These, one may argue, are questions of acting – perhaps Annette Benning [*sic*] just tried too hard and turned herself into a caricature? But she had a lesbian director (!) who finally guided her gestures and expressions and movements and decided which versions and edits would make it into the film. But if Benning's [*sic*] Nic was bad, Julianne Moore's Jules was horrifying, offensive and repulsive (I could add more adjectives, but maybe that's enough?). As the somewhat more femme partner, she nonetheless manufactured the same cartoon mouth thing that was supposed to look "dykey," similar gestures and movements and . . . they made her look really bad in order to make her lesbian. (My pal [Kathryn Bond] Stockton

> began to fear coming home to her lovely girlfriend Shelley White in overalls and a bad sun hat.) Has Cholodenko never seen Wanda Sykes move or Portia de Rossi smile? (Duggan 2010)

While one can certainly find fault with Nic's domineering parenting/partnering and with *Kids*' continuing a representational legacy that softens and effaces female masculinity, Halberstam's and Duggan's comments reduce lesbianism to something verifiable by means of superficial indicators. Claiming that lesbianism is proven via a set of sanctioned looks and behaviours that conform to gendered expectations to be macho (riding motorcycles) or feminine (not wearing overalls) reinforces the same stereotypes that Halberstam and Duggan disparage in the film. As does Halberstam's twin conjecture that 'by not making much of a gender distinction between Nic (vaguely butch) and Jules (vaguely femme)', *Kids* disservices real lesbian couples (Halberstam 2010). Again, this heteronormative positioning of a supposedly not sufficiently butch-femme pair as unbelievable and unappealing overlooks Cholodenko's disidentification with binary-reproducing norms of gender and sexuality.

Also drawing the ire of these and other critics was the aforementioned invocation of 'lesbian bed death' contrasted with rigorous, orgasmic heterophallic sex. What goes missing from these academic bloggers' accounts is a moderate assessment that does not hold the film's representations to such exactingly (and superficial) standards of so-called lesbian legitimacy, but one that does not veer to the opposite extreme by giving the film a pass on its insensitivities and missteps, as does the presumptuous claim in *Cineaste* that 'Of course, only the incorrigibly politically correct will find [Jules' and Paul's] brief romp, which is played mainly for laughs, objectionable' (Porton 2010: 15). Those who take Cholodenko to task for having, as Walters puts it, 'Jules genuflect before Paul's penis', fail to note that in their subsequent sexual encounter, Jules sits astride Paul demanding he pull her hair as she slaps his face until she orgasms – rather queer sex, one could say (Walters 2012: 922). Cholodenko defended her omission of a lesbian sex scene that she claims to have filmed but left out during editing because 'it somehow felt disingenuous. To play it that way would have been to pander – a political maneuver' (Lucia and Porton 2010: 18). Instead, Cholodenko makes explicit reference to lesbian sex with two mentions of cunnilingus (Jules under the covers pleasuring Nic and her joking that after first meeting Nic her 'tongue started working again') that, though 'tastefully' veiled or spoken rather than seen, are unmistakable. After confronting son Laser (Josh Hutcherson) when caught with his moms' stash of gay male porn, Jules' honest explanation of why she and Nic wouldn't prefer 'watch[ing] two women doing it' serves to defend the film's stance as well: 'You would think that. But in most of those movies, they've hired two straight women to pretend and the inauthenticity is just unbearable'.

Interestingly, there is little recognition that a straight white male co-wrote the script with Cholodenko, yet has shouldered little of the criticism. There remain points I could push for the reason that Jasbir Puar and Karen Tongson, in a refreshingly reasonable entry in the blogpost blitz, explain: '[Cholodenko's films] never featured who anyone would call "likeable" characters. All of her films' protagonists have been white, privileged, pretentious and undeniably fucked up . . . [whom Cholodenko] . . . softly, but also scathingly satirises [as] the denizens of queer(ish) urbanity, primarily in Los Angeles' (Puar and Tongson 2012). Echoing their sentiment, I would respond to critics who find that Nic and Jules' partnership replicates the terms of conventional straight marriage – from breadwinner Nic rebuking submissive Jules in front of the children to Jules going down on Nic – that the film hardly endorses their marriage as equilateral and conflict-free, with several scenes given over to Jules expressing her frustration with their marital status quo and her need for greater professional and personal, more than sexual, fulfilment. On the topic of what Halberstam calls *Kids*' 'casual racism', clearly the film does not invite us to applaud (through neither to condemn) Jules for her (as she calls it) 'fucked up' treatment and abrupt dismissal of Latino gardener Luis (Joaquín Garrido) (Halbertam 2010). Nor are we invited to look past Tanya's (Yaya DaCosta) rightful fury when Paul informs his African-American employee/casual sex partner that in 'need[ing] to start thinking about having a family', he must end their extracurricular trysts. From Tanya's first appearance onscreen, when Paul refers to her as 'Foxy' – alluding to the Pam Grier-starring blaxploitation classic *Foxy Brown* (Jack Hill, 1974) – we are made to note Paul's hypersexualisation of her as someone he regards not as mother material, in contrast to Jules, the 'fecund' mother of his children. Although I take issue with these attempts to discipline, from both directions, *Kids*' representational options and our responses to them, there is much to admire about the feminist-queer critique of *Kids*. Collectively these readings illuminate what is troubling about *Kids*: its homonormative endorsement of marriage and family values and the right to defend them at any cost, alongside its complicity in a Hollywood-designed representational system that glosses over questions of class and race. As Puar and Tongson conclude, *Kids* is not an ugly film 'but rather it reveals the ugliness at the heart of queer and bourgeois-bohemian fantasies about being different', and in so doing is compelling precisely because of 'how uncomfortable it makes us feel when we actually *do* experience the tiniest moments of self-recognition within these characters' (Puar and Tongson 2012).

Choosing Security, but Still Courting Controversy

Though it was rumoured that *Kids* was to be developed as a HBO series, it was another project that Cholodenko ultimately brought to fruition at the prestige cable channel: *Olive Kitteridge*, a four-part mini-series adapted from an acclaimed short story collection titled for and focused on an aging matriarch living in a coastal Maine enclave. Frances McDormand bought the rights to Strout's book and developed the project, hiring playwright-screenwriter and out lesbian Jane Anderson to adapt and selecting Cholodenko as director. McDormand plays Olive with a New Englander's exacting resolve and impatience with sentiment and silliness, and in so doing seems affixed to Clara Bradbury-Rance's characterisation that

> Cholodenko's films exhibit many of the outlined traits of postfeminist culture that seem by their very nature to be pitted in opposition to feminist and queer convictions: female temporal anxiety; demonization of purportedly overbearing mother figures; the ultimate privileging of familial – if not biological – relations over friendship-based communities; the girling of femininity and the glorification of youth and naivety; and the representation of older women (who defy that girlification) as jaded. (Bradbury-Rance 2013: 39)

But as Bradbury-Rance is quick to concede, 'Representation does not equate to complicity' (ibid.). Here as in *Laurel Canyon*, had Cholodenko wanted to demonise the mother figure as overbearing, she is undone by McDormand's likeability and the script's shift in point-of-view, dispersed among townspeople in Strout's stories, to sit squarely with Olive so as to reveal her more sympathetically than an outsider's perspective would. Not unlike *Laurel Canyon*'s Jane, McDormand's Olive is a strong-willed, literally unapologetic woman who defies social propriety and gendered dictates to act submissively and to put others' feelings above her own, even as she demonstrates a more finely tuned moral compass than those around her. The 'temporal anxiety' that gnaws at Olive as she watches her only son grow up and move away and the family pharmacy being sold to a corporate chain is mournful but not a denial of aging, such as that which husband Henry (Richard Jenkins) demonstrates in flirting with helpless-acting younger women, whom Olive views with derision. As if still in character, McDormand's stern countenance throughout the Golden Globes ceremony (where her Best Actor nomination for *Olive Kitteridge* was a surprising non-win) was disparaged on social media, indicating the extent to which female celebrities are judged harshly for not exhibiting girlish charm even as they are berated when found not to be 'acting their age'.

Olive proves to be as assailable a role model as Cholodenko's other flawed, non-prescriptively feminist heroines. Made lonely by her husband's death and son's absence, Olive connects with irascible Republican widower Jack Kennison (Bill Murray) in the tellingly titled fourth and final instalment of the mini-series, 'Security'. In a first date dinner conversation that turns divisive upon Jack revealing that he has not spoken to his daughter in two years because she has chosen to live with another woman, Olive is forced to contend with the dilemma of desiring companionship but having no use for heteropatriarchal thinking; in so doing, and as with all her work, Cholodenko integrates discussion of sexual alternatives into the narrative. Their conversation, and date, ends when Jack accuses Olive of being equally judgemental – an allegation that inaccurately equates bigotry with judgement, Olive's strong pronouncements about people never stemming from superficial markers of race, class, or sexual orientation. In choosing to reconcile with Jack, Olive privileges emotional and perhaps (given Jack's wealth) financial security over her misgivings about his character. It is a vexing conclusion given that we heretofore have admired Olive's principled self-sufficiency, but one more courageous and truthful in finding Olive to be entirely human in her need and ultimately akin to other Cholodenko protagonists in balancing the thrill of liberation with the safeness of security.

Cholodenko's latest project, eight-part mini-series *The Slap*, premiered on NBC in February 2015 and focuses on the aftermath of a grown man slapping a young boy at a gathering of family and friends; the boy's parents press charges, and those present find themselves pressured to take sides. Though based on a best-selling novel by Greek-Australian novelist Christos Tsiolkas and adapted for American television by playwright-screenwriter Jon Robin Baitz, both openly gay writers, *The Slap*'s themes echo those of Cholodenko's self-scripted films. Enlisted to document the festivities, budding photographer and gay teen Ritchie (Lucas Hedges), a victim himself of homophobic cyberbullying, becomes key witness given his roving camera's omniscient perspective. Wrestling with how much of one's personal life should be submitted for public scrutiny, forced to confront people he admires and finding them flawed and engaging in escapist behaviour that endangers their loved ones, Ritchie's consternation and ultimate surrendering of 'pictures of these people whom I love trying hard to make it through a day' specifically mirrors Syd's conflicted handing over of photographic proof of her queer desire. In its focus on the multicultural ensemble's conflicting customs, one sees resemblance to *Kids*' exploration of alternative family formations and complex wrangling of security, tradition, and acculturation within a society that remains heteropatriarchal. Though her defiance of patriarchal presumptuousness isn't as showstopping as when Nic in *Kids* tells Paul she needs his observations 'like I need a dick in my ass', *The Slap*'s Anouk (Uma Thurman), a proudly single and childless television director, refuses to be manhandled by the wealthy, hot-blooded Harry (Zachary Quinto) who's facing indictment as a result of the slap. 'You come from a place where men can get away with whatever they want', Anouk informs the second-generation Greek-American turned Westchester County warrior, 'but the world has changed'. Given Anouk's professional role alongside her denouncement of male privilege, we might locate in her another stand-in for Cholodenko.

As *The Slap*'s premise reflects, Cholodenko remains attracted to controversy, and although greeted with increasingly 'mainstream' cachet, her work proves anything but conflict-averse. It may seem deflating to register the trajectory of Cholodenko's career from its initial igniting as New Queer Cinema *cause-célèbre* to its recent retreat into producing others' work, with arguably tepid results, for cable and network television. Without doubt this is a well-trodden path for women directors from Claudia Weill in the 1970s to Angela Robinson in the 2000s, whose early acclaim fizzled after their first features, and who subsequently found a toehold in the relatively impersonal directorship of episodic and series television. Yet Cholodenko's segue seems suggestive of what Mark Duplass, in his keynote address at the 2015 South by Southwest Film Festival, heralds as a transitional moment:

> As the death of the middle class of film has happened, it has been rebirthed in television. The way you used to make really awesome $5m movies that didn't have movie stars in them and had really great, cool original content, that's happening in cable TV right now. (Bakare 2015)

Moreover, Cholodenko challenges artistic or political devaluation of her more recent projects, *Olive Kitteridge* and *The Slap*, in nurturing the work of other women and queer artists across borders of media and nation.

My opening contention that Cholodenko models an industrial in-betweener route for women practitioners in the contemporary US film sphere is undoubtedly challenged by entrenched institutional and ideological barriers to entry and experimentation, as evidenced by Cholodenko's erratic output and recent turn to less personal projects. Yet, as I hope to have indicated here, Cholodenko's authorial signature remains distinct in its in-betweener vision that looks beyond regulatory regimes governing both professional and personal identity. Observing how Cholodenko's disidentification from agreed-upon criteria for queer cinema 'risks her reputation of integrity in [the] queer community', Bradbury-Rance astutely points to how Cholodenko's films 'promote queerness in yet another way, by rejecting the idea of a perfected self and a goal-oriented (read: future-oriented) narrative/life' (Bradbury-Rance 2013: 40). Alongside this embrace of human complexity and the present, Cholodenko similarly affirms desire's incorrigible logic – as Jules describes, 'sometimes human sexuality is counterintuitive' – without granting it free rein. To build fulfilling lives and relationships and to sustain emotional security necessitates a degree of compromise with regard to desire, such that sexual in-betweenness sometimes is harder to perceive but remains irrevocably present within Cholodenko's films and characters. Their, and her, queer sensibility, though representationally muted and politically modulated, is given voice by the industrial in-betweenness that Cholodenko engages so as to remain productive and personal. Embracing the middle road, Cholodenko's work remains reflexive in its questioning of artistic integrity and representational politics and in its negotiations of the culture industry and her position within it.

References

Austerlitz, Saul (2010), 'Same sex – with the same family issues', the *Boston Globe*, 11 July, <http://www.boston.com/ae/movies/articles/2010/07/11/lisa_cholodenko_wanted_her_film_the_kids_are_all_right_to_reflect_every_family_and_every_familys_individual_vulnerabilities/> (last accessed 11 April 2015).

Bakare, Lanre (2015), 'Mark Duplass: "There's no excuse not to make films on weekends with friends"', *The Guardian*, 15 March, <http://www.theguardian.com/film/2015/mar/15/mark-duplass-south-by-southwest-sxsw> (last accessed 11 April 2015).

Bradbury-Rance, Clara (2013), 'Querying Postfeminism in Lisa Cholodenko's *The Kids Are All Right*', in Joel Gwynne and Nadine Muller (eds), *Postfeminism and Contemporary Hollywood Cinema*, Basingstoke: Palgrave Macmillan, pp. 27–43.

Brooks, Jodi (2014), '*The Kids Are All Right*, the Pursuits of Happiness, and the Spaces Between', *Camera Obscura*, 85, 29: 1, pp. 111–35.

Brooks, Jodi (2015), '*Laurel Canyon* (2002): Lacuscular Cinema', in Claire Perkins and Constantine Verevis (eds), *US Independent Film after 1989: Possible Films*, Edinburgh: Edinburgh University Press, pp. 91–100.

Cox, Fiona (2013), 'Fab Lesbianism and Family Values: Costuming of Lesbian Identities in *The L Word* and *The Kids Are All Right*', in Stella Bruzzi and Pamela Church Gibson (eds), *Fashion Cultures Revisited: Theories, Explorations, and Analysis*, 2nd edn, London: Routledge, 249–60.

Duggan, Lisa with Kathryn Bond Stockton (2010), 'Only the Kids Are All Right', *Bully Bloggers*, 30 July, <https://bullybloggers.wordpress.com/2010/07/30/only-the-kids-are-all-right/> (last accessed 11 April 2015).

Halberstam, Jack (2010), 'The Kids Aren't Alright!', *Bully Bloggers*, 15 July, <https://bullybloggers.wordpress.com/2010/07/15/the-kids-arent-alright> (last accessed 14 September 2013).

Lucia, Cynthia and Richard Porton (2010), 'Gay Family Values: An Interview with Lisa Cholodenko', *Cineaste*, 35: 4, Fall, pp. 15–18.

Porton, Richard (2010), Introduction to 'Gay Family Values: An Interview with Lisa Cholodenko', *Cineaste*, 35: 4, Fall, pp. 14–15.

Pramaggiore, Maria (2002), 'High and Low: Bisexual Women and Aesthetics in *Chasing Amy* and *High Art*', *Journal of Bisexuality*, 2: 2/3, pp. 243–66.

Pramaggiore, Maria (2011), 'Kids, Rock and Couples: Screening the Elusive/Illusive Bisexual', *Journal of Bisexuality*, 11: 4, pp. 587–93.

Puar, Jasbir and Karen Tongson (2012), 'The Ugly Truth about Why the Kids Are All Right', revised edition, *VelvetPark*, 20 January, <http://www.velvetparkmedia.com/blogs/ugly-truth-about-why-kids-are-all-right> (last accessed 11 April 2015).

Rich, B. Ruby (1992), 'New Queer Cinema', *Sight & Sound*, 2: 5, September, pp. 30–4.

Rich, B. Ruby (1998), 'A Path of Her Own [interview with Ally Sheedy]', The *Advocate*, 761: 9, June, p. 46, <http://search.proquest.com/docview/215768217?accountid=14953> (last accessed 13 April 2015).

San Filippo, Maria (2013), *The B Word: Bisexuality in Contemporary Film and Television*. Bloomington: Indiana University Press.

Spines, Christine (2010), 'Down to Earth', *Film Comment*, July/August, pp. 40–3.

Wallace, Lee (2009), *Lesbianism, Cinema, Space: The Sexual Life of Apartments*, New York: Routledge.

Walters, Suzanna Danuta (2012), 'The kids are all right but the lesbians aren't: Queer kinship in US culture', *Sexualities*, 15: 8, pp. 917–33.

14. MIRANDA JULY AND THE NEW TWENTY-FIRST-CENTURY INDIE

Kathleen A. McHugh

This essay reframes the masculinist rhetoric that has dominated discussion, both popular and academic, of independent cinema. That rhetoric articulates white male directors and their films as exemplary (e.g., Steven Soderbergh/*sex, lies, and videotape*, Quentin Tarantino/*Pulp Fiction*) and then derives the character and characteristics of indie cinema and its edgy auteurs from these examples. The oft-referenced indie 'maverick' or 'outsider' or 'renegade' clearly invokes a masculine and imperialist American archetype – the Western outlaw hero – who breaks the law in order to save it, who revitalises the staid traditions of Hollywood from its aesthetic and economic margins.

Alongside and within this 'outsider tradition' are 'other' filmmakers, women and people of colour, who are frequently mentioned, but rarely discussed. When they are, critical indie rhetoric articulates these directors and their films either as singular and exceptional or as exemplars for their gender or identity group. This chapter will challenge this critical rhetoric in relation to independent women filmmakers. Despite Barbara Loden's early and brilliant *Wanda* (1970) or Julie Dash's poetic tour de force, *Daughters of the Dust* (1992), or Lizzie Borden's very edgy *Born in Flames* (1983), none have served as exemplars of indie cinema. This essay proposes an experiment that will posit contemporary indie director Miranda July as an exemplar of twenty-first-century indie cinema. What character and characteristics emerge?

LOGICS OF EXEMPLARITY

Whether addressing genre, auteur, counter or independent, national or transnational cinema, film critics and theorists frequently argue from exemplary figures or films whose specificities illustrate or typify their more general conceptual assertions. For example, Peter Wollen's 1972 'Godard and Counter-Cinema: *Vent d'Est*' establishes seven binaries drawn from Godard's films that contrast counter-cinema's fundamental textual practices with those of 'orthodox' cinema. Over forty years later, our categories are much more fraught and multifaceted, but the critical role of the exemplary persists. The scholarship on independent/indie cinema engages critical questions such as: What is it? Who is included and why?

This essay begins with an overview of the recent critical literature on American independent cinema. It traces a genealogy of operative categories by way of scholars' inadvertent but nevertheless racialised and gendered uses of exemplarity. This literature indicates, as might be expected, that the example underwrites the rule in ways that reiterate certain patterns, values, inclusions, and exclusions. From this analysis, I will then discuss Miranda July as exemplary of twenty-first-century independent cinema, extracting from her work, career, fundraising, promotion, and aesthetics the basis of an alternative or hypothetical normative history of American independent cinema.

An early foundational work, Richard Ferncase's *Outsider Features: American Independent Film of the 1980s* (1996), lists and describes ten independent films and their directors in chronologically ordered chapters, the first featuring John Sayles *The Return of the Secaucus Seven* (1980) and the last Michael Moore's *Roger and Me* (1989). In between are Wayne Wang, Susan Seidelman, Jim Jarmusch, Joel and Ethan Coen, Spike Lee, Lizzie Borden, Errol Morris, and Steven Soderbergh. There is no hierarchy; each is equally represented, although the chapters on Wang, Seidelman, and Lee discuss their respective relevance to Asian-American, women's, and African-American filmmaking, whereas the other chapters focus on the filmmakers' individual distinctions.

This approach can be productively compared to Emanuel Levy's subsequent 1999 *Cinema of Outsiders: The Rise of American Independent Film*. As the two titles imply, the former's egalitarian characterisation of film texts becomes the latter's critical mythology and logic of exemplarity. That logic implies chronology, but ends up articulating critical segregations. Levy writes: 'the indie cinema is very much the cinema of the "Other" America' because first, 'its characters are outsiders,' and second, 'the filmmakers themselves are outsiders: members of ethnic minorities, gays and lesbians, and women'. He concludes, 'outsiders also include white male filmmakers who do not belong to the mainstream' (Levy 1999: 52). Six subsequent chapters put the 'also' in front of the 'Other'. Chronologically rendered, these chapters discuss the influence of New Hollywood directors on American independent directors ('Fathers and Sons'); regional aesthetic tendencies ('Regional Cinema', 'The New York School of Indies'); and genre (noir, comedy, and drama). In what is an encyclopaedic tour-de-force, Levy profiles over sixty directors, all white men, save for three Latinos and one Asian-American. Then, the book's last four chapters document the 'Cinema of Diversity,' a complement to but distinct from the 'Cinema of Outsiders' (ibid. p. vii). These four chapters cover non-white, LGBT, and women directors, their significance political and/or identity based; they exist conceptually alongside, but sequentially after the canonical mainstream of American indie cinema, what Chon Noriega refers to as 'the back of the book' – the scholarly analogue to the back of the bus.

Like Levy, many subsequent critics (Biskind 2004, Merritt 2000, Hiller 2001) see the indie cinema that emerges in 1980 as developing from 1960s and 70s New Hollywood Cinema and its 'renegade innovations' and 'maverick' directors. Indeed, the mythos of the indie director as a maverick and an outsider runs throughout the critical literature (Andrew 1999, Ferncase 1996, Hiller 2001, Levy 1999, Merritt 2000, Waxman 2006).[1] This highly masculinised discourse derives from accounts of New Hollywood that culminated in Peter Biskind's seminal 1998 bestseller, *Easy Riders, Raging Bulls*.[2] Tellingly, the New Hollywood maverick was actually an industry insider whose difference was generational. The white male New Hollywood directors came, like Oedipus become cowboy, to supplant and displace their elders; yet in Biskind's Oedipal narrative, the tragedy is leavened by American optimism, with the older generation literally and figuratively going blind (1998:18–19). The maverick also derives from another very well-worn American tradition; he descends from the Western outlaw hero – a white, masculine, and imperialist character beloved by the film industry, who saves the law by existing outside of it.[3]

The brilliant facility of this mythic and longstanding archetype is that it articulates the new, the edgy, the artistic, and the innovative within a familiar white, male, patriarchal order, where the outsider is, by definition, the most privileged insider. Further, it gives rise to a flexible and apparently inclusive binary that nevertheless supports a problematic logic of exemplarity: on the one hand, independent/indie cinema gives us aesthetic, formal, generic, and alt/industrial innovation; and on the other hand, it includes 'transformed representations' of ethnic and racial minorities and lesbian and gays – identity-based outsiders. Many scholars, typified by Hiller (2001), assert that indie cinema sometimes includes 'all these combined' (xi), but two salient problems arise from this model. Women often disappear from or have diminished relevance within this framework – when it comes to exemplarity, white men typically exemplify innovation while ethnic and LGBT directors, often men, exemplify themselves and their identity group. For example, Hiller's introduction to

American Independent Cinema mentions Maya Deren, Shirley Clark, Julie Dash, and Kimberly Pierce, but discusses exemplars that are all men: Robert Altman, Alan Rudolph, John Cassavetes, Andy Warhol, Spike Lee and Greg Araki. The introduction concludes:

> There are entries which could fit elsewhere in the structure. Kobena Mercer's piece on Marlon Riggs in the African-American section could be placed under 'Queers', while Nick James' review of Carl Franklin's *One False Move* [in Generics] would certainly fit under 'African Americans'. Elsewhere it may be too soon to assume that film-makers such as Paul Thomas Anderson, Spike Jonze or Harmony Korinne are really 'mavericks', despite the distinctive individuality of their work so far. (xviii)

Hiller's invaluable and inclusive collection gathers together diverse writers and makers, including several women and people of colour; yet the logic of the maverick confers 'distinctive individuality' only on white men, while men of colour inhabit categories defined by identity or genre. Women, white or of colour, are either denied exemplarity altogether or represent a female/feminist or non-white sensibility.

The clearly racialised and masculinist framework that derives from the logic of the outsider and the forms of exemplarity that have followed from it also extend to issues with genre. Writing after Levy in her 2002 *Cinema and Culture: Independent Film in the United States, 1980–2001*, E. Deidre Pribram observes: 'all genres are not equally represented in independent practice. On the one hand, melodrama and romantic comedy are infrequent unless also used in depicting a subcultural group. Certain genres, such as the gangster or criminal film, are overrepresented' (xv). Her comments register a certain disconnect between understandings of American independent cinema as small and personal, often character-based narratives, and independent cinema as tremendously successful generic homages to exploitation cinema's hyperbolised representations of sex and violence. Indeed, Steven Soderbergh's 1989 *sex, lies, and videotape*, wildly successful and universally credited with transforming indie cinema, is nothing if not an indie version of a domestic melodrama (as are any number of other indie titles directed by white men as well as women and non-white directors). Yet the post-Tarantino years and Tarantino-esque features with their masculinist generic identity have come to typify indie cinema because of their excess and box office success.

Exemplarity necessarily has economic, cultural, political, and methodological as well as ideological origins. Feature filmmaking, even at its very lowest end, is capital intensive. Given the economics, the historical period, and the pervasive and persistent structural inequities that underpin any feature filmmaking (up to the present day), the overwhelming number of American independent feature directors from 1980 to the 2000s are white men, most of them middle or upper class.[4] As the bulk of scholarship on American independent film has focused on features, rather than non-fiction or short films, so obviously has critical exemplarity derived from that demographic. In 1992, Rosa Linda Fregoso wittily addressed this bias: 'In a phallocentric society, power is measured by *big*-ness (as in feature-length films) and in *penetration* (as into the Hollywood industry). These are the crucial markers or signs of success, of "making it", of *coming* ... into fruition' [emphasis hers] (170). King, Molloy and Tzioumakis hypothesise that 'if the term independent is taken to mean any non-studio production in the history of American cinema, it runs the danger of being so inclusive as to be of little value as a specific analytical category' (2013). Yet such inclusion might potentially obviate or mitigate the commercial, cultural, and historical exclusions that, in effect, dictate the logic of methodological exemplarity I have outlined above. Accordingly, I would like to sketch the outlines of an alternative or hypothetically normative history of independent/indie cinema that refuses mandates of relevance based on privilege, quantity, commercial success, visibility, and mass spectatorship by reframing exemplarity. The current state of indie cinema certainly invites such an intervention.

Miranda July: Exemplar of Twenty-first-century Indie Cinema

What are the emerging trends and tendencies for American independent cinema in the twenty-first century's second decade? In *Indie 2.0*, Geoff King argues that new digital technologies ('inexpensive digital video') and online resources for distribution and sales provide 'potentially radical new openings and opportunities for independent filmmakers' (King 2014: 1). If the current moment is auspicious 'for those operating at the lowest-cost end of the spectrum' (King, Molloy, Tzioumakis 2013: 1), it seems particularly apt to select a woman as exemplary of independent cinema in this moment, given women's more compromised access to financial and other resources.[5] Further, from the opportunities King mentions, we could surmise that new, future-oriented mandates of relevance for contemporary independent directors would: eschew hyper-capitalism as the royal road to creative expression; contrive business innovations that serve vision rather than vice-versa; emerge from or build communities or networks through social media rather than articulate niche markets through their work; and seek to engage timely and contemporaneous issues, such as community or environmental concerns or more reflexive issues such as the challenges of intimacy in the age of social media (concerns not readily accommodated by gangster and crime films).

In selecting Miranda July as exemplar of this moment, I choose someone who certainly operates at the lower, if not the lowest, cost end of the indie feature spectrum. In a career spanning twenty years, she has written and directed numerous shorts (*Atlanta* 1996; *The Amateurist* 1997; *Nest of Tens* 1999) and two features (*Me, You, and Everyone We Know* 2005; *The Future* 2011). Significantly, July's identity and her creative practice do not rest solely in film and her aspirations focalise on making work rather than making money (Dunham, Heti). Her self-representation, production, distribution, and exhibition strategies, artistic practice and orientation, and ideological motivation all articulate an independent media profile that is very much of the contemporary zeitgeist. So to the question of exemplarity, 'Why Miranda July?', here are elements of contemporary indie cinema that this director makes manifest:

Miranda July is communally rather than self styled

Miranda July has systematically represented herself and her professional identity in ways dramatically distinct from industry and independent auteurs. Nowhere is this more evident than in the contrast her film school story makes with the industry standard. In the wake of the Miramax years and what Justin Wyatt calls the 'major independents', Internet discourse has necessarily reoriented the criteria for true independence back to directors' biographies, now frequently in relation to film school. Recent online postings and websites rail against the 'film school industrial complex' and proffer examples of industry and indie directors from Steven Spielberg to James Cameron to Quentin Tarantino who either dropped out of film school (Spielberg), who didn't attend but studied in the USC library (James Cameron), or who learned everything about film as a video store clerk (Tarantino) ((LAvideoFilmmaker.com; Renninger; Natasi). No matter in what industrial framework they now work or have always worked, their relative independence from film school secures their identities as true independents/outsiders with innate rather than schooled talents.

Miranda July's film school story articulates a radically different understanding of independence than these very traditional maverick stories. As a sophomore, she dropped out of UC Santa Cruz because she was disappointed that the intro film classes focused on 'mostly guys' (July, '1996: Joanie 4 Jackie'). To teach herself filmmaking, she created her own community of like-minded 'women and girls' through organising and promoting a grassroots video distribution network called Joanie 4 Jackie (hereafter J4J, formerly Big Miss Moviola).[6] She created video chainletters, fifteen in all from 1995–2002, dubbing together her own and other lady filmmakers' work that she then promoted and distributed widely (Bryan-Wilson 2004:184). Her intention was to 'figure out how to make movies and how to create some kind of network that inspired me to do that' (July). In numerous interviews later in her career, July reflected that J4J combatted her own isolation and sense of being totally alone;

through it, she sought to invent 'a place for myself and other women to be' (July; Onstad 2001: 26; Bryan-Wilson 2004:188).

These compilation pieces located July's authorship within an informal distribution network that she credited with creating and facilitating her ability to make films. Thus July represents herself as a communally styled rather than self-styled filmmaker. Disallowing a singular genius, auteur, or maverick myth, she establishes that networking, community and the creation of a 'place for herself and women' were the necessary preconditions for her learning and making film. Indeed, in one interview, she explicitly refers to J4J as her 'film school' (Onstad 2001: 27). Not only does July's example thereby assert and insist upon the often remarked but too often ignored collective and collaborative nature of all filmmaking, from artisanal to blockbuster productions, but it also registers what white male filmmakers have always had and never credit – their own community and place, also known as the film industry, independent or mainstream.

Significantly, in explicitly generating film from and within a named and acknowledged community, July extends and carries on a tradition practiced by other American independent filmmakers, past and present. These include Cheryl Dunye, whose early films *Janine* (1990), *She Don't Fade* (1991), *The Potluck and the Passion* (1993), and first feature, *The Watermelon Woman* (1996) drew from and situated themselves within the black lesbian community in Philadelphia (Juhasz 2001: 291–2; McHugh 2015: 340). Similarly, Ela Troyano's films, *Carmelita Tropicana: Your Kunst is your Waffen* (1994), *Latin Boys Go to Hell* (1997), and *La Lupe: Queen of Latin Soul* (2007), articulate a queer, multicultural Lower East Side community through and as a distinct style (Munoz 1998:119–25). Christina Lane provides a contemporary example in this volume, tracing Susan Seidelman's engagement with community as subject and audience in her recent filmmaking, a tendency of Seidelman's that Ferncase notes goes back to *Smithereens*' (1982) rendering of punk pop subculture (Ferncase 1996: 42–4).

Miranda July is multi- not mono-medial

Recent articles in the popular press and online detail the many indie film directors finding opportunities to work in TV. Notably these stories feature women as exemplary. Gary Susman writes in an article titled: 'How indie filmmakers have transformed TV' that 'Exhibit A is surely Lena Dunham' (Susman 2015). Other innovative indie directors that practice in both media include: Allison Anders, Patricia Cardoso, Lisa Cholodenko, Julie Dash, Jay and Mark Duplass, Carl Franklin, Cary Fukanaga, Sanaa Hamri, Nicole Holofcener, Karyn Kusama, John Ridley, John Sayles, Lynn Shelton, John Singleton, and Mario Van Peebles. While these directors might arguably be moving from the 'margins to the mainstream', to quote Chris Holmlund and Justin Wyatt, Miranda July represents indie makers who eschew both mono-mediality and the mainstream.

July is not of any single medium, her creative work is both diffused and integrated across diverse platforms: she is a film and videomaker, writer, actor, performance, and conceptual artist; she makes web-based pieces, interactive sculpture gardens, online digital photo compilations and appropriates the margins of Hitchcock stills, inserting herself in the place of film extras.[7] July's contemporary profile grounds itself in an aesthetic multi-medial genealogy of American independent cinema, dominated by women, that reaches back to Maya Deren (dance, film, theory, ethnography), Yoko Ono (performance, music, film, installation), Shirley Clarke (dance, film), Yvonne Rainer (dance, performance, film), Lynn Hershman Neeson (performance, film, digital installation and media), and Julie Dash (film, music video, online website designer, writer), among many others. Her aesthetic diversification is not new, but the mono-medial focus of most independent film criticism has obscured this vital tradition – as a tradition – from view. Perhaps more importantly, the contemporary advent of multiple media platforms for creating work makes this tradition more salient and important as a model for indie filmmaking practices in the digital age. Contemporary makers certainly see multimedia practice as now and the future.

Filmmaker, actor, dramaturg, and hybrid media maker Ela Troyano recently observed, 'No one works in just one media anymore. They can't afford to' (interview with author). A recent interview between Miranda July and Lena Dunham echoed and elaborated on these sentiments:

> JULY: I think it's much more thrilling for everyone right now that you're not plunging your energy into the slow mechanism of features . . . it's nice to not have to wait as long to see what you're going to do next.
> DUNHAM: Do you feel frustrated ever about what it takes or how long it takes to make a feature?
> JULY: Yeah. But that's partly why I work in a few different mediums. It's kind of my way around not feeling so pinned or controlled by the slow-moving machines.
> DUNHAM: People sometimes have this idea that there's something schizophrenic about wanting to apply your artistic energy in different places.
> JULY: I do have to say, when interviewers want to spend a lot of time talking about how curious it is that I work in different mediums, I feel like it really dates them – I think, 'Oh, you're an old-timey person.' Which is fine. (July 2013)

Having a multi-media practice allows makers different creative temporalities and opportunities. July approaches different media platforms with the question: 'What would this platform be good for? What would I like it to do?' (Heti 2015). For all media, she believes the task is the same: 'To express something true; to remember you are free; to make a needed space that didn't exist before' (*The Future*, Press Kit 2013).

Miranda July understands indie filmmaking as and through social networking

July's first film project, J4J, integrated and made completely reversible relationships between creator and distributor, audience and author, presenting and sharing work. J4J was for 'each other' – the network of contributors/recipients created by the project. Lucas Hilderbrand astutely notes, 'These tapes created social networks before online "social networking"' (Hilderbrand 2007:197). They provided access, connection, and grassroots communication, often to young adults geographically and/or psychically isolated, as July felt herself to be; they were also 'explicitly interactive' as 'the project calls on its audience to become its participants' (ibid. p. 197 and pp. 218–19). Thus interactivity and social networking were not only the source of July's filmmaking, but also its method. In the press kit for *The Future*, July wrote: 'Remembering that I can exist at all without being online is a daily challenge. How often is there a brand new daily challenge shared by almost every person you know? But as an artist who has always tried to find new ways to feel intimacy with the audience, it also seems useful'.

Miranda July exemplifies indie cinema and its possibilities now and in the future because she understands it, comes to it, not as a (re)presentational medium, but in and as a mode of social networking or communication (July quoted in Kearney 2006: 80). This orientation uniquely apprehends some of the challenges of working in independent film today. It grasps the relevance and challenges of the Internet and social media beyond their basic function as alternative distribution and exhibition sites for film as it always has been. As July writes, online experience is useful 'to find new ways to feel intimacy with the audience'. Social media are interactive; they enable alienated intimacy through networks that connect strangers in various kinds of virtual immersive exchange. Throughout multimedia work, July has focused on the possibilities and failures of mediated intimacy. In her mode of spectatorial address, her films' narrative foci, and her collaborative and networked creative practice, July explores cinema's capacity for social interactivity and virtual intimacy.

July's titular address to audiences is frequently pronominal and deictic: *Learning to Love You More* (with Harrell Fletcher 2002–9); *Me and You and Everyone We Know* (2005); *No One Belongs Here More Than You* (2008); and *It Chooses You* (2012).[8] Significantly, deictic words – in English, pronouns (I, me, you, we), spatial and distil markers (this, that, here, there, nearby, the past, the future) – are at the forefront of digital communications research. 'The

Figure 14.1 John Hawkes in *Me and You and Everyone We Know* (2005).

full understanding of a deictic marker is dependent on the context of utterance' and it thereby 'anchors participants in a shared, virtual space' (Benwell and Stokoe 2006: 255). Because these terms orient meaning and interaction within a presumably shared context, deictic expression has become a central concern for digital literacy and computer-mediated communication. 'Deixis [i]s a strategy for recreating some of the immediate, intimate, community qualities of a speech event with a shared visual environment' (ibid.). Deictic usage in July's titles proposes or infers an implicit, albeit simulated, interactional field.

The insistent use of the deictic second person in July's titles hails individual spectators and articulates them within the 'shared visual environment' of the film. For July, these 'yous' strive to make a connection, to communicate: 'I so desperately want the individual person to really feel like this is for you. I was alone and I made this for us and that's not a marketing ploy. If I put "you" in the title and they'll think "me", then we're halfway there' (Heti 2015). Coupled with July's diegetic appearance as actor/protagonist, impersonating one part of the relation that her titles propose, these titles and the films they designate create or simulate interactivity and cultivate a mediated intimacy with their audiences.

Indie film and intimacy in the age of the Internet

Miranda July's two features, 2005's *Me and You and Everyone We Know* (hereafter *MYEWK*) and 2011's *The Future* both draw their spectators into a 'shared visual environment' comprised of everyday places, including homes, apartments, cars, workplaces, school, the neighbourhood, an art museum, and the Internet. Space does not allow for a close reading of these two complex films; instead I will indicate *MYEWK*'s reflexive engagement with art and intimacy in the age of social media, and the method, promotion, and interactional/intermedial strategies that both produced and derived from *The Future*.[9]

In *MYEWK*, thirteen different characters – children, teenagers, and adults of multiple races – make up the social network referenced by the film's title that, with its deictic address, rhetorically includes the spectator. The films' characters are brought together by 'art, sex, and the Internet' (Murphy 2007:129) in a series of anomalous, if not impossible, pairings. These include: a coprophilic online chat room exchange between a child and an adult woman (who assumes her interlocutor and the initiator of the interaction is also an adult); an adult male almost succumbing to the seductions of two teenage girls; these same girls commandeering a fourteen-year-old boy to judge which of them gives the better blow-job; said contest secretly observed by a nine-year-old neighbourhood girl who then shows this boy her trousseau filled with housewares; an elderly man in love for the first time with a woman who is dying; and an aspiring video artist who falls in love with a shoe salesman just separated from his wife. As these descriptions suggest, most of the film's pairings or connections fail or are inappropriate. Yet it is precisely in those failures that July makes a place for topics largely either unrepresented or morally sensationalised: elderly desire, the sexuality of children and teenagers, and women initiating sexual encounters.

These issues are embedded in a reflexive subplot involving Christine Jesperson (July), the aspiring video artist, and Nancy Herrington (Tracy Wright), an art curator. As Nancy reviews submissions for an upcoming art show, her criteria are demographic ('Is the artist of color? A woman? Local?'), historical ('Could this happen only now?'), and thematic ('What does this tell us about digital culture?') Tellingly, the curator's concerns, while seemingly satirised, actually apprehend the concerns of the film in which they are embedded: *MYEWK* is contemporary, demographically diverse, and engaged with communication and its complex mediations in digital culture. When Christine seeks Nancy out to give her a video art-piece in person, Nancy refuses to take it from her hands. So Christine films a direct message and a challenge to Nancy in the video she sends in. It is this mediated communication, rather than the in-person connection, that leads Nancy to accept Christine's work for the art show. Digital culture facilitates intimacies and understandings not possible through, and often undesirable as, direct contact.[10]

'Have you seen *The Future*?' Critics reviewing July's 2011 film noted that her title wittily re-motivated an everyday question about seeing a film to simultaneously voice another more profound question – do you have a prescient relationship to time? A temporal deictic and a context dependent pun, July's title demonstrates an essential element of her style. Committed to the everyday and the banal, she mines it for profundities of meaning routinely ignored because of their scale, tone, or place: personal, sincere, domestic. In *The Future*, she embeds a planetary, environmental allegory of earth's destruction in the fate of a rescued feral cat: because a slacker couple becomes distracted by their romantic problems, the cat is euthanised. This philosophical uncanny runs through July's work, and indeed, extends beyond it. In an interview, she said 'I think there's something spiritual in very day-to-day mundane experience', and in the creation and production of *The Future*, she hewed to her own insight. Frustrated by fundraising for and completing the film script – this was during the 2008 recession – July became obsessed with people who advertised items in the *PennySaver* magazine. In *It Chooses You*, she writes:

> I really didn't want to return to the computer. Not just to the script, but also the internet, its thrall. So I picked up the phone. The implied rule of the classifieds is you can call the number only to talk about the item for sale. But the other rule, always, is that this is a free country, and I was trying hard to feel my freedom. This might be my only chance to feel free all day. [To] the person who answered, [I said] 'I was wondering if I could interview you about your life and everything about you. Of course I would pay you for your time'. (2011: 11–12)

The interviews with the people who said 'yes' to July resulted in the 2011 book *It Chooses You* and the completion of *The Future*'s screenplay. One of her interviewees also became a crucial character in the film. Further, the texts and projects of film and book can exist independently, but are also completely interdependent. Freedom to interconnect leads to unexpected outcomes.

The Future derived from a network of personal, aesthetic, and philosophical incentives and multimedia practices and interactions that included performance, writing, film, photography, and the US mail. Finally, as I was writing this piece, I discovered that July's exemplarity has already been remarked. In 2009, Corinn Columpar and Sophie Mayer wrote: 'July functions as an exemplar of a contemporary film culture' characterised by mobility of 'people and products' among exhibition venues, 'materials', global locations, 'modes of production' and 'artistic roles" (Columpar and Mayer 2009: 3). Miranda July exemplifies a past and future of indie cinema that is resolutely multi-medial, collaborative, improvisational, and that inhabits and exploits the contradictions of independence – as a mode of communal expression and interaction; as a method of financing; and, perhaps most importantly, as a way of feeling free.

Notes

1. Book titles on independent/indie cinema further indicate the prevalence of this rhetoric: Geoff Andrews, *Stranger than Paradise: Maverick Film-Makers in Recent America Cinema* 1999 and Greg Merritt, *Celluloid Mavericks: A History of American Independent Film* 2000.
2. The 'maverick' Hollywood director has a long history. In Orson Welles' 1975 AFI Lifetime Achievement Award acceptance speech, he received resounding applause when he said, 'This is for all the mavericks', an insider/outsider figure he clearly identified with. See full text at <http://www.wellesnet.com/orson-welles-afi-speech-1975/ accessed 19 April 2015. Similarly, a 1990 AFI documentary titled *Hollywood Mavericks* featured seventeen silent, classical, and New Hollywood directors – all white men.
3. Janet Staiger's 'Independent of what?' article traces an overlap/confusion between New Hollywood cinema and 1960s–70s film which will later be understood 'as the beginnings of American independent/indie cinema,' what she calls a "*dual-track history*"'. Her trenchant overview of these entwined histories summarises numerous scholars, of whom only one, Dave Kehr, references a film made by a woman as exemplary and none mention films made by non-whites. Significantly, Staiger's own examples include Maya Deren and films directed by Greg Nava and Rose Troche, pp. 19 and passim.
4. Michael Newman remarks that 'the creative personnel behind the indie film movement are still demographically of a piece with its audience: mainly urban, educated, middle class, straight, and white' (2009: 22).
5. And women of colour even more so. See Cynthia Baron, Shelley Cobb in this volume.
6. For excellent scholarship on *Joanie 4 Jackie*, see Hilderbrand, Hoffman, and Kearney.
7. Her creative strategies accumulate, appropriate, and assimilate multiple influences. Art historian Julia Bryan-Wilson and film scholar Alison Hoffman associate July with Yoko Ono's instructional/participatory pieces, Carolee Schneeman's body performance and Cindy Sherman's multiple characters and personas (Bryan-Wilson 2004: 182; Hoffman 2009: 22–3). J. Hoberman writes that July has 'a lineage that can be traced back through art-world pop star Laurie Anderson to muscular mind-tripper Yvonne Rainer to the original psychodramatist Maya Deren' in his review of *The Future*. Notably, as written, this lineage is distinctly idiomatic rather than exemplary.
8. I counted eleven such titles on her work diary at MirandaJuly.com.
9. My essay, 'Seeking a Film for the End of the World', includes a close reading of *The Future*.
10. At the same time, I completely agree with Alison Hoffman who perceptively argues that the film's emphasis on bodies and 'hand-touch' relations 'locate agency in a shared openness . . .' and result in a 'commonality of feeling' (2009: 26, 22). July engages these relations and affects and the awkward, if not impossible, nature of human connection and desire in the context of multi and social media.

References

'50 Most Important Indies' (1996), *Filmmaker*, 5: 1, Fall, pp. 40–60.

Andrew, Geoff (1998), *Stranger Than Paradise: Maverick Film-makers in Recent American Cinema*, London: Prion.

Benwell, Bethan and Elizabeth Stokoe (2006), *Discourse and Identity*, Edinburgh: Edinburgh University Press.

Biskind, Peter (1998), *Easy Riders, Raging Bulls: How the Sex-Drugs-And-Rock 'N' Roll Generation Saved Hollywood*, New York: Touchstone.

Bryan-Wilson, Julia (2004), 'Some Kind of Grace: An Interview with Miranda July', *Camera Obscura*, 55, 19: 1, pp. 181–97.

Columpar, Corinn and Sophie Mayer (2009), 'Introduction', in C. Columpar and S. Mayer (eds), *There She Goes: Feminist Filmmaking and Beyond*, Detroit: Wayne State University Press, pp. 1–15.

Dunham, Lena (2015), 'Miranda July in Conversation with Host Lena Dunham', *Brooklyn Academy of Music Talks*, <http://www.bam.org/talks/2015/miranda-july-in-conversation> (last accessed 2 May 2015).

Ferncase, Richard K. (1996), *Outsider Features: American Independent Films of the 1980s*, Westport, CT: Greenwood Press.

Fregoso, Rosa Linda (1992), 'Chicana Film Practices: Confronting the "Many-Headed Demon of Oppression"', in C. Noriega (ed.), *Chicanos and Film: Representation and Resistance*, Minneapolis: University of Minnesota Press, pp. 168–82.

Heti, Sheila (2015), 'Interview with Miranda July', Appel Salon at Toronto Public Library, January 29, <https://www.youtube.com/watch?v=n2KVkYVBCFY> (last accessed 3 May 2015).

Hilderbrand, Lucas (2009), *Inherent Vice: Bootleg Histories of Videotape and Copyright*, Durham, NC: Duke University Press, pp. 195–223.

Hiller, Jim (2001), 'Introduction', in J. Hiller (ed.), *American Independent Cinema: A Sight & Sound Reader*, London: BFI, pp. ix–xviii.

Hoberman, J. (2011), 'Miranda July's *The Future* Reviewed', *LA Weekly*, 4 August, <http://www.laweekly.com/2011-08-04/film-tv/miranda-july-s-the-future-reviewed/full/> (last accessed 15 August 2011).

Hoffman, Allison (2009), 'The Persistence of (Political) Feelings and Hand-Touch Sensibilities', in C. Columpar and S. Mayer (eds), *There She Goes: Feminist Filmmaking and Beyond*, Detroit: Wayne State University Press: 19–33.

Juhasz, Alexandra (2001), 'Cheryl Dunye', in A. Juhasz (ed.), *Women of Vision: Histories in Feminist Film and Video*, Minneapolis: University of Minnesota Press, pp. 291–304.

July, Miranda (2011), *It Chooses You*, San Francisco: McSweeney's.

July, Miranda (1996), 'You Obviously Know What I am Talking About', <http://mirandajuly.com/art/joanie-4-jackie-1996> (last accessed 11 July 2014).

July, Miranda (2013), 'Lena Dunham by Miranda July', *Interview*, <http://www.interviewmagazine.com/film/lena-dunham-february-2013/#page4> (last accessed 11 July 2014).

July, Miranda, 'Miranda July Talks About *The Future*', <https://www.youtube.com/watch?v=11z5SSe9Yko> (last accessed 29 August 2014).

Kearney, Mary Celeste (2006), *Girls Make Media*, London and New York: Routledge.

King, Geoff (2014), *Indie 2.0: Change and Continuity in Contemporary American Indie Film*, New York: Columbia University Press.

King, Geoff, Claire Molloy and Yannis Tzioumakis (2013), 'Introduction', in Geoff King, Claire Molloy, and Yannis Tzioumakis (eds), *American Independent Cinema: Indie, Indiewood and Beyond*, London and New York: Routledge.

Lane, Christina (2005), 'Just Another Girl Outside the Neo-Indie', in Chris Holmlund and Justin Wyatt (eds), *Contemporary Independent Film: From the Margins to the Mainstream*, London and New York: Routledge.

LAvideoFilmmaker.com. 'Should I Go to Film School?', <http://www.lavideofilmmaker.com/filmmaking/the-big-question-for-all-aspiring-filmmakers-should-i-go-to-film-school.html> (last accessed 4 March 2015).

Levy, Emanuel (1999), *Cinema of Outsiders: The Rise of American Independent Film*, New York: New York University Press.

Longworth, Karina (2011), 'Miranda July's New Film *The Future* and MOCA Exhibit "Eleven Heavy Things"', *LA Weekly*, 4 August, pp. 20–3.

Macauley, Scott (2005), 'Everyone She Knew', *Filmmaker*, Spring, <http://filmmaker-magazine.com/archives/issues/spring2005/features/everyone_she_knew> (last accessed 15 March 2015).

McHugh, Kathleen (2015), 'Seeking a Film for the End of the World', *Science Fiction Film and Television*, Fall, 83, pp. 297–319.

McHugh, Kathleen (2007), 'The Experimental "Dunyementary": A Cinematic Signature Effect', in R. Blaetz (ed.) *Women's Experimental Cinema: Critical Frameworks*, Durham, NC and London: Duke University Press, pp. 339–59.

Merritt, Greg (2000), *Celluloid Mavericks: A History of American Independent Film*, New York: Thunder's Mouth Press.

Munoz, Jose (1998), 'Sister Acts', in *Disidentifications: Queers of Color and the Performance of Politics*, Minneapolis: University of Minnesota Press, pp. 119–42.

Murphy, J. J. (2007), *Me and You and Memento and Fargo: How Independent Screenplays Work*, New York and London: Bloomsbury Publishing.

Nastasi, Alison (2013), 'Famous Directors who Never Went to Film School', *Flavorwire*, 1 September, <http://flavorwire.com/412974/famous-directors-who-never-went-to-film- school/10> (last accessed 4 March 2015).

Newman, Michael Z. (2009), 'Indie Culture: In Pursuit of the Authentic Autonomous Alternative', *Cinema Journal*, 48: 3, Spring, pp. 16–34.

Onstad, Katrina (2011), 'Miranda July is Totally Not Kidding', *The New York Times Magazine*, 14 July, pp. 26–9.

Perren, Alisa (2012), *Indie, Inc.: Miramax and the Transformation of Hollywood in the 1990s*, Austin: University of Texas Press.

Pribram, E. Deidre (2002), *Cinema and Culture: Independent Film in the United States, 1980–2001*, New York: Peter Lang.

Renninger, Bryce (2013), 'You Don't Have to Go to Film School to Make it', *Indiewire*, 31 January, <http://www.indiewire.com/article/proving-you-dont-need-to-go-to-film-school-to-make-it-a-list-of-film-schools-2013-sundance-directors-attended> (last accessed 5 March 2015).

Sperri, Brandi (2011), 'Brandi Sperri Interviews Miranda July on *The Future*', *The MacGuffin*, 26 August, <https://www.youtube.com/watch?v=tmfn4DrB2v0> (last accessed 29 August 2013).

Staiger, Janet (2013), 'Independent of What? Sorting Out Differences from Hollywood', in Geoff King, Claire Molloy and Yannis Tzioumakis, eds, *American Independent Cinema: Indie, Indiewood and Beyond*, London and New York: Routledge, pp. 15–27.

Susman, Gary (2015), 'How Indie Filmmakers Have Transformed TV', Moviefone.com, 30 January, <http://news.moviefone.com/2015/01/30/how-indie-filmmakers-have-transformed-tv/> (last accessed 15 April 2015).

'*The Future* Press Kit' (2011), *Métropole Films Distribution*, <http://www.metropolefilms.com/data/ftp/The%20Future/PK_THE%20FUTURE_Metro_Eng.pdf> (last accessed 23 September 2012).

Tzioumakis, Yannis (2006), *American Independent Cinema: An Introduction*, New Brunswick, NJ: Rutgers University Press.

Wyatt, Justin (1998), 'The Formation of the "major independent": Miramax, New Line and the New Hollywood,' in Steve Neale and M. Smith (eds), *Contemporary Hollywood Cinema*, New York: Routledge, pp. 74–90.

PART IV

COLLABORATIONS

15. MUTUAL MUSES IN AMERICAN INDEPENDENT FILM: CATHERINE KEENER AND NICOLE HOLOFCENER, MICHELLE WILLIAMS AND KELLY REICHARDT

Chris Holmlund

Working Together towards a Difference 'for' Others

Muses are typically thought of as women who inspire *male* artists. In film, the list is long: Tilda Swinton and Derek Jarman, Diane Keaton or Mia Farrow and Woody Allen, Tippi Hedren and Alfred Hitchcock, Uma Thurman and Quentin Tarantino, Jennifer Lawrence and David O. Russell and so on. But what of female directors and their stars? When asked by *Variety*, 'Why is it different for women?' Nicole Holofcener replied, tongue in cheek, 'because there are only six of us out there. The world is sexist and racist' (Setoodeh 2013: 85).

This essay examines two female director/actress pairs: Holofcener and Catherine Keener; Kelly Reichardt and Michelle Williams. 'Inspiration' does not adequately describe their relationships: *they* speak of their work in terms of friendship and alliance. Together they bring forward ethical perspectives often missing from action-driven movies, functioning as *mutual* muses. Working on the lower end of the contemporary independent sector, with budgets ranging from $8 million down to less than $300,000, their films focus on quiet, seemingly inconsequential moments. Holofcener has accordingly been associated with a 'female-centric', 'feminine' style of filmmaking by, for example, Claire Perkins (2014), who sets her films in opposition to a male-dominated, Indiewood-backed 'smart' cinema and to a predominantly male mumblecore group.[1]

I am less interested in a 'difference from' that opposes women and men than in a 'difference *for*' others that has ethical implications. To do so, as Caroline Bainbridge (2008) intriguingly also does, I draw on Luce Irigaray, in my case emphasising her more recent writings.[2] I choose to enlist Irigaray because she is concerned with partnerships that respect difference and enact friendship, desire and love, between women and men and between women. In books and essays with titles such as *To Be Two* and *I Love to You*, Irigaray argues for leaving a space, accepting an interval, acknowledging differences, between partners, by partners and between generations. Think of 'I love to you' on a par with 'I talk to you', she says: '"I love to you" is a way to respect your intention and mine' ([1993]/2000: 81).[3] She argues that Western philosophers – among them Freud, Lacan, Marx, Merleau-Ponty, Levinas and Hegel – downplay or ignore gendered difference in favour of 'the one' (man) and 'the multiple'. 'Each woman is annihilated in her identity because she has to remain one among others' ([1990]/2000: 59). 'We are *two human genders*, not just one. We must not confuse gender and species' ([1992]/2000: 90).

Gender, found everywhere, is for Irigaray *the* most basic question that remains to be philosophically thought, politically enacted, in our times.[4] Her writings and lectures stress love between man and woman and foreground communication and communion between two genders. This said, her core argument is 'not about individual sexual preference or the choice of sexual lifestyles' (Cheah and Grosz 1998: 12). 'This other can be of my gender or of another', she comments, though 'it is above all to the other gender as other that I am destined' ([1992]/1996: 34). 'Sexual difference', I would emphasise, is not the same thing as 'heterosexuality'. Moreover, she maintains that the denial of sexual difference 'risks becoming a denial of difference elsewhere' – of class, race and ethnicity, for example (2002b: 79).

Hers is a 'practical ethics, the agent of which is a concrete subject who inhabits a specific social location' (Cheah and Grosz 1998: 10). She signals the historicity of her claims: 'It is not . . . a question of uttering a truth valid once and for all but of trying to make a gesture, faithful to the reality of yesterday and to that of today, that indicates a path towards more continuity . . . concentration, harmony – in me, between me and the living universe, between me and the other(s)' ([1999]/2002c: 22). The establishment of non-hierarchical relationships grounded in respect for difference is central to her project: 'vertical' relationships, whether patriarchal or matriarchal, too often shore up the One: the man, the father, the woman-seen-only-as-reproductive-entity-and-mother, the leader, the one god, the singular truth. 'Oppression [comes] from difference that's functioning hierarchically' ([1979]/2000: 27). Importantly, the 'difference for' others that Irigaray advocates is not, cannot, be exclusive to women. It does, it must, include men engaged with other-oriented optics.

To elucidate how Holofcener/Keener and Reichardt/Williams work as mutual muses and take up ethical positions, I examine *Enough Said* (2013),

Lovely & Amazing (2001), *Friends with Money* (2006), *Wendy and Lucy* (2008) and *Meek's Cutoff* (2013). What Perkins says of *Please Give* is true of Holofcener's other films and of Reichardt's films with Williams: in each, 'characters express and perform attitudes of care. The constant, implicit question of *how* to relate to others is framed by specific situations' (2014: 146). Revolving around women, usually in ensembles, class serves as a prime indicator of difference *among* women in their films more frequently than it does in Irigaray's discussions. Racial, ethnic and generational dissimilarity also come into play more often. Reichardt/Williams portray migrants and immigrants; Holofcener/Keener craft suburbanites and urbanites. Crucially, the actresses translate the ethical dilemmas and choices their characters experience through the minutia of their performance choices. For me, their gestures and delivery, and Holofcener and Reichardt's direction, respond to Irigaray's call to 'find an artistic, musical, touchful way of speaking or saying and of listening . . . not reduced to a simple assistance for remembering meaning or to some code to be respected' ([1994]/2001: 10). In concert, I argue, all four women – in specific social locations – thus make movies that illuminate a gratitude for and appreciation of difference.

Genres and Modalities: Inspiration Goes Both Ways: Nicole Holofcener and Catherine Keener

Time and again critics refer to Catherine Keener as Nicole Holofcener's muse.[5] Holofcener admits she pictures how Keener would say something and writes parts just for her: 'She's fun, she's smart, she makes my scripts better' (Jacobs 2014). Keener, however, says that she doesn't want to be seen as Holofcener's muse: 'That's such a nice word, but I always repel it because I think it might be the other way around' (Taylor 2007).

Not adequately appreciated is the way Keener's improvisational physicality complements Holofcener's loose-knit narratives, enhancing her 'anarchic toughness' by adding a vulnerability and gentleness that Holofcener's words do not on their own suggest (Taylor 2010: 54). To a woman, Keener's characters are flawed, but as Keener plays them they are not unlikeable. At their worst they find themselves in distinctly middle-class muddles and manifest a stereotypically feminine insecurity. At their best they cherish those around them.

When self-absorbed, Keener's characters evoke the boundaries imposed on and accepted by women in the mono-centric male cultures Irigaray critiques. Nonetheless most ultimately appreciate difference – between mothers and daughters, mothers and sons, women friends, female/male partners, female/male friends. Holofcener says they 'all have a searching, questioning quality' (Chocano 2006: E4). In this, too, they recall Irigaray. Her writing is lyrical, exploratory, peppered with ellipses and interrogatives.

As director, Holofcener doesn't take away from the complexity which Keener contributes. Her camera rests on Keener in close-up or medium shot. Editing and framing emphasise relationships. In rehearsal especially Holofcener encourages actors to adjust their lines, more rarely to improvise dialogue. She knows that without their performances her characters are only fantasies; gestures, delivery and timing – together with framing and editing – are key to the success of the throwaway lines she writes and the complicated characters she imagines.

Holofcener's films move from one small story to another small story. Scenes are short; events are interwoven. Judy Blume was a big influence: 'I remember as a kid reading Judy Blume books, and I thought . . . "well, if this little girl's problem [is] her period, or liking some boy and there's food in her teeth, if that can take me through chapter after chapter, then I can write about my stupid problems!"' ('A Conversation' 2006; Chocano 2006: E4).

Bitch Queen: Catherine Keener in *Enough Said*

I begin my discussion of Holofcener and Keener's collaborations with their 2013 film, *Enough Said*, because here the two make Keener's character, Marianne, a female version of the male authoritarian mono-model Irigaray initially indicted. Somewhat atypically, Holofcener did not write Marianne with Keener in mind (Jacobs 2014). She does say that she thought 'it would be fun for Catherine to play . . . a glamorous, narcissistic woman who seems to have no idea of her own shortcomings' ('Promotional materials' 2013: 9).

Marianne's self-absorption is vital to the ethical questions the film poses. A successful poet, Marianne meets the lead character, a masseuse named Eva (Julia Louis-Dreyfus), at an upscale west LA party. The two immediately hit it off. To start Marianne/Keener is outgoing, likeable and attractive in a well-heeled, bohemian kind of way. Her smile is warm; she bobs her head up and down; she enthusiastically waves both hands – even though one is holding a drink – in a gesture that approves of *everything* Eva/Louis-Dreyfus is wearing, from top to toe. 'I *love* your outfit!' she exclaims.

Marianne hires Eva and the two become friends, drinking ice tea and sharing relationship gossip after each massage session in Marianne's beautiful Santa Monica home. But the plot thickens: Eva realises that her new friend was married to Albert (James Gandolfini), the man she is falling in love with. The problem is that Marianne has nothing but bad things to say about her former husband. Eva tells her best friend that Marianne is like a human Trip Advisor. Why not use her as guide? Wouldn't you want to know so you didn't stay in a bad hotel?

A physical actress with a gift for improvisation, Keener is the more unequivocal of the two actresses, swiftly slashing downwards with her right hand as she describes her relationship with her ex-, 'I had *zero* in common with him. I don't know how I *ever* had a real conversation with him'. A few days later, in two-shot on Marianne's patio, Eva confides – without mentioning names – that her new partner's 'middle-agedness is comforting . . . and sexy to me'. Keener utters cooing sounds of agreement, looks into the distance and reminisces. 'I think that my ex-, all he would have wanted for me to accept' – Keener's hands pull in – 'was his belly'. Albert/Gandolfini is fat; her hands move out to make him seem very fat – 'and all his quirks' – her hands gesture wide: there are a lot of quirks. 'In the end I was completely repulsed by him sexually' – she looks disgusted – 'he was kind of terrible in bed'. She wrinkles her nose, looks away briefly, and then holds Eva/Louis-Dreyfus' gaze as her hands involuntarily move out, fingers clenching, for the clincher: 'Very clumsy'. Louis-Dreyfus grimaces.

By film's end the smiles Keener used to introduce Marianne have disappeared: her mouth is down-turned, her eyes hard. This Marianne is full of hate: love and acceptance of difference have no place in her life. As far as she's concerned, it's her way or the highway. Inappreciative of the value of diversity, many women accept and even participate in oppression, Irigaray explains. '[W]e avoid the problem of meeting with . . . the other. We avoid letting ourselves be moved, questioned, modified, enriched by the other as such. We do not look for a way for a cohabitation or a coexistence between subjects of different but equivalent worth' ([1999]/2002c: 125). Eventually Eva realises that, if she is to be happy with Albert, she must appreciate him for who he is, not follow Marianne's example and try to make him into someone he is not. Keener and Holofcener show Marianne's bitterness yet nonetheless somehow manage to render her simultaneously somehow pitiable at the same time. Keener's multi-levelled acting enriches Holofcener's insightful script, and Holofcener's direction of her actress together with her guidance of Xavier Grobet's cinematography and Robert Frazen's editing, adeptly captures the nuances Keener intends.

Shape-shifter: Catherine Keener in *Lovely & Amazing*

Each of Keener's performances is distinct: she melts into her roles and is unconcerned with celebrity. 'If she posed in *Harper's Bazaar* or *Ladies' Home Journal*, she'd be more famous', says Holofcener. 'But I don't think she cares. This is the path she wants to take' (Setoodeh 2010: 49). Although critics and directors frequently praise independent film actors for their insistence on autonomy and resistance of hype, one senses that Holofcener sincerely admires Keener's dedication to her craft (see McDonald 2013 and Holmlund 2017). By the time she was writing *Lovely & Amazing* Keener's versatility was obvious. Holofcener joked that she wanted to give her all the parts. Keener was eager to have the role of Michelle: 'I couldn't pass it up, it was so good and funny and pathetic' ('Getting it going' 2001). She knew Holofcener so well she was sure just what tone Michelle would use ('Playing the part' 2001).

Holofcener's script emphasises relationships among women, across generations and between sisters. Her explorations bring to mind Irigaray's descriptions in *I Love to You* and elsewhere of two sorts of feminine relationships: horizontal (between women friends or sisters) and vertical (between daughter and mother, mother and daughter, tied to instincts and the body as fusion or adherence) ([1996]/2000: 158–9). Together Holofcener and Keener also comment on intergenerational male/female relationships.

For much of the film Keener plays Michelle as immature and self-centred. Holofcener magnifies the pettiness of her exchanges with her mother (Brenda Blethyn) using tight shots. When her mother asks Michelle to take care of her adopted eight-year-old sister Annie (Raven Goodwin) while she recovers from a tummy-tuck, Michelle/Keener agrees to help only after a recalcitrant mumble and a disgruntled 'puff': 'Just don't expect me to do it with joy already'. Resentful of her 'duty to respect and confide in the mother' (Irigaray [1992]/2002c: 107), Michelle resorts to 'private attacks' (Whitford 2003: 33).

The child of a crack-addicted mother, Annie is out of place in her new family. She eats in compensation and, though a dark-skinned African American, tries to make herself look white. Attractively thin, a former home-coming queen, Michelle belittles her for being heavy. But Michelle is insecure, too. Her husband (Clark Gregg) is thoroughly uninterested in, and even steps on, the art-work she tries to sell. They are almost never intimate: indeed, he cheats on her with one of her friends. How, then, might Michelle gain an identity of her own, not just be a 'mom', 'assimilated to a reproductive nature?' (Irigaray [1990]/2000: 58).

It's somewhat understandable that she is pleased when her seventeen-year-old, One-Hour Photo Shop employer, Jordan (Jake Gyllenhaal), takes an interest in her. Jordan is so persuasively adorable and adoring that Michelle cannot help but be charmed. In their 'meet cute' Keener displays her talent for 'hint[ing] at *layers* of personality in a single line of dialogue' – or in this case, a single smile (Fussman 2000: 166). To add emphasis, a hand-held camera follows Michelle/Keener as she marches into the store. Jordan/Gyllenhaal's face lights up. With a thrilled little laugh he says, 'No way'. 'Why not?' Michelle/Keener insists angrily. 'If I haven't developed pictures before will somebody train me?' 'I will', he replies flirtatiously. 'Don't look at me like that', she chides. 'Can I have this job or not? Who do I have to talk to?' 'Well, my dad owns this place'. He leans towards her across the counter. 'Aren't you going to give me a smile or something? If I'm going to give you the job?' Michelle/Keener's expression is exacerbated but she is flattered. Roguishly, she matches Gyllenhaal's head tilt with a single offbeat moue. Pleased with himself, he nonchalantly tosses a roll of film into a container.

A few days later Jordan's mother (Lee Garlington) catches them kissing, and Michelle finds herself arrested and charged with statutory rape. Released from jail hours later, starving, she heads for McDonald's. There she finds Annie eating Happy Meals. Looking at her, Michelle/Keener's face softens. For the first time, she registers that Annie is a person in her own right, both needy *and* talented. Keener's voice lowers. She tells Annie she likes her straightened hair. Annie/Goodwin looks up quickly, says 'Thanks, thanks a lot,' then wipes her mouth daintily and looks up again, expectant. Keener's shifting facial expressions – raised and lowered eyebrows, creased and un-creased forehead, steadfast gaze – evince concern, kindness and sensitivity. Holofcener records Michelle's transformation in shot/reverse shots, her editing translating her characters' newfound appreciation of each other's distinctiveness. Michelle hints that Annie's different genetic make-up – including her crack-head mother's, as well as her father's – could make her different in *good* ways from Michelle, her mother and her sister. Annie rewards her with a sincere smile. What Irigaray would call a horizontal relationship between women, not structured through genealogy, begins between them. That Michelle and Annie are of different races adds dimensions that Irigaray neglects. Over the course of the film Michelle has grown closer to her mother, her own daughter (Ashlynn Rose) and her biological sister Elizabeth (Emily Mortimer), too: she is opening up to others.

Indie Goddess: Catherine Keener in *Friends with Money*

As was the case with *Lovely & Amazing* and *Please Give*, Holofcener wrote *Friends with Money* with Keener in mind. Keener in turn was instrumental in getting many of the other actors onboard ('Director's Commentary' 2006). Like Keener's *Lovely & Amazing* character, Michelle, Keener's character here, Christine, learns that people need to express concern for others and to welcome difference. Irigaray underlines: 'Difference exists. Difference in race, difference in tradition, difference in class, difference in gender . . . The problem is that difference has always been a means for subordination and slavery . . . When women ask for the right to difference, they are asking not to be subjugated to masculine or, more precisely, patriarchal models that paralyse and negate them in their sexual, social and cultural station' ([1979]/2000: 26). In both films, the Keener characters 'grow', rather than, as is the case in *Enough Said*, 'regress' to a female version of an oppressively hierarchical 'One'.

For much of *Friends with Money*, Christine's relationship with her husband, Dave (Jason Isaacs), is dysfunctional. In an early scene she pulls a carton of ice cream from the freezer and starts to eat. Dave/Isaacs saunters in and leafs through the mail. Keener narrows her eyes: something about him is different. Off-handedly he admits to having shaved his beard three weeks ago. Shocked, she apologises for not noticing. He gives her a dismissive half-smile and leaves. Keener salutes his back with her spoon. 'She uses her whole body to play a scene', explains Holofcener. 'She does these things that are so lovely and unique. Things you can't write. Things you can't say to an actress' (Rochlin 2000: 11).

Not only mismatched as spouses, Christine and Dave are also writing partners gone wrong. 'It's like we're writing two different scripts', she says. During one argument Holofcener expressively adds jackhammers to the soundtrack and, as the couple dive deeper into the wreck of their relationship, combines over-the-shoulder takes with shot/reverse shots. First one actor, then the other, is thereby kept in frame to cast a shadow over the other.

World War III launches when Christine realises their neighbours hate them for building an upstairs addition that blocks all their ocean views. Fixing dinner, Christine/Keener accuses Dave/Isaacs: 'You don't care about other people'. She is beside herself, between tears and rage: Keener excels at playing two emotions simultaneously. She burns her hand on the stove but he says nothing. She pretends to be him: 'Are you all right, honey?' He confronts her angrily: 'What are you talking about?' 'I just burned the *fuck* out of my hand! . . . And I politely asked myself if I was all right. Something you seem to be *incapable* of doing!' 'You *are* all right', he replies. She retorts: 'But does it ever occur to you to *ask*?' At the end of his rope, he yells back, 'If you clearly are all right, AS YOU OBVIOUSLY ARE, then WHAT THE FUCK IS THE DIFFERENCE?' Keener flinches, drops her voice and blinks back tears. As an actor, she is an engaged, aggressive listener with 'that rare ability to look as if she was actually listening to her fellow actors' words for the first time' (Andrew 1997: 19).

Only after the two separate does Christine start to regain confidence. One evening she asks their little son Max (Max Burkholder) if the shoes she plans to wear to a fancy dinner with her friends look too clunky. 'What's clunky?' Max wonders. Keener defines the term using body language as well as words, throwing her hands wide and puffing out her cheeks: 'It means, um, heavy, not delicate, you know . . . chunky'. With peals of laughter, Max throws himself forward on her bed: fat shoes! How funny! For the first time since the film's beginning Christine/Keener beams. That Max operates on a different wavelength does gives her joy. She's willing to let him be different, to 'remain a mystery' (Irigaray 2002b: 84).

The last scene rhymes with earlier sequences in which Dave bullied Christine. Alone in what used to be their office, she reads aloud from a script she's writing, stops, and raises her eyes in anticipation of a response. No one answers. She begins to exit but stubs her toe. 'Ow!' she cries. 'You OK, Miss Christine?' the

Mexican maid yells from the next room. Keener stares into the camera, making the moment more of a questioning than an answer. That there is no definitive response accords with Irigaray's sense that 'to protect the duality of subjects requires . . . privileging interrogative transformation rather than negative and above all rather than imperative transformation' ([1992]/2000: 87). At last, ever so slightly, Christine/Keener smiles. Is someone finally listening to her, responding to her, 'loving to her'?"

Bennett Miller comments of Keener's work in *Capote* (2005): 'A lot of her performance comes from understanding and empathy. And that's a hard thing to act' (Chang 2005: 26).[6] For Manohla Dargis, *Friends with Money* is 'one of those films in which the narrative emerges from the characters and through the performances . . . Most of what's here . . . feels startlingly honest' (2006: 12). Keener helps anchor the honesty of Holofcener's script. Their supportive ventures echo, in a filmic register, Irigaray's conviction that ethical, creative relationships to another of one's own gender, not just to the other gender, are possible.

It's What's Happening Between the Lines: Kelly Reichardt and Michelle Williams

Several years younger than Holofcener and Keener, Williams describes 'knowing Kelly' as 'an education in film. Not that she's ever tried to teach me, but just sort of by osmosis, and being her friend, and understanding what she likes, and having her reference movies, and then going and finding them myself, I feel at this point I know how to fill her frame' (Vida 2011).[7] 'My relationship with Michelle is an easy one', says Reichardt (Quart 2001: 43), '[she's] really collaborative' (Chan 2008).

Reichardt and writing partner Jon Raymond did not initially have Williams in mind for the lead characters she plays in *Wendy and Lucy* or *Meek's Cutoff*, yet together they design characters that ask: 'What's our responsibility to each other as complete strangers?' (Roberts 2010). Landscapes play significant roles in the two films: the ethics of acceptance that grounds Williams' characters emerges from nature. More frequently than Holofcener, Reichardt starts with the idea of a place. Even in those scenes marked by human intervention nature functions as a 'cipher that resists the overarching contemporary economy of instrumental reason and calculative exchange of value' (Miller and Cimitile 2007: 13). Reichardt's visualisations resemble Irigaray's imaginings: at times nature is 'a place of life', 'a place of intimacy, prior to and after all family links . . . a place to welcome the other(s)' ([1993]/2002: 82).

Holofcener drafts dialogue that is catchy and candid. For Reichardt 'the language of the film is outside the dialogue. It's where the cut is . . . It's what's happening in between the lines . . . in the landscape' (TORCH n. d.). Ambient sounds matter as much if not more than words. She focuses 'on the moment and the minutiae' (Quart 2010: 42). Her takes are often long; she lets colour and light (or lack thereof) count. She rarely describes her films' overarching ideas or metaphors to her actors. 'I think she . . . knows that for me, as her actor, it's not going to help me tell the story of this person on this particular path at this time to know any sort of underlying message or political overtones . . . she wants that to come across subtly, so she shies away from talking about it explicitly', explains Williams (Kotek 2011: 52).

Reichardt captures Williams' inwardness by using haunting close-ups on her expressive face; what Adam Green calls her 'unadorned truthfulness' at times also emerges in long shot (2011). 'She is one of the few contemporary actresses whose face can communicate so much emotion, so much thought, even when she's simply looking out a window', Vendela Vida concurs (2011). Unlike Keener, Williams underplays her scenes. Differently than Holofcener and Keener, then, Reichardt and Williams foreground relationships and value a 'difference for' others in their films – and through their friendship.

Something Innate: Michelle Williams in *Wendy and Lucy*

Williams brings 'something innate' to the films that she shoots in the West: she comes from Montana. 'I understand what living in that kind of climate and environment does to a person, what living that kind of life looks like on a person's face and in their body' (Fuller 2006: 165). For *Wendy and Lucy* she 'bought her own (and only) costume – a blue hoodie and brown corduroy shorts – at thrift stores' (Setoodeh 2008: 59). Her hair is muddy brown, cut pudding-bowl style. She has no problem making herself unobtrusive, plain. Like Keener, she commits to character.

The film was inspired by the economic displacement that occurred after Hurricane Katrina. Raymond and Reichardt didn't want to write about African Americans, however, they agreed that in the US the class divide is now bigger than the racial divide (Van Sant 2008). Shot in a remote Oregon town, hard luck stories dot the narrative. Wendy stumbles upon an encampment of penniless, train-riding punks and goes to a bottle return where homeless men wait to sell the cans and bottles they have collected.

To be comfortable with playing a 'socially inept' character who is 'holding it in' Reichardt told Williams about a middle-aged Mexican woman she met while location scouting in Texas. The woman's car had blown a tyre – her spare – and had landed in a ditch. She had no shoes and less than $20; her cell phone minutes had expired. Yet she never looked at the big picture or panicked; she just went on to the next thing (TORCH n.d; Van Sant 2008). Reichardt also had Williams watch *Mouchette* (Bresson, 1967) (Chan 2008). Like the woman in the story and Bresson's non-professional modernist 'models', Williams gives a largely flat performance, minimising facial expressions, gestures and movements. We first meet her striding along in a park, throwing a stick for her dog, Lucy. The camera tracks with them, companionably. As Gail Schwab points out, for Irigaray, too, relationships do not only occur between human beings: they may also form with the elements, trees, flowers or birds (2007: 39). The dog disappears. 'Come on back, girl!' Wendy/Williams calls. The line is premonitory. Wendy's car breaks down. Nearly out of food and money, she shoplifts staples for herself and Lucy, gets caught and is taken away in a police car. Released hours later, she takes a bus and runs back to get Lucy. Lucy is gone.

Reichardt coached Williams to use the smallest of gestures, the slightest of changes in posture and stance. Williams is at her most deadpan when Wendy calls home and recounts her travails. Williams speaks in a monotone, her face immobile. She and Reichardt agreed there should be no 'leaking of emotion' (Jones 2008: 44). Bresson similarly utilised the suppression of intentionality, psychology and exteriorisation (Tomlinson 2004, 75), and thereby freed a different 'authenticity' than that conveyed by neo-naturalist performances – for example those Keener gives for Holofcener. Keener's female characters are social types shaped by specific environments. Williams' Wendy lacks psychological 'depth': she is subject to, buffeted by, external circumstances. Thus, with her car in the shop, with no money for a hotel, Wendy tries to sleep in the woods. A crazy homeless man (Larry Fessenden) threatens her. When he leaves she runs into town and bursts into a gas station restroom. Reichardt captures Wendy's terror using rapid editing and handheld shots.

The culmination of the engagement between the trio of Reichardt, Williams and Lucy comes when Lucy is found: turned in to the pound, she has been adopted. Wendy splurges out on a cab but waits until Lucy's foster owner leaves. Largely blank before, emotions now race across Williams' face; her acting becomes transformative. Petting Lucy over the fence, she coos, 'Hi Lu! . . . You miss me?' before she drops to Lucy's level to exchange doggie kisses, then, her face serious, apologises: 'Huh? Lu, I know, I know. Don't be mad'. Lucy's tail wags. Wendy/Williams' mood changes once more: she reaches inside her back-pack, brings out a stick and tosses it for Lucy. They play for several seconds, and Reichardt portrays them as a couple using two-shots and shot-reverse shots. The tone shifts again. Reichardt focuses on Williams as she stops playing and walks slowly along the fence, pondering what her responsibility to Lucy should be. 'So nice here, Lu . . . That man seemed so nice', she says softly. She tears up and squats by the fence to promise her dog, 'I'll come back'. Then she stands and walks away into fields of flowers, her belongings on her back and clutched in her hands. Longingly, Lucy looks after her. What Irigaray would term a 'communication *between* and reciprocity, as well as

Figure 15.1 Michelle Williams and Lucy the dog in *Wendy and Lucy* (Kelly Reichardt, 2008).

respect' ([1992]/1996: 126), here transpires not between genders, but between species; there's an 'alliance with nature' ([1994]/2001: 13).

Always Game: Michelle Williams in *Meek's Cutoff*

In *Meek's Cutoff* Williams again gives an interior performance, her face barely visible under the enormous sun bonnet she wears, and Reichardt and Raymond again proffer a muted left-wing politics through allegories, their story 'unfolding . . . like a dream' (Ficks 2011). Irigaray's writing is similarly evocative: 'Never definitive, always under construction' (2002a: 10). Reichardt compares Meek's claim that he was 'completely successful' – translated in the film as 'we're not lost, just finding our way' – to George W. Bush's bluster about to Iraq: 'Everything went great. Not to worry' (Longworth 2011: 52). Such a narcissistic sense of omnipotence is, says Margaret Whitford, typical of the mono-centric masculinity Irigaray critiques, where 'at least in fantasy, the recognition of dependence, of other people's existence, of needs, and particularly of the need to earn love or esteem' is lacking (2003: 31).

Critical of male-only decision-making and a gendered division of labour, *Meek's Cutoff* is additionally 'in many ways about racism and racist projections on a cipher' (Adams 2011). Reichardt/Williams' film thereby extends Irigaray's concern with racial difference. The plot is spare: three pioneer families and their braggart guide, Stephen Meek (Bruce Greenwood), are lost in the barren expanse of Oregon's western desert. Emily Tetherow (Williams) becomes the party's moral compass. At first she privately shares her negative opinion of Meek with her husband, Solomon (Will Patton). Later, rifle in hand, she forces Meek to back down when he threatens to tries to kill the Cayuse Indian (Rod Rondeaux) he has captured.

To prepare, Reichardt and Williams read diaries by women pioneers. Williams said she felt 'really connected': her grandmother had stowed away from Norway to Ellis Island, then hopped on a covered wagon to Montana (Kotek 2011: 54). Reichardt's response was filtered through film, not personal recollection: for her the diaries called 'to mind Flaherty's *Nanook of the North* more than say Ford's *The Searchers*. You know: build the igloo, catch the fish, make the fire. Or in our case: set up the tent, empty the wagon, build the fire, make the beans . . . [T]he routine of chores . . . the intense silence that falls at night – those things . . . reflect a journey dominated by time and space and repetition' ('Notes on the Film' 2010: 3). The endlessness of the pioneers' journey emerges in Reichardt's choice of a square frame: the cracked earth yawns before them in close-up; the heavens loom above them in long shot. The immensity of nature is palpable, as it sometimes is for Irigaray: 'This interval – and this medium – is first of all nature, as it remains left to itself: air, water, earth, and sun, as fire and light' (2002a: 19). The camera frequently stands still, letting the actors pass in and out of frame, from left to right and right to left, front to back and back to front. An absence of consistent screen direction and smash cuts from night to day subtly convey disorientation. Often shot from the women's perspective, the men's voices are muffled. The soundtrack is hauntingly spare: a wheel squeaks, wagons rattle, utensils clank. Jeff Grace's score is eerie, with distorted string and wind instruments.

Slowly Emily/Williams establishes a relationship with the imprisoned Cayuse man. One day she approaches him carrying a bowl of water. He is carving signs on a rock. She moves deliberately, head bowed respectfully. He stops and drinks. Crouching before him she points insistently at his torn moccasin and makes sewing gestures. He takes off his shoe. She mends it. Without words the two establish trust; the scene does not, however, suggest assimilation occurs. Irigaray would approve: 'any model that implies we are fundamentally similar strips away the difficulty of living with difference' (Deutscher 1998: 139). 'The subject . . . represents only one part of reality and of truth . . . the other is forever a *not I, nor me, nor mine*, and not a *not yet I, not yet mine* to integrate into me or into us' (Irigaray [1999]/2002c: 127). Shooting took a month. Cast and crew travelled over two hours each day in temperatures that ranged from 100+ degree heat to snow ('Notes on the Film' 2010: 5–6). Reichardt was glad of Williams' participation: 'She's very game . . . It helps to have someone like Michelle who is really up for it all so the other actors don't complain about how hard it is' (TORCH n.d.). By the end, everyone was exhausted. Reichardt had fallen in love with a lone tree, dead on top but with branches and leaves underneath. With no rights to the location she pushed her planned final take until the last day. In long shot, the thirsty travellers run, then walk, towards the tree. 'Mama, a tree can't live without water, can it?' Jimmy White (Tommy Nelson), the sole child in the party, asks. 'We're close', says Emily/ Williams softly. 'That's just it. We're close, but we don't know what to,' complains Thomas Gately (Paul Dano). 'We've been through this, we don't know. Either way,' replies Solomon. All look towards Meek, who sits slumped on his horse. He pledges to take orders from Solomon, then grudgingly appends, 'Ms Tetherow'. Turning, he points at the Indian and acknowledges they are all likely to be taking orders from 'him' now.

By the time the actors understood the ambiguity Reichardt was after, the sun was gone. She was out of money. She cut the film without an ending and, months later went back with only a few crew members, Williams and Rondeaux. It was a 'puzzle to finish the scene with only two actors', she admitted (TORCH n.d.). In the final minutes, in long shot, Rondeaux slowly walks across the plain. In close-up Williams appears worried, exhausted. Her lips are parched, her face is streaked with dust. She turns towards Rondeaux. Through the tree's branches they exchange looks. 'The thing I hadn't expected was that kind of quasi-sexual relationship with Rod . . . but toward the end . . . the movie started to take a turn in my own head. I felt like it was about one woman's sexual awakening, a kind of spiritual-sexual experience she was having with this stranger, with this man' (Vida 2011). Rondeaux walks away as strings again sound and the screen fades to black. 'The other is and will remain a mystery to me', 'a mystery which illuminates', says Irigaray ([1994]/2001: 110, 103–12). 'Rather than grasping you – with my hand, with my gaze, with my intellect – I must stop before the inappropriable . . . You do not, then, find yourself reduced to . . . an object of my love' (ibid. p. 19). Is the tree dead or alive? Will Emily and the Indian and the others find water? Will they survive? With the landscape as a third,[8] sharing no language, of differing races, Emily and the Cayuse's loving acceptance of each other, as woman and man, is nonetheless apparent.

Thinking Life as Relation: Commonalities in Commitment, Differences in Direction

Holofcener/Keener and Reichardt/Williams' examples suggest there is no singular model of mutual muse. Holofcener and Reichardt have quite different ways of making films. Keener's improvisational physicality is unlike Williams' interiority. Yet all work towards an ethical, affirmative 'difference for' others. 'She's the funnier, prettier version of me', says Holofcener of Keener (Chocano 2006: E4). Friends for twenty-two years, 'it's so easy to direct her and so easy for her to direct me' ('Behind the Scenes' 2010). 'I never get tired of looking at her face and what it does' (Turan 2010: D4). Keener responds with equal enthusiasm: 'I seek out her advice and sometimes just her ear. That's what's so interesting about her movies, too: she has such a good ear. The way she portrays characters, it's as if she's observing people on the street when they don't realise anybody's watching them' (Mechling 2010: W2). Reichardt and Williams praise each other, too. Williams is 'capable of being really, really still and having so much come through', says Reichardt (Chan 2008: online). 'We have a great amount of trust built up, and that's a situation where I can thrive', Williams rejoins (Vanairsdale 2011). Praise by directors of actors and by actors of directors is common in publicity interviews; the amount of enthusiasm these four express is not.

Importantly, certain women of colour and some women and men also serve as mutual muses. The collaborations of Barbarao and Julie Dash (*Diary of an African Nun* (1977), *Daughters of the Dust* (1991)) – and surely others, too – await exploration. Holofcener, Keener, Reichardt and Williams all regularly work with men, and often with the same men. Keener has repeatedly performed for Tom DiCillo, Spike Jonze and Charlie Kaufmann. Holofcener often enlists editor Robert Frazen. Anthony Bregman has served as producer or executive producer on every film from *Friends with Money* onwards. Reichardt has twice engaged actor Will Oldham, cinematographer Christopher Blauvelt and composer Jeff Grace. She is always backed by Todd Haynes, Larry Fessenden, Neil Kopp, Phil Morrison and Anish Savjani as producers or executive producers. Barbarao twice worked with Haile Gerima.

In this essay I have intermingled subjects and styles – of writing, directing, acting and philosophising. I do not view Holofcener and Keener or Reichardt and Williams' films as mere illustrations of Irigaray's theory; I do intuit shared intentions behind the poetic approaches both they and Irigaray employ. Certainly Williams describes her approach to acting in terms Irigaray would recognise: 'When I'm working, I feel more turned on to life. I'm having outward experiences. I'm looking and grasping and hoping every day for experiences, for little revelations, for help, for signs, for anything. I'm turned on because I'm in the process of trying to make something' (Vida 2011). Compare Irigaray: 'Meeting with the other, the different, this has happened to us. We were surprised, touched, wonderstruck, called beyond or on this side of what we already were. At least if we were a little attentive' (2002a: viii–ix).

In the final analysis, it is up to *us* to critique and deepen Irigaray's postulations, to elaborate what a 'difference for' others means. Irigaray encourages the 'build[ing] of bridges between cultures: . . . through encouraging each man and woman to talk about his or her culture in order to attempt to find similarities and differences to share' (ibid. p. 70). Holofcener/Keener and Reichardt/Williams' partnerships do just this. They emphasise female friendship and collaboration; they create characters who take up and challenge Irigarayan themes in filmic ways. Sexual orientation is not central in their films, though *Friends with Money* flirts with the question of homosexuality through the character of Aaron (Simon McBurney). Several of Holofcener/Keener, Williams/Reichardt's films – in particular *Lovely & Amazing*, *Friends with Money*, *Wendy and Lucy* and *Meek's Cutoff* – do however 'foreground the experience of difference in terms of ethnicity and class' (Bainbridge 2008: 7). The core question all five women pose 'is how to think an identity which is different from the one we know, an identity in which the relationship with the other is inscribed in the pre-given of my body'? All are interested in a 'relationship *between*' that 'does not allow the submission of one to the other' (Irigaray [1994]/2001: 34–5).

Notes

1. See also Hall 2014 and Paskiewicz 2014.
2. Initially Irigaray was more concerned with deconstructing patriarchal philosophical models which position men and women asymmetrically. Now she feels a meeting between men and women is possible and is confident that a female voice exists. See Bostic 2012. Miller and Cimitile hold that, while unified, the later work brings 'the more critical and speculative work into the context of the political'. 2007: 3.
3. To give an idea of the evolution and continuity of Irigaray's engagements I provide the date of initial publication in brackets in my text and bibliography.
4. 'Man and woman are *culturally* different . . . The subjectivity of man and that of woman are structured starting from a *relational identity* specific to each one, a relational identity that is held between nature and culture'. Irigaray (1999)/2002c: 129.
5. See Foreman 2004, Karpel 2010, Setoodeh 2013, Taylor 2007.
6. For more on Keener's performances with other directors see Holmlund 2012.
7. Holofcener was born in 1960, Keener in 1959, Reichardt in 1964, Williams in 1980.
8. Angels as intermediaries and the placenta as a permeable, nourishing membrane serve similarly emblematic, suggestive functions for Irigaray. All facilitate a transcendence, a back and forth wherein 'the duality of the subjectivities and of their own worlds' is possible. 2002b: 84.

References

'A conversation with Nicole Holofcener' (2006), promotional materials for *Friends with Money*, Sony Pictures Classics.

Adams, Sam (2011), 'Interview: Kelly Reichardt and Jon Raymond', *A. V. Club*, 26 April, <http://www.avclub.com/article/kelly-reichardt-and-jon-raymond-55095> (last accessed 29 April 2015).

Andrew, Geoff (1997), 'Women on the verge', *Time Out*, 15 January: 19.

Bainbridge, Caroline (2008), *A Feminine Cinematics: Luce Irigaray, Women and Film*, Basingstoke: Palgrave Macmillan.

'Behind the Scenes' (2010), DVD extra, *Please Give*, Sony Pictures Home Entertainment.

Bostic, Heidi (2012), 'Introduction: the recent work of Luce Irigaray', *L'Esprit Créateur*, 52: 3, pp. 1–10.

Chan, Jason Jude (2008), 'Exclusive: *Wendy and Lucy* filmmaker Kelly Reichardt discusses her slice of life new indie', 10 December, <http://flavorwire.com/5019/exclusive-wendy-and-lucy-filmmaker-kelly-reichardt-discusses-her-slice-of-life-new-indie> (last accessed 28 April 2015).

Chang, Justin (2005), 'Capote', *Variety*, 12 December, p. 26.

Cheah, Pheng and Elizabeth Grosz (1998), 'Of being-two: introduction', *Diacritics*, 28: 1, pp. 3–18.

Chocano, Carina (2006), 'Right on the money,' *Los Angeles Times*, 24 March, pp. E1, E4.

'Director's commentary' (2006), *Friends with Money*, DVD extra, Sony Pictures Home Entertainment.

Dargis, Manohla (2006), 'Three cocooned haves, one aimless have-not', *The New York Times*, 7 April, pp. 1, 12.

Deutscher, Penelope (2007), '*Between East and West* and the politics of "cultural *ingénuité*"', in Maria C. Cimitile and Elaine P. Miller (eds), *Returning to Irigaray*, Albany: State University of New York Press, pp. 137–50.

Ficks, Jesse Hawthorne (2011), 'Northwest Passage: Kelly Reichardt on *Meek's Cutoff*', *San Francisco Bay Guardian*, 3 May, <http://www.sfbg.com/pixel_vision/2011/05/03/northwest-passage-kelly-reichardt-meeks-cutoff> (last accessed 29 April 2015).

Foreman, Liza (2004), '"Money" talks for quartet in Holofcener pic', *Hollywood Reporter*, 29 November, pp. 1, 84.

Fuller, Graham (2006), 'Michelle Williams', *Interview*, March, pp. 160–6.

Fussman, Carl (2000), 'Women we love', *Esquire*, October, pp. 165–6.

'Getting it going' (2001), DVD extra, *Lovely & Amazing*, Lions Gate.

Green, Adam (2011), 'My week with Michelle', *Vogue*, 13 September, <http://www.vogue.com/865411/michelle-williams-my-week-with-michelle/> (last accessed 28 April 2015).

Hall, Dawn (2014), *American Independent Female Filmmakers: Kelly Reichardt in Focus*, Ann Arbor: ProQuest, UMI Dissertations Publishing.

Holmlund, Chris (2017), 'Casing indie acting', in Geoff King (ed.), *A Companion to American Indie Film*, Malden, MA: Wiley-Blackwell.

Holmlund, Chris (2012), 'Niche actors acting gay', in Aaron Taylor (ed.), *Theorizing Film Acting*, London: Routledge, pp. 210–26.

Irigaray, Luce (2002a), *The Way of Love*, London and New York: Continuum.

Irigaray, Luce (2002b), 'Why cultivate difference?', *Paragraph*, 25: 3, November, pp. 79–90.

Irigaray, Luce ([1999]/2002c), *Between East and West: From Singularity to Community*, trans. Stephen Pluháček, New York: Columbia University Press.

Irigaray, Luce ([1994]/2001), *To Be Two*, trans. Monique Rhodes and Marco Cocito-Monoc, New York: Routledge.

Irigaray, Luce ([1996]/2000), 'Thinking life as relation', in Luce Irigaray and Sylvere Lotringer (eds), *Why Different? A Culture of Two Subjects*, trans. Camille Collins, New York: Semiotext(e), pp. 145–67.

Irigaray, Luce ([1993]/2000), 'Different from you/different between us', in Luce Irigaray and Sylvere Lotringer (eds), *Why Different? A Culture of Two Subjects*, trans. Camille Collins, New York: Semiotext(e), pp. 81–4.

Irigaray, Luce ([1992]/2000), 'The question for our time', in Luce Irigaray and Sylvere Lotringer (eds), *Why Different? A Culture of Two Subjects*, trans. Camille Collins, New York: Semiotext(e), pp. 85–92.

Irigaray, Luce ([1979]/2000), 'Mothers and daughters', in Luce Irigaray and Sylvere Lotringer (eds), *Why Different? A Culture of Two Subjects*, trans. Camille Collins, New York: Semiotext(e), pp. 17–27.

Irigaray, Luce ([1990]/2000), 'A bridge between two irreducible to each other', in Luce

Irigaray and Sylvere Lotringer (eds), *Why Different? A Culture of Two Subjects*, trans. Camille Collins, New York: Semiotext(e), pp. 57–62.
Irigaray, Luce ([1992]/1996), *I Love to You*, trans. Alison Martin, New York and London: Routledge.
Jacobs, Matthew (2014), 'Nicole Holofcener on *Enough Said*, her Golden Globe snub, and the TV show she'd most like to direct', *Huffington Post.com*, 8 January, <http://www.huffingtonpost.com/2014/01/08/nicole-holofcener-enough-said_n_4538772.html> (last accessed 27 April 2015).
Jones, Kristin M. (2008), 'The quiet beauty (and radiant desperation) of Kelly Reichardt's *Wendy and Lucy*', *Film Comment*, 6, pp. 44–5.
Karpel, Ari (2010), 'Inspiration goes both ways', *Los Angeles Times*, 30 April, pp. D1, D6.
Kotek, Elliot (2011), 'Michelle Williams: indie trailblazer', *Moviemaker.com*, 18, pp. 50–5.
Longworth, Karina (2011), 'Go west, young women', *LA Weekly*, 15–21 April, p. 52.
McDonald, Paul (2013), *Hollywood Stardom*, Malden, MA: Wiley-Blackwell.
Mechling, Lauren (2010), 'Director and her alter ego', *The Wall Street Journal*, 23 April, p. W2.
Miller, Elaine P. and Maria C. Cimitile (2007), 'Introduction', in Maria C. Cimitile and Elaine P. Miller (eds), *Returning to Irigaray*, Albany: State University of New York Press, pp. 1–24.
'Notes on the film' (2010), Promotional materials for *Meek's Cutoff*, Oscilloscope Productions.
Paskiewicz, Katarzyna (2014), 'G(r)aze encounters: negotiating proximity and distance in Kelly Reichardt's *Meek's Cutoff*', paper presented at the Society for Cinema and Media Studies Seattle Conference.
Perkins, Claire (2014), 'Beyond Indiewood: the everyday ethics of Nicole Holofcener', *Camera Obscura*, 29 [85], pp. 136–59.
'Playing the part' (2001), DVD extra, *Lovely & Amazing*, Lions Gate.
'Promotional materials' for *Enough Said* (2013), Fox Searchlight Pictures.
Quart, Leonard (2011), 'The way west: a feminist perspective', *Cineaste*, Spring, pp. 40–3.
Roberts, Sheila (2010), 'Michelle Williams, Kelly Reichardt interview', <http://www.moviesonline.ca/movienews_15989.html> (last accessed 28 April 2015).
Rochlin, Margy (2000), 'Being Catherine Keener and making it look easy', *The New York Times*, 23 January, p. 11.
Schwab, Gail (2007), 'Reading Irigaray (and her readers) in the twenty-first century', in Maria C. Cimitile and Elaine P. Miller (eds), *Returning to Irigaray*, Albany: State University of New York Press, pp. 25–50.
Setoodeh, Ramin (2013), 'An amazing alliance', *Variety*, 1 October, pp. 84–5.
Setoodeh, Ramin (2010), 'The private life of Catherine Keener', *Newsweek*, 15 April, pp. 49–50.
Setoodeh, Ramin (2008), 'An actress moves on, or tries to', *Newsweek*, 1 December, p. 59.
Taylor, Ella (2010), 'It's complicated', *LA Weekly*, 23 April, p. 54.
Taylor, Ella (2008), 'The wanderers: Michelle Williams finds a safe haven with outsider director Kelly Reichardt on *Wendy and Lucy*', *LA Weekly*, 19–25 December, pp. 26, 36.
Taylor, Ella (2007), 'Mother, flower child, ballbuster', *LA Weekly*, 19 September, <http://www.laweekly.com/film/mother-flower-child-ballbuster-2150523> (last accessed 2 May 2015).
Tomlinson, Doug (2004), 'Performance in the films of Robert Bresson: the aesthetics of

denial', in Cynthia Baron, Sharon Carnicke and Frank P. Tomasulo (eds), *More Than a Method*, Detroit: Wayne State University Press, pp. 71–93.

TORCH (The Oxford Research Centre in the Humanities) (n.d.), 'Kelly Reichardt "in conversation"', <http://torch.ox.ac.uk/kelly-reichardt-conversation> (last accessed 26 February 2015).

Turan, Kenneth (2010), 'Vying for attention', *Los Angeles Times*, 27 January, pp. D1, D4.

Vanairsdale, S. T. (2011), 'Michelle Williams on *Meek's Cutoff*, goodbyes, and getting lost at the movies', 30 March, <http://movieline.com/2011/03/30/michelle-williams-on-meeks-cutoff-goodbyes-and-getting-lost-at-the-movies/> (last accessed 28 April 2015).

Van Sant, Gus (2008), 'Kelly Reichardt', *BOMB* 105, Fall, <http://bombmagazine.org/article/3182/kelly-reichardt> (last accessed 28 April 2015).

Vida, Vendela (2011) 'Michelle Williams', *Interview*, May, <http://www.interviewmagazine.com/film/michelle-williams/> (last accessed 19 November 2015).

Whitford, Margaret (2003), 'Irigaray and the culture of narcissism', *Theory, Culture & Society*, 20: 3, pp. 27–41.

16. THE FEMINIST POLITICS OF COLLABORATION IN LENA DUNHAM'S *TINY FURNITURE*

Corinn Columpar

In her landmark essay 'Women's Cinema as Counter-Cinema' from 1973, Claire Johnston (1999) predicates her model of an oppositional women's cinema on its textual qualities rather than its mode of production. Arguing against her contemporaries who claim that a collectivist approach to the production process inevitably yields a politically oppositional work, she instead identifies a film's capacity to demystify dominant ideology in and through its form and content as the defining attribute of any counter-cinema, including a feminist one. At the time of its publication, this intervention proved extremely productive insofar as it countered facile assumptions about how films make meaning and thereby paved the way for a feminist film criticism steeped in semiotics. At the same time, however, it also foreclosed a potentially generative line of inquiry that has not been pursued in earnest since: one dedicated to an exploration of how collaborative methods actually can, not inevitably, but by design, contribute to a counter-cinematic vision.

For one seeking to pick up where Johnston left off, American independent cinema is an opportune place to start. There are multiple examples of indie filmmakers who regard working relations of affiliation, cooperation, and mutual exchange as not only a necessity (which they are for almost any film production), but also part of a larger aesthetic and/or political programme. For example, one could easily imagine a study of collaboration foregrounding an individual like Jim McKay, who actively incorporates the voices of the communities he films into his work; a partnership like that forged by director Nicole Holofcener and actor Catherine Keener, who have worked together consistently throughout their careers; or a film movement like mumblecore, whose DIY aesthetic goes hand in hand with an expansive social network of creative partners.[1] All of these subjects lend themselves to a discussion of collaborative methods due to their reliance on a cooperative approach to media production that is not only ready but also readily recognised. Rather than taking on such a subject, however, this essay considers the aesthetic and political possibilities of collaboration in relation to a figure of a different sort: Lena Dunham. Not only has her star risen so quickly and decisively that her persona overshadows the community of collaborators with whom she regularly works, but her tendency to move frequently between media platforms and to assume simultaneously multiple roles in her various works, including those of writer, producer, director, and actor, can produce an impression of insular self-sufficiency.

Due to her HBO series *Girls* (2012–), Dunham has in recent years become a mass media sensation and, as such, a figure in acute danger of over-exposure, a topic about which there may be nothing new to say. Yet, in fact, the more Dunham gets discussed, the more evident certain discursive omissions become, confirming that there is a lack of critical paradigms capable of recognising, let alone naming, those aforementioned acts of affiliation, cooperation, and mutual exchange that often condition cultural production, including that engaged in by Dunham. In cinema studies the primary reason for this paucity is the discourse of auteurism, which identifies a film's director as its author and (at least one) locus of textual meaning. Proving one of the most enduring and resilient critical paradigms in the field, it continues to structure the discipline, influencing the creation of curricula, the formation of canons, and the production of knowledge, even in the face of film's indisputably collaborative nature and poststructuralism's designation of the author as dead. In recent years, however, this paradigm has travelled. As evinced by Dunham's career, among others, convergence culture has ensured the movement of not only select auteurs but also the discourse of auteurism across the boundaries drawn between previously discrete media.

The cable television network HBO is particularly noteworthy on this count as it has carefully constructed its brand around an auteurist tradition associated with quality programming and cultural cachet. Thus the challenge it faced upon hiring Dunham was fitting her into this tradition despite her newcomer status. The result, as Taylor Nygaard (2013) has detailed, was a concerted effort on the part of the network to promote Dunham as the rising star of the YouTube generation, and it did so by way of two contradictory strategies. The first involved foregrounding those things about Dunham that would lend her legitimacy among the female audience that HBO was courting with the series *Girls*, such as her personal history; the success of her previous project, the feature film *Tiny Furniture* (2010); and her association with mentor Nora

Ephron. The second strategy, in contrast, served to disavow the gender identity so central to the first by likening Dunham to certain well-established male comedians, including Larry David and Louis C. K., and thereby implicitly acknowledging the specifically masculine lines along which auteurism has historically been conceived.

Despite its attendant tensions, this two-pronged approach has worked extremely well. No matter what position it takes up, criticism of Dunham's work treats her as a singular, and single, artist unified by her stylistic, narrative, and thematic predilections. Indeed, HBO can be credited with furthering an agenda that has been pursued by any number of feminist film critics from Judith Mayne (1990) to Kaja Silverman (1988) to Anneke Smelnik (1998), albeit all in the name of enhancing its brand image and bottom line: it has both adopted and adapted the language of auteurism to accommodate a woman's output. In light of this, one could object that shifting the terms of discussion towards collaborative practice risks ceding the ground that has been gained with the widespread acknowledgement of Dunham – or any woman, for that matter – as an auteur. Nonetheless, the potential rewards of that discursive and methodological shift are arguably much greater: first, the recognition of a more expansive cast of players as well as the contextual factors that shape their work, from the conditions of its creation and circulation to its engagement with various social formations, and, second, a critical practice that is far more responsive to the process of creating counter-cinema than those that take the conventions of auteurist criticism as normative.

To a large extent, Dunham's career since the debut of *Girls* has only served to shore up her status as auteur. After all, with the publication of multiple short stories in *The New Yorker* and the memoir *Not That Kind of Girl: A Young Woman Tells You What She's 'Learned'* (2014) by Random House she has become, in the strictest sense of the word, an author, achieving visibility in a medium that does not depend upon the collective efforts of a creative team. Yet the work through which she gained public exposure prior to *Girls* allows for a different construction of Dunham to emerge. Between numerous short films, the web series *Tight Shots* (2007) and *Delusional Downtown Divas* (2009), and, finally, the feature films *Creative Nonfiction* (2009) and *Tiny Furniture*, Dunham not only began exploring the thematic ground that has become her calling card, namely the lives of twenty-something women who are defined by their cultural literacy, professional limbo, and romantic uncertainty; she also honed a working method that mobilises a network of connections that are both personal and professional in dimension. Of the texts named, the one that lays bare this working method most clearly is *Tiny Furniture*, which was a break-out success at the South by Southwest film festival in 2010 and was subsequently distributed by IFC theatrically and the prestigious Criterion Collection on DVD and Blu-ray. Both reflecting on and performing an investment in multiple communities, it acknowledges collaboration as a horizon of artistic possibility and, in the process, contributes to a vital feminist tradition of cultural production.

Dunham's Web of Relations

Made shortly after Dunham's own graduation from Oberlin College, *Tiny Furniture* features Dunham playing an aspiring filmmaker named Aura, who has just gone through the same rite of passage and returns to her family's home in New York City to figure out her next step. During her 'post-graduate delirium,' Aura drifts apart from her college roommate and puts her creative ambitions on hold while working as a restaurant hostess and spending time with an array of people, including her busy mother, self-possessed sister, and childhood friend, as well as two romantic prospects: an opportunistic video maker and a fickle sous chef. By virtue of this premise, which has Dunham performing a version of herself against the backdrop of Manhattan, *Tiny Furniture* readily lends itself to comparison with the work of Woody Allen. In fact, Dunham herself acknowledges Allen's influence by making intertextual reference to him: in one scene Aura lies in bed with the video artist as he reads a copy of Allen's book *Without Feathers*.

Nonetheless, the filmmaker with whom she shares even more ground is John Cassavetes since it is far more than Dunham as Aura that provides a point of contact between the world of the film and the world of the film's production. Rather, those two worlds interpenetrate each other in such a thoroughgoing fashion that fact and fiction become nearly indistinguishable. Like Cassavetes, Dunham populates *Tiny Furniture* with her friends and family: Dunham's mother, Laurie Simmons, plays Aura's mother, Siri; Dunham's sister, Grace Dunham, plays Aura's sister, Nadine; and Dunham's childhood friend, Jemima Kirk (who also stars as Jessa in *Girls*), plays Aura's childhood friend, Charlotte. What's more, Dunham employs her family home as their stage and draws multiple dramatic details from reality, including Aura's relationship history, Siri's status as a celebrated photographer, Nadine's poetry prize, Charlotte's upbringing, and the journal that Aura reads aloud throughout the film, detailing her mother's early adulthood. Even Dunham's short video *The Fountain* (2007) is folded into the film as one of Aura's creations, which she plays on YouTube for Charlotte and then presents in a group art show.

Due in large part to Cassavetes' tendency to work with his friends and family, George Kouvaros, who has produced the most theoretically nuanced account of the filmmaker's output to date, argues that his work occupies 'an in-between space that is not outside the fiction, yet is not simply contained by it either, a space where actor and character neither have completely fused nor can easily be separated' (x-xi). Yet it is not just the boundary between actor and character and, by extension, life and art that is rendered porous within this space; it is also the boundary between the process of filmmaking, which is open to flux and contingency, and the product of film, with its connotations of fixity and closure. As Kouvaros puts it after taking stock of Cassavetes' entire corpus, 'As an extended network of personal and professional relationships circulate both across the films and 'in real life', the family [at the centre of his work] allows for material contingency (chance, improvisation, the everyday) to inflect the diegetic world of the film' (Kouvaros 2004: 16). In other words, as the diegetic and the nondiegetic become imbricated, Cassavetes' work positions filmmaking as an activity that is not set off from the rest of life, but is part and parcel of it, allowing for the negotiation of relationships, the actualisation of desire, the development of ideas, and the creation of community. For this reason, Kouvaros locates Cassavetes's work in a tradition typically associated with documentary cinema exclusively: Direct Cinema. Following the lead of Jean-Luc Comolli, Kouvaros employs a definition of Direct Cinema that is predicated not on some purported truth-value, but rather on its capacity to '[represent] the moment of mutual implication when the process of filming acts upon the material it records and is, in turn, acted upon and constituted by this material' (ibid. p. 61).

Given the extent to which Dunham also plays at, and with, the boundary between art and life, Kouvaros's comments seem equally applicable to her work. It is precisely this sense of mutual implication that Manohla Dargis (2010) is getting at when she describes *Tiny Furniture* as 'part performance piece, part thought experiment.' One key difference between the work of Cassavetes and Dunham, however, is the extent to which the material implicated in the mutual exchange at issue is animated by a centrifugal or centripetal force. In the case of Cassavetes, the act of filming produces, more often than not, a dispersal, even a decomposition, of its subjects. Between abrupt tonal shifts, a large cast of characters defined foremost by their volatility, and gestural exchanges that, in keeping with Jean François Lyotard's acinematic ideal (1986), resist legibility and productivity, films such as *Faces* (1968) and *Husbands* (1970) showcase a wide array of affectively charged shards. Dunham's work, in contrast, self-consciously engages in a process of accretion and synthesis, a process that allows for the production of a provisional self that is informed by the web of relations in which that self is enmeshed and from which it emerges. Given the extent to which the self at issue is that of Dunham, the performer who both produces and is produced by the work, *Tiny Furniture* fits even more comfortably in another documentary tradition than that of Direct Cinema, one that has proliferated prodigiously in the era of digital media. Namely, it qualifies as the fictional counterpart to 'first person documentaries,' which Elisa Lebow (2012) foregrounds in her recently published anthology, *The Cinema of Me*.

While multiple other cinema studies scholars, including Michael Renov, have discussed the same type of films under the rubric of 'autobiographical documentary', Lebow argues that these films are characterised less by their subject, some autonomous self, than by their mode of address, which may include a speaker conceived of in individual or collective terms. More specifically, referencing the work of Jean-Luc Nancy, she suggests that first person documentaries – both the term and the films that term encompasses – are uniquely capable of bridging the individual and the collective and thereby, potentially at least, speaking in the voice of the 'singular plural'. She writes,

> The grammatical reference reminds us that language itself, though spoken by an individual, is never entirely our own invention, nor anyone else's. Despite the fact that we believe it to express our individuality, it nonetheless also expresses our commonality, our plurality, our interrelatedness within a group, a mass, a sociality, if not a society. This is as true about the expression of individuality and subjectivity in first person films as it is in language itself. (3)

In the case of many of the films discussed in Lebow's collection the cinema of me becomes a cinema of we by virtue of the interpersonal interactions they feature and the publics they, in the process, forge. The same can be said of *Tiny Furniture* in so far as Dunham not only positions Aura at the centre of a network of people, but also thickens the relationships she has with those people by endowing them with a resonance that far exceeds the boundaries of the diegesis. In so doing she implicates the filmmaking process, with all its attendant acts of collaborative negotiation, in the film product.

The most important member of this network is Simmons, her mother. The fact that Simmons is an established and well-respected photographer is germane to the public persona of Dunham as it has taken shape over recent years. Along with the similar success of her father, painter Carroll Dunham, her mother's status is most often noted as a biographical footnote to a discussion of Dunham's work or as the grounds from which a critique of her privilege and resulting myopia is launched. What such accounts occlude, however, is the extent to which Dunham engages in active, strategic, and generative exchange with her mother in a couple of different ways. First, she has enlisted the efforts of Simmons throughout her career: Simmons appears not only in *Tiny Furniture*, but also in multiple shorts and one episode of *Girls*, and she produced *Creative Nonfiction*. Second, Dunham makes intertextual reference to Simmons' work throughout *Tiny Furniture*, thereby grounding an act of self-expression in interlocution. The result is a film characterised by dialogic form, which allows Dunham to define herself in terms of a multi-layered relationship that has several dimensions, a relationship not only between mother and daughter, but also between fellow visual artists and self-defined feminists, albeit ones riding different waves.

Like Mother, Like Daughter

In the liner notes for the Criterion Collection's DVD of *Tiny Furniture*, writer Phillip Lopate (2010) astutely argues that *Tiny Furniture* is 'at heart a mother-daughter story,' citing as evidence Aura's multiple attempts, over the course of the film, to get something from her mother, be it attention, affection, reassurance, or guidance. To some extent, she finds these things in Siri's old journal, which provides an account of Siri's life when she was Aura's age, but it is present-day Siri with whom Aura most wants a close bond. In light of this narrative priority, the final scene offers closure of sorts in so far as it provides Aura with the intimacy and reciprocity she seeks, at least provisionally; as Lopate notes, it allows Aura to 'return to the comfort of her mother's body' and finally 'feel that her mother needs her, if only for a brief moment'. Yet as much as *Tiny Furniture* depicts a relationship between a fictional mother and daughter, it also enacts one between Dunham and Simmons, and in the context of that latter, real-life relationship the film's development and resolution have implications that extend beyond the personal to encompass the professional and the political as well. That is, with *Tiny Furniture*, Dunham negotiates her relationship not only to Simmons but also to the feminist legacy of her work.

With her film's title, Dunham gestures towards one of the defining materials that Simmons has used to create her photographic corpus since the mid-1970s: dolls' house furniture. From her earliest experiments in both black & white and colour photography to series such as 'Deluxe-Redding House' (1998), 'Kaleidoscope House' (2000–2), and 'Long House' (2002–4), Simmons has made that furniture a fixture in the worlds she creates and then captures, presenting it on its own or in concert with other props, including female figures in the form of dolls or paper cut-outs.[2] The result is the representation of domestic spaces that are miniature in dimension, fantastic in nature, and evocative, either literally or by association, of a carefully constructed femininity. Like Cindy Sherman, with whom Simmons is often coupled due to their membership in the so-called Pictures Generation of photographers, Simmons produces imagery that has a mimetic relationship to reality, but is nonetheless steeped in artifice and thus capable of exposing the conventions that condition female identity. At the same time, however, her work is also deeply personal, compelled by her own childhood experiences and therefore infused with emotional resonance; as Calvin Tompkins puts it in a profile on Simmons for *The New Yorker*, 'The strange emotional pull in each photograph comes from the artist's obsessive need to make it' (2012: 36).

Simmons' work with tiny furniture features in the film *Tiny Furniture* in two pointed ways. First, Dunham puts it in the hands of the fictional Siri and thereby contributes to the blurring of boundaries between actor and character, between fiction and reality already discussed. Second, she, in concert with

Figure 16.1 Laurie Simmons' photograph in Lena Dunham's film *Tiny Furniture* (2010).

director of photography Jody Lee Lipes, reproduces it on her own cinematic terms in order, like her mother before her, to explore the affective possibilities it houses. This act of reproduction is evident in the film's first scene, in which Aura returns from college and finds Siri and Nadine busy with a photo shoot: Siri is behind the camera photographing Nadine's feet as she stands like a hyper-feminine giant in the middle of an arrangement of miniature living room furniture. While narratively the scene serves to foreshadow the needy dynamic that Lopate identifies – immediately upon seeing the shoot Aura asks her mother, 'How come you never use me in any pictures?' – aesthetically it serves to create a very different relationship between mother and daughter since it is Dunham who is, in this instance, using Simmons: appropriating her mother's aesthetic through the film's form, she presents her home (which houses both her actual family and her fictional one) in such a manner that it mirrors the worlds that Simmons has made a career of building. Specifically, the *mise-en-scène* is dominated by a white decor punctuated with bursts of colour and illuminated with high key lighting, and it is shot with a static camera and framed so as to emphasise rectilinearity and the ordered segmentation of space. The result is images characterised by clean lines and hard edges that serve either to encompass their subjects in highly stylised tableaux or to fragment human forms as they move across unyielding frame lines. In subsequent scenes, Dunham uses other compositional strategies drawn from Simmons' work as well: in select shots she films two rooms (and their occupants) simultaneously such that the wall that separates them bisects the frame vertically, and even more frequently she produces frames within frames, enclosing her characters in doorways or openings of another kind. In all of these ways, Simmons' aesthetic exerts a structuring influence on certain scenes in the film, dictating the formal choices Dunham makes.

At the same time, however, the formal approach established at the outset of *Tiny Furniture* and developed thereafter gives way to others on occasion. On the night of her return home, for example, Aura attends a party at a friend's apartment, and for the first time in the film a style similar to that seen earlier prevails, but with a key difference: the footage is captured by a handheld camera and thus the static shots are only relatively static, continuously moving ever so slightly while capturing the narrative action and thereby infusing the scenes with a kind of restless energy. Handheld camerawork of this kind characterises multiple subsequent scenes as well, some of them locating Aura out in the world (at Charlotte's apartment and at work, for instance) and others taking place when she brings people she encounters there back to her family home. Furthermore, in a radical departure from the formal precedent established initially, the camera moves dramatically during two relatively fraught scenes that occur late in the film. In the first, Aura and Nadine have an explosive fight in front of a roomful of Nadine's friends as Aura attempts to assert her authority over her sister and Nadine responds by characterising Aura as desperate and attention seeking. In the second, Aura disposes of her dead hamster, who has come to serve as a synecdoche for everything associated with college life. While both of these scenes represent occurrences that enhance Aura's sense of dislocation, the fact that they are rendered with an unprecedented amount of camera movement heightens their disruptive effect.

In light of the stylistic progression described above, one that begins with static framing and builds to incorporate more, and more dramatic, camera movement as the film develops, one could read *Tiny Furniture* as an exercise in individuation, an attempt on Dunham's part to distinguish herself from her mother, as both a woman and an artist. That is, one could argue that the use of hand-held camerawork allows Dunham to supplant her mother's worldview with one of her own. While there is textual evidence for such a reading, perhaps even more persuasive is an extratextual factor: as Charlotte Brunsdon (2005) has noted, dramas of 'dis-identification' are rampant in popular culture, particularly in the contemporary intellectual and creative work of women. Yet in *Tiny Furniture* a different dynamic is afoot. Far from severing ties with her mother, Dunham instead shores them up. Not only does she return to Simmons' aesthetic time and again throughout the film but she concludes with it as well, in a final scene that has Aura taking reassuring comfort in her mother's company.

Feminist through Lines

Brunsdon introduces the notion of disidentification in her contribution to a *Cinema Journal* dossier on postfeminism from 2005 when she describes a phenomenon in both academia and popular culture wherein contemporary women contrast themselves with their feminist predecessors by defiantly claiming their stake in those things they imagine the second wave to have rejected entirely, most importantly pleasure and femininity. In an academic context this tendency has resulted in what Brunsdon calls the 'Ur feminist article,' wherein an author juxtaposes two readings of a female-centred text: on the one hand, a supposedly orthodox feminist one and, on the other, her own, more flexible one. While the immediate goal of such a move is to (re)value, at least in part, that text and its fans, the broader effect is to realise a general shift in the tenor of feminist criticism by promoting the celebration of feminine culture rather than its censorship, the negotiation of gender roles rather than their refusal, and the indulgence of spectatorial pleasure rather than its destruction. Similarly, in popular culture the same rhetorical move is evident in those public figures who implicitly or explicitly invoke a feminist precedent in order to then define themselves against it.

In making these claims, Brunsdon does not dwell on, or even broach, the difference between third-wave feminism and postfeminism, seemingly subsuming both under the latter term, which is the subject of the dossier. Moreover, her argument does not compel her to disentangle the two phenomena since she regards acts of disidentification to be a defining feature of both. To wit, the examples she provides of those who engage in disidentification are quite diverse, ranging from herself, a self-identified feminist who has written a typical Ur feminist article, to Nigella Lawson, domestic goddess and exemplar of postfeminist popular culture. It follows then that her language is extremely inclusive: she writes, 'Disidentity – not being like that, not being like those other women, not being like those images of women – is constitutive of feminism, and constitutive of feminism in all its generations' (112). Yet as much as disidentification is integral to every iteration of feminism, including the 'post-' variety, it, according to Brunsdon, functions differently in a contemporary context than it did for previous generations. Rather than target patriarchal constructions of women or even oneself in an act of self-reflexive critique, recent feminist and postfeminist acts of disidentification take second-wave feminism as their abject object. As Brunsdon continues,

> For if second-wave feminists were not like the housewives and sex objects they saw in the media, they were in turn othered by the postcolonial critique of the 1980s. As second-wave feminism interrogated itself, those in the next generation of feminists felt compelled to declare their lack of identity with second-wave feminists. Second-wave feminism is remembered, and demonised, as personally censorious, hairy, and politically correct. (112)

In other words, recent acts of disidentification entrench a hard-and-fast distinction between us and them, between past and present that denies the continuity of feminist thought and action over time and instead produces a history of women's output predicated on rupture and rejection. For those who identify with the label feminist, as Dunham does, that distinction is one between the second and third waves; for those who do not, it is one between feminism and postfeminism.

To a certain extent, both Aura and Dunham take part in the shift that Brunsdon identifies. By virtue of their age and social location, they are the beneficiaries of many decades of feminist activity and thus necessarily have a different relationship from what their foremothers had to any number of institutional and social phenomena. For example, the same impulse that fuels the Ur feminist article is the one that allows Aura's (and presumably Dunham's) friends at Oberlin to take self-aware pleasure in activities associated with a stereotypical femininity, including baking and building miniature 1950s dinette sets out of balsa wood. It is also the same one that allows Dunham, in all of her work, to employ certain tropes associated with mainstream cultural forms, such as romantic comedies and melodrama, in order to explore with biting wit the complexities of women's lives. Yet as much as *Tiny Furniture* both represents and constitutes such acts of reappropriation and thus bespeaks Dunham's third-wave status, the film's final scene, in both its form and its content, lays bare that it is not invested in the kinds of distinctions and divisions that Brunsdon observes elsewhere.

In that scene Aura climbs into bed with Siri at the end of a long night that includes a humiliating date with the sous chef and a tense exchange between mother and daughter. As Aura rubs Siri's aching back, the two talk frankly about a range of topics, from Aura's sexual experiences to her career ambitions, and the result is as Lopate describes: a satisfaction of Aura's desire to be close to her mother and thus a consolidation of their bond. At the same time, however, the scene also serves to consolidate Siri as a character and Simmons as her real-life counterpart. Over the course of the conversation Aura reveals that she has been reading Siri's old journal (again, Simmons' actual journal) and then asks about the various people mentioned in it. In Siri's responses, which draw on Simmons' personal history, she creates a through line from the past to the present by recounting and commenting on the events that Aura has been reading about, thereby placing them in the context of a life that is still being lived, of a narrative that continues to unfold. Similarly, *Tiny Furniture* makes connections between past and present as well: as Dunham incorporates into her own film the photographic series Simmons initiated in the period of time the journals document, she forges a profound connection with her mother as well as an entire legacy of feminist cultural production. Moreover, in so doing she, as heir to that legacy, resignifies the aesthetic that she and her mother share. Rather than evoking the confinement and conformity conditioning women's lives that Simmons comments on in her work involving tiny furniture,. *Tiny Furniture* evokes the work itself, a material artifact of artistic agency, women's labour, and feminist critique. It evokes a history – personal, professional, and political – that remains both relevant and alive as it fuels Dunham's collaborative efforts.

Notes

1. In vol. 91, No. 1 (2016) of *Camera Obscura*, I discuss collaboration in the case of yet another subject related to American independent cinema: John Cameron Mitchell's *Shortbus* (2006).
2. A catalogue of Simmons' work, including the photographic series mentioned here, is available online at <http://www.lauriesimmons.net>

References

Brunsdon, Charlotte (2005), 'Feminism, Postfeminism, Martha, Martha, and Nigella', *Cinema Journal*, 44: 2, pp. 110–16.

Columpar, Corinn (2016), 'A Permeable Practice: Shortbus and the Politics of Cinematic Collaboration', *Camera Obscura*, 90: 1.

Dargis, Manohla (2010), 'Girl Undefined: Post-College but Pre-Real World', *The New York Times*, 11 November, <http://www.nytimes.com/2010/11/12/movies/12tiny.html?_r=0> (last accessed 13 April 2015).

Dunham, Lena (2014), *Not That Kind of Girl: A Young Woman Tells You What She's 'Learned'*, New York: Random House.

Johnston, Claire ([1973]/1999), 'Women's Cinema as Counter-Cinema', in Sue Thornham (ed.), *Feminist Film Theory: A Reader*, New York: New York University Press, pp. 31–40.

Kouvaros, George (2004), *Where Does It Happen? John Cassavetes and Cinema at the Breaking Point*, Minneapolis: University of Minnesota Press.

Lebow, Alisa (2012), 'Introduction', in Alisa Lebow (ed.), *The Cinema of Me: The Self and Subjectivity in First-Person Documentary*, New York: Columbia University Press, pp. 1–12.

Lopate, Phillip (2010), '*Tiny Furniture*: Out There', Lena Dunham (director), *Tiny Furniture* [DVD], USA: Criterion.

Lyotard, Jean-François (1986), 'Acinema', in Philip Rosen (ed.), *Narrative, Apparatus, Ideology: A Film Theory Reader*, New York: Columbia University Press, pp. 349–74.

Mayne, Judith (1990), *The Woman at the Keyhole*, Bloomington: Indiana University Press.

Nygaard, Taylor (2013), 'Girls Just Want to be "Quality": HBO, Lena Dunham, and *Girls*' conflicting brand identity', *Feminist Media Studies*, 13: 2, pp. 370–4.

Silverman, Kaja (1988), *The Acoustic Mirror*, Bloomington: Indiana University Press.

Smelnik, Anneke (1998), *And the Mirror Cracked: Feminist Cinema and Film Theory*, New York: Palgrave.

Tompkins, Calvin (2012). 'A Doll's House', *The New Yorker*, 10 December, pp. 34–41.

17. THE DIRECTOR AS FACILITATOR: COLLABORATION, COOPERATION AND THE GENDER POLITICS OF THE SET

John Alberti

'One of the things I wanted to explore was: could I keep the intimate feeling of my tiny, family-style film sets where everybody is really excited to be there and on the same page, and it's a really positive experience for everybody?' (Rochlin 2013: 2). The indie director Lynn Shelton's concerns about how her low-budget filmmaking style would translate into her work on an episode of *Mad Men* speaks to a central structural issue surrounding the 'difference' of female indie filmmakers and the radically hierarchical workplace practices that still govern both mainstream and indie movie production, practices that define the director as the central voice of authority on the set. In this essay I will argue that it is these practices, understood in their gendered and ideological context, that contribute to the seemingly intractable gender imbalance of who gets to direct movies.

While the loose matrix of production practices, aesthetic conventions, and cultural signifiers that define 'indie' moviemaking has been relatively more open to women directors than mainstream Hollywood production, this difference results as much from the dismally low bar set by the major studios as from anything even closely approaching gender equality in the indie film world.[1] Drawing from an extended interview with Shelton on her own collaborative approach to moviemaking as well as the examples of other indie directors who challenge the dominant dictatorial and antagonistic models of set management, I argue that questioning the gendered assumptions informing the traditionally masculine signifier of the auteur can help us reframe the binary of individualist versus collectivist as models of the production process.

Instead, the more dialectical idea of the auteur/director as collaborator and facilitator provides a strategy of feminist critique that opens up the connections between the maintenance of gender inequality and top-down (and often abusive) production practices that impede both the creative potential and economic efficiency of the traditional movie set.

Celluloid Ceiling: Theory and Practice

Although the issues of the celluloid ceiling and the glaring gender imbalance in the director's chair are a focus of scrutiny within both the movie industry and academic cinema studies, this scrutiny takes different forms within each. Most entertainment industry and media discussion of the barriers that continue to exclude women from film and television direction, for example, tend to concentrate on the need to change individual attitudes among production executives. *The New York Times* critic Manohla Dargis's three-part investigative and advocacy series – 'Making History: With "Selma," Ava DuVernay Seeks a Different Equality'; 'In Hollywood, It's a Men's, Men's, Men's World'; 'Lights, Camera, Taking Action: On Many Fronts, Women Are Fighting for Better Opportunity in Hollywood' – provides a case in point (DuVernay 2014a; 2014b; 2015).

Beginning with an on-set profile of indie director Ava DuVernay's work on the major motion picture *Selma* (2014), Dargis pointedly deploys the cultural capital of *The New York Times* to foreground the persistent gender discrimination in Hollywood movie production. Using the work of Stacey L. Smith at the University of Southern California, who along with Martha M. Lauzen at San Diego State University has been a leader in painstakingly and empirically documenting the bias against women in movie and television production, Dargis challenges the explanations offered by production executives, especially women executives, that either minimise the problem or point to the few examples of women-directed productions as hopeful signs of progress. When Amy Pascal, the then-co-chairwoman of Sony Pictures Entertainment asserts that the studio is '"committed to making movies about women"', Dargis expresses her frustration with the answer and with what seems to be the intractable gender politics of mainstream Hollywood: 'I can't let Ms. Pascal off the hook. But women in power, often the beneficiaries of male munificence, tend to be treated harshly when they betray that gift by failing. That may help explain why female executives as a group are not better advocates for female directors' (Dargis 2014b: 3).

Demanding greater accountability and action from well-paid movie executives who plead helplessness is an important and necessary task of journalistic activism. At the same time, the potential circularity of this approach – frustration with decision-makers leads to frustration with the decision-making process, leading back to frustration with decision-makers – points to the need for a more extensive theoretical engagement with the material practices of movie production as part of any strategic plan for change. Dargis recognises this point when she begins her final article in the series with the declaration that the 'American movie mainstream needs a revolution' (Dargis 2015: 1). Recognising that laudable projects aimed at providing more funding for women filmmakers, while necessary, will 'only go so far,' Dargis highlights the need for 'filmmaking values and habits' to change (only now in terms of evolution rather than revolution):

> Even as women have directed more movies, the profession remains heavily coded as masculine, from its white-collar male auteurs to its blue-collar laborers. It has a production culture developed over time by men, and if more women are to join its ranks, that culture will need to evolve, including dealing with the crushing hours that are especially difficult if you're the primary caretaker of your kids. (Dargis 2015: 5)

It is at precisely this intersection between ideological critique and production culture that I wish to situate the collaborative directorial practices of Shelton and other women directors in indie film. While this larger theoretical focus on feminist praxis clearly seems more the purview of academic cinema studies than journalism, feminist film theory has only recently begun to take the gendered politics of material production practice into consideration.

It has become a commonplace to divide the academic study of the movies into two broad camps: one historicist and empirical, focused on production and industrial practices; the other formalist and theory-based, focused on the hermeneutic analysis of movies-as-texts. This theory/praxis divide has its correlate in the evolution of feminist film studies since the 1960s. Catherine Grant (2001), Jane M. Gaines (2004), and Kelly Hankin (2007), for example, all cite this divide as both a historical reality and a challenge for contemporary feminist theory. Gaines writes that

> [a]n earlier orthodoxy that prohibited empirical work was unable to imagine the intertwining of approaches that defines the contemporary moment. Still, feminist film theory itself requires more, not less, historical situating, for the apparent division between theory and history that characterized feminist developments in the 1970s also defined the larger field at this formative moment. (115)

Similarly, in her overview of twenty-first-century documentaries chronicling the work of contemporary women directors, Hankin argues, 'if feminist film scholarship has been slow to discuss the female director, it has been even slower to talk about the materiality of film production vis-à-vis women. Feminist film scholarship has had very little to say about the material ways in which sexuality and gender affects women's roles and possibilities as directors, leaving most of the discussion to journalism' (72).

The usual suspects in this reluctance of feminist film scholarship to explore 'the material ways in which sexuality and gender affects women's roles and possibilities as directors' are various offshoots of poststructuralist psychoanalytic criticism; in particular, what we might call the School of Mulvey after the enduring significance of Laura Mulvey's 1975 landmark essay, 'Visual Pleasure and Narrative Cinema'. But there is nothing about poststructuralist theories in their various manifestations that preclude their application to material production practices, an application that can counter, for example, overly reified ideas about gender and sexual identity that limit many journalistic descriptions of the gender divide in contemporary cinema.

A more relevant theoretical impasse identified by Grant in her essay on 'Women's Film Authorship' is the continuing vexed status of the amorphous yet culturally enduring idea[l] of the auteur. Dargis, for example, makes this connection when moving to a more structural analysis of the gender ideology of movie production: 'the profession remains heavily coded as masculine, from its white-collar male auteurs to its blue-collar laborers'. As Grant and others note, the justified suspicion of auteur theory as an essentialist cult of personality can also undermine the struggle for women filmmakers to establish recognised subjectivities within the industrial practices and critical machinery that constitute the contemporary cinema complex. But approaching auteurism as a commercial and marketing strategy and, even more usefully, as what Grant refers to a kind of 'postmodernist author-function' can help us discuss the collaborationist directing practices of certain indie women directors such as Shelton as not (or not only) personal style but as a form of political intervention into the 'coded' practices that Dargis refers to (Grant 2000: 102).

Traditional critiques of auteur theory focus, understandably, on the mystification involved in reducing the inescapably collaborationist nature of movie production to the will of a single personality. My argument in this essay is not with auteur theory per se – except in terms of how Dargis's reference to the 'male auteur' is actually redundant in terms of how consistently gendered the idea of the auteur has been – whether as a theoretical concept or a commercial brand. From the perspective of material production, the way that the ideological keyword of 'the auteur' operates to resist collaborationist and egalitarian approaches to media production demonstrates how the 'masculine code' that Dargis refers to maintains the persistence of the celluloid ceiling in the form of regressive labour practices.

Lynn Shelton: Director, Facilitator, Curator

If indie filmmaking, however nebulous the term, represents a cinematic subculture relatively more open to women-directed productions than the 'mainstream' (an equally baggy term) movie industry, it also continues to signify the idea of the alternative and the experimental, despite the growing body of criticism detailing how 'indie film' has become a marketing category as formally constrained as the Hollywood tentpole blockbuster (indeed, the Library of Congress continues to list work on indie cinema under the category 'Experimental films – History and Criticism'). Indie cinema thus at least still has the potential to function – and in the case of Lynn Shelton, is functioning – as an arena not just for new directors to learn conventional production practices in the service of 'alternative' narratives, but for those material practices themselves to come under challenge, especially in regard to the conventional top-down (male) auteurist model of movie production.

The auteur model has particular resonance for indie filmmaking, as the low-budget and all-hands-on-deck mystique of indie production can if anything intensify the myth of the solitary visionary filmmaker, as with the generation of 1990s male auteurs who emerged from the indie renaissance at the end of the twentieth century. My own approach in this essay likewise follows an auteurist model in my focus on Shelton as the focal point for my discussion. Shelton herself does not shy away from the centrality and authority of the director's position. Although two of her most recent movies – *Touchy Feely* (2013) and *Laggies* (2014) – were fully scripted projects, as are the episodes of television series that she directs, she is most well known for her use of improvisation in constructing her movies, providing actors with plot outlines but relying on collaboration with them to create the final narrative. In the case of *Humpday* (2009), her reimagining of the bromance, she left the outcome of the final scene completely up to the two main actors Mark Duplass and Joshua Leonard, including the resolution of the central premise of the narrative involving two old college friends who decide to make an alternative porn film featuring themselves as 'straight' guys having 'gay' sex.

In spite of such directorial practices that would seem to almost consciously undermine the auteurist model, Shelton still describes herself as a 'control freak': 'for a long time I made a dozen movies really all by myself, and it was both because I was too kind of shy or proud or something to ask people for help, but I also was terrified of losing control, I didn't want to give anybody any of my control up, over any element'. In finally moving on to making feature-length movies, she found that the practical exigencies of movie production required her to cede control to others, a process that - significantly - she found 'beautiful' rather than terrifying, even in terms of the standard industrial and military metaphors that have become commonplaces of conventional moviemaking: 'I got the experience of being just one cog in this beautiful well-oiled machine, and I realised that, "Oh, I'm not responsible", there is a hierarchical army-like structure of the division of labor, it's all really logical'.

It is just this understanding of the structural and material conditions of movie production, I would argue, that defines Shelton's critical awareness of the politics of the film set, an awareness that leads her not to internalise or naturalise the subject position of director but to describe the director as 'just one cog', a dismantling of the will-to-power version of auteurism that does not privilege the director's position within the ideological apparatus of the film set. The 'director', from this point of view, is no more of an Ayn Rand-like autonomous free agent than any other 'cog', her authority in the production process deriving from and ultimately beholden to larger structures of power and control involving the financing and market operations of the movie industry, operations that equally govern indie and mainstream movie production.

The tension between the desire for a kind of auteurist personal autonomy and the inescapability of these larger structures, whether economic, familial, or romantic, resonates throughout Shelton's filmography. Shelton's movies typically feature characters in crisis and isolation (sometimes physical, sometimes psychological, sometimes both), and *Humpday* in particular focuses on an 'auteurist' male artist named Andrew (played by Joshua Leonard) who, in his early 30s, has styled himself as a bohemian free spirit but whom we discover is adrift and plagued by his lack of productivity. At the beginning of the film, he arrives in the middle of the night on the doorstep of his former best friend from college, Ben (Mark Duplass), who works for the city of Seattle and has settled into a comfortable yuppie marriage. As alluded to above, Andrew and Ben decide to enter an amateur porn film festival run by the local alternative arts newspaper.

While Shelton intended *Humpday* as a deconstruction of the bromance and an analysis of masculine gender performance, it is also very much a story about the material practice of artistic and specifically movie production. The conflict between male competitiveness and vulnerability that marks the arc of Andrew and Ben's friendship reflects Andrew's own auteurist orientation towards creativity and the subject position of the 'artist'. Andrew desperately wants to claim the mantle and, most importantly, the cultural capital of the artist, a role he defines in competition with Ben's status as middle-class professional. Their porn movie is both a collaboration and pointedly Andrew's movie, a conflict reinforced repeatedly throughout the movie, as when Ben, for example, chickens out of explaining his central role in the project to his wife Anna (Alycia Delmore) by claiming to simply be Andrew's assistant.

Significantly, the two friends come up with the idea for the movie during a stoned brainstorming session set in a party held at a local kind of artists' commune. The brainstorming is simultaneously collaborative and competitive, as Andrew and Ben challenge each other's capacity for transgression and thus 'true' artistic credibility. While one of the women hosting the party (whose lover is played by Shelton herself) commends the idea as a beautiful expression of their genuine love and affection for each other, Andrew and Ben continue to frame their artistic collaboration in terms of ironic macho one-upsmanship. This occurs most comically in a basketball game in which their mutual athletic ineptitude leads to a confrontation over who is the most open-minded and adventurous, with the self-styled 'free spirit' Andrew challenging Ben's middle-class conventionality as a form of artistic emasculation.

The price of Andrew's artistic isolation and the insecurity at the heart of his auteurist braggadocio becomes increasingly apparent over the course of the movie, most poignantly in a late night heart-to-heart in which each friend admits to his own vulnerability and fears. Andrew confesses that he has never successfully completed a single artistic project, an admission that results in the brilliant final sequence of the movie, in which Andrew and Ben – and the actors Joshua Leonard and Mark Duplass – forgo a top-down auteurist production model and engage in an open-ended collaborative creative process to make their porn movie, a process that again mirror's Shelton's own improvisatory approach to filmmaking.

In the end, the characters/actors do not follow through on their original premise, realising not only that they don't want to have sex with each other but also that the premise itself was built on a kind of competitive will-to-power, as when they hilariously confront the logistics of the sex act in terms of who will be 'dominant' and who 'submissive'. Instead, they wind up creating an affectionate and bittersweet record of realising that they are, as Ben puts it, 'morons', rather more intent on preserving their fragile ego identities than working together to create an emotionally compelling narrative.

Their project does not turn out to be a complete failure, however. In the movie's final shot – or more accurately, in the improvisatory take that Shelton decided on as the movie's final shot – a melancholy Andrew almost by chance reviews the footage he and Ben had just shot on their inexpensive camcorder, the same sequence that the movie audience of *Humpday* had just experienced. Rather than a depressing confirmation of yet another of his artistic failures, Andrew begins to laugh with delight at their absurd yet also endearing false bravado and transparent anxiety caught on tape. Here the movie *Humpday* conflates with Ben and Andrew's movie, just as Andrew's laughter conflates with Joshua Leonard's 'genuine' laughter in the unscripted scene, as Andrew realises the comic energy that emerged from their collaborative improvisation far exceeds the cramped egotism of their original premise. Similarly, *Humpday*'s conclusion swerves the viewer's attention and emotional investment away from an obsession with the teleology of whether Andrew and Ben will actually have sex and towards how their project served as a way to avoid

Figure 17.1 Mark Duplass and Joshua Leonard in *Humpday* (2009).

coming to terms with their respective early mid-life crises. By focusing on a film project, Shelton embeds this realisation within the material practices of artistic production, turning *Humpday* itself into a meta-commentary on the interconnection of the production process with issues of gender and the ideology of the lone wolf auteur.

This awareness of the political and cultural implications of the material practices that determine the 'hierarchical army-like structure of the division of labor' in the production process distinguishes the view of the auteur as subject-position from the naturalised view of the auteur as controlling genius. We can see the gendered dimensions of this distinction at play in comparing Shelton's description of her initial reluctance to assume and aspire to the role of director with her experiences teaching in a digital filmmaking programme involving mostly recent high school graduates. As she describes it, her trepidation about going to film school after her early career as an actor was not the result of any artistic insecurity but instead her quite correct understanding of the economics of the movie industry: 'I knew that feature films cost millions of dollars and that was terrifying to me, you know that you're responsible for somebody else's millions of dollars, it just all was too kind of overwhelming'. Rather than seeing the director's position as one of power, authority, and autonomy, she instead focused on the responsibility and accountability (literally so in terms of the large sums of money involved) that defined the position. Compare this reaction to her experience with the 'entitled attitude' of some of the teenage male students she encountered as a teacher, whom she described as freely claiming the title of 'director' despite their complete lack of experience, in contrast to the reluctance shown by more accomplished female colleagues to do so.

The entitled attitude that Shelton encountered in these young men indicates a different orientation to the subject-position of the director than her own more structurally aware understanding. Instead of understanding the director's role as that of a 'cog' that therefore demands a level of skill and functionality in order to contribute to overall operation of the machinery, these young men responded to the idea of the director as a position of social power, as a source of autonomy and control. Like the failed artist Andrew in *Humpday*, their definition of themselves as 'directors' seems more a metaphor for their understanding of and desire for personal autonomy – for the mystique of the naturalised 'auteur' – than actual confidence over their levels of skill and craft.

This pseudo-confidence, of course, is one definition of masculine privilege within a patriarchal system, a circular cultural (tauto)logic that bases masculine centrality on an essential masculine authority that both justifies and is justified by that cultural centrality. One possible tactical response to the gendered entitlement gap that Shelton describes would be a kind of 'lean in' approach that encourages young women to emulate this entitlement, to 'out-auteur' the male auteurs by proving their own ability to dominate the film set.[2]

But the most useful implication for the effective feminist practice of Shelton's discussion of her experiences of teaching these young men may not be envy for their sense of entitlement. Rather, it's the recognition that this entitlement, as with Andrew's fetishisation of the role of the artist as prophetic auteur, acts as an impediment to the creative and artistic development of these young filmmakers, who are too mystified by the idea of directorial power to understand the need for successful collaborative management skills on the movie set, skills that are as much (or perhaps should be as much) a part of the craft of direction as any reified concept of 'personal vision'. Rather than a source of weakness or a barrier to directorial success, Shelton's initial reluctance to immediately take on the subject-position of director, along with that of the other women she refers to, actually informs their ability to transform the director as auteur into the director as facilitator, a structural intervention that can both undermine the gendered biases and practices that constitute the celluloid ceiling and lead to more efficient, sustainable, and artistically compelling forms of moviemaking.

Shelton does not place collaboration in opposition to the subject-position of the author. Instead, she emphasises the tactical importance of that subject position in fostering a more collaborative, less combative workplace: 'the culture of the set comes from the top'. Her position – that the 'main thing is that the people at the top level are the ones responsible for setting the tone and the culture of the set' – is less an endorsement of hierarchy than a recognition of how the hierarchical structure of the conventional movie set can be used to counteract the agonistic model of workplace interaction that defines so much of contemporary movie production, an agonism that reflects the gendered and reified idea of auteur as despot.

Shelton's critical vantage point – her ability both to understand and work within the conventional power structures of the movie set and to maintain a critical distance which has allowed her to develop an alternative collaborative practice as an indie auteur - derives from her initial reluctance to enter film school, a reluctance that can function as a key psychic structure in maintaining the celluloid ceiling. Instead, Shelton credits her self-made 'funny back road/route into feature filmmaking' as 'my own film school', one that developed from pursuing her different creative interests, from acting to photography to editing, in a way that allowed her to mature and develop as a filmmaker outside of institutionalised cultural pressures based on gendered work practices.[3]

As a result, Shelton's introduction into filmmaking was through her work as a skilled editor, itself a traditionally gendered role in movie production and one that has historically been more open to women within mainstream Hollywood practice. In part, this openness can be seen as stemming from stereotypes of women as supportive of others and the idea of the editor as 'serving' the director's unifying vision. For Shelton, though, the editor's position was a model of 'what a good collaboration looks like . . . I became really invested in the work and it felt like our project and not just their project'.

For Shelton, her editing career did not lead to feelings of subservience to the auteur but of satisfaction at becoming a co-creator, the transformation of 'their' project into 'our' project. In becoming a director herself, the 'independence' of indie production practices allowed her to develop her collaborative practice almost organically. Having only been involved in post-production, she came to the set unconditioned by previous production practice. Instead, she found herself 'going around introducing myself to everybody and getting people's names and then saying "What do you do, oh, you're the gaffer, and what does the gaffer do?" You know, it was really crazy, so that was the intensive last module of my film school'.

This reorientation of the masculinist auteur model towards valuing and respecting the skills and creativity of the entire production team is central to the redefinition of the director as facilitator. The term that Shelton uses, one that combines the idea of director as structural locus of decision-making with a non-hierarchical collaborative approach to artistic collaboration, is 'curator', a term she used both in our conversation and in a recent essay she published on improvisation in *Moviemaker* magazine:

> But I know I'll always return to working with improvisation. Directing an improvised film takes the collaborative nature of narrative moviemaking to its highest degree. It forces me to let go of ego, to keep my

> micromanaging, control-freak nature in check, and to become the kind of director I most want to be: a *curator* of the best ideas, whether they come from my own brain or the magnificent minds of my collaborators. (Shelton 2014b, emphasis hers)

Of course, the subject position of the curator is not without its gendered inflection and history within the patriarchal structures of the visual art world, but it shares with the structurally analogous subject-position of editor within text publishing a destabilised locus of institutional authority stemming from the necessarily dependent nature of both the curator and editor. In some ways, Shelton's use of the term as a replacement for 'director' extends the equally 'dependent' creative status of the movie editor (without raw footage, there's nothing to edit) to the director as a way of affirming the essentially 'collaborative nature of narrative moviemaking': without actors, without a crew, there is nothing and no one to 'direct'.

The Personal and the Structural

A clear danger with this utopian revisioning of the director as facilitator, collaborator, and curator is the degree to which it recapitulates and reinforces essentialist stereotypes about women in movie production. In 'Exploring the Barriers and Opportunities for Independent Women Filmmakers', Smith and her co-researchers define the cultural 'double-bind' that impedes women gaining access to the director's chair. To begin with, there is the stereotype against women in leadership roles. In their qualitative survey, 'a woman's confidence and ability to command a group of people to achieve her vision' was repeatedly questioned (Smith 2013: 27). The words of one movie executive are quoted below as a representative expression of this attitude:

> So they have to be seen as the leaders of large crews of people, many of whom are working-class middle-aged guys who drive trucks and set lights and things like that. And I would bet that there's a kind of built-in bias against prospective female directors starting out that people don't project them into that position as easily as they project younger males. (Smith 2013: 27)

On the other hand, if women do display assertive, director-as-dictator behaviour,

> . . . females may be evaluated poorly if they violate stereotypes about their gender or stereotypes about the role they play in production . . . individuals in our sample indicated that women are naturally more col-

> laborative, nurturing, or helpful, and gravitate to those roles. When women demonstrate aptitude as assistants, it may be difficult for them to move out of stereotyped positions into those with more authority in film production. (Smith 2013: 27)

If the transformation of the director into a collaborative facilitator, a 'curator of the best ideas', only refers to a change in personal affect or temperament, then it risks validating the binary described here between the 'tough' (male) director able to assert his will and the 'nurturing' (female) director who, 'by nature', subordinates her will to the needs of the group. But approaching the director as a subject position, as a specific functional nexus within the material structure of the production process, recasts our understanding of the director in dialectical fashion, as a leadership role that is at the same time subordinated, as are all subject-positions within the production process, to the needs of the overall project. It is this structural transformation of the subject-position of the director that is specifically what is most revolutionary about the approach Shelton is advocating and practising.

Shelton expresses this 'revolutionary' mission in describing how intentionally she and her fellow Seattle indie filmmaker Megan Griffiths have sought to transform their larger filmmaking community in Seattle:

> I feel like we've really made it our mission in this community, in Seattle's community, to kind of make sure that all of our productions that we were involved with are as positive as possible. [This approach has] really spread through the entire filmmaking community here in general.

Dargis likewise implies the radical implications of redefining the subject position of the director in the rhetorical structure of her article chronicling Ava DuVernay's work on *Selma*. She contrasts, on the one hand, the way she 'was struck by how Ms. DuVernay had made the leap from low-budget filmmaking with a handful of people to commanding hundreds' with her later observation that she was watching

> a very smart filmmaker command a veritable army partly with hugs. Movie sets can be very unfriendly spaces for women, as she knows. Before she started shooting, she recalled, she sat down with 'every single person' on the crew and said, "I'm inviting you to work with me, so this is going to run in the way that I want it to run"'. (Dargis 2014a: 5)

That Dargis sees – or, more accurately, understands that her readers will see – this conjunction of the ability to 'command a veritable army' with 'hugs' as oppositional or even contradictory, points to how deeply embedded gendered assumptions about leadership, motivation, and efficiency are in the conventional model of directing practice. This model separates the ability to understand and respond to the needs of individual members of the cast and crew from the ability to 'command', relegating the former to the merely 'personal' and the latter to the structural. Hence, qualities cited in the 'Exploring Barriers' report above that could be considered management assets, such as a propensity to be 'collaborative, nurturing, or helpful', are instead seen as impediments to dealing with 'working-class middle-aged guys who drive trucks', as if these members of the set, by virtue of their age, gender and class identity, have no personal, emotional, or work/life management needs.

In discussing and recommending her own collaborative management style, Shelton is quick to emphasise that her approach is as structural and pragmatic as it is a matter of personal temperament (let alone any 'natural' gender orientation): 'for me, I'd rather be empathetic with my actors, help them out a little, and then ultimately it's going to be good, it's going to be good for me, because I'm going to have a better product as a filmmaker.' She does not see a contradiction between being empathetic and being assertive in terms of maintaining her vision for the film: 'it's all selfishness, I mean it's not like I'm just doing it because I'm a nice gal . . . I'm doing it because I get the best work out of people and that they're all going to be helping fulfill this, this vision of mine.' In describing the 'collaborative, nurturing, or helpful' culture on her set as all a part of her 'control freak' nature, Shelton invokes the more dialectical understanding of the director as functional subject-position. From this perspective, the gendered model of the control freak as screaming dictator is as dysfunctional, in the strictest sense of the term, as failing to efficiently carry out the functionality of the director as part of the production process.

The greater practical functionality of Shelton's facilitative approach, as well as the dialectical connection between nurturing and leading, is borne out in her discussion of work on episodic television, an environment very different from the culture of indie production and one steeped in the more toxic culture of traditional Hollywood practice. In reporting on the positive response she has received from veteran Hollywood crews, Shelton sees no contradiction between her 'friendly' personal approach and the need to fulfill the leadership demands of the director subject-position:

> I also get feedback about, 'You know what you need, and you know when to move on, and you're very decisive, and you're not just sort of showing up on set unprepared and saying "Oh, what are we doing now?" and so it's not just my personal warmth that I might have, it's also, I've been told by, externally validated as a, "No, you're really like a good director, you're a pro, you really know, you know what you need, and you're respectful in asking people for help in getting what you need."'[4]

The practical functionality of both Shelton's and DuVernay's approaches, their ability to translate a collaborative, feminist indie production ethic to mainstream television and movie production, defines their potential to offer more than a simply theoretically utopian alternative to the celluloid ceiling. It is no accident that as the lines between the televisual and the cinematic continue to blur, 'television' work has allowed indie women directors to maintain both access to funding and industry visibility as directors, creating entry points for transformational production practices. Both Shelton and DuVernay regularly cross the lines between movies and television, as have directors such as Nicole Holofcener and Lisa Cholodenko, with Lena Dunham serving as a paradigm for a feminist redefinition of 'auteur' that focuses more on shared communities of practice than the individual will-to-power. The development and evolution of these feminist workplace practices overlap with the collaborative culture of the early twentieth century mumblecore movement as well, a shared genealogy reflected in Shelton's longtime collaboration with the mumblecore auteurs Mark and Jay Duplass.[5]

As the executive quoted above from 'Exploring Barriers' exemplifies, filmmaking management has long used working-class men as surrogates and excuses for the maintenance of the celluloid ceiling, even though that same class status mitigates their supposedly vast influence. Yet as the examples of Shelton and DuVernay demonstrate, even 'working-class middle-aged guys' respond positively to the model of the director as facilitator, not surprising if we view gender and class issues as completely intertwined, as Shelton does when she observes that 'the eight-hour work day just sort of passed by the entire film industry'. Shelton's comment connects the 'work life balance' issues cited in the 'Exploring Barriers' report as an impediment to aspiring women directors with the long and fraught history of labour organising in Hollywood, linking the concerns of women filmmakers with the 'working-class middle-aged guys' on the film crew.

The collaborative approach developed by Shelton and others connects aesthetics, economics, and ideology as part of a deliberate political intervention into production practices that to date have continued to privilege the subject-position of the lone white male director. Rather than a matter of personal style or an expression of a 'natural' female sensibility, these collaborative practices, the reimagining of auteur director into the subject-position of facilitator and curator, actually reflect a depersonalised critique of the material structure of movie production, a critique necessary for any aspiring director whose own designated gender subject-position automatically disqualifies her from conventional practice. Through a structural intervention into these practices, Shelton and others create an environment more conducive to a wider range of aesthetic practice and a wider range of practitioners. As Shelton describes this new model: 'you're creating this invisible but sturdy container for the creativity to flow within, and you're setting boundaries, you're setting parameters . . . you're going to get great results, because people are going to really own it, and they're going to feel ownership and investment that they wouldn't have felt otherwise if you were just trying to stick your hand up their ass and make them into a puppet, right?'

In the end, the developing feminist model of the director-as-facilitator potentially represents a strategic evolution in the structural practice of movie production that may in fact lead to the kind of revolution that Manohla Dargis calls for. As the digital age of visual media production continues to blur lines between the mainstream and indie, between the televisual and the cinematic, women indie directors such as Shelton are taking advantage of this destabilising of 'traditional' workplace practices to move easily across these boundaries in ways unimaginable even twenty years ago.

Just as digital technologies and delivery systems demand a reconceptualisation of the Hollywood business model on screens both large and small, this new wave of feminist directors are reimagining and restructuring the material and aesthetic practices of Hollywood to demonstrate the economic efficiency of more inclusive and democratic production methods. As Shelton reports, the early returns on her question that began this essay – could she translate 'the intimate feeling of my tiny, family-style film sets where everybody is really excited to be there and on the same page, and it's a really positive experience for everybody' to mainstream television production – suggest that these new models of moviemaking provide a much needed sign of hope for challenging the seeming intractability of the celluloid ceiling.

Notes

1. According to Martha M. Lauzen's annual 'Celluloid Ceiling' report on the top 250 movies of 2014, issued by the Center for the Study of Women in Television and Film at San Diego State University, 'women accounted for 7% of directors' (Lauzen 2015: 1). By comparison, 'Women accounted for 23% of *directors* working on documentaries and 18% of *directors* working on narrative features' that were presented at 'high profile film festivals in the United States in 2013–14' (Lauzen 2014: 1, emphasis hers). Similarly, the Women Filmmakers Initiative study 'Exploring the Barriers and Opportunities for Independent Women Filmmakers' points out that while '4.4% of directors were female across the top 100 box office films each year from 2002 to 2012', 'female directors comprised 22.2% of the narrative Competition categories' at the Sundance Film Festival (Smith et al: 2013).
2. By 'lean in', I am of course referring to Sheryl Sandberg's *Lean In: Women, Work, and the Will to Lead* (2013), which has become a recent cultural touchstone in relation to the question of women in positions of institutional power, including the argument over the extent to which her approach represents a changing of or capitulation to the gendered hierarchical models of corporate organisation.
3. How film school curricula and practice reinforce gendered and agonistic production practice remains an understudied area for cinema studies. At the same time, anecdotal feminist analyses of filmmakers' school experiences provide critical openings for

this work, such as Erica Rose's *Indiewire* blog entry (2014) about her time at New York University.

4. In response to her question about whether she could maintain a 'family-style' environment on the set of *Mad Men*, Shelton reports a similarly positive reaction: 'People of all different stripes from different departments from high to low, were coming up to me and saying, "Usually by this time on a production someone is driving me out of my mind and I want to strangle them, I can't wait to finish. But this? The weeks have flown by",' recalls Shelton. 'People just had a great time and it made me really happy to hear that' (Rochlin 2013: 2),
5. I explore the gendered and feminist dimensions of mumblecore in 'The Emergence of the Anxious Romance: Mumblecore, Neorealism, and Gender Play', Chapter 3 (2013).

References

Alberti, John (2013), *Masculinity and the Contemporary Romantic Comedy: Gender as Genre*, London and New York: Routledge.

Dargis, Manohla (2014a), 'Making History: With "Selma", Ava DuVernay Seeks a Different Equality', *The New York Times*, 3 December, <http://nyti.ms/1yMC7g3> (last accessed 23 February 2015).

Dargis, Manohla (2014b), 'In Hollywood, It's a Men's, Men's, Men's World', *The New York Times*, 24 December, <http://nyti.ms/1wkTAb3> (last accessed 23 February 2015).

Dargis, Manohla (2015), 'Lights, Camera, Taking Action: On Many Fronts, Women Are Fighting for Better Opportunity in Hollywood', *The New York Times*, 21 January, <http://nyti.ms/1ErPC78> (last accessed 23 February 2015).

Gaines, Jane M. (2004), 'Film History and the Two Presents of Feminist Film Theory', *Cinema Journal*, 44: 1, pp. 113–19.

Grant, Catherine (2000), 'www.auteur.com?', *Screen*, 41: 1, pp. 101–8.

Grant, Catherine (2001), 'Secret Agents: Feminist Theories of Women's Film Authorship', *Feminist Theory*, 2: 1, pp. 113–30.

Hankin, Kelly (2007), 'And Introducing . . . the Female Director: Documentaries about Women Filmmakers as Feminist Activism', *NWSA Journal*, 19: 1, pp. 59–88.

Mulvey, Laura (1975), 'Visual Pleasure and Narrative Cinema', *Screen*, 16: 3, pp. 6–18.

Rochlin, Margy (2013), 'Let's Make a Movie', *DGA Quarterly*, Winter 2013, <http://www.dga.org/Craft/DGAQ/All-Articles/1301-Winter-2013/Independent-Voice-Lynn-Shelton.aspx> (last accessed 29 February 2013).

Rose, Erica (2014), 'The Unspoken Biases in Film School', *Indiewire*, 4 September, <http://blogs.indiewire.com/womenandhollywood/the-unspoken-biases-in-film-school-20140904> (last accessed 19 February 2015).

Sandberg, Sheryl and Nell Scovell (2013), *Lean In: Women, Work, and the Will to Lead*, New York: Knopf.

Shelton, Lynn (2014a), personal interview, 16 September.

Shelton, Lynn (2014b), 'Writing for Improvisation: An Oxymoron', *Moviemaker 2015 Guide to Making Movies*, 21: 110, pp. 24–6.

Smith, Stacy L., Katherine Pieper and Marc Choueiti (2013), *Exploring the Barriers and Opportunities for Independent Women Filmmakers*, Women Filmmakers Initiative, <http://annenberg.usc.edu/Faculty/Communication%20and%20Journalism/~/media/7C43F5337F154F7EB5A5FD67C7120C52.ashx> (last accessed 26 February 2015).

18. BEYOND THE SCREEN: ON CONTEMPORARY FEMINIST MEDIA RE-ARTICULATIONS

Claudia Costa Pederson and
Patricia R. Zimmermann

Feminist Media Ecologies

Fifteen screen megaplex theatres showcase comic book-inspired tentpoles with male superheroes and special effects, playing to teenage boys chomping on Twizzlers. Four decades of feminist film agitation seems to have happened on a remote planet in another universe. Arthouses present a more character-and-dialogue driven cinema of cinematographic complexity and narrative ambiguity. Whether you argue that *Birdman* (Alejandro Gonzáles Iñárritu, 2014) unfurls breakthrough cinematography or revivifies male patriarchal fantasies perhaps is insignificant: its months-long exhibition runs bankrolled independent art cinemas. The powerful, pathos-inducing, historical biopic about Martin Luther King, *Selma* (2014), directed by African-American film director Ava DuVernay, generated enormous press and attention. But it did not enjoy *Birdman*'s extended runs. Feminist independent media is frequently categorised as 'indie' work outside the studio system. Most festival programmers and museum curators mobilise a heterogeneity that decentres white male, Euro- and American-centric privilege, and gender, race, nation, and sexualities as key programming strategies. Feminist debates swirl around the transnational corporate-produced, male action genre films of Katherine Bigelow (*The Hurt Locker*, 2008; *Zero Dark Thirty*, 2012), the first woman to win an Academy Award for directing. *Obvious Child* (Gillian Robespierre, 2014), a narrative film about a young woman's decision to have an abortion which was independently-produced, engages feminist issues more explicitly (Weaver 2010).

A University of Southern California study done in 2013 and entitled 'Exploring the Barriers and Opportunities for Independent Women Film Directors' reviewed 11,197 directors, writers, cinematographers, and editors of films screened at the Sundance Film Festival from 2002–12. Women directed only 29% of these films. Of the top 100 box office films, women directed only 4.4% (Beck 2013). Even *Variety* pondered whether Hollywood was sexist (Setoodeh 2014). A July 2014 article in the *Guardian* contended gender inequality and bias in blockbusters: production crews were 75% male (Peterson 2014). In December 2014, an *Indiewire* article decried the 'abysmal number of women in the film industry' while heralding a few key breakout women-directed narrative films of that year: *A Girl Walks Home Alone at Night* (Ana Lily Amirpour), *Selma* (DuVernay), *Beyond the Lights* (Gina Prince-Bythewood) (Silversteen and King 2014). *The New York Times* film reviewer Manohla Dargis noted that women comprise only 15% of protagonists in narrative films and represent only 30% of speaking parts in her aptly headlined story, 'In Hollywood, It's a Men's, Men's, Men's World' (Dargis 2014).

Improvement regarding the position of women in film and media depends on what screens you might be looking at and how you define the independent media arts ecology. Moving beyond the single movie screen to the multiple screens, interfaces, and performances of new media arts, the position of women does not seem locked in a forty-year time warp. New media arts ecologies reroute this discourse on women in film. They reframe feminist film theory towards engaging newly emerging coordinates. These practices push film theory to account for practices beyond ingrained ideas about cinema residing in linear narratives, the auteur, the star system and industrial models. Feminist video of the 1970s provides a precedent, as it combined art and activist contexts. The practices this essay analyses expand these histories. They insist on distributed or non-auteurial modes. They cross film with new media platforms, engaging spectatorship beyond the gaze. They create new spaces for participatory knowledge. Collectives, collaborations, transmedia and interfaces rearticulate feminist practices within a more complex intersectionality beyond who directed a film and who speaks in it. In these new ecologies, feminist practices flourish. They redefine how we identify feminist media. Conceptual interventions, they reroute feminist media theory away from representation towards rearticulations of feminist encounters, designs and engagement strategies.

If the definition of the independent media arts ecology can dispense with the extremely limited, legacy media ideology of how many feature-length narrative and documentary films by women infiltrated Sundance and expand to include the multiplication of screens and interfaces recalibrating this dynamic, subaltern media arts ecology, then a more optimistic landscape comes into focus (Wong 2011). Sundance functions as the under-resourced farm team for the transnational media industries, a market for boutique distributors. This other media arts ecology reframes the infrastructural domains of feminist media practices towards a more heterogeneous set of coordinates beyond the long-form feature-length film, now looking more and more like a brontosaurus – unsustainable, unscalable, and risking extinction. Instead, this new transnational media arts ecology reveals plural, layered, intersecting, dynamic ecologies that cross media platforms, algorithms and encounters. They recalibrate the relationship between production, practice, distribution, exhibition and engagement (Hudson and Zimmerman 2015). These works unsettle feminist film theory: they theorise the movement of women and feminist conceptualisations through many matrices and intersections.

The Finger Lakes Environmental Film Festival: New Ecologies and Exhibition Spaces

As programmers of the Finger Lakes Environmental Film Festival (FLEFF), a multi-disciplinary, multi-arts and cross-platform festival exploring the intersections between human rights, nature, diversity, labour, gender, class, environment, and conflict now entering its nineteenth year, we have observed provocative new vectors for feminist media practices beyond the analog feature film. In the 1980s and 1990s, Ithaca College programmed a stand-alone feminist film series. By the 2000s, when the college assumed full sponsorship of FLEFF, the question of feminist media practice became a central operating tenet of heterogeneous, intersectional programming philosophies. Because we have lived and worked in upstate New York, a region with a long history of media arts and technology innovation and a vibrant, internationally renowned locale for new media innovation, we have witnessed the more sustainable and scalable parallel alternative universe to the feature film in our festival programming work.[1]

As a curated festival that focuses on sustainability and thinking about the environment differently, FLEFF operates not as a market like Sundance, but as a place for curatorial interventions to create a dialectic between the local and the global across different platforms, representing our upstate New York media ecology (Iordanova 2013; Fischer 2013). New media production, exploration, critical writing, and exhibition permeate our region and constitute a key focus of FLEFF. Conceptualising the environment in terms of interdependencies and interconnections between humans, media and ecologies, FLEFF programmes feminist new media work. The festival provides space for alternative exhibitions of international works in difficult modalities that could not access a week-long arthouse run. As a result, feminist new media work in different platforms has emerged as a programming goal. The festival has had the luxury, given its location in a college, to explore exhibition formats beyond cinema's flat screens.

The works featured in FLEFF reroute this argument about the paucity of women directors into one that engages many new media platforms and interfaces which are expanding the democratic promise imbedded in media practices. These works ask different questions – beyond representation, narrative, and what gender worked above and below the line. They function as speculations: they rework feminism, issues, community, exhibition and production in much more fluid, responsive, iterative ways. These works marshall collaborative, relational, and participatory new media models. They restructure the singular role of director into the multiplicities of designer, collaborator and convener (De Michiel and Zimmerman 2013).

Cartographies of New Feminist Media Ecologies: Four Case Studies

The projects analysed below reject the notion of a fixed object like a film. Instead, they open into interactive, fluid, changing spaces for encounters to generate dialogue in provisional public spaces. These projects also emphasise intersectionality between feminism and other issues such as healthy food, immigration, war, toxicity, sexualities, region and history. They range across media platforms: from *The Lunch Love Community Project* (a mosaic online project about healthy food in public schools) to *The Veterans Book Project* (a collaborative publishing venture on war and gender) to *Children of Srikandi* (a collaborative LBGT project in Indonesia), *Maiden Voyages* (a collaboratively-sourced, distributed, storytelling project rethinking the intersection of feminist and Muslim identities) and *Dream Addictive* (a Mexican/transnational project linking sustainability, bio-technics, and open source culture).

Each example defines and maps feminist media arts ecologies: we look at form (heterogeneous crossovers of media) and content (food; war/conflict; Muslim queer culture; post-colonial gender geographies; technology and ecology). The *Lunch Love Community Project* figures ecology/feminism/community as a 'mosaic'. The *Veterans Book Project* reconsiders the war on terror and enacts a foundational feminist film concern to render visible marginalised stories and archives. *Children of Srikandi* suggests the continuing importance of bearing testimony beyond the West, queering history and the nation. This project intersects with long-standing theorisation of feminist media correctives to official histories. The *Maiden Voyages Project* disrupts homogenous images of Muslim women by combining the networks of globalisation with diaries for transnational dialogues. Dream Addictive realises the concept of ecology in radical ways: it produces new interfaces to disrupt imaginaries of the environment as outside the body. It places us within ecologies, blending organic and machinic components to extend feminist community science debates.

These projects reconsider the relationship between designer/facilitator and audience, focusing on creating adaptive, inviting architectures for place-based encounters. At the festival, many of these groups/designers have not only presented formally in the more traditional artists'/filmmakers' question and answer sessions, but have also crafted smaller workshops that engaged interaction, dialogue, and embodied convening. These projects transpose the notion of the audience that is so deeply entrenched within the transnational media consumerist economies into the construct of the participant being in a provisionally opened-up space.

Leslie Garcia focuses on developing open-source tools to expand shared techniques, knowledge, and agency. She engages the public via the Internet and through face-to-face workshops, like the one she produced for FLEFF. Similarly, Monica Haller expands on photography by bringing invisible archives of veterans and civilians of recent wars into the public realm via museum, gallery showings, and workshops with high school and college students. FLEFF online exhibitions also exemplify this notion of the multiplication of screens. Hird's work – consisting of animated diaries on the web created together with four (anonymous) women from different countries over a period of three years – is profoundly humanising in the context of Muslim women represented as helpless victims in need of rescue.

Many invited FLEFF artists like Laura Coppens, Helen De Michiel, and Monica Haller redirect the traditional post-screening experience away from the singularity of auteurism and into the multiplicities of intersectionality. They reimagine a screening as a platform that provides space for community convenings around issues of significance, such as healthy food in the public schools (the *Love Lunch Community* project). Similarly, *Children of Srikandi* by the Srikandi collective is the first film documenting the LGBT community in Indonesia. But it is also a collaboration between Laura Coppens and the women involved who learned documentary filmmaking techniques as part of the process.

Exhibiting Community

The *Lunch Love Community*, a collaborative community-based new media project probing healthy food in public schools in Berkeley California, provides an example of feminist transmedia that moves beyond the fixity and preciousness of analog forms and conventional exhibition practices. Inspired by the chef Alice Waters, the Berkeley School Lunch Initiative substitutes healthy food for processed food. This project advances a participatory feminist documentary practice, revising a confrontational mode with a more inviting encounter to facilitate dialogue and to open public space for discussion about food and schools.

Lunch Love Community focuses on place and people rather than abstractions. The shooting style exemplifies this conceptual political strategy, with carefully lit, lush, colourful close-ups of food, hands, plants, faces, desks, soil and kitchen surfaces, suggesting a heteronomic rather than hermetic spatiality of food and schools. It visually maps the two conceptual metaphors 'ground-up' and 'community-based'. The teachers, students, parents, cooks, and gardeners portrayed in the shorts double the mosaic structure of the website: no one voice holds the final analysis, but all voices join together, articulating food issues as connected to people, multi-linearity and layers of discourses and practices.

The exhibition of these shorts differs from conventional documentary: they are screened in highly constructed media socials, customised for specific community needs. They showcase not the filmmaker but people involved in a particular community's school food issue. The media socials emphasise dialogue rather than authorial intentionality. The project describes its strategy as putting 'a human face on food policy reform'. Designed by Helen De Michiel, *Lunch Love Community* employs a mosaic model, with short films around five minutes long on different Berkeley public school food topics: *Labor of Lunch* (labour), *The Whole World in a Small Seed* (gardening), *Parent Factor* (families), *If They Cook It, They Will Eat It* (vegetables and meals). Moving across social media and narrowcasting public exhibition for parents, educators, nutritionists and policy makers (rather than the *Variety* top grossing films list), the films were designed for social media shareability.

In contrast to feature-length films like *Food Inc.* which portray the repulsions of commercial food production, the *Lunch Love Community* chronicles how teachers, students, parents, cooks, and food workers came together to change how children engage with food in school. While many feature films on food use horror genre emplotment strategies on the macrolevel, *Lunch Love Community* reframes food from the microlevel of one school district that enacted different food practices and policies. Instead of critiquing the food system, the project maps the myriad, small engagements that offer forward action and social change: kids burning Cheetos to check chemical content, cooks discussing the meals they craft, a teacher planting seeds with children in a garden. Each film enacts a hyperlocal strategy.

Making Visible

The *Veterans Book Project* (2009–12) is a library of fifty books authored by US veterans and Iraqi refugees with direct experiences of American-led wars. The books were created in fourteen workshops led by the photographer Monica Haller over three years. The archival materials are the photographs and memories of the authors. Haller provided the container in which to arrange these materials, a software template designed by graphic designer Matthew Rezac. The books form a public repository which is available online and shown at libraries, museums, public reading rooms in universities and schools. The books can also be purchased on demand. These books migrate across spaces, places, and platforms.

Fragmented and poetic, The *Veterans Book Project* shuns the linear, objective coding of the archive used to legitimise the Iraq war. The archive, as curator and theorist Okwui Enwezor contends, was central for the justification of the Iraq war. Search for evidence of weapons of mass destruction included scouting seized Iraqi archives 'for documents containing evidence of a weapons system's many components: designs, bills of procurement, building plans, site maps, photographs of laboratories' (Enwezor 2008). Notwithstanding evidence gathered by inspectors showing that the building of a weapons program was abandoned, the burden of proof was placed on the Iraqi regime. Invoking Derrida's science of the archive, Enwezor underscores how the historical monopoly on gathering and interpreting data is central to imperial power, and continues to be fundamental to the nation-state (Enwezor 2008: 44). The *Veterans Book Project* challenges the self-evidentiary aura and hermeneutic authority produced by linking photography, the archive, and empire. Its use of personal photographic archives and war memories points to both the tenuous relationship between the photograph, memory and the real, as well as to the ultimate aim of the project, the use of photography and narrative to activate alternative forms of collectivisation opposed to the comprehensive totality of the official archive (Pederson 2013).

The *Veterans Book Project* began as a collaborative book project with Iraq war veteran Riley Sharbonno, Haller's college friend, who served as a nurse at Abu Ghraib prison in Iraq. Sharbonno returned with hundreds of digital images shot while he was deployed, most of which he does not remember taking. The result, *Riley and His Story* (2009), is a book that became the framework for the forty-nine volumes that followed. Alongside dislocated and, at times, graphic photographs, Riley's fragmented narrative contrasts sharply with the sanitised jargon of officials and mainstream media depictions of the war. To drive home this point – of using collage for juxtaposition to generate new, more critical meanings – militarised terms like tactical and deployment were re-appropriated. The back jacket of his book presents it as an 'object for deployment' designed for 'tactical' reading.

Initially, Haller sought out veterans by placing calls to community organisations ranging from activist veterans groups and VA centres to art spaces. Later, and as the project developed, veterans and refugees came to the workshops via word of mouth. During initial interviews, Haller discussed her role as an 'editor, designer, and organizer', emphasising the time commitment (each workshop spanned ten days), potential traumatising impact, and vision of the project as a platform for aligning personal and collective memory. During workshops participants gathered materials (personal photos, diaries, mail) selected and organised content, designed the book, and revised. The completed library is fragmented: some books are conflicting, some are very personal, some attest to views contrary to those of the artist (for example, a participant insisted on using the language of 'fighting for freedom'). In the end, Haller sees this fragmentation as both a reflection of personal and collective trauma, as well as 'key to the expansion of the social sphere'.

As embodied interaction is a central component of the work, Haller decided to limit access to the software upon completion of the work. The library, however, has generated a variety of public engagements mostly in educational settings. Professors and students at various institutions have used the books and the software to develop class and artistic projects around personal and collective narratives of war. Haller's FLEFF workshop (2011) marked her second visit to Ithaca, New York, where she had previously worked on a book with the Iraq veteran Drew Cameron. Cameron runs the Combat Paper Project, an ongoing series of papermaking workshops in the US, Canada, and Britain, in which veterans are taught how to transform their army uniforms into paper. In the sanctuary's library, books by several veterans are highly suggestive of theirs, and thus of the crux of Haller's project, as both intersect on the bearing of poetics to undercut the use of images and words for war.

Queering Testimony

Children of Srikandi or *Anak-Anak Srikandi* (2012) by the Srikandi collective, is the first film documenting the LGBTQ community in Indonesia. Conceived as a collaboration between two German filmmakers, Laura Coppens and Angelika Levi, and the Srikandi collective, a group of queer women based in Jakarta, the film is equally remarkable for its expressive take on queer life in Jakarta, which straddles documentary, fiction, and experimental film, as for its collective authorship. The film emerged out of a collective effort involving crowd-funding (funds came from various organisations, family, friends and supporters), and from a collaborative framework conceived to intertwine the women's control over the various facets of filmmaking with their bearing testimony to their individual and shared stories about queer life in Jakarta, Indonesia.

Named after the story of Srikandi, a female figure from the Indian Mahabharata epic who changes gender to become a warrior, the film is divided into eight episodes interwoven with scenes from the epic in the form of traditional *wayang* puppetry which is performed and narrated by two transgender women (known as the *waria*). The episodes span personal narratives about growing up queer in a popular neighbourhood and coming out in a predominantly Muslim society (as Indonesia has the largest Muslim population in the world), to social and group dynamics around violence within (by

Figure 18.1 *Children of Srikandi* (2012) http://www.childrenofsrikandi.com/

queer women) and against queer communities (by religious extremist groups and police).

Set against the urbanity of Jakarta, the film stresses the community's deep-rooted connection to the country's cultural traditions (apart from *wayang* puppetry, the film makes reference to folk tales, gamelan play, and Indonesian dance), as well as its quirkiness (from a Western point-of-view), on show in the collective sing-along and synchronised dancing at the local lesbian disco. While embracing its local queer flair, the film also takes on the assertion that queer identity is 'Western' that is often levelled by local fundamentalist groups against non-Western queer individuals. Represented by the shots of the mall and references to fashion in the later part of the film, Western queer categories of femme, butch, and the like are directly addressed and rejected in the film as restrictive fashion labels by the women involved. Instead, they frame the complexity of contemporary queer identity in Indonesia as an extension of the gender fluidity that can be traced to the roots of the country's diverse cultural traditions.

As the scholar Benedict Anderson has pointed out, historically the *wayang* tradition is particularly significant in this regard, as it was used by Sukarno, Indonesia's first president and recognised leader of the nation's independence, to illustrate and teach diversity and tolerance at the onset of the nation's post-colonial era (Anderson 1965: 5). *Children of Srikandi* de-emphasises the framing of gender on individualistic and autonomous notions of the self, in favour of linking gender issues with larger social and power dynamics in present day Indonesia. As a result, the project gives primacy to the celebration of diversity that underlies historical cultural traditions such as the *wayang* theatre rather than to the Western gaze.

In part a reflection of the democratisation of Indonesia's post–Suharto era of the *Reformasi* or Reformation movement, post-1998, *Children of Srikandi* also responds to the complexities and pitfalls facing democratic sentiment in Indonesia in the wake of a long legacy of authoritarianism which itself can be traced back to colonisation. Queer lives in Indonesia are precarious. For example, harsh anti-gay laws were recently institutionalised in Aceh, a province under the rule of sharia law imposed by Islamist extremists in government. This precariousness correlates, as the film underscores, with the instability brought about by the military's continual vying for power, growing Islamism in politics and society, and separatist conflict. Homophobia is ultimately only one of the various forms that fear and harassment take as regressive forces vie for political power. In short, *Children of Srikandi* is a retort to those that exclude queer communities based on the understanding of queerness as 'Western'. Contrary to this narrative, the film shows that queer culture is native, while homophobia is a more recent 'import', a regressive relic holdover of colonialism. In the current climate, *Children of Srikandi* stands as a corrective to the distortion of local queer communities and as part of larger efforts to mobilise filmmaking to protect vulnerable individuals and communities in Indonesia. The film was screened at various venues in the country and in the Asian region as well as in Europe and the United States. The visibility and skills acquired in this process harbour the potential for the future development of Indonesian film itself.

Gazing Re-framed

Valerie Hird's *Maiden Voyages Project* (2007–10) represents a collaboration between the artist and four women in Jordan, Iran, Egypt, and the Palestinian West Bank. The project consists of five diaries by Hird and each of the women, a series of hand-drawn illustrations and large-scale drawings, and animated graphics based on the diaries for the Internet. The project began with Hird's requests to colleagues in various cities in the Middle East, asking for suggestions for potential collaborators in the project. Her only specifications were that participants would be willing to contribute a diary entry via email on the first day of the month for a year. Four women were selected because of the likelihood of their commitment to these requirements. The resulting diaries consist of sparse texts (in English and Arabic), enlivened by Hird's drawings (based on the women's emails), animated features (online), and by music pieces chosen by each of the women.

Hird's interest in Middle-Eastern culture can be traced to her being brought up surrounded by her grandparents' collection of artefacts from the region. For twenty-five years, Hird has travelled extensively throughout the area as an archaeological illustrator and later as a guest documentarian of semi-nomadic groups in Egypt, Turkey, Morocco, and Central Asia. With the ongoing North American military presence in the region in the last thirteen years, this project has come to a halt because of the risks to her hosts, and this has led Hird to shift focus towards exploring dominant perceptions about the Middle East in the West.

Underscored by Hird's wry mobilisation of a gendered literary genre, the diary, the *Maiden Voyages Project* upends perceptions of the 'Middle-Eastern' woman, historically rooted in the orientalising gaze of European imperialism. Long a subject in literature, painting, photography, and cinema in the West, as famously discussed by the late Edward Said, the narrative and image of the 'Middle-Eastern woman' continues to stand in for the East's difference and exoticism. As the Iraqi author and activist Haifa Zangana asserts, in the aftermath of the 'women rights' rhetoric accompanying North American military intervention in Iraq in 2001: 'The main misconception is to perceive Iraqi women as silent, powerless victims in a male-controlled society in urgent need of 'liberation.' This image fits conveniently into the big picture of the Iraqi people being passive victims who would welcome the occupation of their country. The reality is different' (Zangana 2014).

Contrary to the homogenising image of 'Middle-Eastern' women in Western media, the diaries of the *Maiden Voyages Project* suggest shared identity but also strong differences across geographic and national boundaries. Simply marked with initials (DB, KK, NS, SK, and VH), the diaries honour the women's requests for anonymity due to various concerns including family circumstances, religious affiliation and job security issues. In a short introductory text, each woman's diary identifies her solely by location, occupation, religious affiliation, and sometimes by her hobbies and fashion tastes. A Coptic Christian, DB lives in Cairo with her parents, wears jeans and bikinis, plays the guitar and studies Islamic art. KK lives in Amman with her family, is a devout Muslim and was a visiting instructor of Arabic at Earlham College in the United States where she joined the gospel choir. A Muslim, NS is a student at the Tehran University with a fascination for Classical Persian painting, American culture and shopping. SK is a primary and secondary school teacher living in Bethlehem. Her entries revolve around her humiliating experiences crossing Israeli checkpoints to Nazareth, where her boyfriend lives, and avoiding her mother's attempts to arrange a marriage to one of the local young men. Hird's own diary documents mundane life in the United States as a drawing teacher, art student, partner and homeowner.

Most significantly, the diaries were conceived to function as catalysts for cross-cultural discussions. In one post-Arab spring event, two of the women involved contributed to a public discussion via Skype at the Center for Book Arts in Manhattan, New York. According to Hird, the tone of this event highlighted the persistence of orientalist views: the American audience consistently questioned the on-remote participants about the oppression of women in the Middle East. In response, one of the women (KK) pointed to the scarce number of publications by Middle Eastern women authors available in English, remarking that most of the books published focus on female oppression.

Opening Interfaces

Leslie Garcia's interests in art and electronics traces to her involvement with Dream Addictive Lab (2003–11), a Tijuana-based collective she co-founded with Carmen Gonzalez. For eight years, the pair created interactive public sculptures straddling sound, sustainability issues, and open-source collectivist culture. Inspired by Soviet-era legacies of Constructivism's geometric forms and the theremin, an early electronic instrument invented by the Russian physicist Leon Theremin in 1928, these works were designed to be played by the public. They were fashioned from recycled materials and operated on solar radiation. In an update of communist aesthetics, the programming of the sculptures as musical interfaces also underscored collectivism and involved the sharing of code made available on the collective's site for others to use. At present, Garcia works solo and as a member of Astrovandalistas, a collective based in Mexico City that she co-founded in 2011. Like Dream Addictive, Garcia's and the Astrovandalistas' focus on the development of open-source interfaces reflects the core belief of their work: that to collectivise artistic and technological knowledge is to enable social agency.

Garcia's *Pulsum Plantae* (2012–ongoing) echoes the concept and design of Dream Addictive's public sculptures. It fuses organic and non-organic components such as plants and electronics. Garcia describes *Pulsum Plantae* 'as self-sustainable sonic devices designed as hybrid systems that integrate a living organism (a plant) and an electronic interface (biosensors) to create a network based on code and sonic frequencies'. Like a theremin, prepared moss and cacti with attached sensors can be played without physical contact and because the interaction with the work creates the illusion of organic aliveness, Garcia hopes that such interaction will ultimately trigger attentiveness to non-human life in the environment. In this regard, the project evokes the sculptures of Dream Addictive, inflecting a broader emergence of ecological themes in media art in Latin America. Similarly, *Pulsum Plantae* involves documenting and sharing production processes online and through free and low-cost workshops at various venues, including academic and art institutions, independent spaces, and festivals. For instance, at FLEFF 2011, Garcia hosted such a workshop, teaching students the rudiments of Pure Data, an open-source sound environment used in *Pulsum Plantae*.

With Astrovandalistas, Garcia's work likewise involves adapting existing digital technologies to enable collective access to the public sphere. Beginning with poetic sound sculptures in public spaces, the group increasingly brought sound to a more political level. Its first public intervention, *Unentitled 1* (2011) was a sonic installation designed to provide a chance encounter with contemporary art in a popular neighbourhood in Mexico City where the community is disconnected from art institutions but familiar with digital consumer product technologies. The piece consists of thirty-six headphones salvaged from a closing-down inventory and hanging from wires alongside an open-air restaurant. The soundscape was provided by fellow artists working in poetry and sound. The piece was later installed in La Galeria de Comercio, an independent arts organisation that lends legitimacy to free-culture art projects in Mexico City. *El Abismo no nos Detiene (The abyss won't stop us)* (2012), a modified video environment that allows collaborative audiovisual narratives followed.

Framed as 'an exercise in collective memory', the project recompiles an archive of audio and video contributed by the public via a website and Twitter in response to the following questionnaire: 'What is the Mexican Spring?'; 'Who was involved in the 2012 mobilizations in Mexico?'; 'What catalysed the mobilizations in the country?' and 'What happened after the mobilizations in Mexico?' The group's remix in the form of a video-essay counters assertions by Enrique Peña Nieto, then the Institutional Revolutionary Party's (PRI) presidential candidate and now the current president, that the protesters were paid off by his opponent. Contrary to these allegations, contributions demonstrate historical awareness about the PRI's members' involvement in systemic violence against the Mexican population, with participants sending in images of the Zapatista uprisings of 1994 and more recent footage taken at student protests in 2012 denouncing the party's hold on media channels and engagement in electoral fraud. The work was presented at various commercial sound festivals in the country.

The group is currently conducting workshops in Mexico City which teach the public how to create autonomous wireless networks, or *redes libres*, essentially wireless nodes operating independent of mainstream providers. Garcia's and the Astrovandalistas' works converge on what the late media artist Beatriz da Costa called 'tactical biopolitics', or practices dedicated to the investigation, critique, and creation of resistant 'forms of collective production, distribution, and deployment of knowledge that engages with history and culture, academia and the public, technoscience and everyday life' (Costa and Phillips 2008: xviii). Garcia's and Astrovandalistas' projects take opportunity, in the increasing penetration of information and communications technology in Mexico, to connect digital technologies with social energies working to change the current cultural imaginary around ecological, social, and political conditions.

Beyond the Screen

Transnational feminist new media practices such as *Lunch Love Community*, *Veterans Book Project*, *Children of Srikandi*, the *Maiden Voyages Project*, and the Dream Addictive collective push us to consider a much wider conceptualisation of women's indies beyond the industrial practices of analog feature length, long-form film for Sundance, the art cinemas, or megaplexes. All of these projects refuse the double bind of reducing questions of feminist media to how many women worked behind the scenes and how many woman have speaking roles in a female-led conventional narrative. These projects operate beyond the screen. They rearticulate new media as an engagement between communities and technologies that shift and adjust across multiple spaces and places, sometimes in a fixed form like a short films programmed in different ways for their fungibility, or a book downloadable online, or a performance of bio-politics. They move within a much more dynamic, fluid, multi-platformed media ecology where content adapts to specific groups, locales, and collaborations, shape-shifting across the analog, the digital, and the embodied. They rearticulate feminist media practices as collaborative, open, iterative, malleable, adaptive. Instead of one screen, they propose the embodied, the performative, the analog, the digital and the collaborative ecologies of multiple screens.

Note

1. For a timeline on the history of media, technology, and innovation in upstate New York, see the internationally renowned Experimental Media Center, formerly in Owego, New York, Video History Project, at <http://www.experimentaltvcenter.org/video-history-project> (last accessed 26 November 2015).

References

Anderson, Benedict (1965), *Mythology and the Tolerance of the Javanese*, Ithaca, NY: Modern Indonesia Project, Southeast Asia Program, Cornell University.

Beck, Laura (2013), 'There's only 1 Female Film Director for every 15.24 Male ones, and Things aren't Getting Any Better', *Jezebel*, 22 January, <http://jezebel.com/5977854/there-are-1524-male-film-directors-for-every-1-female-film-director-any-better> (last accessed 10 June 2015).

da Costa, Beatriz and Kavita Phillips (eds) (2008), *Tactical Biopolitics: Art, Activism, and Technoscience*, Cambridge, MA: MIT Press.

Dargis, Manohla (2014), 'In Hollywood, It's a Men's Men's Men's World,' *The New York Times*, 24 December, <http://www.nytimes.com/2014/12/28/movies/in-hollywood-its-a-mens-mens-mens-world.html?_r=0> (last accessed 9 July 2015).

De Michiel, Helen and Patricia R. Zimmermann (2013), 'Documentary as Open Space',

in Brian Winston (ed.), *The Documentary Film Book*, London: British Film Institute, pp. 366–75.
Dina Iordanova (ed.) (2013), *The Film Festival Reader,* St Andrews: University of St Andrews.
Enwezor, Okwui (2008), 'Archive Fever: Photography between History and the Monument', in *Archive Fever: Uses of the Document in Contemporary Art*, exhibition catalogue, New York and Gottingen: International Center of Photography and Steidl publishers, pp. 11–58.
Fischer, Alex (2013), *Sustainable Projections: Concepts in Film Festival Management*, St Andrews: University of St Andrews.
Hudson, Dale and Patricia R. Zimmermann (2015), *Thinking Through Digital Media: Transnational Environments and Locative Places,* New York and London: Palgrave Macmillan.
Pederson, Claudia (2013), 'The Veterans Book Project: A Conversation with Monica Haller', *Afterimage: The Journal of Media Arts and Cultural Criticism*, 2: 41, pp. 21–5.
Peterson, Hannah Ellis (2014), 'Gender Bias in the Film Industry: 75% of Block Buster Crews are male', *The Guardian*, 22 July, <http://www.theguardian.com/film/2014/jul/22/gender-bias-film-industry-75-percent-male> (last accessed 9 July 2015).
Setoodeh, Ramin (2014), 'Hollywood Sexist? Female Directors Still Missing in Action', *Variety*, 2 January, <http://variety.com/2014/biz/features/the-top-10-grossing-films-of-2013-directed-by-women-is-a-sad-sad-list-1201021712/> (last accessed 9 July 2015).
Silversteen, Melissa and Inkoo King (2014), 'The Best Women Directed Films of 2014', *Indiewire*, 18 December, <http://blogs.indiewire.com/womenandhollywood/the-best-women-directed-films-of-2014-20141218 > (last accessed 9 July 2015).
Wong, Cindy Hing-Yuk (2011), *Film Festivals: Culture, People, and Power on the Global Screen,* New Brunswick, NJ: Rutgers University Press.
Weaver, Matthew (2010), 'Kathryn Bigelow Makes History as First Woman to Win Best Director Oscar', *The Guardian*, 8 March, <http://www.theguardian.com/film/2010/mar/08/kathryn-bigelow-oscars-best-director> (last accessed 9 July 2015).
Zangana, Haifa (2004), 'Quiet, or I'll Call Democracy', *The Guardian*, 21 December, <http://www.theguardian.com/world/2004/dec/22/iraq.gender> (last accessed 5 November 2014).

INDEX

Note: page numbers in *italics* indicate illustrations; those followed by 'n' refer to notes